Stories of Piety and Prayer

Deliverance Follows Adversity

Letter from the General Editor

The Library of Arabic Literature makes available Arabic editions and English translations of significant works of Arabic literature, with an emphasis on the seventh to nineteenth centuries. The Library of Arabic Literature thus includes texts from the pre-Islamic era to the cusp of the modern period, and encompasses a wide range of genres, including poetry, poetics, fiction, religion, philosophy, law, science, travel writing, history, and historiography.

Books in the series are edited and translated by internationally recognized scholars. They are published as hardcovers in parallel-text format with Arabic and English on facing pages, as English-only paperbacks, and as downloadable Arabic editions. For some texts, the series also publishes separate scholarly editions with full critical apparatus.

The Library encourages scholars to produce authoritative Arabic editions, accompanied by modern, lucid English translations, with the ultimate goal of introducing Arabic's rich literary heritage to a general audience of readers as well as to scholars and students.

The Library of Arabic Literature is supported by a grant from the New York University Abu Dhabi Institute and is published by NYU Press.

Philip F. Kennedy
General Editor, Library of Arabic Literature

الفرج بعد الشدّة

المحسّن بن عليّ التنوخيّ

LIBRARY OF ARABIC LITERATURE
المكتبة العربية

Stories of Piety and Prayer

Deliverance Follows Adversity

AL-MUḤASSIN IBN ʿALĪ AL-TANŪKHĪ

Edited and translated by
JULIA BRAY

Volume editor
SHAWKAT M. TOORAWA

NEW YORK UNIVERSITY PRESS
New York

NEW YORK UNIVERSITY PRESS
New York

Library of Congress Cataloging-in-Publication Data

Names: Tanūkhī, al-Muḥassin ibn ʿAlī, 940?-994, author. | Bray, Julia, translator. | Toorawa, Shawkat M., editor. | Tanūkhī, al-Muḥassin ibn ʿAlī, 940?-994. Faraj baʿda al-shiddah.
Title: Stories of piety and prayer : deliverance follows adversity / al-Muḥassin ibn ʿAlī al-Tanūkhī ; edited and translated by Julia Bray ; volume editor Shawkat M. Toorawa.
Other titles: Faraj baʿda al-shiddah. English
Description: New York, NY : New York University Press, [2019] | Includes bibliographical references and index. | In English and Arabic; English translated from original Arabic. | Description based on print version record and CIP data provided by publisher; resource not viewed.
Identifiers: LCCN 2018052776 (print) | LCCN 2018056625 (ebook) | ISBN 9781479850242 (ebook) | ISBN 9781479820658 (ebook) | ISBN 9781479855964 (hardcover : alk. paper)
Subjects: LCSH: Islamic ethics--Early works to 1800.
Classification: LCC BJ1291 (ebook) | LCC BJ1291 .T3613 2019 (print) | DDC 297.5/7--dc23
LC record available at https://lccn.loc.gov/2018052776

New York University Press books are printed on acid-free paper, and their binding materials are chosen for strength and durability.

Series design by Titus Nemeth.

Typeset in Tasmeem, using DecoType Naskh and Emiri.

Typesetting and digitization by Stuart Brown.

Manufactured in the United States of America
c 10 9 8 7 6 5 4 3 2 1

Table of Contents

To the memory of D. S. Margoliouth, ʿAbbūd al-Shāljī,
A. F. L. Beeston, and Dominique Sourdel.

Acknowledgments

Al-Tanūkhī is one of the most lastingly popular of Arabic authors, which made his *al-Faraj baʿd al-shiddah* (*Deliverance Follows Adversity*) an early candidate for inclusion in the Library of Arabic Literature. Three great scholars, D. S. Margoliouth (d. 1940, a notable supporter of women's suffrage in addition to his other distinctions), ʿAbbūd al-Shāljī (whom I met in London shortly before his death in 1996, and who gave me his blessing), and my own teacher, A. F. L. Beeston (d. 1995), were instrumental in bringing him to a modern readership. Dominique Sourdel (d. 2014) is the other pioneering Tanūkhī scholar who must be acknowledged here. Margoliouth and Beeston handed on the baton of Tanūkhī studies in Oxford, where I now teach in my turn. Sourdel has notable francophone successors. Al-Shāljī was obliged to flee Iraq, and his intellectual heirs are correspondingly scattered.

Circumstances delayed the project of editing and translating *Deliverance* for the Library, and I must express my gratitude for the help I received on the final lap from the typist who so quickly produced a fair copy of the Arabic text, and from the external reviewer, who gave valuable advice on presenting the translation.

I am deeply grateful to the editors of the Library of Arabic Literature for their patient support, encouragement, and material help in enabling me to complete this first volume, *Stories of Piety and Prayer*, and above all, as always, to Shawkat Toorawa, a debt that is both a pleasure and an honor. Finally, I must thank Stuart Brown for the knowledge and understanding he brings to Arabic typesetting, Keith Miller for copyediting, and Lucie Taylor, who was recently my student and is now on the staff of the Library, for easing the volume's final steps.

Introduction

Al-Tanūkhī

Al-Faraj baʿd al-shiddah (*Deliverance Follows Adversity*) was written in Iraq in the second half of the tenth century AD by al-Muḥassin ibn ʿAlī al-Tanūkhī, born in 327/939, the son of ʿAlī ibn Muḥammad al-Tanūkhī, a judge and leading literary figure in the city of Basra. Basra, long a center of learning, agricultural wealth, and Indian Ocean trade, had become politically important during al-Tanūkhī's childhood. It was one of the theaters where the unraveling of the Abbasid caliphs' authority played out against the rise of the Shiʿi Buyid warlord dynasty. Al-Tanūkhī's father had a modest part in these events.[1] From his father, al-Tanūkhī inherited land and family connections in neighbouring Ahwaz in what is now Iran, as well as strong family ties in Baghdad thanks to his father's marriage into a famous legal family there. His writings are full of references to his father's local friends and colleagues, and to his Baghdad relatives, some of whom had held posts in the old caliphal bureaucracy. He does not mention his mother or any brothers or sisters. His father gave him an excellent education and was clearly a great influence on him.

The key figures in al-Tanūkhī's life were all exceptionally gifted, and they left their mark on his writings. Al-Tanūkhī was fifteen when his father died in 342/953. At eighteen, in 346/957, he already held the position of inspector of the mint in Sūq al-Ahwāz (§19.1). Not long afterward, he was taken under the wing of his father's friend and patron, the vizier al-Muhallabī.[2] Thanks to him, al-Tanūkhī studied in Baghdad with Abū l-Faraj al-Iṣfahānī, one of the greatest literary historians who ever lived,[3] and was given a number of administrative posts and judgeships in southern Iraq. (We do not know how he trained to become a judge.) Al-Muhallabī died in 352/963, when al-Tanūkhī was in his early twenties, and he was less lucky under his successors, losing his positions and having his estates confiscated, as he mentions several times (§§0.5, 8.7, 18.3, 42.1, 59.2–4, 80.1–8). Reinstated in 366/977, al-Tanūkhī joined the court of the greatest of the Buyid emirs, ʿAḍud al-Dawlah, where we find him in 367/977, aged thirty-eight, taking part in a Hadith session convened by the ruler in private audience while he was on a military campaign (§31.4). Two years later, when ʿAḍud al-Dawlah married his daughter to the caliph al-Ṭāʾiʿ in Baghdad in 369/979, al-Tanūkhī gave the wedding address. This was the zenith of his career. But the caliph refused to consummate the marriage, and al-Tanūkhī, who had been ordered to recall him to his duty, wriggled out of the task and was disgraced. After ʿAḍud al-Dawlah's death, he seems to have spent the last ten years of his life quietly in Baghdad,[4] dying there in 384/994. *Deliverance* and his other work, *Nishwār al-muḥāḍarah* (*The Table Talk of a Mesopotamian Judge*), were probably written during this period, or at any rate put into their final form then.[5]

The theme of *Deliverance* and al-Tanūkhī as author

The message of *Deliverance*, spelled out in al-Tanūkhī's introduction, is that our lives are full of tribulations and reversals, but if we trust in God's kindness and love Him steadfastly, He will make everything come right. Al-Tanūkhī wrote *Deliverance* for people like himself: members of the Iraqi upper bourgeoisie and service aristocracy who for centuries had been adept at surviving regime change. A lot of the stories in *Deliverance* are indiscreet first-person gossip about ups and downs in the careers of just such grandees, keyhole history that reflects their worldly and self-interested attitudes to patronage, politics, money, and success. In *Stories of Piety and Prayer*, which consists of the first three chapters of *Deliverance*, stories of this sort (§§14.4, 17.1–4, 65.1–6, 73.1–18, 78.1–7, 82.1–5, 100.1–4, 103.1–4, 111.1–4) rub shoulders with legendary examples of sanctity or moral heroism, and are interwoven with prayers of great spirituality—and others of guaranteed talismanic efficacy—together with reflections on key passages from the Qur'an. This mix of ingredients, some of them common property, some composed by al-Tanūkhī, and the whole organized by him into a vision of his own, reflects al-Tanūkhī's idea of authorship, which is in some ways what we would call academic and in others autobiographical. Equally, it reflects his background, his theoretical adherence to the rationalist Muʿtazilī religious thought that ran in his family, and his immersion in Tradition (also a family speciality), which acts as hinge between his intellectual allegiances and his longing for comfort and hope. What *Stories of Piety and Prayer* offers is not the idealized belief and practice of prescriptive writings. Rather, it gives a rare insight into the complexities of lived religion. When al-Tanūkhī's sophistication is confounded by another man's blind faith, he notes the fact with irony (§80.8). His own acts of blind faith are recorded with no irony at all.

Compilation as autobiography

Al-Tanūkhī wrote *Deliverance* not only for a readership of people like himself; he also wrote it for himself and about himself, as a spiritual exercise and a setting in which to relate and give meaning to his own experiences. Such items form a minority, but much if not most of the material in *Deliverance* came to him through people with whom he was on intimate terms, especially his father. Al-Tanūkhī cites his father fourteen times in Chapters One to Three (§§20.1, 20.2, 20.3, 20.4, 20.5, 21.1, 23, 25.1, 25.2, 40 (twice), 59.6, 65.1, 111.4; he is also cited indirectly at §106.1). The connections between al-Tanūkhī and many of his informants would probably have been evident to his intended readers. Nevertheless, because he is a literary scholar and a man of law, he names them formally—publicly, as it were—before identifying any personal relationship, and often stops short of explaining the connection. Most notably in the case of his mother's family, the Buhlūlids, he never clarifies the family link, although he repeatedly cites the members of the family. This family link, which was first noticed by Margoliouth but ignored by subsequent scholars, explains al-Tanūkhī's access to inside information about the caliphal court and government offices in Baghdad, and helps us understand certain aspects of his piety.[6] Buhlūlid family sources not identified as such in *Stories of Piety and Prayer* are Abū l-Ḥasan Aḥmad ibn Yūsuf the Blue-Eyed, son of Yaʿqūb ibn Isḥāq ibn al-Buhlūl al-Tanūkhī, al-Tanūkhī's cousin on his mother's side, much cited by him in later parts of *Deliverance* and in *Table Talk*, who died when al-Tanūkhī was about twelve (§76.1); the famous judge Abū Jaʿfar Aḥmad ibn Isḥāq ibn al-Buhlūl al-Tanūkhī, al-Tanūkhī's great-grandfather (§106.1); his son Abū Ṭālib Muḥammad ibn Aḥmad ibn Isḥāq ibn al-Buhlūl, al-Tanūkhī's grandfather, who took a hand in his education and was closely involved with his father (§§83.1, 84.1); his son, al-Tanūkhī's uncle, Judge Jaʿfar ibn Abī Ṭālib Muḥammad ibn Abī Jaʿfar Aḥmad (§§31.12, 59.5); and his great-great-grandfather, the famous traditionist Isḥāq ibn al-Buhlūl al-Tanūkhī (§92.1). A different branch of maternal relatives is mentioned at §74.2.

For modern readers, al-Tanūkhī's reticence has obscured the more general significance of the personal element in his writings. Teachers, friends, and associates, some not overtly identified as such in *Stories of Piety and Prayer*, are his father's friend Abū l-Faraj ʿAbd al-Wāḥid ibn Naṣr ibn Muḥammad al-Makhzūmī of Naṣībīn, the state scribe and poet known as the Parrot (§§16.1, 42.1–7); Abū ʿAqīl al-Khawlānī, who taught al-Tanūkhī's father in his youth in Antioch (§25.1); his father's deputy Ibn Khallād of Rāmhurmuz (§§26.3, 63.1); Ayyūb, son of the vizier al-Jarjarāʾī (al-ʿAbbās ibn al-Ḥasan ibn Ayyūb of Jarjarāyā) (§34.1); the literary historian Abū Bakr al-Ṣūlī (§§55.3, 64.1, 111.5); the critic al-Ḥātimī (Muḥammad ibn al-Ḥasan ibn al-Muẓaffar) (§§13.5, 94.1, 95.1, 105.12, 108.2, 111.5); and the vizier al-Muhallabī (§61).

In more ways than scholars have yet examined, al-Tanūkhī writes himself into *Deliverance*, expressing his identity and allegiances by the channels through which he cites his materials. This is particularly true of one of the previous books on the subject of deliverance that he acknowledges as an inspiration and source. He could have quoted it directly, but instead he cites it via a personal informant. Thus in Chapters One to Three, he transmits forty-eight items from Ibn Abī l-Dunyā without naming his *Book of Deliverance*, instead quoting a personal informant, ʿAlī ibn al-Ḥasan ibn ʿAlī ibn Muṭrif of Rāmhurmuz (of whom, unfortunately, we know little) as citing Ibn al-Jarrāḥ citing Ibn Abī l-Dunyā (§§11.3, 13.2–4, 13.7–8, 13.11, 20.1, 21.2, 22, 26.2, 28, 30, 31.1, 31.6–11, 31.13, 35.1–4, 37, 38.1, 59.5, 68.6, 69.1, 85.1–2, 85.3, 85.5, 85.6, 86.1–3, 87.1, 88.1, 89, 91, 92.1, 93.1, 96.1, 96.3, 97.1, 98.1, 105.5, 105.9, 110.4. There is also one mention of Ibn Abī l-Dunyā with no onward chain of transmitters to al-Tanūkhī, §36). ʿAlī ibn al-Ḥasan's informant, Ibn al-Jarrāḥ (Aḥmad ibn Muḥammad Ibn al-Jarrāḥ), was also a personal connection of the Tanūkhī family. He lived in Baghdad and knew al-Tanūkhī's son, to whom he described himself in these terms: "My books are worth ten thousand dirhams; so is my mistress and so are my arms and my horses." Fully accoutered, he engaged in tourneys with other cavaliers in the *maydān* or "Great Square" in Baghdad.[7] Other noteworthy personal informants are the aforementioned al-Ḥātimī, state scribe and poet as well as literary critic (§§13.5, 94.1, 105.12, 108.2, and 111.5); Abū ʿUmar Muḥammad ibn ʿAbd al-Wāḥid, known as "Thaʿlab's Pupil," with whom al-Tanūkhī had studied (§§13.5, 108.2); and the state scribe Abū l-Faḍl Muḥammad ibn ʿAbd Allāh ibn al-Marzubān, whom al-Tanūkhī had known at the court of al-Muhallabī (§18.1). The chains of transmitters (*isnād*s) that identify al-Tanūkhī's informants and their sources are discussed in more detail below in the Note on the Text.

A century of reading al-Tanūkhī

With its promise that all life's woes and perils can lead to happy outcomes, not to mention thrilling stories of romance and adventure involving brigands, caliphs, amateur detectives, and even animals, *Deliverance* appealed for many centuries to a wide readership, and when it first appeared in print in the twentieth century, the editions were based on manuscripts in which scribes no longer recognized the names of most of the protagonists, and the anecdotes, now blurred and generic, had become much like *Thousand and One Nights* tales—in the course of time, a number of them were in fact absorbed into the *Thousand and One Nights*. These versions of *Deliverance* gave the impression of a naive feast of optimism difficult to reconcile with the rationalist, disillusioned *Table Talk*, which mirrors tenth-century Iraqi life in all its aspects, from tax collecting to teenage neurosis, with a strong emphasis on absurdities, and is quoted by countless medieval authors. How did al-Tanūkhī manage to write two such different bestsellers? And how could *Deliverance* be a devotional work, as he claims, when so often it is about morally flawed characters?

Our image of al-Tanūkhī, and especially of *Deliverance*, has developed over the past century. Alfred Wiener published the first study of the deliverance-story genre and al-Tanūkhī's precursors and sources in 1913,[8] and in 1955 Rouchdi Fakkar produced the first monograph on *Deliverance* itself.[9] Meanwhile, in the 1920s and 1930s, D. S. Margoliouth brought out an edition and English translation of what survives of *Table Talk*, which had hitherto been unknown to modern readers. In 1920, Margoliouth had translated Miskawayh's history of the times in which al-Tanūkhī and his father lived,[10] and in 1928, Harold Bowen's *The Life and Times of ʿAlí ibn ʿÍsà* drew a lively picture of the high politics that some of al-Tanūkhī's maternal relatives had witnessed or been involved in. In 1937, Adam Mez's *The Renaissance of Islam*, co-translated by Margoliouth, provided a wealth of information on the social, literary, and material culture of the period. Together, these books gave (and still give) readers of *Deliverance* and *Table Talk* an unusual amount of detailed historical background in accessible form.[11] In the 1950s, Dominique Sourdel, working from two unpublished manuscripts in the Bibliothèque nationale de France, showed that *Deliverance* is itself a major source for Abbasid political history.[12] Finally, in 1978, the Iraqi scholar ʿAbbūd al-Shāljī published a richly annotated critical edition of *Deliverance* from previously unused manuscripts and drew attention to the mass of information it contains on people, places, institutions, food, music, medicine, local customs, and language. Above all, his edition makes visible its high literary quality and shows the importance of its form and compositional techniques.

Al-Tanūkhī's compositional techniques

The way al-Tanūkhī cites books reflects his literary training. He sometimes dates and localizes the encounters that provided his literary material, such as the teaching sessions with Abū Bakr al-Ṣūlī which he attended as a boy (§§55.3, 64.1, 111.5). The same applies when he cites Tradition. These are compositional techniques insofar as they frame and connect items. Al-Tanūkhī's attributions of variant tellings of a story and his identification of poetic variants—which he records scrupulously even when they are minor—are likewise techniques of connection and closure as well as marks of literary scholarship. Among his contemporaries, al-Tanūkhī is unusually rigorous and consistent in his use of such devices and, as he says in his introduction, he makes it a point of honor to acknowledge material quoted from his predecessors in the *faraj* genre. In Chapters One to Three, besides his single major source, Ibn Abī l-Dunyā, whom (as we have already seen) he quotes through a personal informant, he quotes six items from al-Madāʾinī (§§58.2–3, 104.1, 105.1, 108.1, and 110.1; see also §108.2) and ten from Judge Abū l-Ḥusayn (§§19.3, 58.4, 60.1, 90.1, 106.2, 107.3, 108.1, 109.1, 110.1, 111.1), whose father is also cited (§109.1).

As a literary practitioner, al-Tanūkhī uses rhymed prose (*sajʿ*) for his chapter headings, perhaps for its mnemonic qualities. He does not use it elsewhere as a stylistic resource, but his introduction illustrates his command of expository and argumentative structures, and of complex analytical phrasing. These are found again in his densely written passages of Qur'anic exegesis. A compositional feature of *Stories of Piety and Prayer* (but not of *Deliverance* as a whole) is al-Tanūkhī's use of recurrent vocabulary to establish an intertextual connection between the three chapters. This is discussed further in the Note on the Text.

The form and structure of *Deliverance*

The form of *Deliverance* is all-important—its division into themed chapters, and the way the chapters explore subthemes. Besides the overarching theme of deliverance (*faraj*), thirteen out of the fourteen chapters deal with a specific type of adversity and deliverance, as announced by al-Tanūkhī in his table of contents (§0.14). Sometimes the chapter contents are also specific to a genre:

for example, Qur'anic stories in Chapter One, or medical stories in Chapter Ten. Within each chapter's theme, particular motifs and narrative schemas are highlighted and explored. For example, "toying with grapes, tyrant taunts captive but is struck down before he can eat them," in Chapter Three (§§105.2–3), is an elaboration of "tyrant taunts captive with the Angel of Death and is killed in his place" (§§105.6–8). This technique, applied to a range of sources—the Qur'an, histories, life writing, letter writing, and Abū l-Faraj al-Iṣfahānī's *Book of Songs* are just a few—makes *Deliverance* a pattern book of Arabic storytelling and a virtual motif index of one of the richest periods of Arabic writing. It has been used as such by folklorists,[13] but it ought to be used much more widely as a guide to plots, themes, and materials that occur across Arabic genres.

I have used numbered paragraphs to emphasize the book's motif index aspect, breaking down each piece into units that correspond to a theme, situation, or narrative function. Its analytical structure makes *Deliverance* a revolution in Arabic narratology and literary theory, but the theory is embedded in al-Tanūkhī's method, not expressed separately. He was conscious of his own originality, but too close to it to do it full justice. As he says in his introduction, his book is, in every way, bigger and better organized than anything written on the subject before. But though he expresses exasperation at having spent so long writing and rewriting it, he makes nothing of the fact that *Deliverance* is more than a themed anthology: It is in fact an epitome of a culture, in this sense a rival to his teacher Abū l-Faraj al-Iṣfahānī's *Book of Songs*, from which it differs in that it does not content itself with setting down the complexities of human experience but tries to reconcile them.

Al-Tanūkhī's notion of *faraj*

The comprehensiveness of *Deliverance* is due to al-Tanūkhī's conception of affliction and divine rescue. His predecessors had thought of deliverance in conventionally devotional terms. Al-Tanūkhī's notion of deliverance embraced most kinds of human situation and many ways of writing about them. There are few limits to what qualifies as a rescue story in *Deliverance*. Under the storytelling rules that emerge as one reads, deliverance must be earned, sometimes heroically, or deserved, sometimes by the truly deserving; but often it takes only a very little faith or hope for someone to be plucked from misery, and luck in all its forms, including that of unexpected human kindness, plays a major part. In this moral economy, one person's merit may rub off on another. The ultimate example of this is asking someone whose prayers are known to be answered to pray in your stead, as at §74.1.

This is where the structure of the book and the plot structures it foregrounds work together to express al-Tanūkhī's ideas about God and society. Many of al-Tanūkhī's family members—his father and relatives on his mother's side—prided themselves on their inquiring, scientific minds. Theologically they were Muʿtazilīs, believing in a just and rational deity whose workings and providence can be rationally apprehended.[14] With al-Tanūkhī, inquiry blossomed into inquisitiveness and a delight in the variety and surprises of God's world, and he thought (or hoped) that God's providence was not only just, but merciful to the point of indulgence, and likely to operate in the unlikeliest situations. In an ideal society as al-Tanūkhī's tales depict it, God's mercy to the afflicted is channeled through the established customs of generosity and mutual obligation that permeate social hierarchy and social exchange. Money, which is so prominent in many of his stories, even in *Stories of Piety and Prayer*, is a tangible sign of God's goodness. It should be freely given and gratefully received, for networks of giving and receiving money and favors are the fabric of a good society. Coincidence belongs to this order of things. The wise recognize it as an opportunity to be generous (§§71.4–5); the wicked misread it as a sanction for their evil acts (§§105.2, 105.10). Invoking God, which everyone does, including the wicked, as an everyday habit of speech, never fails in these stories to bring about some operation of divine justice: God is truly present.

It could be argued that the early chapters of *Deliverance*—those translated in this volume—are the most genuinely religious since they focus on the Qur'an and prayer, and that as the book proceeded, worldliness got the better of al-Tanūkhī, or that he observed a certain decorum by placing an increasing distance between sacred and worldly material. The contrast between the earlier and later materials has been seen as hierarchical (downward from the divine to the human)[15] or stylistic (upward from the archaic and schematic material that forms the bulk of the first three chapters to the contemporary realism of the following ones).[16] If hierarchy there is, it is complicated by what seems to be al-Tanūkhī's conviction that the present and everyone in it is as immediate to God as is the sacred past of prophets and saints. The evidence of God's providential mercy is manifest in all lives, and all afflictions are important and morally productive if God responds to them with mercy. The happy accidents that prove this increase in frequency as the book proceeds.

Does this confirm the traditional view of *Deliverance* as optimistic? In his introduction, al-Tanūkhī insists we must believe that, with faith, all will be well. But the examples he gives from his own experience are mixed, and the letter of consolation sent to him by Abū l-Faraj "the Parrot," which argues that good and bad fortune alternate cyclically (§§42.1–7), offers no lasting comfort if the argument is followed to its conclusion. Scripture, parables, and fiction affirm the optimistic, deliverance-follows-adversity paradigm. Life writing, on the other hand, conforms more to the paradigm of circularity or alternation. Thus X, whose friendship saves his colleague Y from ruin (§§73.9–18), is a threat to Z, who is saved when X drops dead of a stroke (§§103.1–4); and in real life, as al-Tanūkhī knew from his own checkered career, benevolence has limits and deliverance is a respite. The information on protagonists in the Glossary shows that many of the people held up as examples of deliverance in *Stories of Piety and Prayer* met a sticky end in real life.

The contradiction between the two paradigms is unresolved, and their juxtaposition points to *Deliverance*'s dark side. Al-Tanūkhī lived in dangerous times, and the experience of fear and loss is as much part of the book as the theme of hope. The emotional immediacy of autobiographical narrators' reactions to fear, grief, and pain is heightened by the deliberate eschewing of distinctions of proportion and time that places an anecdote about the worries of a civil servant (§§17.1–4) in the same chapter as the ordeals of prophets, or al-Tanūkhī's unabashedly self-pitying reminiscences of his own misfortunes (§§59.2–4) next to the Prophet's and the Alids' teachings on fortitude.

Stories of Piety and Prayer

The first three chapters of *Deliverance*, which we have called *Stories of Piety and Prayer* for convenience, combine literary genres, which makes it both self-consistent and a foretaste of *Deliverance* as a whole. Its dominant genres, not found in other parts of *Deliverance*, are Tradition; prayers; paraphrases of and glosses on the Qur'an; Qur'anic exegesis and theological discussions that, typically, expand condensed expressions, explain imagery, and clarify grammatical rules, citing authorities where appropriate, and adducing key passages of the Qur'an to prove the necessity of faith and the efficacy of prayer. Some glosses are specifically Muʿtazilī in their concern to demonstrate that God is just and that believers, including prophets, earn their own destinies by making rational moral choices (§§4.6, 8.5, 9.3). The prayers quoted range from short, talismanic supplications to complex meditations. A large component of *Stories of Piety and Prayer* is Tradition, both Prophetic and Alid (an index of the former has been provided). Aphorisms, popular proverbs, admonitions, and edifying epistles are seemingly accorded the same moral authority as Tradition. Uniquely for al-Tanūkhī, there is also a story involving a demon (§§16.1–7).

The scattered examples of the genres typical of the rest of *Deliverance* include occasional poetry; anecdotes about sicknesses and cures; supposedly real-life autobiographical narratives (the default mode of Abbasid storytelling and historiography) involving Abbasid bureaucracy and politics; and stories that afford glimpses of Abbasid urban and rural domestic and economic life. These last are of special interest, for medieval Islamic social and economic history remains the least developed area of modern scholarship. Hints at the connections between Abbasid political structures, officeholding, landholding, agricultural and manufacturing production, distribution, trade, and taxation can be gleaned from stories such as §§73.1–18, 77.1–3, 78.6–7, 80.1–8, 82.1–5, 103.1–2, 106.1–2.

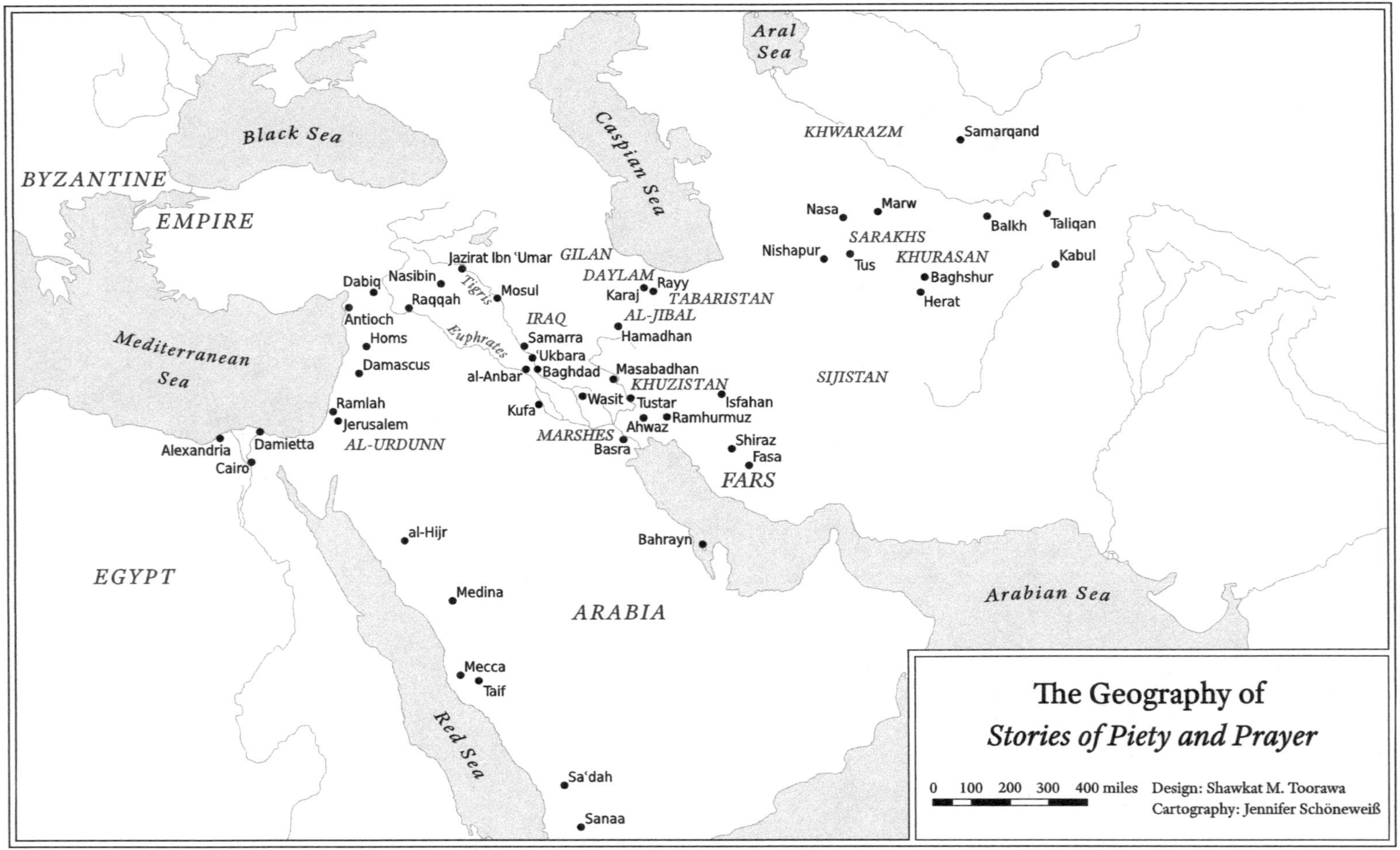
The Geography of
Stories of Piety and Prayer
0 100 200 300 400 miles
Design: Shawkat M. Toorawa
Cartography: Jennifer Schöneweiß
Black Sea
Caspian Sea
Aral Sea
Mediterranean Sea
Red Sea
Arabian Sea
BYZANTINE EMPIRE
EGYPT
ARABIA
KHWARAZM
SARAKHS
KHURASAN
SIJISTAN
GILAN
DAYLAM
TABARISTAN
AL-JIBAL
IRAQ
KHUZISTAN
MARSHES
FARS
AL-URDUNN
Tigris
Euphrates
Samarqand
Nasa
Marw
Balkh
Taliqan
Nishapur
Tus
Kabul
Baghshur
Herat
Jazirat Ibn ʿUmar
Dabiq
Nasibin
Mosul
Raqqah
Antioch
Homs
Damascus
Rayy
Karaj
Hamadhan
Samarra
ʿUkbara
Baghdad
al-Anbar
Masabadhan
Isfahan
Wasit
Tustar
Kufa
Ramhurmuz
Ahwaz
Basra
Shiraz
Fasa
Ramlah
Jerusalem
Alexandria
Damietta
Cairo
al-Hijr
Bahrayn
Medina
Mecca
Taif
Sa'dah
Sanaa

Note on the Text

The Arabic edition

ʿAbbūd al-Shāljī's five-volume edition of *al-Faraj baʿd al-shiddah* (Beirut: Dār Ṣādir, 1978) is the first to use a range of manuscripts and identify its sources clearly. It numbers the items, enabling comparison of the sequence in which they occur in different manuscripts. It is the standard edition, and I take it as my base text. It is described more fully below.

The two previous printed editions are:

1. *Al-Faraj baʿd al-shiddah*. 2 vols. Cairo: Maṭbaʿat al-Hilāl, 1903–4. Edited by Shaykh Muḥammad al-Zuhrī Ghamrāwī from a MS in the library of the grandfather of Maḥmūd Efendī Riyāḍ, collated with another in the Khedivial Library (see title page and p. 2).
2. *Al-Faraj baʿd al-shiddah*. 1 vol. No editor named. Cairo: Maktabat al-Khānjī, 1955. Based on a MS in Dār al-Kutub al-Miṣriyyah (see title page).[17]

The texts of these two editions agree. For example, neither contains al-Tanūkhī's list of chapter headings following his Introduction (§0.14). In the Introduction, both quote only one version of the *rajaz* line by al-Aghlab al-ʿIjlī (§0.3). In Chapter Thirteen, they have the same *isnād*s and share the sequence: numbers 473–76, 479, 477, 478, 480, 489, 490, 491, 492, 481, 482, 488, 485, 483, 486, 484, 487 (compared to al-Shāljī's numbering).

Al-Shāljī's edition has held the field for nearly forty years as the only critical edition. It contains 492 items, as against 360 in the Cairo editions. It uses the Cairo 1955 edition and five MSS. It is a composite, which shows where a given manuscript is fuller than the others (that is, has longer, more detailed, or extra *isnād*s, adds phrases or items, or gives historically identifiable forms of names). It does not attempt to establish stemmas, and indeed there is no evident relationship between the MSS used by al-Shāljī, which were simply those he could gain access to or photocopy. Nor does al-Shāljī tabulate the differences in sequence between his MSS. Instead he uses in-text folio references. This method has merit in light of our current knowledge of the manuscripts and state of the text of *al-Faraj baʿd al-shiddah,* which is still very incomplete.

What does al-Shāljī's edition achieve? It does not reconstruct an urtext, but by recording variants that restore the names of transmitters and protagonists to their original form, it gives us more authoritative readings than those of the previous editions and puts the text in its proper historical perspective. Without trying to relate them critically to each other, it presents a spectrum of different states of the text and adds to the previous shorter published texts a considerable amount of material that can reasonably be attributed to al-Tanūkhī—for it makes sense to assume that more circumstantial *isnād*s and whatever items they are prefixed to are not scribal but are due to al-Tanūkhī, given that most of his informants were not well known outside his own circle. Al-Shālji's text, therefore, is not definitive but it is a good working text from which to improve our understanding of *Faraj.* In the section on the translation below, I give reasons why a definitive text may not be achievable.

Al-Shāljī identifies and describes his five MSS in *Faraj,* vol.1, pp. 21–28, and illustrates folios of each of them in *Faraj,* vol.1, between pages 32 and 33. They are:

1. for "Part I," extent unspecified, a Damascus Ẓāhiriyyah MS (al-Shāljī's readings do not always coincide with Sourdel's readings of Damascus MS Ẓāhiriyyah *adab* 34, see below);
2. for "Part II," extent unspecified, a Rabat MS dated 849/1445–46;
3. for the whole text, Escorial MS 714 dated 975/1567–68, Manchester John Rylands MS Arabic 667 (306), dated 1050/1640–41, and Cairo Dār al-Kutub MS *bāʾ* 22959 (1945/2170, 13225 Add.), dated 1212/1797–98.

It will require a lot more research to find and examine all, or a critical number of, MSS of *Faraj,* and to establish any certainties or reasonable probabilities as to what families of MSS exist and how to interpret the differences between them. Alfred Wiener drew attention to the discrepancies between the Cairo 1903–4 edition and the MSS examined by him.[18] Dominique Sourdel studied these discrepancies more closely, with particular reference to *isnād*s and narrative passages absent from the Cairo 1955 edition and present in one or the other of the Paris MSS Ar. 3483 and 3484, Damascus MS Ẓāhiriyyah *adab* 34, and Berlin MSS Ahlwardt 8737 and 8738.[19] Neither Wiener nor Sourdel examined the differences in the sequences of their manuscripts' contents and their distribution within or between chapters, and a number of manuscripts in accessible libraries escaped their attention. Furthermore, generally speaking, Middle Eastern and European Tanūkhī manuscript studies have not meshed. The field is open to much further exploration.

This edition therefore attempts only to be transparent, cogent, and consistent, not definitive. While adopting the substance of al-Shāljī's text, I have departed from his edition in several ways. He provides a full apparatus, critical and explanatory, in footnotes.[20] My apparatus is much lighter. As regards the translated English text, I give summary explanations in endnotes. General information about persons (transmitters and protagonists) is given in the Glossary, where everyone cited has an entry, even if I have not been able to identify them more than minimally, or, in the case of some Hadith transmitters, at all. Information about realia, institutions, dynasties, concepts, and places is also given in the Glossary.

In the Arabic text, I have removed the identificatory titles al-Shāljī gave to the stories, which are not found in any of the manuscripts, while retaining his numbering of the stories, which is essential for purposes of reference and comparison, even though it cannot always reflect all the articulations of the text. (For example, in terms of their content, in al-Shāljī's no. 20, which I have sub-numbered, §§20.1–4 clearly form one sequence, but §20.5 belongs to the next, al-Shāljī's no. 21.) Al-Shāljī's numbering nevertheless allows us to see how al-Tanūkhī organized items according to a combination of content and source. Thus most of the items cited at §§20.1–25.2 may be considered a sequence in that all but three have al-Tanūkhī's father as informant. Similarly, §§20.1–40, with their dozens of transmitters and careful recording of variants, form a sequence displaying al-Tanūkhī's, and his father's, technical credentials as transmitters of early Muslim tradition. In contrast, the lack of such technical apparatus marks out §§41–57 as a sequence drawing on a broader mixture of both older and more recent traditions.

As well as al-Shāljī's numbering, I have retained all the pious words and phrases that accompany the name of God and references to the Prophet in his base text, even though it is rarely possible to say whether we owe them to al-Tanūkhī or to copyists. In al-Tanūkhī's introduction, §0.1, for example, the words "Lord, «ease» my task" are probably the scribe's, since they occur in different forms in different manuscripts. (For other such variants, see §13.1.)

I have removed most of al-Shāljī's modernizations of the text by reducing voweling to a minimum except in poetic and Qur'anic quotations and deleting almost all punctuation (punctuation is not, of course, original to the MSS, and tends to impose a single interpretation where more than one may be possible).

I have organized each of al-Shāljī's numbered items into numbered subparagraphs so as to foreground recurrent narrative motifs, schemas, and functions. I have not specified which of al-Shāljī's MS readings contribute to each item unless proposing a reading of my own in footnotes. For details of al-Shāljī's readings, the reader is referred back to his edition.

For this particular section of *Deliverance, Stories of Piety and Prayer,* I have examined both Paris MSS, the Manchester John Rylands MS, and microfilms of both Berlin MSS. (An important but incomplete Oxford MS, Pococke 64, does not include the chapters in this volume.) I have consulted a printout of a microfilm of Escorial 714, and five MSS not available to al-Shāljī, which for this volume have yielded a small number of variants or additions. (In subsequent volumes, the proportion will be higher.) They are footnoted in Arabic, and endnoted in English if they are of narrative interest, that is, in the case of this part of the book, which has great cross-sectarian devotional appeal, if they represent variants that testify to the breadth of the reception of the text (see "A variable text" in the section on the translation below). This approach will not satisfy scholars who expect an editor to establish a stable text controlled by a single-minded or at any rate organized author. My editorial approach arises out of my understanding of the current state of Arabic book studies and its acceptance of the frequent messiness of manuscript publication—which is no greater than the messiness of print publication—and what it tells us about authors and readers in an artisan knowledge economy.

Sigla

ب Berlin Ahlwardt 8738. It covers the whole text of *Faraj.* Its first *juz'* is dated 1012/1603–4. In the English notes to this volume, I refer to it as "the" Berlin MS, although it is one of two.

بن Bibliothèque nationale, Paris, 3483. It covers the whole text of *Faraj* and is dated 1126/1714. In the English notes to this volume, I refer to it as "the" Paris MS, although it is one of two.

س Istanbul Sülemaniye (Reisulküttab Mustafa Ef.) 864. Complete, dated 776?/1374–75?. (Printout of microfilm.) In the English notes to this volume, I refer to it as the Sülemaniye MS.

أ	Istanbul Sülemaniye (Ahmed III) 2629. Ostensibly complete, but there is missing and misplaced material. Undated. (Printout of microfilm.) In the English notes to this volume, I refer to it as the Sultan Ahmet MS.
ل	Leiden Cod. Or. 61. Complete, dated 22 Shaʿbān 890/1485.
غ	Escorial 714. Complete.
ش	Al-Shāljī's edition.

The translation

Translating emotions

Just as the range of plots and situations surveyed in *Deliverance* makes it a pattern book of storytelling, so the range of emotions in the passages of first-person life writing makes it a prime source for exploring how al-Tanūkhī's society thought about feelings.[21] What he and his narrators are prepared to reveal about their despair, cowardice, anger, and so on, falls far short of the perfect equanimity that they take as their ideal, giving historians of the emotions new perspectives on the conventions of the exemplary writings that alternate with such passages in *Deliverance*.

That *Deliverance* is so rich a potential source for the history of emotions has led me to particular choices as translator. Arabic vocabulary, and especially the vocabulary of emotions, has a fluid range of meanings that can be narrowed down by context but is often deliberately left open, so that words like *shiddah* and *faraj* can express anything from physical sensations of constraint and release, or psychological feelings of anguish and relief, to emotional judgments: that a situation constitutes an "adversity" or a process amounts to a "deliverance." As yet, such gradations have barely been investigated by scholars and are treated intuitively by translators, who usually vary the rendering freely according to context and to a vocabulary set derived from their own cultural background. In *Stories of Piety and Prayer*, however, al-Tanūkhī's introduction lays down a set of keywords, a number of them derived from the Qur'anic passages in Chapter One, which then reverberate throughout Chapters Two and Three.[22] In an attempt to capture this recurrence and emotional layering, and at the same time avoid imposing subjective interpretations, I have opted for fixed English translations in this particular section of *Deliverance*. Instead of using existing translations, I have translated the Qur'anic passages myself so that the keywords contained in them do not vary. This of course poses the problem of finding words that sit convincingly in different contexts. Examples of fixed translations are my choice of "acceptance" for the Qur'anic *ṣabr*, the attitude that one should ideally maintain in adversity in hope of deliverance (§§0.3, 0.4, 0.6, 1.9, 1.10, 4.4, 9.8–9, 10, 11.1, 11.3, 13.7, 20.5, 22, 23, 34.2, 42.1, 42.5, 44.1–2, 47.1, 47.4, 48, 49.4, 50.3, 50.5, 50.7, 51.1, 52.2–3, 54.5, 55.2–3, 56, 58.1, 60.2, 60.4, 66.1, 74.1), and, of course, "deliverance" to render *faraj* and "adversity" for *shiddah* (neither of them Qur'anic terms). Other examples that carry echoes of the Qur'an or of Prophetic or Alid hadith include "loss" or "hurt" for *ḍarr* (§§0.2, 0.3, 1.6, 7.1, 11.3, 13.5, 34.2, 47.7, 47.10, 60.4, 72), "constraint" for *ḍayq/ḍīq* (§§0.2, 0.11, 1.2, 2.3, 26.1, 34.2), "hardship" for *ʿusr* (§§1.1–4, 13.7, 19.3, 20.5, 22, 42.6, 59.1–3, 59.5–6, 60.1–2, 62, 107.1–3, 108.1), "care" or "grief" for *ghamm* (§§0.6, 1.2, 1.10, 2.3, 8.4, 16.1, 19.1, 31.7, 31.9, 31.11, 34.2–3, 45.2, 66.1, 97.1), "affliction" for *karb* or *kurbah* (§§0.11, 0.14, 1.6, 1.10, 2.3, 3.2, 11.3, 13.4, 15.1, 17.3, 19.2, 20.5, 22, 24, 25.1–2, 28, 31.2, 31.4, 31.8–10, 31.12–13, 33, 34.2, 38.2, 52.3, 67.4, 68.2, 69.1, 86.3, 110.3), "trial" or "ordeal" for *miḥnah* (§§0.2, 0.4, 0.5, 0.14, 2.1–2, 6, 9.10, 12.3, 34.3, 42.1–2, 42.5, 49.4, 50.1–3, 50.5, 55.1–2, 57, 58.1, 60.4, 66.1, 72, 80.5), and "sorrow" or "anxiety" for *hamm* (§§0.4, 0.6, 2.3, 19.1, 26.1, 26.2, 31.7–8, 31.11, 32, 34.2, 42.1, 47.11, 52.1, 58.3, 85.3, 91, 95.1, 98.1, 99).

I have also used fixed formulas to translate all the pious words and phrases that accompany the name of God and references to the Prophet. I have not pruned them to make the translation smoother, even though such phrases may generally be regarded as optional, to be multiplied or removed at will by readers and copyists, because in this part of *Deliverance* I think they have special emotional weight.

I hope that the use in this volume of consistent renderings rather than free variation will afford a reliable script for anyone wishing to investigate Arabic emotions in their historical context.

Language and literary conventions

The written literary Arabic of this period is a book language. Even in dialogue, the vernacular is not used. However natural some of the speeches may seem, their verisimilitude is artful: Al-Tanūkhī, or his sources, have not "reproduced" the words of protagonists or narrators; they have translated them into formal written Arabic, or invented them in that language. Al-Tanūkhī's readers would assume that the Prophet, ʿAlī ibn Abī Ṭālib, other exemplary early figures, and the Bedouin spoke formal Arabic, complete with case endings, as their natural tongue, but they would know that ordinary characters made to speak in this way would not have done so in real life.

There are two other literary conventions connected with dialogue. First, Arabic dialogue is almost always direct speech. It is very rarely reported. I have followed this convention, never substituting (for example) "They asked if they should memorize it" for " 'Should we memorize this?' they asked," so that on the rare occasions when indirect speech is used, it stands out. Second, the Arabic dialogue cue is always "he said" or "she said," prefixed to a speech. This corresponds to Arabic reading habits. I believe that al-Tanūkhī and his contemporaries would have read aloud to themselves. As in a radio play, they would have "performed" dialogue and not read out the cues, which were there simply to guide the eye, separating dialogue from non-dialogue on the page (text was written continuously, with no paragraphs, indentations, or quotation marks). Modern readers read silently, and expect the author to tell them through varied dialogue cues what the tone of a speech should be. In deference to silent reading habits, I have sometimes varied the verb or positioned it after the speech. More often it is otiose and I have left it out altogether.

Translating isnād*s*

My translation retains in full al-Tanūkhī's chains of transmitters (*isnād*s), which would have been integral to the experience of reading the original and to al-Tanūkh's processes of composition: to reading or hearing and then, mentally or in writing, recording and classifying source materials, before reusing them in new configurations. This was a complex operation, as can be seen from comparing the items in one of al-Tanūkhī's main sources, Ibn Abī l-Dunyā's *Book of Deliverance*, with the way he selected, split, and regrouped them. In the history of Arabic literature and book culture, *isnād*s are vital evidence.[23]

There are several reasons why al-Tanūkhī himself attached great importance to chains of transmitters and lists of sources. In the case of sacred material, they serve as a continuous living link to the Prophet and other holy people, and have a devotional, emotional, and sometimes a magical function. For other materials, they are an acknowledgement of literary paths of transmission, of sources and copyright, as it were, and are part of the learned apparatus of scholarship, like modern footnote citations and bibliographies.[24] Very often, they are also witnesses to a personal link between al-Tanūkhī and his teachers, friends, or family members, so that he quotes from books, such as those of his predecessors in the *faraj* genre, through *isnād*s that face two ways, showing both where the books got their materials and whom al-Tanūkhī studied the books with. This gives his citations a social and personal dimension. Lastly, some *isnād*s show off al-Tanūkhī's technical competence as a traditionist. His family on both sides were well-known transmitters of Hadith, and al-Tanūkhī indulges in occasional virtuoso displays of *isnād* scholarship, comparing or commenting on lines of transmission. Many kinds of social and scholarly capital are compounded in these performances.[25]

A variable text

There is a great deal of near-repetition and variation on subthemes in *Deliverance*. Some previous translators of *Deliverance* into European languages have chosen to keep just one or two representative versions of a story, tale type, or (especially) prayer. I have kept them all. *Deliverance* deliberately explores variants and alternatives and is intrinsically analytical, so a true picture of how the author's mind worked can be given only by translating the complete text.

By "complete," however, I mean two slightly different things. I mean nonselective, in the sense of retaining *isnād*s and variants; and I mean maximalist, in the sense of translating as much of the text as can be found in a reasonable selection of accessible manuscripts. Manuscripts of *Deliverance* are numerous. They have not all been identified, and many of the known ones have not been studied. To have tried to trace all of them would have delayed the translation indefinitely. To do so in hopes of establishing a definitive text might be a perverse endeavor, for on the available evidence it seems likely there never was a definitive text. In his introduction, al-Tanūkhī looks back over the process of composing *Deliverance* and says that it went through two phases: accumulation and cutting. He does not mention that part of the process involved the adaptation of some particularly vivid items that he also used in *Table Talk*, and overall his description may be formulaic and conventional. He may have tinkered with his text rather than cutting it. Traces of multiple revisions can be followed in a number of manuscripts. Some contain extra items. Some reorganize the analytical sequences in which the items are presented within chapters, or move them between chapters. There are manuscripts with expanded *isnād*s adding personal details about al-Tanūkhī's informants, or with passages that interpolate narrative variants into the body of a story or add alternative endings complete with their own *isnād*s.[26] The sum of the evidence tends to suggest that al-Tanūkhī added more than he cut, and that he did so at various times without ever quite making up his mind (like Proust with *À la recherche du temps perdu*), and either that he himself put revised portions of his book into circulation while he was still drafting or rewriting the next installment, or else that any drafts he left behind were copied indiscriminately after his death. As it is not yet possible to reconstruct the sequence of the revised versions, I have adopted the same solution as al-Shāljī: a composite text. My additions to al-Shāljī's edition, using manuscripts to which he did not have access, become significant only in the volumes following this one, however. In *Stories of Piety and Prayer*, the additions or noteworthy variants signaled in the footnotes and endnotes at §§9.4, 13.8, 67.1, and 112 bear witness to the process of folklorization mentioned in the Introduction, which is important for the reception history of *Deliverance*, and even more so for our growing understanding of the interdependence of what were once thought to be the quite separate spheres of elite and popular Arabic literature.

Interpretation

Finally, what of my translation of the title as *Deliverance Follows Adversity*? Previous English renderings, such as *Relief after Distress*, or the German *Ende Gut, Alles Gut*, have tended to attenuate it, and to slant the purpose of the *faraj* paradigm toward the literary pleasure readers gain from unexpected reversals and the resolution of suspense. Pleasure there certainly is, but there is also meant to be pain. Empathy with the stricken, with how they experience their plight, and their different reactions to suffering, is fundamental to the way readers are expected to respond to *Deliverance*, and so I have opted for a translation that lingers on this process rather than cutting straight to the happy endings. These are, after all, a literary trick, by which al-Tanūkhī adapts to the *faraj* paradigm much material that belongs to the alternation or circularity paradigm that I described in the Introduction. Al-Tanūkhī's original readers would have known this, for they were as familiar as he was with the lives and deaths of figures such as the vizier Ibn Muqlah.

Did al-Tanūkhī really believe in happy endings, or did he only try to make himself believe in them? This is open to interpretation. But no reader can fail to notice that the emotion that dominates *Deliverance*, and especially *Stories of Piety and Prayer*, is fear: fear of sickness, pain, poverty, injustice, torture, and execution. The history of al-Tanūkhī's times shows just how much there was to be afraid of. We should remember this if we want to understand why *Deliverance* was written and why people were eager to read it.

Notes to the Introduction

1 See Miskawayh, *The Eclipse of the Abbasid Caliphate*, vol.1, 388, 430, 435.

2 For al-Muhallabī's vizierate, see Donohue, *The Buwayhid Dynasty*, 139–47.

3 On Abū l-Faraj al-Iṣfahānī and his huge, unfinished masterpiece, *Kitāb al-Aghānī* (*The Book of Songs*), see Kilpatrick, *Making the Great Book of Songs*.

4 The chronology of al-Tanūkhī's life has been clarified by Ghersetti and is summarized by her in the foreword to *Sollievo*, 12–16. Further details have been uncovered by Franssen, "Une copie en *maġribī*," 45–49.

5 Two further works have been attributed to al-Tanūkhī, a collection of examples of generosity, *al-Mustajād min fa'lāt al-ajwād* (*Admirable Acts of Generosity*), and a collection of aphorisms, *'Unwān al-ḥikmah wa-l-bayān* (*The Epitome of Wisdom and Eloquence*). The attributions are now thought to be spurious. See Franssen, "Une copie en *maġribī*," 50.

6 See Bray, "Place and Self-Image: The Buhlūlids and Tanūẖids," 63.

7 Al-Khaṭīb al-Baghdādī, *Tārīkh Baghdād*, vol. 5, 81–82.

8 Wiener, "Die *Farağ ba'd aš-Šidda*-Literatur."

9 Fakkar, *At-Tanûẖî et son livre: La Délivrance après l'angoisse*. Fakkar in fact adds little to Wiener. There are three recent European-language monographs, one of a them a still-unpublished PhD thesis: Moebius, "Narrative Judgments: The *Qāḍī* al-Tanūkhī and the *Faraj* Genre in Medieval Arabic Literature"; Özkan, *Narrativität im Kitāb al-Farağ ba'da aš-Šidda*; and Khalifa, *Hardship and Deliverance*.

10 Miskawayh, *The Eclipse of the Abbasid Caliphate*. The life of Miskawayh (ca. 320–421/932–1030) overlapped that of al-Tanūkhī's father (278–342/892–953) as well as al-Tanūkhī's (327–84/939–94).

11 Since the 1930s, "Tanūkhī studies" have grown, in the fields of both history and literature. See the bibliography of Özkan, *Narrativität im Kitāb al-Farağ ba'da aš-Šidda*, and Key, review of Khalifa, *Hardship and Deliverance*, 212, 214–16.

12 Sourdel, *Vizirat*, 35–36.

13 See *Enzyklopädie des Märchens*.

14 See Bray, "Place and Self-Image: The Buhlūlids and Tanūẖids," and "Practical Mu'tazilism."

15 Franssen, "Une copie en *maġribī*," 57; Beaumont, "In the Second Degree," 127; Ghersetti, "Il *qāḍī* et il *faraǧ*," 43–45.

16 Schippers, "Changing Narrativity in a Changing Society."

17 There is also an abridged edition, or an edition of an abridgment, which does not identify its source: *Al-Faraj baʿd al-shiddah li-l-waqāʾiʿ al-gharībah wa-l-asrār al-ʿajībah.* 1 vol. Edited by Khalīl ʿImrān al-Manṣūr. Beirut: Dār al-Kutub al-ʿIlmiyyah, 1997.

18 Wiener, "Die *Faraǧ baʿd aš-Šidda*-Literatur," 398–400.

19 See Sourdel, *Vizirat*, passim, and idem, "Une lettre inédite de ʿAlī b. ʿĪsā (317/929)," "Fragments d'al-Ṣūlī sur l'histoire des vizirs ʿAbbāsides," "Nouvelles recherches," and review of Fakkar, *At-Tanûhî et son livre*.

20 Objections to the copiousness of al-Shāljī's annotations have been rebutted by Garulo, "Erudición y nostalgia."

21 See Behzadi, "Standardizing Emotions."

22 On cumulative emotional resonance in the Qur'an itself, see Bauer, "Emotion in the Qur'an," 3, 22–25.

23 Starting with Schoeler, *Ecrire et transmettre*, studies of medieval Arabic are increasingly informed by awareness of how the processes of composition and the physical structure of books influenced structures of writing and thinking. See also *Putting the House of Wisdom in Order* and al-Ṣūlī, *The Life and Times of Abū Tammām*, introduction, xvii–xviii.

24 Moebius, "Narrative Judgments: The *Qāḍī* al-Tanūkhī and the *Faraj* Genre in Medieval Arabic Literature," pays particular attention to this type of *isnād*.

25 I have done my best to identify the traditionists cited in the *isnād*s, but many of them are obscure or of uncertain identity.

26 See [Ashtiany] Bray, "*Isnād*s and Models of Heroes," 26, 28–29; Franssen, "A *Maġribī* Copy," 75–77; and "Une copie en *maġribī*," 69–71 for some of these features.

الفــرج بعد الشــدّة

Deliverance Follows Adversity

١،٠ بسم الله الرحمن الرحيم

رب يسّر

٢،٠ قال الفقيه القاضي أبو عليّ المحسّن بن القاضي أبي القاسم عليّ بن محمّد بن أبي الفهم التنوخيّ رحمه الله تعالى الحمد لله الّذي جعل بعد الشدّة فرجاً ومن الضرّ والضيق سعةً ومخرجاً ولم يُخْلِ محنةً من منحة ولا نقمة من نعمة ولا نكبة ورزيّة من موهبة وعطيّة وصلّى الله على سيّد المرسلين وخاتم النبيّين محمّد وآله الطيّبين.

٣،٠ أمّا بعد فإنّي لمّا رأيت أبناء الدنيا متقلّبين فيها بين خير وشرّ ونفع وضرّ ولم أرَ لهم في أيّام الرخاء أنفع من الشكر والثناء ولا في أيّام البلاء أنجع من الصبر والدعاء لأنّ من جعل الله عمره أطول من عمر محنته فإنّه سيكشفها عنه بتطوّله ورأفته فيصير ما هو فيه من الأذى كما قال من مضى ويروى للأغلب العجليّ أو غيره [رجز]

أَلْغَمَرَاتُ ثُمَّ يَنْجَلِينَا   ثُمَّتَ يَذْهَبْنَ وَلا يَجِينَا

ويُروى

أَلْغَمَرَاتُ ثُمَّ يَنْجَلِينَهْ   ثُمَّتَ يَذْهَبْنَ وَلا يَجِينَهْ

فطوبى لمن وُفّق في الحالين للقيام بالواجبين.

٤،٠ ووجدتُ أقوى ما يفزع إليه من أناخ الدهر بمكروه عليه قراءة الأخبار التي تنبّي عن تفضّل الله عزّ وجلّ على من حصل قبله في محصله ونزل به مثل بلائه ومعضله

Author's Introduction

In the name of God, full of compassion, ever compassionate. 0.1
Lord, «ease» my task.[1]

The author of this work, the learned judge Abū ʿAlī al-Muḥassin, son of Judge Abū l-Qāsim ʿAlī ibn Muḥammad ibn Abī l-Fahm al-Tanūkhī, may God Exalted show him compassion, says: 0.2

Praise God, Who has made deliverance follow adversity, comfort and relief follow loss and constraint, Who lets no trial be devoid of gain, no blow be devoid of blessing, and Who makes all calamities and bereavement yield bountiful gifts. God bless the chief of all His emissaries, Muḥammad, Seal of the Prophets, and his noble kin.

Now I come to my topic. I have seen that humankind's passage through this world is an alternation of good and ill, profit and loss, and that in good times nothing is more profitable than thankfulness and praise, and in bad times nothing more salutary than acceptance and prayer, since if God lets a sufferer outlive his trials, once His generosity and mercy have preserved him from his woes, they will seem, in the words of a bygone poet (al-Aghlab al-ʿIjlī according to some): 0.3

> A sea of troubles; but it withdraws,
> ebbs, and comes not back again

or:

> A sea of troubles; but it withdraweth,
> ebbeth, and cometh not back again.[2]

Blessed, therefore, are those to whom it is granted in both good times and bad to behave as befits.

To those enduring fate's injuries, nothing, I find, affords more powerful solace than reading accounts of God's graciousness, Mighty and Glorious is 0.4

بما أتاحه له من صنع أمسك به الأرماق ومعونة حلّ بها من الخناق ولطف غريب نجّاه وفرج عجيب أنقذه وتلافاه وإن خفيت تلك الأسباب ولم تبلغ ما حدث من ذلك الفكر والحساب فإنّ في معرفة الممتحن بذلك شحذ بصيرته في الصبر وتقوية عزيمته على التسليم إلى مالك كلّ أمر وتصويب رأيه في الإخلاص والتفويض إلى من بيده مُلك النواصِ وكثيرًا ما إذا علم الله تعالى من وليّه وعبده انقطاع آماله إلّا من عنده لم يكِله إلى سعيه وجهده ولم يرض له باحتماله وطوقه ولم يخله من عنايته ورفقه.

وأنا بمشيئة الله تعالى جامع في هذا الكتاب أخبارًا من هذا الجنس والباب أرجو بها انشراح صدور ذوي الألباب عند ما يدهمهم من شدّة ومصاب إذكنت قد قاسيت من ذلك في محن دُفعت إليها ما يحنو بي على الممتحنين ويحدوني على بذل الجهد في تفريج غموم المكروبين.

٥،٠ وكنت وقفت في بعض محني على خمس أو ستّ أوراق جمعها أبو الحسن عليّ بن محمّد المدائنيّ وسمّاها كتاب الفرج بعد الشدّة والضيقة وذكر فيها أخبارًا يدخل جميعها في هذا المعنى فوجدتها حسنة لكنّها لقلّته أنموذجُ صبرة فلم يأت بها ولا سلك فيها سبل الكتب المصنّفة ولا الأبواب الواسعة المؤلّفة مع اقتداره على ذلك ولا أعلم غرضه في التقصير ولعلّه أراد أن ينهج طريق هذا الفنّ من الأخبار ويسبق إلى فتح الباب فيه بذلك المقدار واستثقل تخريج جميع ما عنده فيه من الآثار.

٦،٠ ووقع إليّ كتاب لأبي بكر عبد الله بن محمّد بن أبي الدنيا قد سمّاه كتاب الفرج[١] في نحو عشرين ورقة والغالب عليه أحاديث عن النبيّ صلّى الله عليه وسلّم وعلى آله وأخبار عن الصحابة والتابعين رحمهم الله يدخل بعضها في معنى طلبته ولا يخرج عن قصده وبغيته وباقيها أحاديث وأخبار في الدعاء وفي الصبر وفي الأرزاق والتوكّل والتعوّض عن الشدائد بذكر الموت وما يجري مجرى التعازي ويتسلّى به عن طوارق الهموم ونوازل الأحداث والغموم بما يستحقّ فيها من الثواب في الأخرى مع التمسّك بالحزم

١ ش: كاتب الفرج بعد الشدّة.

He, toward those who have previously suffered the same plight and undergone the same tribulations and perplexities, for they show how those at their last gasp have been preserved through the working of His ordinance, those sore beset succored, or saved by an extraordinary grace, or freed by a marvelous deliverance that made all come right again. How these things came to pass may not be evident; what happened may not be susceptible to reasoning or calculation. Nevertheless, knowing that such things *have* happened hones the sufferer's perception of what acceptance of God's will means. His resolve to consign himself to the Lord Omnipotent is strengthened. He sees that his proper course is to love Him with all his heart and commit himself to the One in Whose hand lies the «governance» of all creatures.[3] And so it often happens that God Exalted, understanding that His friend and servant has placed all his hope in Him, will not leave him to his own endeavors, is pleased not to let him struggle alone under his burden, and does not withhold from him His kindly providence.

In this book, if God Almighty wills, I shall gather accounts of this sort, which I hope will open out the breasts[4] of the discerning when adversity and mishaps befall them. As a result of trials that have overtaken me, I have been through experiences that make me feel for my fellow sufferers and move me to exert myself to relieve the sorrows of others who are afflicted.

In the course of one such trial, I came across five or six folios put together 0.5
by Abū l-Ḥasan ʿAlī ibn Muḥammad al-Madāʾinī to which he had given the title *The Book of Deliverance following Adversity and Straits*. All the items it contained were on this theme, and I thought it was good, but too slim to be more than a random sample. He did not organize the contents by topic, as he might have done, or compose chapters of any length. I do not know why he failed to do so. Perhaps he meant to pioneer the genre[5] but could not be bothered to compile all the relevant traditions he knew, and intended his small amount of material to serve as a door opening the way.

I also came upon a book by Abū Bakr ʿAbd Allāh ibn Muḥammad Ibn Abī 0.6
l-Dunyā, which he called *The Book of Deliverance*.[6] It is about twenty folios long, and consists mostly of reports about the Prophet, God bless and keep him and his kin, and accounts of the Companions and Successors, God show them compassion. Some were relevant, or not irrelevant, to my own undertaking; but the rest consisted of reports and accounts concerning prayer, acceptance, trusting in God to provide, and compensation for misfortunes. There

في الأولى وهو عندي خالٍ من ذكر فرج بعد شدّة غير مستحقّ أن يدخل في كتاب مقصور على هذا الفنّ وضمّن الكتاب نبذاً قليلة من الشعر وروى فيه شيئاً يسيرًا جدًّا ممّا ذكره المدائنيّ إلّا أنّه جاء بإسناد له لا عن المدائنيّ.

٧،٠ وقرأت أيضاً كتاباً للقاضي أبي الحسين عمر بن القاضي أبي عمر محمّد بن يوسف القاضي رحمهم الله في مقدار خمسين ورقة قد سمّاه كتاب الفرج بعد الشدّة أودعه أكثر ما رواه المدائنيّ وجمعه وأضاف إليه أخباراً أخر أكثرها حشو[1] وفيها غير ما هو مماثل عندي لما عزاه ولا مشاكل لما نحاه وأتى في أثنائها بأبيات شعر يسيرة من معادن لأمثالها جمّة كثيرة ولم يلمّ بما أورده ابن أبي الدنيا ولا أعلم أتعمّد ذلك أم لم يقف على الكتاب.

٨،٠ ووجدت أبا بكر بن أبي الدنيا والقاضي أبا الحسين لم يذكرا أنّ للمدائنيّ كتاباً في هذا المعنى فإن لم يكونا عرفا هذا فهو طريف وإن كانا تعمّدا ترك ذكره تنفيقاً لكتابيهما وتغطية على كتاب الرجل فهو أطرف ووجدتهما قد استحسنا استعارة لقب كتاب المدائنيّ على اختلافهما في الاستعارة وحيدهما عن أن يأتيا بجميع العبارة فتوهّمتُ أنّ كلّ واحد منهما لمّا زاد على قدر ما أخرجه المدائنيّ اعتقد أنّه أولى منه بلقب كتابه فإن كان هذا الحكم ماضياً والصواب به قاضياً فيجب أن يكون من زاد عليهما فيما جمعاه أولى منهما بما تعبا في تصنيفه ووضعاه.

٩،٠ فكان هذا من أسباب نشاطي لتأليف كتاب يحتوي من هذا الفنّ على أكثر ممّا جمعه القوم وأشرح وأبين للمغزى وأكشف وأوضح وأن أخالف مذهبهم في التصنيف وأعدل عن طريقتهم في الجمع والتأليف فإنّهم نسقوا ما أودعوه كتبهم جملة واحدة وربّما صادفت ملاً من سامعيها أو وافقت سآمة من الناظرين فيها فرأيت أن أنوّع الأخبار وأجعلها أبواباً ليزداد من يقف على الكتب الأربعة بكتابي من بينها إعجاباً وأن أضع ما في الكتب الثلاثة في مواضعه من أبواب هذا الكتاب إلّا ما أعتقد

[1] حشو: كذا في أ، ب، س. وفي ش: حسن.

were also thoughts on death, and various kinds of consolation and solace for use on occasions of deep sorrow and when grievous accidents and cares befall, telling of the reward these things earn in the hereafter, and how in this life they should be met with a stout heart. In my opinion none of this has anything to do with deliverance following adversity, and there is no place for it in a book of which that is the sole topic. Ibn Abī l-Dunyā's book contains a few bits of poetry. He transmits a very small part of al-Madāʾinī's material, but substitutes his own chains of transmitters for al-Madāʾinī's.

I have also read a work by Judge Abū l-Ḥusayn ʿUmar, son of Judge Abū ʿUmar Muḥammad, whose father was Judge Yūsuf, may God show them all compassion.[7] It is fifty folios long, and he entitled it *The Book of Deliverance following Adversity*. It contains most of al-Madāʾinī's material, together with additional items, which are largely padding and are all, in my opinion, beside the point and irrelevant. He inserted a few lines of poetry from sources that could have yielded much more, and included none of Ibn Abī l-Dunyā's material. I do not know if this was by design or because he did not know his book. 0.7

I noticed, however, that neither Ibn Abī l-Dunyā nor Judge Abū l-Ḥusayn mentions that al-Madāʾinī wrote a book on the subject. It would be strange if neither of them knew about it, and stranger still if they deliberately kept quiet about it in order to promote their own books by concealing his. At all events, they were happy enough to borrow versions of the title of al-Madāʾinī's book without reproducing it exactly. No doubt each believed he had a better claim to it by virtue of having included more material than al-Madāʾinī. If this is deemed to set a valid and binding precedent, then it follows that anyone who collects more material than they did must have a better claim to what they labored to set down. 0.8

That is one reason why I have been eager to compose a book that contains more on the topic than any previous work and is more detailed, pertinent, analytical, and intelligible. Unlike my predecessors, I organize my matter thematically, and again unlike them, I arrange it coherently, whereas they lumped everything together, which is apt to bore and irk listeners and readers. I have chosen to classify my materials and divide them into chapters, so that anyone comparing the four books will admire mine all the more, and to assign quotations from my three precursors' books to the appropriate chapters in my own. I have left out what I thought irrelevant or best omitted and substituted more 0.9

أنّه لا يجب أن يدخل فيه وأنّ تركه وتعدّيه أصوب وأولى والتشاغل بذكر غيره ممّا هو داخل في المعنى ولم يذكره القوم أليق وأحرى وأن أعزو ما أخرجه ممّا في الكتب الثلاثة إلى مؤلّفيها تأديةً للأمانة واستيثاقاً في الرواية وتبييناً لما آتي به من الزيادة وتنبيهاً على موضع الإفادة.

١٠.٠ فاستخرت الله عزّ ذكره وبدأت بذلك في هذا الكتاب ولقّبته بكتاب الفرج بعد الشدّة تيمّناً لقارئه بهذا الفال وليستسعد في ابتدائه بهذا المقال ولم أستبشع إعادة هذا اللقب ولم أحتشم تكريره على ظهور الكتب لأنّه قد صار جارياً مجرى تسمية رجل اسمه محمّداً أو محموداً أو سعداً أو مسعوداً فليس لقائل مع التداول لهذين الاسمين أن يقول لمن سمّي بهما الآن إنّك انتحلت هذا الاسم أو سرقته.

١١.٠ ووجدتني متى أعطيت كتابي هذا حقّه من الاستقصاء وبلغت به حدّه من الاستيفاء جاء في ألوف أوراق لطول ما مضى من الزمان وإنّ الله بحكمته أجرى أمور عباده وأغذياء نعمته منذ خلقهم وإلى أن يقبضهم على التقلّب بين شدّة ورخاء ورغد وبلاء وأخذ وعطاء ومنع وصنع وضيق ورحب وفرج وكرب علماً منه تعالى بعواقب الأمور ومصلحة الكافّة والجمهور وأخبار ذلك كثيرة المقدار عظيمة الترديد والتكرار وليست كلّها بمستحسنة ولا مستفادة ولا مستطابة الذكر والإعادة.

١٢.٠ فاقتصرت على كتْب أحسن ما رُويتُ من هذه الأخبار وأصحّ ما بلغني في معانيها من الآثار وأملح ما وجدتُ في فنونها من الأشعار وجعلت قصدي الإيجاز والاختصار وإسقاط الحشو وترك الإكثار وإن كان المجتمع من ذلك جملة يستطيلها الملول ولا يتفرّغ لقراءتها المشغول.

١٣.٠ وأنا أرغب إلى من يصل كتابي هذا إليه وينشط للوقوف عليه أن يصفح عمّا يعثر به من زلل ويصلح ما يجد فيه من خطأ وخلل والله أسأل السلامة من المعاب والتوفيق لبلوغ المحاب والإرشاد إلى الصواب ويفعل الله ذلك بكرمه إنّه جواد وهّاب.

suitable and relevant items that have not been cited before. I acknowledge my predecessors whenever I quote from them. This is honest, establishes reliable readings, shows clearly what I have added, and draws attention to any points of significance.

I began my book by seeking God's guidance, mighty is His name, giving it 0.10 the title *Deliverance Follows Adversity* so that the reader would be gladdened by the presage and anticipate good fortune from its opening words. Nor am I loath or ashamed to reuse the title on the grounds that other books have borne it before, for this has become a commonplace,[8] equivalent to calling someone by his given name, Muḥammad or Maḥmūd, Saʿd or Masʿūd. Both forms of each are used so widely that no one would say to those now called by them,"Your name is usurped or plagiarized."

But when in due course I had made the book as exhaustive as it deserved 0.11 to be and explored the subject to its limits, so much time had passed that I realized it was thousands of folios long. This is because from the moment He creates His servants, the partakers of His blessings, until He gathers them to Himself, God in His wisdom takes and gives, denies and bestows, which causes us to alternate between adversity and prosperity, opulence and tribulation, constraint and freedom, and between deliverance and affliction—for He knows, exalted is He, the outcome of events and what is best for each and all. Consequently, there are many stories to this effect, and they are very repetitive. Not all are exemplary or edifying, and some are better not mentioned or cited.

I therefore confined myself to transcribing the best stories I had been told, 0.12 the soundest accounts I knew, and the most pleasing verse I had come across on the subject. This time my aim was pith and concision, without padding or superfluity. Even so, those who are easily bored may find the whole thing too long, and busy people may not have time to read it.

It is my hope that those into whose hands my book may fall and who take 0.13 the trouble to read it will forgive any errors they happen upon and correct any mistakes or flaws. I pray to God, such is His goodness and unstinting generosity, to preserve me from blame, and to grant that, thanks to His guidance, my book will achieve its purpose and be well received.

تسمية أبواب الكتاب وهي أربعة عشر باباً: ١٤،٠

الباب الأوّل: ما أنبأ الله تعالى به في القرآن من ذكر الفرج بعد البؤس والامتحان.

الباب الثاني: ما جاء في الآثار من ذكر الفرج بعد اللأواء وما يتوصّل به إلى كشف نازل الشدّة والبلاء.

الباب الثالث: من بُشّر بفرج من نطق فال ونجا من محنة بقول أو دعاء أو ابتهال.

الباب الرابع: من استعطف غضب السلطان بصادق لفظ أو استوقف مكروهه بموقظ بيان أو وعظ.

الباب الخامس: من خرج من حبْس أو أسر أو اعتقال إلى سراح وسلامة وصلاح حال.

الباب السادس: من فارق شدّة إلى رخاء بعد بشرى منام لم يشب صدق تأويله كذب الأحلام.

الباب السابع: من استنقذ من كرب وضيق خنّاق بإحدى حالتي عمد أو اتّفاق.

الباب الثامن: من أشفى على أن يُقتل فكان الخلاص إليه من القتل أعجل.

الباب التاسع: من شارف الموت بحيوان مهلك رآه فكفاه الله سبحانه ذلك بلطفه ونجّاه.

الباب العاشر: من اشتدّ بلاؤه بمرض ناله فعافاه الله تعالى بأيسر سبب وأقاله.

الباب الحادي عشر: من أُمتحن من لصوص بسرق أو قطع فعُوِّض منه الارتجاع والخلف بأجمل صنع.

الباب الثاني عشر: من ألجأه خوف إلى هرب واستتار فأُبدل بأمن ومستجدّ نعمة ومسارّ.

الباب الثالث عشر: من نالته شدّة في هواه فكشفها الله تعالى عنه وملّكه من يهواه.

الباب الرابع عشر: ما اختير من ملح الأشعار في أكثر معاني ما تقدّم من الأمثال والأخبار.

The book's fourteen chapter headings are as follows: 0.14

Chapter One. In the Qur'an, God Exalted reveals how deliverance follows suffering and ordeals.

Chapter Two. What Tradition relates of deliverance following desolation and how one may be rescued from sore adversity and tribulation.

Chapter Three. Presages bringing tidings of delivery to those saved from ordeals by speech, prayer, or entreaty.

Chapter Four. Speaking truth to power and averting its fury or checking death with an eloquent homily.

Chapter Five. After prison, concealment, or captivity finding wellbeing, safety, and liberty.

Chapter Six. Exchanging adversity for prosperity after dreams of good tiding untainted by figments misguiding.

Chapter Seven. Those saved from affliction or straitened circumstance either by design or by happenstance.

Chapter Eight. Those about to be killed whose death was forestalled.

Chapter Nine. Those by beasts given chase spared death by God's grace.

Chapter Ten. Those in sore tribulation from disease whom God Exalted cured with perfect ease.

Chapter Eleven. The trials of brigandage and burglary recouped and compensated by God's agency.

Chapter Twelve. Those resorting, in fear, to flight and hiding who found instead security, blessings, and joy abiding.

Chapter Thirteen. Lovers frustrated in their hearts' affection on whom the Almighty bestowed the object of their affections.

Chapter Fourteen. Choice poetic samples illustrating most of these examples.

الباب الأوّل

ما أنبأنا به الله تعالى في القرآن من ذكر الفرج بعد البؤس والامتحان

١،١ قال الله تعالى وهو أصدق القائلين وهو الحقّ اليقين ﴿بِسْمِ ٱللَّهِ ٱلرَّحْمَٰنِ ٱلرَّحِيمِ أَلَمْ نَشْرَحْ لَكَ صَدْرَكَ وَوَضَعْنَا عَنكَ وِزْرَكَ ٱلَّذِىٓ أَنقَضَ ظَهْرَكَ وَرَفَعْنَا لَكَ ذِكْرَكَ فَإِنَّ مَعَ ٱلْعُسْرِ يُسْرًا إِنَّ مَعَ ٱلْعُسْرِ يُسْرًا فَإِذَا فَرَغْتَ فَٱنصَبْ وَإِلَىٰ رَبِّكَ فَٱرْغَب﴾.

٢،١ فهذه السورة كلّها مُفصحة بإذكار الله عزّ وجلّ رسوله عليه السلام منّته عليه في شرح صدره بعد الغمّ والضيق ووضع وزره عنه وهو الإثم بعد إنقاض الظهر وهو الإثقال أي أثقله فنقض العظام كما ينتقض البيت إذا صوّت للوقوع ورفع جلّ جلاله ذكره بعد أن لم يكن بحيث جعله الله مذكوراً معه والبشارة له في نفسه عليه السلام وفي أمّته بأنّ مع العسر الواحد يسرين إذا رغبوا إلى الله تعالى ربّهم وأخلصوا له طاعاتهم ونيّاتهم.

٣،١ وروي عن عبد الله بن عبّاس أو عن عليّ بن أبي طالب عليه السلام أنّه قال لا يغلب العسر الواحد يسرين يريد أنّ العسر الأوّل هو الثاني وأنّ اليسر الثاني هو غير الأوّل وذلك أنّ العسر معرفة فإذا أُعيد فالثاني هو الأوّل لأنّ الألف واللام لتعريفه ويسر بلا ألف ولام نكرة فإذا أُعيد فالثاني غير الأوّل وهذا كلام العرب فإذا بدأت بالاسم النكرة ثمّ أعادته أعادته معرفةً بالألف واللام ألا ترى أنّهم يقولون قد

Chapter One

In the Qur'an, God Exalted reveals how deliverance follows suffering and ordeals

God Exalted, Who alone is wholly truthful, and is Himself absolute truth, says, «In the name of God, full of compassion, ever compassionate, have We not opened out your breast and taken from you your burden, which made your back groan, and raised up your good name? So, the hardship shall bring ease; the hardship shall bring ease, and when you have labored, turn again with all your strength to your Lord.»[9] 1.1

The whole of this chapter of the Qur'an shows plainly how God, Mighty and Glorious, bade His messenger, on whom be peace, bear in mind the favors He had shown him, to wit, the opening out of his breast after grief and constraint, the removal of his burden (namely sin) after it had made his back groan (meaning weighed it down, that is, weighed down his back so that the bones groaned, just as a tent makes a groaning noise when it collapses), and the raising up by God, Whose glory be extolled, of his name, which had been nothing, and which God caused to be uttered together with His own. The chapter gives the good tidings to the Prophet himself, and to his people, that each single hardship shall be doubly attended with ease if they turn with all their strength to the Lord their God and show Him sincere and heartfelt obedience. 1.2

Either 'Abd Allāh ibn 'Abbās, or 'Alī ibn Abī Ṭālib, may God be pleased with him, is reported to have said, "The single «hardship» is no match for «ease» twice over," meaning that the first and second «hardship» in the Qur'anic verse are identical, but the first and second «ease» are not; for «the hardship» is defined by the article, whereas «ease» is undefined, so that the second «ease» refers to a separate instance, according to the linguistic usage of the 1.3

جاءني الرجل الذي تعرفه فأخبرني الرجل بكذا وكذا فالثاني هو الأوّل فإذا قالوا جاءني رجل وأخبرني رجل بكذا وجاءني رجل فأخبرني رجل بكذا وكذا فالثاني غير الأوّل ولوكان الثاني في هذا الموضع هو الأوّل لقالوا فأخبرني الرجل بكذا وكذا كما قالوا في ذلك الموضع.

٤،١ وقال الله تعالى ﴿سَيَجْعَلُ ٱللَّهُ بَعْدَ عُسْرٍ يُسْرًا﴾ وقال ﴿وَمَن يَتَّقِ ٱللَّهَ يَجْعَل لَّهُۥ مَخْرَجًا وَيَرْزُقْهُ مِنْ حَيْثُ لَا يَحْتَسِبُ وَمَن يَتَوَكَّلْ عَلَى ٱللَّهِ فَهُوَ حَسْبُهُۥٓ﴾ وقال تعالى ﴿أَوْ كَٱلَّذِى مَرَّ عَلَىٰ قَرْيَةٍ وَهِىَ خَاوِيَةٌ عَلَىٰ عُرُوشِهَا قَالَ أَنَّىٰ يُحْىِۦ هَٰذِهِ ٱللَّهُ بَعْدَ مَوْتِهَا فَأَمَاتَهُ ٱللَّهُ مِاْئَةَ عَامٍ ثُمَّ بَعَثَهُۥ قَالَ كَمْ لَبِثْتَ قَالَ لَبِثْتُ يَوْمًا أَوْ بَعْضَ يَوْمٍ قَالَ بَل لَّبِثْتَ مِاْئَةَ عَامٍ فَٱنظُرْ إِلَىٰ طَعَامِكَ وَشَرَابِكَ لَمْ يَتَسَنَّهْ وَٱنظُرْ إِلَىٰ حِمَارِكَ وَلِنَجْعَلَكَ ءَايَةً لِّلنَّاسِ وَٱنظُرْ إِلَى ٱلْعِظَامِ كَيْفَ نُنشِزُهَا ثُمَّ نَكْسُوهَا لَحْمًا فَلَمَّا تَبَيَّنَ لَهُۥ قَالَ أَعْلَمُ أَنَّ ٱللَّهَ عَلَىٰ كُلِّ شَىْءٍ قَدِيرٌ﴾.

٥،١ فأخبر الله تعالى أنّ الذي مَرَّ عَلَىٰ قَرْيَةٍ استبعد أن يكشف الله تعالى عنها وعن أهلها البلاء لقوله ﴿أَنَّىٰ يُحْىِۦ هَٰذِهِ ٱللَّهُ بَعْدَ مَوْتِهَا فَأَمَاتَهُ ٱللَّهُ مِاْئَةَ عَامٍ ثُمَّ بَعَثَهُۥ﴾ إلى آخر القصّة. فلا شدّة أشدّ من الموت والخراب ولا فرج أفرج من الحياة والعمارة فأعلمه الله عزّ وجلّ بما فعله به أنّه لا يجب أن يستبعد فرجاً من الله وصنعاً كما عمل به وأنّه يحيي القرية وأهلها كما أحياه فأراه بذلك آياته ومواقع صنعه.

٦،١ وقال عزّ وجلّ ﴿أَلَيْسَ ٱللَّهُ بِكَافٍ عَبْدَهُۥ وَيُخَوِّفُونَكَ بِٱلَّذِينَ مِن دُونِهِۦ﴾ وقال تعالى ﴿وَإِذَا مَسَّ ٱلْإِنسَٰنَ ٱلضُّرُّ دَعَانَا لِجَنۢبِهِۦٓ أَوْ قَاعِدًا أَوْ قَآئِمًا فَلَمَّا كَشَفْنَا عَنْهُ ضُرَّهُۥ مَرَّ كَأَن لَّمْ يَدْعُنَآ إِلَىٰ ضُرٍّ مَّسَّهُۥ كَذَٰلِكَ زُيِّنَ لِلْمُسْرِفِينَ مَا كَانُوا۟ يَعْمَلُونَ﴾ وقال عزّ وجلّ ﴿هُوَ ٱلَّذِى يُسَيِّرُكُمْ فِى ٱلْبَرِّ وَٱلْبَحْرِ حَتَّىٰٓ إِذَا كُنتُمْ فِى ٱلْفُلْكِ وَجَرَيْنَ بِهِم بِرِيحٍ طَيِّبَةٍ وَفَرِحُوا۟ بِهَا جَآءَتْهَا رِيحٌ عَاصِفٌ وَجَآءَهُمُ ٱلْمَوْجُ مِن كُلِّ مَكَانٍ وَظَنُّوٓا۟ أَنَّهُمْ أُحِيطَ بِهِمْ دَعَوُا۟ ٱللَّهَ مُخْلِصِينَ لَهُ ٱلدِّينَ لَئِنْ أَنجَيْتَنَا مِنْ هَٰذِهِۦ لَنَكُونَنَّ مِنَ ٱلشَّٰكِرِينَ فَلَمَّآ أَنجَىٰهُمْ إِذَا هُمْ يَبْغُونَ فِى ٱلْأَرْضِ بِغَيْرِ ٱلْحَقِّ﴾ وقال تعالى في موضع

Arabs,[10] whereby if they first use an undefined noun and then repeat it, they give it the definite article. This is proved by the fact that when the Arabs say "*the* man"—that is, the man whom you know—"came to me, and *the* man told me such and such," the two men are identical; but when they say "*a* man came to me; *a* man told me such and such" or "*a* man came to me, and *a* man told me such and such," they are not identical. If they were, the Arabs would say "and *the* man told me such and such," as in my first example.

God Exalted also says, «After hardship, God will give ease»,[11] and «Who- 1.4
ever reveres God, He will give him relief, and give him provision whence he least expects it; for whoever trusts only in God needs nothing else»;[12] and, further: «Or like him who, passing a city empty and roofless, said, "It is dead. How can God make it live again?" God made *him* die a hundred years, then resurrected him. He asked, "How long have you been here?"—"I have been here a day, or even less." God said, "You have been here a hundred years; but look at your food and drink: they have not spoilt; and now at your donkey—for we shall make you a sign to humankind. See its bones, how We gather them up and then clothe them in flesh." And when he perceived this, he said, "I know that God has power over all things."»[13]

In the words «How can God make it live again?» God Exalted tells how the 1.5
man «passing a city» could not believe that He, Exalted, could save it and its inhabitants from their tribulation. That is why God «made him die a hundred years, then resurrected him,» and so on. Now there is no greater adversity than death and destruction, and no greater deliverance than to live and thrive. By using the man as He did, God, Mighty and Glorious, taught him through his own experience that he should never have doubted God's deliverance and what He can bring about, and that He could give life to the city and its inhabitants just as He delivered the man and gave life to him. Thus did He show him His signs and His workings.

Mighty and Glorious, He also says, «Shall not God suffice His servant, 1.6
though they threaten you with false gods?»[14] and says, exalted is He: «When loss strikes someone, he will pray to Us on his side, or sitting, or standing, but once We have saved him from it, off he goes as if he had never prayed for Our help when loss struck him. Thus do the profligate delude themselves»[15] and«It is He Who lets you travel by land and by sea; but once you are shipborne, running with a fair wind and rejoicing, a stormy wind comes upon them; waves come upon them from everywhere, and they think themselves

آخر ﴿قُلْ مَن يُنَجِّيكُم مِّن ظُلُمَٰتِ ٱلْبَرِّ وَٱلْبَحْرِ تَدْعُونَهُۥ تَضَرُّعًا وَخُفْيَةً لَّئِنْ أَنجَىٰنَا مِنْ هَٰذِهِۦ لَنَكُونَنَّ مِنَ ٱلشَّٰكِرِينَ قُلِ ٱللَّهُ يُنَجِّيكُم مِّنْهَا وَمِن كُلِّ كَرْبٍ ثُمَّ أَنتُمْ تُشْرِكُونَ﴾ .

٧،١ وقال تعالى ﴿وَقَالَ ٱلَّذِينَ كَفَرُوا۟ لِرُسُلِهِمْ لَنُخْرِجَنَّكُم مِّنْ أَرْضِنَآ أَوْ لَتَعُودُنَّ فِى مِلَّتِنَا فَأَوْحَىٰٓ إِلَيْهِمْ رَبُّهُمْ لَنُهْلِكَنَّ ٱلظَّٰلِمِينَ وَلَنُسْكِنَنَّكُمُ ٱلْأَرْضَ مِنۢ بَعْدِهِمْ ذَٰلِكَ لِمَنْ خَافَ مَقَامِى وَخَافَ وَعِيدِ﴾ وقال عزّ وجلّ ﴿وَنُرِيدُ أَن نَّمُنَّ عَلَى ٱلَّذِينَ ٱسْتُضْعِفُوا۟ فِى ٱلْأَرْضِ وَنَجْعَلَهُمْ أَئِمَّةً وَنَجْعَلَهُمُ ٱلْوَٰرِثِينَ وَنُمَكِّنَ لَهُمْ فِى ٱلْأَرْضِ وَنُرِىَ فِرْعَوْنَ وَهَٰمَٰنَ وَجُنُودَهُمَا مِنْهُم مَّا كَانُوا۟ يَحْذَرُونَ﴾ .

٨،١ وقال عزّ وجلّ ﴿أَمَّن يُجِيبُ ٱلْمُضْطَرَّ إِذَا دَعَاهُ وَيَكْشِفُ ٱلسُّوٓءَ وَيَجْعَلُكُمْ خُلَفَآءَ ٱلْأَرْضِ أَءِلَٰهٌ مَّعَ ٱللَّهِ قَلِيلًا مَّا تَذَكَّرُونَ﴾ وقال جلّ من قائل ﴿وَقَالَ رَبُّكُمُ ٱدْعُونِىٓ أَسْتَجِبْ لَكُمْ﴾ وقال عزّ من قائل ﴿وَإِذَا سَأَلَكَ عِبَادِى عَنِّى فَإِنِّى قَرِيبٌ أُجِيبُ دَعْوَةَ ٱلدَّاعِ إِذَا دَعَانِ فَلْيَسْتَجِيبُوا۟ لِى وَلْيُؤْمِنُوا۟ بِى لَعَلَّهُمْ يَرْشُدُونَ﴾ .

٩،١ وقال تعالى ﴿وَلَنَبْلُوَنَّكُم بِشَىْءٍ مِّنَ ٱلْخَوْفِ وَٱلْجُوعِ وَنَقْصٍ مِّنَ ٱلْأَمْوَٰلِ وَٱلْأَنفُسِ وَٱلثَّمَرَٰتِ وَبَشِّرِ ٱلصَّٰبِرِينَ ٱلَّذِينَ إِذَآ أَصَٰبَتْهُم مُّصِيبَةٌ قَالُوٓا۟ إِنَّا لِلَّهِ وَإِنَّآ إِلَيْهِ رَٰجِعُونَ أُو۟لَٰٓئِكَ عَلَيْهِمْ صَلَوَٰتٌ مِّن رَّبِّهِمْ وَرَحْمَةٌ وَأُو۟لَٰٓئِكَ هُمُ ٱلْمُهْتَدُونَ﴾ وقال جلّ جلاله ﴿ٱلَّذِينَ قَالَ لَهُمُ ٱلنَّاسُ إِنَّ ٱلنَّاسَ قَدْ جَمَعُوا۟ لَكُمْ فَٱخْشَوْهُمْ فَزَادَهُمْ إِيمَٰنًا وَقَالُوا۟ حَسْبُنَا ٱللَّهُ وَنِعْمَ ٱلْوَكِيلُ فَٱنقَلَبُوا۟ بِنِعْمَةٍ مِّنَ ٱللَّهِ وَفَضْلٍ لَّمْ يَمْسَسْهُمْ سُوٓءٌ وَٱتَّبَعُوا۟ رِضْوَٰنَ ٱللَّهِ وَٱللَّهُ ذُو فَضْلٍ عَظِيمٍ﴾ .

١٠،١ وروي عن الحسن البصريّ أنّه قال

عجباً لمكروب غفل عن خمس وقد عرف ما جعل الله لمن قالهنّ قوله تعالى ﴿وَلَنَبْلُوَنَّكُم بِشَىْءٍ مِّنَ ٱلْخَوْفِ وَٱلْجُوعِ وَنَقْصٍ مِّنَ ٱلْأَمْوَٰلِ وَٱلْأَنفُسِ وَٱلثَّمَرَٰتِ وَبَشِّرِ

surrounded and pray to God with wholehearted faith: "If You save us from this, we will be truly thankful!" but as soon as We have saved them, they go wayward about the earth, ungratefully».[16] Elsewhere He says, exalted is He: «Say, Who saves you from the darknesses of land and sea? You pray to Him humbly and secretly: "If You save us from them, we will be truly thankful!" Say, God saves you from them and from all other afflictions—and then you associate other gods with Him!»[17]

He says, exalted is He, «The unbelievers said to the messengers sent to them: "We will drive you out of our land unless you return to our creed." But their Lord gave them a revelation: "We will destroy the unjust and We will give you the earth to dwell in after them. This shall be for whoever fears My rank and fears My threat."»[18] And, Mighty and Glorious, He says, «Yet We will favor those deemed powerless. We shall make them leaders; We shall make them the inheritors and establish them in the land; and make them make Pharaoh and Haman and their hosts see what they dreaded.»[19] 1.7

Mighty and Glorious, He also says, «He Who answers the needy when they pray to Him, and saves from evil, and makes you successors in the earth—is there a god beside God? Little do you reflect!»[20] Glorious in His utterances, He says, «Your Lord has said, Pray to Me; I will heed you»[21] and, mighty in His utterances, He says, «If My servants ask you about Me, I am near. When he prays, I answer the prayer of him who prays to Me. So let them also heed Me and believe in Me, that they may be rightly guided.»[22] 1.8

He says, Exalted, «We will test you with some fear and famine, and lessening of herds, life, and crops; but give good tidings to those who show acceptance; who when they suffer a misfortune say, "To God we belong, and to Him we shall return." On such shall be blessings from their Lord and compassion; such are led aright,»[23] and He says, Mighty and Glorious, «Those whom the people told: "The people have joined against you; therefore be afraid of them." But this only increased their faith and they said, "God is all we need, the best of guardians." And now they had blessings from God, and bounty; they were not struck by evil; they had followed God's pleasure, and God's bounty is immense.»[24] 1.9

Ḥasan of Basra[25] is reported to have said: 1.10

I wonder that anyone suffering affliction could neglect these five passages of the Qur'an, knowing how God dealt with those who recited them: His words, exalted is He: «We will test you with some fear and famine, and lessening of

ٱلصَّٰبِرِينَ ٱلَّذِينَ إِذَآ أَصَٰبَتۡهُم مُّصِيبَةٞ قَالُوٓاْ إِنَّا لِلَّهِ وَإِنَّآ إِلَيۡهِ رَٰجِعُونَ أُوْلَٰٓئِكَ عَلَيۡهِمۡ صَلَوَٰتٞ مِّن رَّبِّهِمۡ وَرَحۡمَةٞۖ وَأُوْلَٰٓئِكَ هُمُ ٱلۡمُهۡتَدُونَ﴾ وقوله تعالى ﴿ٱلَّذِينَ قَالَ لَهُمُ ٱلنَّاسُ إِنَّ ٱلنَّاسَ قَدۡ جَمَعُواْ لَكُمۡ فَٱخۡشَوۡهُمۡ فَزَادَهُمۡ إِيمَٰنٗا وَقَالُواْ حَسۡبُنَا ٱللَّهُ وَنِعۡمَ ٱلۡوَكِيلُ فَٱنقَلَبُواْ بِنِعۡمَةٖ مِّنَ ٱللَّهِ وَفَضۡلٖ لَّمۡ يَمۡسَسۡهُمۡ سُوٓءٞ﴾ وقوله ﴿فَسَتَذۡكُرُونَ مَآ أَقُولُ لَكُمۡۚ وَأُفَوِّضُ أَمۡرِيٓ إِلَى ٱللَّهِۚ إِنَّ ٱللَّهَ بَصِيرُۢ بِٱلۡعِبَادِ فَوَقَىٰهُ ٱللَّهُ سَيِّـَٔاتِ مَا مَكَرُواْ﴾ وقوله ﴿وَذَا ٱلنُّونِ إِذ ذَّهَبَ مُغَٰضِبٗا فَظَنَّ أَن لَّن نَّقۡدِرَ عَلَيۡهِ فَنَادَىٰ فِي ٱلظُّلُمَٰتِ أَن لَّآ إِلَٰهَ إِلَّآ أَنتَ سُبۡحَٰنَكَ إِنِّي كُنتُ مِنَ ٱلظَّٰلِمِينَ فَٱسۡتَجَبۡنَا لَهُۥ وَنَجَّيۡنَٰهُ مِنَ ٱلۡغَمِّۚ وَكَذَٰلِكَ نُـۨجِي ٱلۡمُؤۡمِنِينَ﴾ وقوله ﴿وَمَا كَانَ قَوۡلَهُمۡ إِلَّآ أَن قَالُواْ رَبَّنَا ٱغۡفِرۡ لَنَا ذُنُوبَنَا وَإِسۡرَافَنَا فِيٓ أَمۡرِنَا وَثَبِّتۡ أَقۡدَامَنَا وَٱنصُرۡنَا عَلَى ٱلۡقَوۡمِ ٱلۡكَٰفِرِينَ فَـَٔاتَىٰهُمُ ٱللَّهُ ثَوَابَ ٱلدُّنۡيَا وَحُسۡنَ ثَوَابِ ٱلۡأٓخِرَةِۗ وَٱللَّهُ يُحِبُّ ٱلۡمُحۡسِنِينَ﴾

وروي عن الحسن أيضاً أنّه قال: ١١،١

من لزم قراءة هذه الآيات في الشدائد كشفها الله عنه لأنّه قد وعد وحكم فيهنّ بما جعله لمن قالهنّ وحكمه لا يُبطل ووعده لا يُخلف.

١،٢ وقد ذكر الله تعالى فيما اقتصّه من أخبار الأنبياء شدائد ومحناً استمرّت على جماعة من الأنبياء عليهم السلام وضروباً جرت عليهم من البلاء وأعقبها بفرج وتخفيف وتداركهم فيها بصنع جليل لطيف.

٢،٢ فأوّل ممتحن رضي فأُعقب بصنع خفيّ وأغيث بفرج قويّ أوّل العالم وجوداً آدم أبو البشر صلّى الله عليه كما ذكر فإنّ الله خلقه في الجنّة و﴿عَلَّمَ﴾ ه ﴿ٱلۡأَسۡمَآءَ كُلَّهَا﴾ وأسجد له ملائكته ونهاه عن أكل الشجرة فوسوس له الشيطان وكان منه ما قاله الرحمٰن في محكم كتابه: ﴿وَعَصَىٰٓ ءَادَمُ رَبَّهُۥ فَغَوَىٰ ثُمَّ ٱجۡتَبَٰهُ رَبُّهُۥ فَتَابَ عَلَيۡهِ وَهَدَىٰ﴾ هذا بعد أن أهبطه الله إلى الأرض وأفقده لذيذ ذلك الخفض فانقضت عادته

herds, life, and crops; but give good tidings to those who show acceptance, who when they suffer a misfortune say, "To God we belong, and to Him we shall return." On such shall be blessings from their Lord and compassion, and such are led aright»[26] and: «Those whom the people told: "The people have joined against you; therefore be afraid of them." But this only increased their faith, and they said: "God is all we need, the best of guardians." And now they had blessings from God, and bounty; they were not struck by evil; they had followed God's pleasure, and God's bounty is immense»;[27] «"I commit myself to God, for God sees His servants,"[28] and God protected him from their evil devices»;[29] «How Jonah[30] went angrily on his way, thinking We would not straiten[31] him, and then cried out in the darkness, saying, "There is no god but You. Glory to You! I am unjust." And We heeded him and saved him from grief; so We save believers»;[32] and: «Their only words were to say, "Lord, forgive us our misdeeds and our profligacy. Make us stand firm, and help us overcome the unbelieving people." And God gave them the reward of this world and the good reward of the next world, for God loves those whose works are good.»[33]

Ḥasan of Basra is also reported to have said: 1.11

Whoever continually recites these verses in time of misfortune will be saved by God. In them He has given a promise and a judgment by dealing as He did with those who spoke them. His ruling cannot be overturned, nor can His promise be broken.

Among the accounts that God, Exalted, gives of the prophets in the stories 2.1
He tells are the evils and trials that beset so many of them, peace be on them all, and the various kinds of affliction they endured, the outcome of which He ensured would be deliverance and remission. Through His glorious and gracious workings, He gave them reparation.

The first person to submit to his trials and be saved by a great deliverance 2.2
through the hidden workings that ensued was Adam, the first creature to exist on earth, the father of humankind, may God bless him, as Scripture relates. God created him in Paradise «and taught him the names, all of them»,[34] and made His angels bow down before him,[35] and forbade him to eat of the Tree; but the Devil tempted him.[36] What then became of him is described in the Qur'an in unambiguous terms by the One Who is full of compassion: «And Adam disobeyed his Lord and erred, but afterward his Lord took him

وغلظت محنته وقتل أحد ابنيه الآخر وكانا أوّل أولاده فلمّا طال حزنه وبكاؤه واتّصل استغفاره ودعاؤه رحم الله عزّ وجلّ تذلّله وخضوعه واستكانته ودموعه فتاب عليه وهداه وكشف ما به ونجّاه.

٣،٢ فكان آدم عليه السلام أوّل من دعا فأجيب وامتُحن فأثيب وخرج من ضيق وكرب إلى سعة ورحب وسلّى همومه ونسي غمومه وأيقن بتجديد الله عليه النعم وإزالته عنه النقم وأنّه تعالى إذا استُرحم رحم.

٤،٢ فأبدله تعالى بتلك الشدائد وعوّضه من الابن المفقود والابن العاقّ الموجود نبيّ الله شيت صلّى الله عليه وهو أوّل الأولاد البررة بالوالدين ووالد النبيّين والصالحين وأبو الملوك الجبّارين الذي جعل الله ﴿ذُرِّيَّتَهُۥ هُمُ ٱلۡبَاقِينَ﴾ وخصّهم من النعم بما لا يحيط به وصف الواصفين.

٥،٢ وقد جاء في القرآن من الشرح لهذه الجملة والتبيان بما لا يحتمله هذا المكان وروي فيه من الأخبار ما لا وجه للإطالة به والإكثار.

١،٣ ثمّ نوح عليه السلام فإنّه امتُحن بخلاف قومه عليه وعصيان ابنه له والطوفان العامّ واعتصام ابنه بالجبل وتأخّره عن الركوب معه وبركوب السفينة ﴿وَهِىَ تَجۡرِى بِهِمۡ فِى مَوۡجٍ كَٱلۡجِبَالِ﴾. وأعقبه الله الخلاص من تلك الأهوال والتمكّن ﴿فِى ٱلۡأَرۡضِ﴾ وتغييض الطوفان وجعله شبيهاً لآدم لأنّه أنشأ ثانياً جميع البشر منه كما أنشأهم أوّلاً من آدم عليه السلام فلا ولد لآدم إلاّ من نوح.

٢،٣ قال الله تعالى: ﴿وَلَقَدۡ نَادَىٰنَا نُوحٌ فَلَنِعۡمَ ٱلۡمُجِيبُونَ وَنَجَّيۡنَٰهُ وَأَهۡلَهُۥ مِنَ ٱلۡكَرۡبِ ٱلۡعَظِيمِ وَجَعَلۡنَا ذُرِّيَّتَهُۥ هُمُ ٱلۡبَاقِينَ وَتَرَكۡنَا عَلَيۡهِ فِى ٱلۡأٓخِرِينَ﴾ ﴿وَنُوحًا إِذۡ نَادَىٰ مِن قَبۡلُ فَٱسۡتَجَبۡنَا لَهُۥ فَنَجَّيۡنَٰهُ وَأَهۡلَهُۥ مِنَ ٱلۡكَرۡبِ ٱلۡعَظِيمِ﴾.

again to Himself, and pardoned him and guided him»,[37] having first cast him down upon the earth and bereft him of his former joys. His old ways were undone, and he was sorely tried. One of his firstborn sons murdered the other. Such were his grieving and weeping, and constant praying and pleading for forgiveness, that God, Mighty and Glorious, at last took pity on his abasement and humiliation, his laments and mortification, and pardoned him and guided him, removed his woes and saved him.

Thus Adam, peace on him, was the first person ever to pray and have his prayer answered, the first to be put to the test and requited, the first to quit constraint and affliction for ease and freedom. He found solace for his sorrows and forgetfulness of his cares in the certain knowledge that God would renew His bounty toward him, shield him from blows, and, exalted is He, mercifully grant his prayers for mercy. 2.3

Exalted is He, He compensated Adam for the evils he had suffered, and in place of the son he had lost and of the undutiful son who remained to him, He gave him Seth,[38] the prophet of God, God bless him. Seth was the first child to show duty to his parents; he begot the prophets and God-fearing men, and was father of the mighty kings of old. «God made his seed survive»,[39] and blessed them especially beyond all description. 2.4

(More is said of all this in the Qur'an, in far more detail than I have space for, and more tales have been told about it than there is need to dwell upon.)[40] 2.5

Next is Noah, peace on him. He was tried by his people's opposition and the disobedience of his son, who took refuge in the mountain and was too late to embark,[41] by the universal flood, and by sailing in the ark, «which carried them between billows like mountains».[42] But God caused this to be followed by release from these terrors, «established him in the land»,[43] made the flood ebb, and made him like Adam, for He produced the whole of the human race afresh from Noah, as He first produced it from Adam, on whom be peace. All Adam's offspring are descended from Noah. 3.1

God Exalted says, «Noah called out to Us—well was he answered, and We saved him and his kin from the great affliction and made his seed survive, and left peace on him in posterity»,[44] and He says, «Also Noah. When he called out of old, We heeded him. We saved him and his kin from the great affliction.»[45] 3.2

٤،١ ثمّ إبراهيم صلّى الله عليه وسلّم وما دُفع إليه من كسر الأصنام وما لحقه من قومه من محاولة إحراقه فجعل الله تعالى عليه النار ﴿بَرْدًا وَسَلامًا﴾ وقال ﴿قَالُواْ حَرِّقُوهُ وَٱنصُرُوٓاْ ءَالِهَتَكُمْ إِن كُنتُمْ فَٰعِلِينَ قُلْنَا يَٰنَارُ كُونِى بَرْدًا وَسَلَٰمًا عَلَىٰٓ إِبْرَٰهِيمَ وَأَرَادُواْ بِهِۦ كَيْدًا فَجَعَلْنَٰهُمُ ٱلْأَخْسَرِينَ وَنَجَّيْنَٰهُ وَلُوطًا إِلَى ٱلْأَرْضِ ٱلَّتِى بَٰرَكْنَا فِيهَا لِلْعَٰلَمِينَ وَوَهَبْنَا لَهُۥٓ إِسْحَٰقَ وَيَعْقُوبَ نَافِلَةً وَكُلًّا جَعَلْنَا صَٰلِحِينَ وَجَعَلْنَٰهُمْ أَئِمَّةً يَهْدُونَ بِأَمْرِنَا﴾.

٤،٢ ثمّ ما كلّفه الله تعالى إيّاه من مفارقة وطنه بالشام لمّا غارت عليه سارة من أمّ ولده هاجر فهاجر بها وبابنه منها إسماعيل الذبيح عليهما السلام ف﴿أَسْكَنَ﴾هما ﴿بِوَادٍ غَيْرِ ذِى زَرْعٍ﴾ نازحين عنه بعيدين منه حتّى أنبع الله تعالى لهما الماء وتابع عليهما الآلاء وأحسن لإبراهيم فيهما الصنع والفائدة والنفع وجعل لإسماعيل النسل والعدد والنبوّة والمُلك. هذا بعد أن كلّف سبحانه إبراهيم أن يجعل ابنه إسماعيل بسبيل الذبح.

٤،٣ قال الله تعالى فيما اقتصّه من ذكره في سورة الصافّات ﴿فَبَشَّرْنَٰهُ بِغُلَٰمٍ حَلِيمٍ فَلَمَّا بَلَغَ مَعَهُ ٱلسَّعْىَ قَالَ يَٰبُنَىَّ إِنِّىٓ أَرَىٰ فِى ٱلْمَنَامِ أَنِّىٓ أَذْبَحُكَ فَٱنظُرْ مَاذَا تَرَىٰ قَالَ يَٰٓأَبَتِ ٱفْعَلْ مَا تُؤْمَرُ سَتَجِدُنِىٓ إِن شَآءَ ٱللَّهُ مِنَ ٱلصَّٰبِرِينَ فَلَمَّآ أَسْلَمَا وَتَلَّهُۥ لِلْجَبِينِ وَنَٰدَيْنَٰهُ أَن يَٰٓإِبْرَٰهِيمُ قَدْ صَدَّقْتَ ٱلرُّءْيَآ إِنَّا كَذَٰلِكَ نَجْزِى ٱلْمُحْسِنِينَ إِنَّ هَٰذَا لَهُوَ ٱلْبَلَٰٓؤُاْ ٱلْمُبِينُ وَفَدَيْنَٰهُ بِذِبْحٍ عَظِيمٍ وَتَرَكْنَا عَلَيْهِ فِى ٱلْءَاخِرِينَ سَلَٰمٌ عَلَىٰٓ إِبْرَٰهِيمَ﴾.

٤،٤ فلا بلاء أعظم من بلاء يشهد الله تعالى أنّه بلاء ﴿مُبِين﴾ وهو تكليف الإنسان أن يجعل بسبيل الذبح ابنه وتكليفه وتكليف المذبوح أن يؤمنا ويصبرا ويسلّما ويحتسبا. فلمّا أدّيا ما كُلّفا من ذلك وعلم الله عزّ وجلّ منهما صدق الإيمان والصبر والتسليم والإذعان فدى الابن ﴿بِذِبْحٍ عَظِيمٍ﴾ وجاز الأب بابن آخر على صبره ورضاه بذبح ابنه الذي لم يكن له غيره قال الله عزّ وجلّ ﴿وَبَشَّرْنَٰهُ بِإِسْحَٰقَ نَبِيًّا مِّنَ

Then there is Abraham, God bless and keep him, and how he was impelled to break the idols[46] and was persecuted by his own people. They tried to burn him, but God Exalted made the fire «coolness and safekeeping»[47] to him and said, «We had already given Abraham his guidance, for We knew him.»[48] Then, exalted is He, He tells Abraham's story up to His words «They said, "Burn him and help your gods, if you will act." We said, O fire, be coolness and safekeeping to Abraham. Then they tried to trick him, but We made them the greater losers and brought him and Lot safe to the land that We had blessed for all, and over and above this gave him Isaac and Jacob, and made all of them God-fearing, and made them leaders, to lead aright by Our command.»[49] 4.1

Next in this chapter is the burden that God Exalted laid upon Abraham of leaving his homeland in Syria, when Sarah grew jealous on account of his concubine, Hagar, and how he emigrated[50] with her and his son by her, Ishmael the sacrificial victim, peace on them both, and «settled» them both «in a valley where no crops were sown»[51] far away, distant from where he was; and how at last God Exalted made water gush for them,[52] and gave them bounty after bounty, and for Abraham's sake worked for their good, advantage, and profit, and gave Ishmael issue and increase, prophethood and governance—all this, may He be glorified, after laying on Abraham the burden of offering up Ishmael to Him in the guise of a blood sacrifice. 4.2

What follows is part of Abraham's story as God Exalted relates it in the surah of The Ranks: «We gave him the good tidings of a patient boy. When he was old enough to work at his side, he said, "Dear child, I see in a dream that I am to sacrifice you. What think you?" He said, "Dear father, do as you are commanded. God willing, you will find me accepting." But once they had submitted, and he flung him facedown, We called to him, saying, "Abraham, you have fulfilled the vision." Thus do We recompense those who act well. This was the clear tribulation. We ransomed him with a great sacrifice and made all generations say, "Peace on Abraham!"»[53] 4.3

There can be no greater tribulation than one that God Exalted Himself testifies is «clear», namely, to lay on a person the burden of offering up his son in the guise of a blood sacrifice, and to lay on both him and the victim the burden of showing faith and acceptance and of yielding and resigning themselves to the death of a child. Yet, when both had done what had been laid upon them, and God, Mighty and Glorious, knew that they were true in their faith, accepting, and utterly resigned, He ransomed the son «with a great sacrifice», and in 4.4

﴿ٱلصَّٰلِحِينَ﴾ إلى قوله ﴿لِنَفۡسِهِۦ مُبِينٞ﴾ وخلّصهما بصبرهما وتسليمهما من تلك الشدائد الهائلة.

٥،٤ وقد ذهب قوم إلى أنّ إبراهيم إنّما كُلّف ذبح ابنه في الحقيقة لا على ما ذُهب إليه من ذلك أنّ الذي كُلّفه أن يجعل ابنه بسبيل الذبح لا أن يذبحه في الحقيقة.

٦،٤ واستدلّ الحسن البصريّ على أنّ إسماعيل هو الذبيح لا إسحاق وأنّ المأمور به كان الذبح في الحقيقة بقوله تعالى ﴿فَبَشَّرۡنَٰهَا بِإِسۡحَٰقَ وَمِن وَرَآءِ إِسۡحَٰقَ يَعۡقُوبَ﴾ فحصلت لإبراهيم البشرى بأنّه سيُرزق إسحاق وأنّ إسحاق سيرزق يعقوب ولا يجوز للنبيّ أن يشكّ في بشارة الله تعالى فلو كان إسحاق هو الذبيح ما صحّ أن يأمره بذبحه قبل خروج يعقوب من ظهره لأنّه كان إذا أمر بذلك علم أنّ البشرى الأوّلة[1] تمنع من ذبح إسحاق قبل ولادة يعقوب وكان لا يصحّ تكليفه ذبح من يعلم أنّه لا يموت أو يخرج من ظهره من لم يخرج بعد ومتى وقع التكليف على هذا لم يكن فيه ثواب وفي قوله تعالى ﴿إِنَّ هَٰذَا لَهُوَ ٱلۡبَلَٰٓؤُاْ ٱلۡمُبِينُ﴾ دليل على عظم ثواب إبراهيم وصحّة الأمر بالذبح يبيّن ذلك قوله تعالى ﴿فَلَمَّآ أَسۡلَمَا وَتَلَّهُۥ لِلۡجَبِينِ﴾ أي استسلما لأمر الله وهما لا يشكّان في وقوع الذبح على الحقيقة حتّى فداه الله تبارك وتعالى فهذا دليل على أنّ الذبيح غير إسحاق ولم يكن لإبراهيم ولد غير إسحاق إلاّ إسماعيل صلّى الله عليهم أجمعين.

٥ ومن هذا الباب قصّة لوط عليه السلام لمّا نهى قومه عن الفاحشة فعصوه وكذّبوه وتضيفه الملائكة فطالبوه فيهم بما طالبوه فخسف الله بهم أجمعين ونجّى لوطاً وأثابه ثواب الشاكرين وقد نطق بهذا كلام الله العظيم في مواضع من الذكر الحكيم.

[1] كذا.

return for the father's acceptance and willingness to sacrifice his only son recompensed him with another son—God says, Mighty and Glorious, in the verses ending «while others clearly wronged themselves»: «We gave him tidings of Isaac, a prophet and a God-fearing man»[54]—and in return for their acceptance and resignation, He released them both from those terrible misfortunes.

Opinions are divided as to whether the burden laid on Abraham was that of actually sacrificing his son or whether he was charged with slaughtering him not in fact but solely in the guise of a sacrifice. 4.5

Ḥasan of Basra cited the following passage of the Qur'an as proof not only that the sacrifice was meant to be real, but that the intended victim was Ishmael and not Isaac: «We gave her[55] the good tidings of Isaac, and, after Isaac, Jacob»,[56] after which the tidings reached Abraham also that Isaac was to be his provision, and Jacob Isaac's.[57] Now, a prophet may not doubt tidings imparted by Almighty God Himself.[58] Had Isaac been the sacrificial victim, God would not have commanded Abraham to sacrifice him before Isaac had begotten Jacob—for if He had, Abraham would have known that the initial tidings received by him meant that it was impossible for Isaac to be sacrificed before the birth of Jacob, since God would not have laid on him the burden of sacrificing someone he knew could not die before he had begotten someone as yet unbegotten. Moreover, if these had been the circumstances, the burden laid upon him would have merited no reward, whereas the words of God Exalted, «This was the clear test,» prove how great would be Abraham's reward, and that he was really ordered to make the sacrifice, as is shown clearly by His words, exalted is He: «But once they had submitted, and he flung him facedown» which mean: "once they had yielded themselves to God's command, never doubting, until the very moment that God, blessed and exalted is He, ransomed him, that the sacrifice would really take place." All of which goes to prove that the victim was not Isaac, but Ishmael, Abraham's only other child. God's blessings on them all! 4.6

To this first chapter also belongs the story of Lot, his forbidding his people to commit abominations, their disobedience and disbelief, his entertaining of the angels, and what his people demanded that he let them do.[59] God made the earth swallow them all up but saved Lot and bestowed on him the reward of the thankful. Almighty God has spoken of this in several passages of Holy Scripture.[60] 5

٦ ويعقوب ويوسف عليهما السلام فقد أفرد الله تعالى بذكر شانهما وعظيم بلواهما وامتحانهما سورة محكمة بيّن فيها كيف حسد إخوة يوسف يوسفَ على المنام الذي بشّره الله تعالى فيه بغاية الإكرام حتّى طرحوه في الجبّ فخلّصه الله تعالى منه بمن ﴿فَأَدْلَىٰ دَلْوَهُ﴾ ثمّ استُعبد فألقى الله تعالى في قلب من صار إليه إكرامه واتّخاذه ولدًا ثمّ مراودة امرأة العزيز إيّاه عن نفسه وعصمة الله له منها وكيف جعل عاقبته بعد الحبس إلى ملك مصر وما لحق يعقوب من العمى لفرط البكاء وما لحق إخوة يوسف من التسرّق وحبس أحدهم نفسه ﴿حَتَّىٰ يَأْذَنَ﴾ له أبوه ﴿أَوْ يَحْكُمَ ٱللَّهُ﴾ له وكيف أنفذ يوسف إلى أبيه قميصه فردّه الله به بصيرًا وجمع بينهم وجعل كلّ واحد منهم بالباقين وبالنعمة مسرورًا.

١٫٧ وأيّوب عليه السلام وما امتُحن من الأسقام وعظم اللأواء والدود والأدواء وجاء القرآن بذكره ونطقت الأخبار بشرح أمره قال الله تعالى ﴿وَأَيُّوبَ إِذْ نَادَىٰ رَبَّهُۥٓ أَنِّى مَسَّنِىَ ٱلضُّرُّ وَأَنتَ أَرْحَمُ ٱلرَّٰحِمِينَ فَٱسْتَجَبْنَا لَهُۥ فَكَشَفْنَا مَا بِهِۦ مِن ضُرٍّ وَءَاتَيْنَٰهُ أَهْلَهُۥ وَمِثْلَهُم مَّعَهُمْ رَحْمَةً مِّنْ عِندِنَا وَذِكْرَىٰ لِلْعَٰبِدِينَ﴾.

٢٫٧ وأخبرنا أبو عليّ الحسن بن محمّد بن عثمان الفسويّ قراءة عليه بالبصرة سنة سبع وثلاثين وثلثمائة قال حدّثنا يعقوب بن سفيان الفسويّ قال حدّثنا عمرو بن مرزوق قال حدّثنا شعبة عن قتادة عن النضر بن أنس عن بشير بن نهيك عن أبي هريرة عن النبيّ صلّى الله عليه وسلّم قال:

لمّا عافى الله عزّ وجلّ أيّوب عليه السلام أمطر عليه جرادًا من ذهب قال فجعل يأخذه ويجعله في ثوبه فقيل له يا أيّوب أما تشبع قال ومن يشبع من رحمة الله.

Also Jacob and Joseph, on both of whom be peace, to whom and to whose ordeals and trials God devoted an unambiguous surah of the Qur'an[61] in which He shows how Joseph's brothers so envied Joseph, because of the dream in which He gave him the good tidings that he should attain the highest honor, that they threw him into the well, from which God Exalted released him through the agency of «him who let down his bucket»,[62] only for him to be sold into slavery, whereupon God Exalted moved his new masters to use him honorably and adopt him as their son. Potiphar's wife[63] then tried to seduce him, but God preserved him blameless from her. He tells how He made it the consequence of Joseph's imprisonment that he became ruler of Egypt, how Jacob became blind with much weeping,[64] and how Joseph's brothers became pilferers, and one of them bound himself prisoner «until his father should give him leave, or until God should give judgment for him»;[65] how Joseph sent his shirt to his father and through it God restored his sight;[66] and how He reunited them all, and made each of them rejoice in the others and in His blessing. 6

Also in this chapter belongs Job, on whom be peace, and the sicknesses and great desolation, the maggots[67] and the maladies with which he was tried. He is mentioned in the Qur'an,[68] and various other accounts give details of his story. God Exalted says, «Consider also Job, when he called out to his Lord: "Loss has struck me; but none is more compassionate than You." We rescued him from his loss and, through Our mercy and as a reminder to the devout, gave him back his household and as many again.»[69] 7.1

In the year 337 [948–49],[70] in Basra, I read back to Abū ʿAlī al-Ḥasan ibn Muḥammad ibn ʿUthmān of Fasā, for verification, his report in which he cited Yaʿqūb ibn Sufyān of Fasā, citing ʿAmr ibn Marzūq, citing Shuʿbah, quoting Qatādah, quoting al-Naḍr ibn Anas, quoting Bashīr ibn Nahīk, quoting Abū Hurayrah, quoting the Prophet, God bless and keep him, who said: 7.2

After God, Mighty and Glorious, had cured Job, He rained down on him locusts of gold,[71] which Job began to pick up and store in his robe. When asked, "Job! Can you still be greedy for more?" he replied, "Who can ever have enough of God's mercy?"

ويونس عليه السلام وما اقتصّ الله تعالى من قصّته في غير موضع من كتابه ذكر فيها التقام الحوت له وتسبيحه في بطنه وكيف نجّاه الله عزّ وجلّ فأعقبه بالرسالة والصنع. ١،٨

قال الله تعالى ﴿وَإِنَّ يُونُسَ لَمِنَ ٱلْمُرْسَلِينَ إِذْ أَبَقَ إِلَى ٱلْفُلْكِ ٱلْمَشْحُونِ فَسَاهَمَ فَكَانَ مِنَ ٱلْمُدْحَضِينَ فَٱلْتَقَمَهُ ٱلْحُوتُ وَهُوَ مُلِيمٌ فَلَوْلَآ أَنَّهُۥ كَانَ مِنَ ٱلْمُسَبِّحِينَ لَلَبِثَ فِى بَطْنِهِۦٓ إِلَىٰ يَوْمِ يُبْعَثُونَ فَنَبَذْنَٰهُ بِٱلْعَرَآءِ وَهُوَ سَقِيمٌ وَأَنۢبَتْنَا عَلَيْهِ شَجَرَةً مِّن يَقْطِينٍ وَأَرْسَلْنَٰهُ إِلَىٰ مِاْئَةِ أَلْفٍ أَوْ يَزِيدُونَ﴾. ٢،٨

قال صاحب الكتاب ٣،٨

﴿أَوْ﴾ هاهنا ظاهرها الشكّ وقد ذهب إلى ذلك قوم وهو خطأ لأنّ الشكّ لا يجوز على الله تعالى العالم لنفسه العارف بكلّ شيء قبل كونه. وقد رُوي عن ابن عبّاس وهو الوجه أنّه قال ﴿أَوْ يَزِيدُونَ﴾ بل يزيدون وقال كانت الزيادة ثلاثين ألفاً. ورُوي عن ابن جبير ونوف الشاميّ أنّهما قالا كانت الزيادة سبعين ألفاً. فقد ثبت أنّ ﴿أَوْ﴾ هنا بمعنى بل وقد ذهب إلى هذا الفرّاء وأبو عبيدة وقال آخرون إنّ ﴿أَوْ﴾ هاهنا بمعنى و يزيدون.

ومنها قوله تعالى ﴿وَذَا ٱلنُّونِ إِذ ذَّهَبَ مُغَٰضِبًا فَظَنَّ أَن لَّن نَّقْدِرَ عَلَيْهِ فَنَادَىٰ فِى ٱلظُّلُمَٰتِ أَن لَّآ إِلَٰهَ إِلَّآ أَنتَ سُبْحَٰنَكَ إِنِّى كُنتُ مِنَ ٱلظَّٰلِمِينَ فَٱسْتَجَبْنَا لَهُۥ وَنَجَّيْنَٰهُ مِنَ ٱلْغَمِّ وَكَذَٰلِكَ نُـۨجِى ٱلْمُؤْمِنِينَ﴾. ٤،٨

قال بعض المفسّرين معنى ﴿لَن نَّقْدِرَ عَلَيْهِ﴾ لن نضيّق عليه وهذا مثل قوله ﴿وَمَن قُدِرَ عَلَيْهِ رِزْقُهُۥ فَلْيُنفِقْ مِمَّآ ءَاتَىٰهُ ٱللَّهُ﴾ أي ضيّق عليه ومثل قوله ﴿قُلْ إِنَّ رَبِّى يَبْسُطُ ٱلرِّزْقَ لِمَن يَشَآءُ مِنْ عِبَادِهِۦ وَيَقْدِرُ لَهُۥ وَمَآ أَنفَقْتُم مِّن شَىْءٍ فَهُوَ يُخْلِفُهُۥ﴾ وقد جاء ﴿قُدِرَ﴾ بمعنى ضيّق في القرآن في مواضع كثيرة ومن هذا قيل للفرس الضيّق الخطو فرس أقدر لأنّه لا يجوز أن يهرب من الله تعالى نبيّ من أنبيائه والأنبياء ٥،٨

Also Jonah, on whom be peace, whose story God Exalted tells in several passages of His book, relating how he was swallowed by the fish and glorified Him in its belly, and how God Mighty and Exalted saved him, and in consequence made him a messenger who experienced His workings. 8.1

God says, Exalted is He, «Jonah too was a messenger. He ran away to the laden vessel, cast lots and was confounded, swallowed by the fish, for he was at fault. And had he not glorified Me, there he would have stayed until the Resurrection. But We flung him down sick on the bare ground, made a gourd tree grow above him, and sent him as a messenger to a hundred thousand or more.»[72] 8.2

The author remarks: 8.3

«Or», in «a hundred thousand or more», has the appearance of expressing doubt, and indeed this is how some have interpreted it. But this is false, for doubt may not be imputed to God Exalted, Who knows Himself and has knowledge of everything before it comes into being. Ibn ʿAbbās is reported to have glossed «or more» correctly as "rather, more," and to have said that there were thirty thousand more, while Ibn Jubayr and Nawf of Syria say that there were seventy thousand more. All of this establishes that in this case «or» means "rather," as al-Farrāʾ and Abū ʿUbaydah agree.[73] Others, however, say that «or» is here used to mean "*and* more."

Another such passage is: «When Jonah went angrily on his way thinking We would not straiten him, and then cried out in the darkness, saying, "There is no god but You. Glory to You! I am unjust," and We heeded him and saved him from grief; and so We save believers.»[74] 8.4

One interpretation of «thinking We would not straiten him»[75] is that it means "straiten," by analogy with «Let the man whose provision God has *straitened* spend according to what He has given him»,[76] and with «Say: My Lord makes ample or *strait* provision to whichever of His servants He wishes; whatever you spend, He will replace.»[77] This is a frequent usage in the Qur'an (hence the common expression "a straitened horse" for one that takes short steps). The reason for this interpretation is that no prophet may flee from God Exalted, nor can a prophet be a miscreant. Now, anyone who thought that God Exalted "had no power over him," that is, could not catch him, or that he could escape Him by fleeing, would be a miscreant; and prophets, peace 8.5

لا يكفرون ومن ظنّ أنّ الله تعالى لا يقدر عليه أي لا يدركه أو أنّه يُعجز الله هربًا فقد كفر والأنبياء عليهم السلام أعلم بالله سبحانه من أن يظنّوا فيه هذا الظنّ الذي هو كفر.

وقد رُوي أنّ من أدام قراءة قوله عزّ وجلّ ﴿وَذَا ٱلنُّونِ إِذ ذَّهَبَ مُغَٰضِبًا﴾ الآية إلى قوله ﴿ٱلْمُؤْمِنِينَ﴾ في الصلاة وغيرها في أوقات شدائده عجّل الله له منها فرجًا ومخرجًا. ٦،٨

وأنا أحد من واصلها في نكبة عظيمة لحقتني يطول شرحها وذكرها عن هذا الموضع وكنت قد حبست وهدّدت بالقتل ففرّج الله عنّي وأطلقت في اليوم التاسع من يوم قبض عليّ فيه. ٧،٨

وموسى بن عمران عليه السلام فقد نطق القرآن بقصّته في غير موضع منها قوله تعالى ﴿وَأَوْحَيْنَآ إِلَىٰٓ أُمِّ مُوسَىٰٓ أَنْ أَرْضِعِيهِ فَإِذَا خِفْتِ عَلَيْهِ فَأَلْقِيهِ فِى ٱلْيَمِّ وَلَا تَخَافِى وَلَا تَحْزَنِىٓ إِنَّا رَآدُّوهُ إِلَيْكِ وَجَاعِلُوهُ مِنَ ٱلْمُرْسَلِينَ فَٱلْتَقَطَهُۥٓ ءَالُ فِرْعَوْنَ لِيَكُونَ لَهُمْ عَدُوًّا وَحَزَنًا إِنَّ فِرْعَوْنَ وَهَٰمَٰنَ وَجُنُودَهُمَا كَانُوا۟ خَٰطِـِٔينَ وَقَالَتِ ٱمْرَأَتُ فِرْعَوْنَ قُرَّتُ عَيْنٍ لِّى وَلَكَ لَا تَقْتُلُوهُ عَسَىٰٓ أَن يَنفَعَنَآ أَوْ نَتَّخِذَهُۥ وَلَدًا وَهُمْ لَا يَشْعُرُونَ وَأَصْبَحَ فُؤَادُ أُمِّ مُوسَىٰ فَٰرِغًا إِن كَادَتْ لَتُبْدِى بِهِۦ لَوْلَآ أَن رَّبَطْنَا عَلَىٰ قَلْبِهَا لِتَكُونَ مِنَ ٱلْمُؤْمِنِينَ وَقَالَتْ لِأُخْتِهِۦ قُصِّيهِ فَبَصُرَتْ بِهِۦ عَن جُنُبٍ وَهُمْ لَا يَشْعُرُونَ وَحَرَّمْنَا عَلَيْهِ ٱلْمَرَاضِعَ مِن قَبْلُ فَقَالَتْ هَلْ أَدُلُّكُمْ عَلَىٰٓ أَهْلِ بَيْتٍ يَكْفُلُونَهُۥ لَكُمْ وَهُمْ لَهُۥ نَٰصِحُونَ فَرَدَدْنَٰهُ إِلَىٰٓ أُمِّهِۦ كَىْ تَقَرَّ عَيْنُهَا وَلَا تَحْزَنَ وَلِتَعْلَمَ أَنَّ وَعْدَ ٱللَّهِ حَقٌّ وَلَٰكِنَّ أَكْثَرَهُمْ لَا يَعْلَمُونَ﴾. ١،٩

فلا شدّة أعظم من أن يُبتلى الناس بملك يذبح أبناءهم حتّى ألقت أمّ موسى ابنها في البحر مع طفوليّته ولا شدّة أعظم من حصول طفل في البحر فكشف الله تبارك اسمه ذلك عنه بالتقاط آل فرعون له وما ألقاه في قلوبهم من الرقّة عليه حتّى استحيوه وتحريم المراضع عليه حتّى ردّوه إلى أمّه وكشف عنها الشدّة من فراقه وعنه الشدّة في حصوله في البحر. ٢،٩

on them, know God better than to think such disbelieving thoughts of Him, Glory to Him.

It has been said that if one continually repeats the words of God, Mighty and Glorious: «When Jonah went angrily on his way . . .» up to «believers» during the ritual prayers and other devotions, in times of great misfortune, God will bring forward the hour of one's deliverance and relief. 8.6

I am one of those who have done so. I suffered a great calamity, of which there is not space to give the details here. I was in prison under threat of death, and God delivered me. I was set free only nine days after my arrest. 8.7

To this chapter also belongs Moses, peace on him, the son of ʿImrān, whose story the Qur'an tells in several places, as when God Exalted says, «We gave a revelation to the mother of Moses, saying, "Suckle him, and if you fear for him, throw him into the deep, and do not fear or grieve. We will return him to you, and will make him an emissary." And so it was that Pharaoh's kin gathered him up, for an enemy and a grief to themselves, for Pharaoh, Haman, and their army were wicked. But Pharaoh's wife said, "A comfort to us both! Do not kill him. He may profit us, or we may take him as our son"—they were all unaware—and the heart of Moses's mother grew desolate, so that she would have betrayed him had We not strengthened her heart to make her a believer, and she said to his sister, "Find him." She watched him from a distance—they were all unaware—and because We had forbidden him to take the breast of a nurse, she said, "Shall I show you a highborn household that will rear him for you?" And thus We returned him to his mother, to be her comfort, so that she should not grieve, and should understand that God's promise is true—which most do not understand.»[78] 9.1

There can be no greater adversity than for people to suffer the tribulation of a king who slaughters their sons—the mother of Moses preferred to throw her son into the flood, infant though he was—nor any greater adversity than for an infant to fall into the flood. But God, blessed is His name, rescued Moses from this by making Pharaoh's kin «gather him up» and filling their hearts with tenderness for him so that they spared his life, and by «forbidding him to take the breast of a nurse», whereby they returned him to his mother and He rescued her from the adversity of losing him, and him from that of falling into the flood. 9.2

٣،٩ ومعنى قوله تعالى ﴿لِيَكُونَ لَهُمْ عَدُوًّا وَحَزَنًا﴾ أي يصير عاقبة أمره معهم إلى عداوة لهم وهذه لام العاقبة كما قال الشاعر [وافر]

لِدُوا لِلْمَوْتِ وَٱبْنُوا لِلْخَرَابِ وَكُلُّكُمْ يَصِيرُ إِلَى ذَهَابِ

وقد علم أنّ الولادة لا يقصد بها الموت والبناء لا يقصد به الخراب وإنّما عاقبة الأمر فيهما تصير إلى ذلك وعلى الوجه الأوّل قوله تعالى ﴿وَلَقَدْ ذَرَأْنَا لِجَهَنَّمَ كَثِيرًا مِّنَ ٱلْجِنِّ وَٱلْإِنسِ﴾ أي إنّ عاقبة أمرهم وفعلهم واختيارهم لنفوسهم يصيّرهم إلى جهنّم فيصيرون لها لأنّ الله عزّ وجلّ لم يخلقهم ليقصد تعذيبهم بالنار في جهنّم عزّ الله عن هذا الظلم.

٤،٩ وجعل الله عاقبة أمر موسى عليه السلام من تلك الشدائد وشدائد بعدها نالته يأتي ذكرها أن بعثه نبياً وأنقذ به بني إسرائيل من الشدائد التي كانوا فيها مع فرعون.

٥،٩ فقال عزّ وجلّ في تمام هذه القصّة ﴿وَجَآءَ رَجُلٌ مِّنْ أَقْصَا ٱلْمَدِينَةِ يَسْعَىٰ قَالَ يَٰمُوسَىٰٓ إِنَّ ٱلْمَلَأَ يَأْتَمِرُونَ بِكَ لِيَقْتُلُوكَ فَٱخْرُجْ إِنِّى لَكَ مِنَ ٱلنَّٰصِحِينَ فَخَرَجَ مِنْهَا خَآئِفًا يَتَرَقَّبُ قَالَ رَبِّ نَجِّنِى مِنَ ٱلْقَوْمِ ٱلظَّٰلِمِينَ﴾ فهذه شدّة أخرى كشفها الله عزّ وجلّ.

٦،٩ قال تعالى ﴿وَلَمَّا تَوَجَّهَ تِلْقَآءَ مَدْيَنَ قَالَ عَسَىٰ رَبِّىٓ أَن يَهْدِيَنِى سَوَآءَ ٱلسَّبِيلِ وَلَمَّا وَرَدَ مَآءَ مَدْيَنَ وَجَدَ عَلَيْهِ أُمَّةً مِّنَ ٱلنَّاسِ يَسْقُونَ وَوَجَدَ مِن دُونِهِمُ ٱمْرَأَتَيْنِ تَذُودَانِ قَالَ مَا خَطْبُكُمَا قَالَتَا لَا نَسْقِى حَتَّىٰ يُصْدِرَ ٱلرِّعَآءُ وَأَبُونَا شَيْخٌ كَبِيرٌ فَسَقَىٰ لَهُمَا ثُمَّ تَوَلَّىٰٓ إِلَى ٱلظِّلِّ فَقَالَ رَبِّ إِنِّى لِمَآ أَنزَلْتَ إِلَىَّ مِنْ خَيْرٍ فَقِيرٌ﴾ فهذه شدّة أخرى لحقته بالاغتراب والحاجة إلى الاضطراب في المعيشة والاكتساب فوفّق الله تعالى له شعيباً قال الله عزّ وجلّ في تمام هذه القصّة ﴿فَجَآءَتْهُ إِحْدَىٰهُمَا تَمْشِى عَلَى ٱسْتِحْيَآءٍ قَالَتْ إِنَّ أَبِى يَدْعُوكَ لِيَجْزِيَكَ أَجْرَ مَا سَقَيْتَ لَنَا فَلَمَّا جَآءَهُۥ وَقَصَّ عَلَيْهِ ٱلْقَصَصَ قَالَ لَا تَخَفْ نَجَوْتَ مِنَ ٱلْقَوْمِ ٱلظَّٰلِمِينَ﴾.

The meaning of His words, exalted is He, «for an enemy and a grief to themselves» is that the consequence was that he and they would become enemies, a use of "for" exemplified in a line by the poet:[79] 9.3

Beget for death, build for decay:
you all are bound to pass away.

The poet knew very well that the purpose of birth is not death, nor is the purpose of building ruin. These are simply their consequences. It is in this light that we must read God's word, exalted is He: «We have engendered for hell many jinn and men.»[80] This means that the consequence of their own actions and their exercise of their free will will send them to hell, and there they shall go. God Mighty and Glorious did not create them for the express purpose of torturing them in hellfire, for He is beyond any such injustice, mighty is He!

As the consequence of the above misfortunes, and of others that he suffered 9.4
subsequently[81] and that will be related in due course, God made Moses, peace on him, a prophet, and caused him to free the Children of Israel from the misfortunes Pharaoh had inflicted on them.

God, Mighty and Glorious, tells the story: «Then a man came running from 9.5
the end of the town, saying, "Moses, the nobles are plotting against you to kill you. Flee! I give you good counsel." And Moses fled, looking about him fearfully and saying, "Lord! Save me from an unjust people!"»[82] This was another adversity from which God, Mighty and Glorious, rescued him.

God Exalted says, «Turning his face toward Midian, he said, "It may be 9.6
that my Lord will lead me on an even path," and coming to the well of Midian, he found a company of people watering their flocks there, and beyond them two women holding back theirs. "What is this?" he asked. They replied, "We may not go down to the water until the shepherds have come back up, because our father is an old man." So he watered their sheep for them and then went into the shade, saying, "Lord, I stand in need of whatever good You can bestow on me."»[83] This was a further adversity, that of exile and having to toil to gain a living. But God Exalted granted him Shuʿayb. God, Mighty and Glorious, says, «Then one of the women walked up to him shyly. She said, "My father asks you to come and be paid the hire of watering for us"; and when he came and told him the story, he said, "Do not be afraid. You are safe from the unjust people."»[84]

٧،٩ ثمّ أخبر الله تعالى في هذه القصّة كيف زوّجه شعيب ابنته بعد أن استأجره ثماني حجج وأنّه خرج بأهله من عند شعيب فرأى النار فمضى يقتبس منها فكلّمه الله تعالى وجعله نبيّاً وأرسله إلى فرعون فسأله أن يرسل معه أخاه هارون فشدّ الله تعالى ﴿عَضُدَهُ بِ﴾ ه وجعله نبيّاً معه فأيّ فرج أحسن من فرج أتى رجلاً خائفاً هارباً فقيرًا قد آجر نفسه ثماني حجج بالنبوّة والملك.

٨،٩ قال الله تعالى في سورة الأعراف ﴿وَقَالَ ٱلْمَلَأُ مِن قَوْمِ فِرْعَوْنَ أَتَذَرُ مُوسَىٰ وَقَوْمَهُۥ لِيُفْسِدُوا۟ فِى ٱلْأَرْضِ وَيَذَرَكَ وَءَالِهَتَكَ قَالَ سَنُقَتِّلُ أَبْنَآءَهُمْ وَنَسْتَحْىِۦ نِسَآءَهُمْ وَإِنَّا فَوْقَهُمْ قَٰهِرُونَ﴾ فهذه شدّة لحقت بني إسرائيل فكشفها الله عنهم قال سبحانه ﴿قَالَ مُوسَىٰ لِقَوْمِهِ ٱسْتَعِينُوا۟ بِٱللَّهِ وَٱصْبِرُوٓا۟ إِنَّ ٱلْأَرْضَ لِلَّهِ يُورِثُهَا مَن يَشَآءُ مِنْ عِبَادِهِۦ وَٱلْعَٰقِبَةُ لِلْمُتَّقِينَ قَالُوٓا۟ أُوذِينَا مِن قَبْلِ أَن تَأْتِيَنَا وَمِنۢ بَعْدِ مَا جِئْتَنَا قَالَ عَسَىٰ رَبُّكُمْ أَن يُهْلِكَ عَدُوَّكُمْ وَيَسْتَخْلِفَكُمْ فِى ٱلْأَرْضِ فَيَنظُرَ كَيْفَ تَعْمَلُونَ﴾.

٩،٩ وقال تعالى في تمام هذه القصّة في هذه السورة بعد آيات ﴿وَتَمَّتْ كَلِمَتُ رَبِّكَ ٱلْحُسْنَىٰ عَلَىٰ بَنِىٓ إِسْرَٰٓءِيلَ بِمَا صَبَرُوا۟ وَدَمَّرْنَا مَا كَانَ يَصْنَعُ فِرْعَوْنُ وَقَوْمُهُۥ وَمَا كَانُوا۟ يَعْرِشُونَ﴾ فأخبر تعالى عن صنعه لهم وفلقه البحر حتّى عبروه يبساً وإغراقه فرعون لمّا اتّبعهم.

١٠،٩ وكلّ هذه أخبار عن محن عظيمة انجلت بمنح جليلة لا يؤدّى شكر الله عليها ويجب على العاقل تأمّلها ليعرف كنه تفضّل الله عزّ وجلّ بكشف شدائده وإغاثته بإصلاح كلّ فاسد لمن تمسّك بطاعته وأخلص في خشيته وأصلح من نيّته فسلك هذه السبيل فإنّها إلى النجاة من المكاره أوضح طريق وأهدى دليل.

Then God Exalted relates how Shuʿayb married Moses to his daughter after hiring him for eight years, and how he took his household and left Shuʿayb, saw the fire, and took a brand from it.[85] Then God Exalted spoke to him and made him a prophet and sent him to Pharaoh.[86] Moses asked Him to send his brother Aaron with him, and «God» Exalted «strengthened» his «arm by means of» his brother[87] and made him a prophet also. What deliverance could be finer than one that brings both prophethood and governance to a man who, fleeing in fear and in need, had been eight years a hireling? 9.7

God Exalted says in the surah entitled The Heights: «The nobles of Pharaoh's nation said, "Will you leave Moses and his people to be corrupt in the land and abandon you and your gods?" He answered, "We will put their sons to death but let their women live. We will triumph over them!"»[88] This was an adversity that befell the Children of Israel and from which God rescued them. He says, glory to Him, «Moses said to his people, "Ask God's help, and show acceptance. The earth is God's; whichever of His servants He wills shall inherit it, and the outcome shall benefit those who revere Him!" They replied, "We have been hurt since before you came to us and since your coming." He said, "It may be that your Lord will destroy your enemy and make you successors in the land and scrutinize how you act then!"»[89] 9.8

A few verses later in the same surah, concluding this episode, God Exalted says, «And the excellent word of your Lord was fulfilled on the Children of Israel in return for their acceptance: We razed the works and buildings of Pharaoh and his people»,[90] going on to tell, exalted is He, what He brought to pass for them, parting the sea so they might cross it dry-shod, and drowning Pharaoh when he followed them. 9.9

All these are accounts of grave trials dispelled by glorious gains, for which God can never be given enough thanks, and which every rational person should contemplate in order to understand the inwardness of that graciousness by which God, Mighty and Glorious, rescues him from his misfortunes and succors him, making good whatever has gone wrong for all of sound intent who tenaciously obey and wholeheartedly fear Him and follow this path, which is the plainest and surest way to be saved from injury. 9.10

١٠ وذكر الله سبحانه وتعالى في ﴿وَٱلسَّمَآءِ ذَاتِ ٱلْبُرُوجِ﴾ أصحاب الأخدود وروى قوم من أهل الملل المخالفة للإسلام عن كتبهم أشياء من ذلك فذكرت اليهود والنصارى أنّ أصحاب الأخدود كانوا دعاة إلى الله وأنّ ملك بلدهم أضرم لهم ناراً وطرحهم فيها فاطّلع الله تعالى على صبرهم وخلوص نيّاتهم في دينه وطاعته فأمر النار أن لا تحرقهم فشوهدوا فيها قعوداً وهي تضطرم عليهم ولا تحرقهم ونجوا منها وجعل الله ﴿دَآئِرَةُ ٱلسَّوْءِ﴾ على الملك وأهلكه.

١٠١١ وذكر هؤلاء القوم أنّ نبيّاً كان في بني إسرائيل بعد موسى عليه السلام بزمان طويل يقال له دانيال وأنّ قومه كذّبوه فأخذه ملكهم فقذفه إلى أُسد مجوّعة في جبّ فلمّا اطّلع الله تعالى على حسن اتّكاله عليه وصبره طلباً لما لديه أمسك أفواه الأُسد عنه حتّى قام على رؤوسها برجليه وهي مذلّلة غير ضارّة له.

٢٠١١ فبعث الله تعالى إرميا من الشام حتّى تخلّص دانيال من هذه الشدّة وأهلك من أراد إهلاك دانيال.

٣٠١١ وعضدت روايتهم أشياء رواها أصحاب الحديث منها ما حدّثناه عليّ بن أبي الطيّب الحسن بن عليّ بن مطرف الرامهرمزيّ قال حدّثناه أحمد بن محمّد بن الجرّاح قال حدّثنا أبو بكر عبد الله بن محمّد بن أبي الدنيا القرشيّ قال حدّثنا أحمد بن عبد الأعلى الشيبانيّ قال إن لم أكن سمعته من شعيب بن صفوان فحدّثنا بعض أصحابنا عنه عن الأجلح الكنديّ عن عبد الله بن أبي الهديل قال

ضرّى بخت نصر أسدين فألقاهما في جبّ وجا[١] بدانيال فألقاه عليهما فلم يهيجاه فمكث ما شاء الله ثمّ اشتهى ما يشتهي الآدميّون من الطعام والشراب فأوحى الله إلى إرميا وهو بالشام أن أعدّ طعاماً وشراباً لدانيال فقال.

١ كذا.

In the surah «By the sky with its constellations»[91] God Exalted, glory to Him, mentions «the People of the Pit». Members of those creeds that do not acknowledge Islam have related some of what their own scriptures say about them. Thus Jews and Christians say that the People of the Pit called people to God, and that the king of their country lit a fire and flung them into it, but God, cognizant of their acceptance and the wholehearted intent of their faith in Him and obedience to Him, commanded the fire not to burn them, so that they were seen sitting in it safe and untouched as the flames burned above them, while God made «the evil turn of fortune»[92] turn against the king and destroyed him. 10

These same Jews and Christians say that there was among the Children of Israel, many years after Moses, peace on him, a prophet named Daniel, and that his people called him a liar, and that their king seized him and tossed him to hungry lions in a pit; but God Exalted, cognizant of the perfect trustfulness that Daniel placed in Him and the acceptance with which he made petition in his plight, not only stayed the lions' jaws but enabled Daniel to set his foot on their bowed heads without suffering harm. 11.1

Then God Exalted sent Jeremiah from Syria to free Daniel from this adversity, and destroyed those who would have destroyed Daniel. 11.2

These narratives are supported by the accounts of the Traditionists, notably a report transmitted to us by ʿAlī ibn Abī l-Ṭayyib al-Ḥasan ibn ʿAlī ibn Muṭrif of Rāmhurmuz,[93] citing Aḥmad ibn Muḥammad Ibn al-Jarrāḥ,[94] citing Ibn Abī l-Dunyā, who cites Aḥmad ibn ʿAbd al-Aʿlā al-Shaybānī, who says: 11.3

Even though I did not personally hear this from Shuʿayb ibn Ṣafwān, nevertheless it was cited to me by a fellow Traditionist, from al-Ajlaḥ al-Kindī, from ʿAbd Allāh ibn Abī l-Hudayl, who said:

Nebuchadnezzar baited two lions and threw them into a pit, then had Daniel brought and threw him to the lions, but the lions would not attack him. After he had remained there at God's pleasure, Daniel began to feel hungry and thirsty, as any human would. God therefore told Jeremiah in Syria to prepare food and drink for Daniel.

"Lord," replied Jeremiah, "I am in the Holy Land, and Daniel is in Iraq, in the land of Babylon. "

يا ربّ أنا بالأرض المقدّسة ودانيال بأرض بابل من أرض العراق فأوحى الله تعالى إليه أن أعدّ ما أمرناك به فإنّا سنرسل إليك من يحملك ويحمل ما أعددت ففعل فأرسل الله إليه من حمله وحمل ما أعدّ حتّى وقف على رأس الجبّ. فقال دانيال من هذا قال أنا إرميا قال ما جاء بك قال أرسلني إليك ربّك قال وذكرني قال نعم.

قال الحمد لله الذي لا ينسى من ذكره والحمد لله الذي لا يخيّب من رجاه والحمد لله الذي من توكّل عليه كفاه والحمد لله الذي من وثق به لم يكله إلى غيره والحمد لله الذي يجزي بالإحسان إحسانًا وبالسيّئات غفرانًا والحمد لله الذي يجزي بالصبر نجاة والحمد لله الذي يكشف ضرّنا بعد كربنا والحمد لله الذي هو ثقتنا حين تسوء ظنوننا بأعمالنا والحمد لله الذي هو رجاؤنا حين تنقطع الحيل منّا.

١،١٢ وقد ذكر الله تعالى في محكم كتابه الشدّة التي جرت على محمّد صلّى الله عليه وعلى آله الأخيار فيما اقتصّه من قصّه الغار فقال سبحانه ﴿ إِلَّا تَنصُرُوهُ فَقَدْ نَصَرَهُ ٱللَّهُ إِذْ أَخْرَجَهُ ٱلَّذِينَ كَفَرُوا۟ ثَانِىَ ٱثْنَيْنِ إِذْ هُمَا فِى ٱلْغَارِ إِذْ يَقُولُ لِصَٰحِبِهِۦ لَا تَحْزَنْ إِنَّ ٱللَّهَ مَعَنَا فَأَنزَلَ ٱللَّهُ سَكِينَتَهُۥ عَلَيْهِ وَأَيَّدَهُۥ بِجُنُودٍ لَّمْ تَرَوْهَا وَجَعَلَ كَلِمَةَ ٱلَّذِينَ كَفَرُوا۟ ٱلسُّفْلَىٰ وَكَلِمَةُ ٱللَّهِ هِىَ ٱلْعُلْيَا وَٱللَّهُ عَزِيزٌ حَكِيمٌ ﴾.

٢،١٢ وروى أصحاب الحديث ما يطول إعادته بألفاظه وأسانيده أنّ

النبيّ صلّى الله عليه وسلّم لمّا خاف أن يلحقه المشركون حين سار عن مكّة مهاجرًا دخل الغار هو وأبو بكر الصدّيق فاستخفى فيه فأرسل الله عنكبوتًا فنسج في الحال على باب الغار وحمامة عشّشت وباضت وفرّخت للوقت فلمّا انتهى المشركون إلى الغار رأوا ذلك فلم يشكّوا أنّه غار لم يدخله حيوان منذ حين وإنّ رسول الله صلّى الله

God Exalted told him to do as he had been commanded: "We will have you and the food carried there."

Jeremiah obeyed, and God had them borne to the mouth of the pit, whence Daniel called out, "Who is there?"

Jeremiah replied, "I, Jeremiah."

"Why are you here?" asked Daniel.

"I was sent to you by your Lord," said Jeremiah.

Daniel asked, "Did He utter my name?"

"He did," said Jeremiah, and Daniel said, "Praise God, Who does not forget those who utter *His* name. Praise God, Who does not fail those who put their hope in Him. Praise God, Who preserves those who put their trust in Him; and praise God, Who Himself takes charge of those who place their confidence in Him. Praise God, Who recompenses good with good and evil with pardon. Praise God, Who recompenses acceptance with salvation. Praise God, Who takes away the losses we have suffered in our afflictions. Praise God, in Whom we confide when we doubt our own works; and praise to the One Who is our hope when we are at our wits' end."

In an unambiguous passage of His Book where He tells the story of the cave, **12.1** God Exalted, glory to Him, relates the adversity that beset Muḥammad, God bless him and his exemplary kin, saying, «Though you will not help him, God is his helper, as when the miscreants drove him out, the second of two,[95] when they were both in the cave, when he said to his companion, "Do not grieve; God is with us," and God sent down His tranquility upon him and strengthened him with armies invisible to you and brought low the word of the miscreants, for the word of God is far above it, and God is mighty and wise.»[96]

The Traditionists, whose versions are too long to repeat word for word with **12.2** their chains of transmitters, relate that:

The Prophet, God bless and keep him, fearing that the idolaters[97] would catch him as he traveled into exile from Mecca, went and hid inside the cave together with Abū Bakr the Undoubting, whereupon God sent a spider, which at once spun a web over the mouth of the cave, and a pigeon, which built a nest, laid eggs, and immediately hatched them. When the idolaters arrived and saw this, they were convinced that it was a cave long uninhabited by any living thing; yet Abū Bakr and the Prophet, God bless and keep him, could see

عليه وسلّم وأبا بكر ليريان أقدامهم ويسمعان كلامهم فلمّا انصرفوا وأبعدوا وجاء الليل خرجا فسارا نحو المدينة فورداها سالمين.

٣،١٢ وروى أصحاب الحديث أيضاً من شرح حال النبيّ صلّى الله عليه وسلّم في المحن التي لحقته من شقّ الفرث عليه ومحاولة أبي جهل وشيبة وعتبة ابني ربيعة وأبي سفيان صخر بن حرب والعاص بن وائل وعقبة بن أبي معيط وغيرهم قتله وما كانوا يكاشفونه به من السبّ والتكذيب والاستهزاء والقدع والتأنيب ورميهم إيّاه بالجنون وقصدهم إيّاه غير دفعة بأنواع الأذى والعضيهة والاقتراء وحصرهم إيّاه صلّى الله عليه وسلّم وجميع بني هاشم في الشعب وتخويفهم إيّاه وتدبيرهم أن يقتلوه حتى بعُد وبيّت عليّاً عليه السلام على فراشه ما يطول اقتصاصه ويكثر شرحه.

٤،١٢ ثم أعقبه الله تعالى من ذلك بالنصر والتمكين وإعزاز الدين وإظهاره على كلّ دين وقمع الجاحدين والمشركين وقتل أولئك الكفرة المارقين والمعاندين وغيرهم من المكذّبين الكاذبين الذين كانوا عن الحق ناكثين وبالدين مستهزئين وللمؤمنين مناصبين متوعّدين وللنبيّ صلّى الله عليه وسلّم مكاشفين محاربين وأذلّ من بقي منهم بعزّ الإسلام بعد أن عاذ بإظهاره وأضمر الكفر في إسراره فصار من المنافقين الملعونين ﴿ٱلْحَمْدُ لِلَّهِ رَبِّ ٱلْعَٰلَمِينَ﴾.

١،١٣ فـهذه أخبار جاءت في آيات من القرآن وهي تجري في هذا الباب وتضاف إليه.

٢،١٣ حدّثنا عليّ بن أبي الطيّب بن مطرف قال حدّثنا أحمد بن محمّد بن الجرّاح قال حدّثنا أبو بكر عبد الله بن محمّد القرشيّ المعروف بابن أبي الدنيا قال حدّثنا إبراهيم بن راشد قال حدّثنا عبد الرحمٰن بن حمّاد الشعيثيّ قال حدّثنا كهمس بن الحسن عن أبي السليل قال قال أبو ذرّ

the Meccans' feet and hear what they were saying. Once they were far away and night had fallen, the two of them came out and made their way safely to Medina.

The Traditionists also speak at length and with much commentary in expounding the circumstances of the trials undergone by the Prophet, God bless and keep him. Excrement from animals' split entrails was poured over him. Abū Jahl; the two sons of Rabīʿah, Shaybah and ʿUtbah; Abū Sufyān Ṣakhr ibn Ḥarb; al-ʿĀṣ ibn Wāʾil; ʿUqbah ibn Abī Muʿayṭ, and others all tried to murder him, and went on to persecute him with ridicule and violence, cursing him and calling him a liar, shunning him and claiming that he was possessed. They repeatedly made him the butt of all kinds of hurt, slander, and calumny, detaining him, God bless and keep him, and the whole clan of Hāshim in a valley outside Mecca, threatening him and making attempts on his life, until he withdrew, leaving behind ʿAlī ibn Abī Ṭālib, peace on him, in his bed in his place. 12.3

But the outcome of this was that God Exalted gave him help and strength, made the faith mighty, and caused it to triumph over every other. He subdued the infidels and the idolaters and slew the renegade and obdurate miscreants, those liars who had called Muḥammad a liar, who broke their word and mocked the faith, showed malice to the believers and menaced them, and who had persecuted the Prophet and made war on him. Those who remained, who had sought refuge in a show of faith while secretly harboring unbelief, He abased through the glory of Islam, and they were accursed as hypocrites. «Praise God, Lord of all!»[98] 12.4

The following are accounts connected with Qurʾanic verses.[99] They belong in this chapter, and should be added to it. 13.1

We cite ʿAlī ibn al-Ḥasan, citing Ibn al-Jarrāḥ, citing Ibn Abī l-Dunyā, citing Ibrāhīm ibn Rāshid, citing ʿAbd al-Raḥmān ibn Ḥammād al-Shuʿaythī, citing Kahmas ibn al-Ḥasan, quoting Abū l-Salīl, who cited Abū Dharr as follows: 13.2

كان نبيّ الله صلّى الله عليه وسلّم يتلو هذه الآية ﴿وَمَن يَتَّقِ ٱللَّهَ يَجْعَل لَّهُۥ مَخْرَجًا وَيَرْزُقْهُ مِنْ حَيْثُ لَا يَحْتَسِبُ وَمَن يَتَوَكَّلْ عَلَى ٱللَّهِ فَهُوَ حَسْبُهُۥٓ إِنَّ ٱللَّهَ بَٰلِغُ أَمْرِهِۦ﴾ ثمّ يقول يا أبا ذرّ لو أنّ الناس كلّهم أخذوا بها لكفتهم.

٣،١٣ وحدّثنا عليّ بن الحسن قال حدّثنا ابن الجرّاح قال حدّثنا ابن أبي الدنيا قال حدّثنا إسحاق بن إسماعيل قال حدّثنا سفيان عن مسعر عن عليّ بن بَذِيمة عن أبي عبيدة قال

جاء رجل إلى النبيّ صلّى الله عليه وسلّم فقال إنّ بني فلان أغاروا عليّ فذهبوا بإبلي وابني فقال رسول الله صلّى الله عليه وسلّم إنّ آل محمّد لكذا وكذا أهل ما فيهم مُدّ من طعام أو صاع من طعام فسَل الله عزّ وجلّ فرجع إلى امرأته فقالت ما قال لك رسول الله صلّى الله عليه وسلّم فأخبرها فقالت نِعْمَ ما ردّك إليه. فما لبث أن ردّ الله عليه إبله أوفر ما كانت فأتى النبيّ صلّى الله عليه وسلّم فأخبره فصعد النبيّ صلّى الله عليه وسلّم المنبر فحمد الله وأثنى عليه وأمر الناس بمسألة الله عزّ وجلّ والرجوع إليه والرغبة فيه وقرأ عليهم ﴿وَمَن يَتَّقِ ٱللَّهَ يَجْعَل لَّهُۥ مَخْرَجًا وَيَرْزُقْهُ مِنْ حَيْثُ لَا يَحْتَسِبُ﴾.

٤،١٣ وحدّثني عليّ بن أبي الطيّب قال حدّثنا ابن الجرّاح قال حدّثنا ابن أبي الدنيا قال حدّثنا أبو عبد الرحمٰن الفرسيّ عن إسحاق بن سليمان عن معاوية بن يحيى عن يونس بن ميسرة عن أبي إدريس الخولانيّ عن أبي الدرداء

وسئل عن هذه الآية ﴿كُلَّ يَوْمٍ هُوَ فِى شَأْنٍ﴾ قال سئل عنها رسول الله صلّى الله عليه وسلّم فقال إنّ من شأنه أن يغفر ذنبًا ويكشف كربًا ويرفع أقوامًا ويضع آخرين.

٥،١٣ أخبرني محمّد بن الحسن بن المظفّر الكاتب قال أنبأنا محمّد بن عبد الواحد أبو عمر قال حدّثنا بشر بن موسى الأسديّ قال حدّثنا أبو بكر الأسديّ قال حدّثنا أبو حاتم الرازيّ قال حدّثنا محمّد بن عبد الكريم قال سمعت سعيد بن عنبسة يقول

The Prophet, God bless and keep him, used to intone the verse: «Whoever reveres God, He will give him relief, and give him provision whence he least expects it; for whoever trusts only in God needs nothing else. God accomplishes His purpose».[100]

Then he would say: "Abū Dharr! If only everyone were to do this, it would suffice them!"

We cite ʿAlī ibn al-Ḥasan, citing Ibn al-Jarrāḥ, citing Ibn Abī l-Dunyā, citing Isḥāq ibn Ismāʿīl, citing Sufyān,[101] quoting Misʿar, quoting ʿAlī ibn Bidhaymah, quoting Abū ʿUbaydah, who said: 13.3

A man came to the Prophet, God bless and keep him, and said, "Such and such a tribe have raided me and carried off my camels and my son."

The Prophet, God bless and keep him, replied, "The House of Muḥammad, for some moons, has owned not a quart nor a bushel of grain. Ask alms of God, Mighty and Glorious!"

The man went back to his wife, and when he told her what the Prophet, God bless and keep him, had said, she said, "He gave you good advice."

Before long, God gave him back his camels as numerous as could be.

The man went and told the Prophet, God bless and keep him, who mounted the pulpit and praised and extolled God, telling the Muslims to ask for alms from God, Mighty and Glorious, to rely on Him and desire only Him, and recited to them the verse: «Whoever reveres God, He will give him relief: and give him provision whence he least expects it.»[102]

I cite ʿAlī ibn al-Ḥasan, citing Ibn al-Jarrāḥ, citing Ibn Abī l-Dunyā, citing Abū ʿAbd al-Raḥmān al-Farasī,[103] quoting Isḥāq ibn Sulaymān, quoting Muʿāwiyah ibn Yaḥyā, quoting Yūnus ibn Maysarah, quoting Abū Idrīs al-Khawlānī, quoting Abū l-Dardāʾ: 13.4

Abū l-Dardāʾ, questioned about the verse «Every day He has some great task,»[104] said, "When the Prophet, God bless and keep him, was asked what it meant, he replied, 'His task is forgiving a misdeed, taking away an affliction, raising up some nations and humbling others.'"

I cite the state scribe Muḥammad ibn al-Ḥasan ibn al-Muẓaffar, who quotes Abū ʿUmar Muḥammad ibn ʿAbd al-Wāḥid, citing Bishr ibn Mūsā al-Asadī, citing Abū Bakr al-Asadī, citing Abū Ḥātim of Rayy, citing Muḥammad ibn ʿAbd al-Karīm, who said, I heard Saʿīd ibn ʿAnbasah say: 13.5

بينما رجل جالس وهو يعبث بالحصى ويحذف بها إذ رجعت حصاة منها فصارت في أذنه فجهد بكلّ حيلة فلم يقدر على إخراجها فبقيت الحصاة في أذنه دهرًا تؤلمه فبينما هو ذات يوم جالس إذ سمع قارئًا يقرأ ﴿أَمَّن يُجِيبُ ٱلْمُضْطَرَّ إِذَا دَعَاهُ وَيَكْشِفُ ٱلسُّوٓءَ﴾ الآية فقال الرجل يا ربّ أنت المجيب وأنا المضطرّ فاكشف ضرّ ما أنا فيه فنزلت الحصاة من أذنه.

٦،١٣ قال مؤلّف هذا الكتاب: وقد لقيت أنا أبا عمر محمّد بن عبد الواحد المعروف بغلام ثعلب وبالزاهد وحملت عنه وأجاز لي جميع ما يصحّ عندي من رواياته ولم أسمع هذا الخبر منه إلاّ أنّه قد دخل في الإجازة.

٧،١٣ حدّثنا عليّ بن أبي الطيّب قال حدّثنا ابن الجرّاح قال حدّثنا ابن أبي الدنيا قال حدّثنا خالد بن خداش قال حدّثنا عبد الله بن زيد بن أسلم عن أبيه زيد عن أبيه أسلم أنّ

أبا عبيدة حُصر فكتب إليه عمر مهما نزل بامرئ من شدّة يجعل له الله بعدها فرجًا ولن يغلب عسر يسرين فإنّه يقول ﴿ٱصْبِرُواْ وَصَابِرُواْ وَرَابِطُواْ وَٱتَّقُواْ ٱللَّهَ لَعَلَّكُمْ تُفْلِحُونَ﴾.

٨،١٣ حدّثنا عليّ بن أبي الطيّب قال حدّثنا ابن الجرّاح قال حدّثنا ابن أبي الدنيا قال حدّثنا الحسن بن عليّ قال حدّثنا أحمد بن صالح قال حدّثنا عبد الله بن وهب قال حدّثنا أبو صخر أنّ يزيد الرقاشيّ حدّثه قال سمعت أنس بن مالك ولا أعلم إلاّ أنّ أنسًا يرفع الحديث إلى النبيّ صلّى الله عليه وسلّم إنّ

يونس عليه السلام حين بدا له أن يدعو الله عزّ وجلّ بالظلمات حين ناداه وهو في بطن الحوت فقال اللّهمّ ﴿لَّآ إِلَٰهَ إِلَّآ أَنتَ سُبْحَٰنَكَ إِنِّى كُنتُ مِنَ ٱلظَّٰلِمِينَ﴾ فأقبلت الدعوة نحو العرش فقالت الملائكة يا ربّ هذا صوت ضعيف مكروب من بلاد غربة فقال أما تعرفون ذاك قالوا ومن هو قال ذاك عبدي يونس الذي لم يزل يُرفع له عمل

A man once sat playing with some pebbles, and as he tossed them around, one of them flew backward and lodged in his ear. He tried everything to get it out, without success, and there the pebble stuck painfully for some time until one day when all of a sudden he heard a voice recite the verse: «. . . Who answers the hard-pressed when he prays to Him and takes away evil.»[105]

The man exclaimed,"O Lord, You are the answerer of prayers, and I am that hard-pressed person! Take away my present hurt!" and the pebble dropped from his ear.

The author observes: I myself met Abū ʿUmar Muḥammad ibn ʿAbd al-Wāḥid, also known as Thaʿlab's Pupil and as the Ascetic, and studied under him, obtaining permission to transmit all the material of his I deemed sound. I never heard him tell this story himself. It does, however, form part of the corpus that he authorized me to transmit. 13.6

We cite ʿAlī ibn al-Ḥasan, citing Ibn al-Jarrāḥ, citing Ibn Abī l-Dunyā, citing 13.7
Khālid ibn Khidāsh, citing ʿAbd Allāh ibn Zayd ibn Aslam, quoting his father Zayd, quoting his father Aslam:

Abū ʿUbaydah ibn al-Jarrāḥ, on being besieged, received the following missive from ʿUmar ibn al-Khaṭṭāb:

"Whatever adversity may beset a man, God will afterward give him deliverance. A single hardship can never be a match for ease twice over, for He has said, «Show acceptance; vie with each other in acceptance; be steadfast; revere God, and you shall prosper.»"[106]

We cite ʿAlī ibn al-Ḥasan, citing Ibn al-Jarrāḥ, citing Ibn Abī l-Dunyā, citing 13.8
al-Ḥasan ibn ʿAlī, citing Aḥmad ibn Ṣāliḥ, citing ʿAbd Allāh ibn Wahb, citing Abū Ṣakhr as saying that Yazīd al-Raqqāshī told him that he heard, from Anas ibn Mālik, who may well have attributed it to the Prophet, God bless and keep him, that:

When Jonah, on whom be peace, saw fit to call on God, Mighty and Exalted, in the darkness, crying out to Him from the belly of the fish: "O God! «There is no God but You. Glory to You! I am unjust!»"[107] his supplication went up toward[108] the throne of God. The angels exclaimed:

"Lord, this is the voice of a weak and afflicted man from a distant land!"

"Do you not recognize him?" God asked.

"Who is he?" they answered.

متقبّل ودعوة مجابة قالوا يا ربّ أفلا ترحم ما كان يصنع في الرخاء فتنجيه من البلاء قال بلى فأمر الحوت فطرحه ﴿بِٱلْعَرَآءِ﴾.

قال أبو صخر فأخبرني أبو سعيد بن بسيط وأنا أحدّثه بهذا الحديث أنّه سمع أبا هريرة يقول ٩،١٣

طُرح ﴿بِٱلْعَرَآءِ﴾ فأنبت الله عليه اليقطينة قلنا يا أبا هريرة وما اليقطينة قال شجرة الدبّاء.

قال أبو هريرة هيّأ الله تعالى له أروية وحشيّة تأكل من حشيش الأرض فتجيء فتفشّج له وترويه من لبنها كلّ عشيّة وبكرة حتّى نبت يعني لحمه.

وقال أميّة بن أبي الصلت قبل الإسلام في ذلك بيتاً من الشعر [طويل] ١٠،١٣

فَأَنْبَتَ يَقْطِيناً عَلَيْهِ بِرَحْمَةٍ   مِنَ اللهِ لَوْ لَا ٱللهُ أُلْفِيَ ضَاحِيا

حدّثنا عليّ بن الحسن قال حدّثني ابن الجرّاح قال حدّثنا ابن أبي الدنيا قال حدّثنا يوسف بن موسى قال حدّثنا عبيد الله بن موسى عن إسرائيل عن أبي إسحاق عن عمرو بن ميمون قال حدّثنا عبد الله بن مسعود في بيت المال قال ١١،١٣

لمّا ابتلع الحوت يونس عليه السلام أهوى به إلى قرار الأرض فسمع يونس تسبيح الحصى في الظلمات ظلمات ثلاث بطن الحوت وظلمات الليل وظلمة البحر فنادى في الظلمات ﴿أَن لَّآ إِلَٰهَ إِلَّآ أَنتَ سُبْحَٰنَكَ إِنِّى كُنتُ مِنَ ٱلظَّٰلِمِينَ﴾ ﴿فَنَبَذْنَٰهُ بِٱلْعَرَآءِ وَهُوَ سَقِيمٌ﴾ قال كهيأة الفرخ الممعوط الذي ليس له ريش.

God said, "He is my servant Jonah, from whom ever rise pleasing works and supplications that I answer."

"Lord," said the angels, "will You not pity him for the sake of how he acted in prosperity, and save him from this tribulation?"

"Even so," answered God, and commanded the fish to cast him up «on the bare ground.»[109]

Abū Ṣakhr said, When I was relating this report to Abū Saʿīd ibn Basīṭ, he related to me that he had heard Abū Hurayrah say: 13.9

"He was cast up «on the bare ground», and God made the gourd tree grow over him."

Asked what the gourd tree was, Abū Hurayrah replied, "A squash."

Abū Hurayrah also said, "God Exalted provided Jonah with a female mountain goat, to eat the herbage of the place and come to him each evening and morning and part her hind legs to give him her milk to drink, until it grew (meaning Jonah's flesh)."

There is a line of poetry on this subject composed by Umayyah ibn Abī l-Ṣalt before Islam: 13.10

> God in his mercy grew a gourd above him.
> Had He not done so, heatstroke would have killed him.

We cite ʿAlī ibn al-Ḥasan, citing Ibn al-Jarrāḥ, citing Ibn Abī l-Dunyā, citing Yūsuf ibn Mūsā, citing ʿUbayd Allāh ibn Mūsā, quoting Isrāʾīl, from Abū Isḥāq, quoting ʿAmr ibn Maymūn, who said, ʿAbd Allāh ibn Masʿūd related to me, in the public treasury:[110] 13.11

After the fish swallowed Jonah, on whom be peace, it plunged down to the seafloor, and Jonah heard the pebbles glorifying God in the three darknesses, that of the fish's belly, that of the night, and that of the sea.

He cried out in the darkness: "«There is no God but You. Glory to You! I am unjust!»"[111] whereupon «We flung him down sick on the bare ground»[112] like a featherless plucked fledgling.

حدّثني فتى من الكتّاب البغداديّين يعرف بأبي الحسن بن أبي الليث وكان أبوه من كتّاب الجبل يتصرّف مع لشكرورز بن سهلان الديلميّ أحد الأمراء كان في عسكر معزّ الدولة قال ١،١٤

قرأت في بعض الكتب إذا دهمك أمر تخافه فبِتْ وأنت طاهر على فراش طاهر وثياب كلّها طاهرة واقرأ ﴿وَٱلشَّمْسِ وَضُحَىٰهَا﴾ إلى آخر السورة سبعاً و﴿وَٱلَّيْلِ إِذَا يَغْشَىٰ﴾ إلى آخر السورة سبعاً ثمّ قل اللّهمّ اجعل لي فرجاً ومخرجاً من أمري فإنّه يأتيك في الليلة الأوّلة[1] أو الثانية وإلى السابعة آتٍ في منامك يقول لك المخرج منه كذا وكذا.

قال فحُبست بعد هذا بسنين حبسة طالت حتّى أيست من الفرج فذكرته يوماً وأنا في الحبس ففعلت ذلك فلم أر في الليلة الأوّلة[2] ولا الثانية ولا الثالثة شيئاً فلمّا كان في الليلة الرابعة فعلت ذلك على الرسم فرأيت في منامي كأنّ رجلاً يقول لي خلاصك على يد عليّ بن إبراهيم. ٢،١٤

فأصبحت من غد متعجّباً ولم أكن أعرف رجلاً يقال له عليّ بن إبراهيم فلمّا كان بعد يومين دخل إليّ شابّ لا أعرفه فقال لي قد كفلت بما عليك فقم وإذا معه رسول إلى السجّان بتسليمي إليه فقمت معه فحملني إلى منزلي وسلّمني فيه وانصرف فقلت لهم من هذا فقالوا رجل بزّاز من أهل الأهواز يقال له عليّ بن إبراهيم يكون في الكرخ قيل لنا إنّه صديق الذي حبسك فطرحنا أنفسنا عليه فتوسّط أمرك وضمن ما عليك وأخرجك. ٣،١٤

قال مؤلّف هذا الكتاب ٤،١٤

فلمّا كان بعد سنين جاءني عليّ بن إبراهيم هذا وهو معاملي في البزّ منذ سنين كثيرة فذاكرته بالحديث فقال

١ كذا. ٢ كذا.

A Baghdadi state scribe known as Abū l-Ḥasan ibn Abī l-Layth, whose father was a state scribe in Gīlān and worked for a former commander in the army of Muʿizz al-Dawlah, Lashkarwarz ibn Sahlān the Daylamī, told me: Somewhere or other I read: 14.1

In any crisis, you should spend the night in a state of ritual purity, on a bed that is ritually pure, in clothes all of which are ritually pure, and recite the whole of the surah: «By the sun and its morning light»[113] seven times, and the whole of the surah «By the night when it descends,»[114] also seven times. Then say,

"O God! Give me deliverance and relief!" and on the first or second night, or any night up to the seventh, you will have a dream in which you will be told,

"This or that thing or person shall be your relief."

Abū l-Ḥasan ibn Abī l-Layth continued: 14.2

Some years after this, I was imprisoned for so long that I gave up hope of deliverance. Then one day I remembered what I had read, and acted on it.

On the first, second, and third nights I saw nothing. On the fourth night, after performing the rite, I dreamed I saw a man who said to me,"Your release will be effected by ʿAlī ibn Ibrāhīm."

The next morning I awoke in amazement, for I knew no one called ʿAlī ibn Ibrāhīm. 14.3

Two days later, a young man who was a stranger to me came to my cell and said, "I was told to stand surety for you. Come!" With him was a messenger with orders to the warder to release me to him. He took me to my house, saw me inside, and left.

"Who is he?" I asked my people.

"A cloth merchant called ʿAlī ibn Ibrāhīm from Ahwaz, who has a shop in al-Karkh," they replied. "We were told he was a friend of the man who put you in jail, so we threw ourselves on his mercy, and he interceded, posted bail for you, and got you out."

The author adds: 14.4

Some years later, this ʿAlī ibn Ibrāhīm, who had been my partner in the cloth trade for many years, came to see me, and I reminded him of the story. He confirmed it, saying:

نعم كان هذا الفتى قد حبسه عبدوس بن أخت أبي عليّ الحسن بن إبراهيم النصرانيّ خازن معزّ الدولة وطالبه بخمسة آلاف درهم كانت عليه من ضمان ضمنه عنه وكان عبدوس لي صديقاً فجاءني من سألني خطابه في أمر هذا الرجل وجرى الأمر على ما عرّفك.

وما أعجب هذا الخبر فإنّي قد وجدته في عدّة كتب بأسانيد وبغير أسانيد على اختلاف الألفاظ والمعنى قريب وأنا أذكر أصحّها عندي. ١،١٥

وجدت في كتاب محمّد بن جرير الطبريّ الذي سمّاه كتاب الآداب الحميدة والأخلاق النفيسة حدّثني محمّد بن عمارة الأسديّ قال حدّثنا عبد الله بن يزيد قال أنبأنا أنيس ابن عمران النافعيّ أبو يزيد عن رَوح بن الحارث بن حبش الصنعانيّ عن أبيه عن جدّه أنّه قال لبنيه

يا بنيّ إذا دهمكم أمر أو كربكم فلا يبيتنّ أحد منكم إلاّ وهو طاهر على فراش طاهر في لحاف طاهر ولا تبيتنّ معه امرأة ثمّ ليقرأ ﴿وَٱلَّيۡلِ إِذَا يَغۡشَىٰ﴾ سبعاً ﴿وَٱلشَّمۡسِ وَضُحَىٰهَا﴾ سبعاً ثمّ ليقل ٱللّٰهمّ اجعل لي من أمري فرجاً ومخرجاً فإنّه يأتيه آت في أوّل ليلة أو في الثالثة أو في الخامسة وأظنّه قال أو في السابعة فيقول له المخرج ممّا أنت فيه كذا وكذا.

قال أنيس ٢،١٥

فأصابني وجع لم أدرِ كيف أزيله ففعلت أوّل ليلة هكذا فأتاني اثنان فجلس أحدهما عند رأسي والآخر عند رجلي ثمّ قال أحدهما لصاحبه جسّه فلمس جسدي كلّه فلمّا انتهى إلى موضع من رأسي قال احجم ها هنا ولا تحلق ولكن اطلِه بغرا ثمّ التفت إليّ أحدهما أو كلاهما فقالا لي كيف لو ضممت إليهما ﴿وَٱلتِّينِ وَٱلزَّيۡتُونِ﴾.

This man had been put in prison by ʿAbdūs—Muʿizz al-Dawlah's treasurer, the son of the sister of Abū ʿAlī al-Ḥasan ibn Ibrāhīm the Christian—who demanded that he pay him five thousand dirhams, which he owed him according to a tax-farming contract he held from him.[115] ʿAbdūs was a friend of mine. Someone came and asked me to have a word with him about this man, and what followed was just as he told you.

Here is a wonderful story that I have read in several books, with and without chains of transmitters and with different wording, although the sense remains similar. I shall relate what seems to me the soundest version: 15.1

I read in the book by Muḥammad ibn Jarīr al-Ṭabarī entitled *The Book of Praiseworthy Behavior and Valuable Principles*: I cite Muḥammad ibn ʿUmārah al-Asadī, citing ʿAbd Allāh ibn Yazīd, who quotes Abū Yazīd Unays ibn ʿImrān al-Nāfiʿī, quoting Rawḥ ibn al-Ḥārith ibn Ḥabash of Ṣanʿāʾ, quoting his father, quoting his grandfather,[116] as saying that he said to his sons:

My sons, should some affliction suddenly befall you, spend the night in a state of ritual purity, on a ritually pure bed with a ritually pure covering. You must have no woman with you. Then recite, seven times, «By the sun and its morning light» and «By the night when it descends,»[117] also seven times. Then say, "O God! Give me deliverance and relief!"

Then, on the first, third, or fifth night (and I believe he said: "or on the seventh") you will be told:

"This or that thing shall be your relief from your plight."

Abū Yazīd Unays said: 15.2

When I developed a pain that I did not know how to get rid of, I did this on the first night, and two beings came to me and sat one at my head, the other at my feet.

One of them said to the other, "Examine him!" and felt my body all over. When he reached a certain spot on my head, he said, "Have yourself cupped here. Don't shave off the hair—use plant gum."

Then one or both of them turned to me and said, "Why don't you add «By the fig and the olive»?"[118]

قال فلمّا أصبحت سألت أيّ شيء الغرا فقيل لي الخطميّ أو شيء تستمسك به المحجمة فاحتجمت فبرئت وأنا ليس أحدّث بهذا الحديث أحدًا إلاّ وجد فيه الشفاء بإذن الله تعالى وأضمّ إليها ﴿وَٱلتِّينِ وَٱلزَّيْتُونِ﴾ . ٣،١٥

ووجدت في كتاب أبي الفرج المخزوميّ عبد الواحد بن نصر عن أبي القاسم عبد الرحمٰن بن العبّاس قال حدّثني أبو ساعدة بن أبي الوليد بن أحمد بن أبي دؤاد قال حدّثني أبي قال حدّثنا إبراهيم بن رباح قال حدّثنا أبو عبد الله أحمد بن أبي دؤاد قال حدّثنا الواثق قال حدّثنا المعتصم ١،١٦

أنّ قومًا ركبوا البحر فسمعوا هاتفًا يهتف بهم من يعطيني عشرة آلاف دينار حتّى أعلّمه كلمة إذا أصابه غمّ أو أشرف على هلاك فقالها انكشف ذلك عنه فقام رجل من أهل المركب معه عشرة آلاف دينار فصاح أيّها الهاتف أنا أعطيك عشرة آلاف دينار وعلّمني فقال ارم بالمال في البحر فرمى به وهو بدرتان فيهما عشرة آلاف دينار فسمع الهاتف يقول إذا أصابك غمّ أو أشرفت على هلكة فاقرأ ﴿وَمَن يَتَّقِ ٱللَّهَ يَجْعَل لَّهُ مَخْرَجًا وَيَرْزُقْهُ مِنْ حَيْثُ لَا يَحْتَسِبُ وَمَن يَتَوَكَّلْ عَلَى ٱللَّهِ فَهُوَ حَسْبُهُ إِنَّ ٱللَّهَ بَٰلِغُ أَمْرِهِ قَدْ جَعَلَ ٱللَّهُ لِكُلِّ شَىْءٍ قَدْرًا﴾ فقال جميع من في المركب للرجل لقد ضيّعت مالك فقال كلاّ إنّ هذه لعظة ما أشكّ في نفعها.

قال فلمّا كان بعد أيّام كسر بهم المركب فلم ينجُ منهم أحد غير ذلك الرجل فإنّه وقع على لوح. ٢،١٦

فحدّث بعد ذلك قال ٣،١٦

طرحني البحر على جزيرة فصعدت أمشي فيها فإذا بقصر منيف فدخلته فإذا فيه كلّ ما يكون في البحر من الجواهر وغيرها وإذا بامرأة لم أر قطّ أحسن منها.

Next morning I asked what plant gum was, and was told: "Marsh mallow,[119] or anything that will make the cupping glass stick." 15.3

I had myself cupped, and was cured.

Everyone I have told about this has found that it cured him, by God's leave, exalted is He; and I personally add «By the fig and the olive».

I read, written down by Abū l-Faraj ʿAbd al-Wāḥid ibn Naṣr al-Makhzūmī, quoting Abū l-Qāsim ʿAbd al-Raḥmān ibn al-ʿAbbās, who said, I cite Abū Sāʿidah son of Abī l-Walīd ibn Aḥmad ibn Abī Du'ād, citing his father, citing Ibrāhīm ibn Rabāḥ, citing Abū ʿAbd Allāh Aḥmad ibn Abī Du'ād, citing the caliph al-Wāthiq, citing the caliph al-Muʿtaṣim:[120] 16.1

A company of seafarers heard a disembodied voice[121] call out: "Who will buy? Ten thousand dinars for something that will save you from any grief or mortal peril when you say it!"

Up jumped one of the travelers who happened to have the money. "I will!" he cried. "Here's ten thousand dinars."

"Throw the money into the sea," said the voice.

The man tossed two purses into the sea, and heard the voice say, "In any grief or mortal peril that may befall you, recite: «Whoever reveres God, He will give him relief, and give him provision whence he least expects it; for whoever trusts only in God needs nothing else. God accomplishes His purpose. God has set a measure for all things»."[122]

At this, the man's fellow travelers all said, "What a waste of money!" but he replied,

"Not at all. I'm sure this will prove very profitable."

Some days later they were shipwrecked. He clung to a plank and was the only one saved. 16.2

This is the story he told afterward: 16.3

The sea cast me up on an island. As I made my way inland, I saw a lofty castle, which I entered. I discovered that it contained not only all the jewels and treasures of the sea, but the most beautiful woman I had ever seen.

٤،١٦ فقلت لها من أنت وأيّ شيء تعملين ها هنا قالت أنا بنت فلان بن فلان التاجر بالبصرة وكان أبي عظيم التجارة وكان لا يصبر عنّي فسافر بي معه في البحر فانكسر مركبنا فاختطفت حتّى حصلت في هذه الجزيرة فخرج إليّ شيطان من البحر يتلاعب بي سبعة أيّام من غير أن يطأني إلاّ أنّه يلامسني ويؤذيني ويتلاعب بي ثمّ ينظر إليّ ثمّ ينزل إلى البحر سبعة أيّام وهذا يوم موافاته فاتّق الله في نفسك واخرج قبل موافاته و إلاّ أتى عليك.

٥،١٦ فما انقضى كلامها حتّى رأيت ظلمة هائلة فقالت قد والله جاء وسيهلكك فلمّا قرب منّي وكاد يغشاني قرأت الآية فإذا هو قد خرّ كقطعة جبل إلاّ أنّه رماد محترق فقالت المرأة هلك والله وكفيت أمره من أنت يا هذا الذي منّ الله عليّ بك.

٦،١٦ فقمت أنا وهي فانتخبنا ذلك الجوهر حتّى حملنا كلّ ما فيه من نفيس وفاخر ولزمنا الساحل نهارنا أجمع فإذا كان الليل رجعنا إلى القصر قال وكان فيه ما يؤكل فقلت لها من أين لك هذا فقالت وجدته ها هنا.

٧،١٦ فلمّا كان بعد أيّام رأينا مركبًا بعيدًا فلوّحنا إليه فدخل فحملنا فسلّمنا الله تعالى إلى البصرة فوصفت لي منزل أهلها فأتيتهم فقالوا من هذا فقلت رسول فلانة بنت فلان فارتفعت الواعية وقالوا يا هذا لقد جدّدت علينا مصابنا فقلت اخرجوا فخرجوا فأخذتهم حتّى جئت بهم إلى ابنتهم فكادوا يموتون فرحًا وسألوها عن خبرها فقصّته عليهم وسألتهم أن يزوّجوني بها ففعلوا وحصّلنا ذلك الجوهر رأس مال بيني وبينها وأنا اليوم أيسر أهل البصرة وهؤلاء أولادي منها.

"Who are you," I asked her, "and what are you doing here?" 16.4

She replied, "I am the daughter of such and such, son of so and so, a merchant of Basra. My father was a great trader who could not bear to be parted from me and took me with him when he sailed. Our ship was wrecked, and I was swept away to this island, where a demon comes out of the sea and fondles me for seven whole days. Though he does not lie with me, he caresses me and paws me painfully. Then he gazes at me and goes back into the sea for the next seven days. He will return this very day, so beware, and leave before he comes, or he will destroy you."

No sooner had she spoken these words than I beheld a terrifying shadow. 16.5

"Here he is! He's going to kill you!" the woman cried.

The shadow bore down on me and was about to envelop me when I recited the Qur'anic verse. At once the demon collapsed like a rockfall, leaving nothing behind but burnt ashes.

"By God, he's dead and I'm saved!" cried the woman. "My godsend, who are you?"[123]

Together we sorted through the jewels and made up a load of the most valuable and splendid. During the day we kept to the shore, returning to the castle only at night for food. "Where did you get it?" I asked. 16.6

"It was already here," she replied.

After some days, we spied a ship in the distance and signaled to it. The vessel came in and took us off, and God Exalted brought us safely to Basra. The woman told me where her people lived. "Who are you?" they asked when I presented myself. "A messenger from such and such, the daughter of so and so," I said. 16.7

They wailed: "O sir! You only remind us of our misfortune!" but I replied,

"Come with me," and took them to where their daughter was.

Half dead with joy, they listened as she told her story, and when I asked them to marry her to me, they agreed.

She and I used the jewels we had brought with us as joint capital.[124] Today I am one of the richest men in Basra, and these are the children I have had by her.[125]

وذكر أبو عبد الله محمّد بن عبدوس الجهشياريّ في كتابه كتاب الوزراء أنّ المعلّى بن عبد الله بن المعلّى بن أيّوب حدّثه عن أبيه قال قال لي المعلّى بن أيّوب ١،١٧

أعنتني الفضل بن مروان ونحن في بعض الأسفار وطالبني بعمل طويل يعمل في مدّة بعيدة واقتضانيه في كلّ يوم مرارًا إلى أن أمرني عن المعتصم بالله أن لا أبرح إلاّ بعد الفراغ منه.

٢،١٧ فقعدت في ثيابي وجاء الليل فجعلت بين يديّ نفّاطة وطرح غلماني أنفسهم حولي وورد عليّ همّ عظيم لأنّني قلت ما تجاسر على أن يوكّل بي إلاّ وقد وقف على سوء رأي فيّ من المعتصم.

٣،١٧ فإنّي لجالس وذقني على يدي وقد مضى الليل وأنا متفكّر فحملتني عيناي فرأيت كأنّ شخصًا قد مثل بين يديّ وهو يقول ﴿قُلْ مَن يُنَجِّيكُم مِّن ظُلُمَٰتِ ٱلْبَرِّ وَٱلْبَحْرِ تَدْعُونَهُۥ تَضَرُّعًا وَخُفْيَةً لَّئِنْ أَنجَىٰنَا مِنْ هَٰذِهِۦ لَنَكُونَنَّ مِنَ ٱلشَّٰكِرِينَ قُلِ ٱللَّهُ يُنَجِّيكُم مِّنْهَا وَمِن كُلِّ كَرْبٍ﴾.

٤،١٧ ثمّ انتبهت فإذا أنا بمشعل قد أقبل من بعيد فلمّا قرب منّي كان وراءه محمّد بن حمّاد دنقش صاحب الحرس وقد أنكر نفّاطتي فجاء يعرف سببها فأخبرته خبري فمضى إلى المعتصم فأخبره فإذا الرسل يطلبوني فدخلت إليه وهو قاعد ولم يبق بين يديه من الشمع إلاّ أسفله فقال لي ما خبرك فشرحته له فقال ويلي على النبطيّ يمتهنك وأيّ يد له عليك أنت كاتبي كما هو كاتبي انصرف. فلمّا ولّيت ردّني واستدناني ثمّ قال لي تمضي مديدة ثمّ ترى فيه ما تحبّ قال فانصرفت وبكّرت إلى الفضل على عادتي لم أنكر شيئًا.

١،١٨ وحدّثني أبو الفضل محمّد بن عبد الله بن المرزبان الشيرازيّ الكاتب في المذاكرة في خبر طويل لست أقوم على حفظه

Abū ʿAbd Allāh Muḥammad ibn ʿAbdūs al-Jahshiyārī in his *Book of Viziers*[126] relates that al-Muʿallā ibn ʿAbd Allāh ibn al-Muʿallā ibn Ayyūb cited his father as saying: 17.1

Al-Muʿallā ibn Ayyūb told me:[127]

I was on a progress[128] with al-Faḍl ibn Marwān. He victimized me, setting me a lengthy task that needed time to complete, but which he demanded several times a day. Finally he ordered me, in the caliph al-Muʿtaṣim's name, not to stir until it was done.

Overcome with apprehension—for I said to myself, "He would never dare do this to me unless he had discovered that al-Muʿtaṣim was displeased with me"—when night fell I set a naphtha lantern[129] before me and stayed up fully dressed while all around me the junior clerks laid themselves down to sleep. 17.2

As I sat musing, chin in hand, the night passed away and my eyelids drooped. Then it seemed to me that a figure appeared before me and said, «Say, Who saves you from the darknesses of land and sea? You pray to Him humbly and secretly: "If You save us from them, we will be truly thankful!" Say, God saves you from them and from all other afflictions.»[130] 17.3

I woke up to see a torch approaching in the distance. As it drew near, I saw that it was borne before Muḥammad ibn Ḥammād Danqash, the captain of the guard,[131] who had thought my light looked suspicious and come to investigate. 17.4

When I told him my story, he went straight to al-Muʿtaṣim. He sent for me and I discovered that he had not been to bed either, for the candles before him were burnt down to stumps.

"Explain yourself," he commanded.

When I had done so, he exclaimed, "I am mortified that that peasant[132] should humiliate you like this. What right has he? You are my clerk,[133] and so is he. You may go."

But as I was leaving he called me back, commanded me to approach, and said to me, "You will soon be on good terms again."

My mind at rest, I withdrew, and went to the office in the morning as usual.

In the course of a conversation, as part of a long anecdote I can no longer remember, the state scribe Abū l-Faḍl Muḥammad ibn ʿAbd Allāh ibn al-Marzubān of Shiraz told me: 18.1

أنّ رجلاً كانت بينه وبين رجل متمكّن من أذاه عداوة فخافه خوفاً شديداً وأهمّه أمره ولم يدرِ ما يصنع فرأى في منامه كأنّ قائلاً يقول له اقرأ في كلّ يوم في إحدى ركعتي صلاة الفجر ﴿أَلَمْ تَرَ كَيْفَ فَعَلَ رَبُّكَ بِأَصْحَٰبِ ٱلْفِيلِ﴾ إلى آخر السورة.

٢،١٨ قال فقرأتها فما مضت إلاّ شهور حتّى كفيت أمر ذلك العدوّ وأهلكه الله تعالى فأنا أقرؤها إلى الآن.

٣،١٨ قال مؤلّف هذا الكتاب

دُفعت أنا إلى شدّة لحقتني شديدة من عدوّ فاستترت منه فجعلت دأبي قراءة هذه السورة في الركعة الثانية من صلاة الفجر في كلّ يوم وأنا أقرأ في الأوّلة[١] منها ﴿أَلَمْ نَشْرَحْ لَكَ صَدْرَكَ﴾ إلى آخر السورة لخبر كان بلغني أيضاً فيها فلمّا كان بعد شهور كفاني الله أمر ذلك العدوّ وأهلكه الله من غير سعي لي في ذلك ولا حول ولا قوّة إلاّ بالله وأنا أقرؤها في ركعتي الفجر إلى الآن.

١،١٩ وأمّا الخبر في ﴿أَلَمْ نَشْرَحْ لَكَ صَدْرَكَ﴾ فإنّ أبا بكر بن شجاع المقرئ البغداديّ الذي كان يخلفني على العيار في دار الضرب بسوق الأهواز في سنة ستّ وأربعين وثلثمائة وكان خازن المسجد الجامع بها وكان شيخاً محدّثاً ثقةً نبيلاً من أمناء القاضي الأحنف وهو محمّد بن عبد الله بن عليّ بن محمّد بن أبي الشوارب حدّثنا بإسناد له ذكره لم أحفظه ولا المتن بلفظه وبُعد عن يدي إخراجه من الأصل وقد تحرّيت مقاربة اللفظ بجهدي ولعلّه يزيد أو ينقص

أنّ بعض الصالحين ألحّ عليه الغمّ وضيق الصدر وتعذّر الأمور حتّى كاد يقنط فكان يوماً يمشي وهو يقول [وافر]

أَرَى ٱلْمَوْتَ لِمَنْ أَمْسَى عَلَى ٱلذُّلِّ لَهُ أَصْلَحْ

---

١ كذا.

A man was on bad terms with another man who had it in his power to harm him. He was very worried, and very frightened of him, but did not know what to do.

Then he had a dream in which he was told: "Every day, during one of the two sequences of the dawn prayer, recite the whole of the surah that begins: «Have you not seen how your Lord dealt with the Men of the Elephant?»"[134]

I did so (he said), and after only a few months I was preserved from my enemy, whom God destroyed. I continue to recite the surah to this day. 18.2

The author remarks: 18.3

I too was once made to suffer great adversity by an enemy to escape whom I went into hiding. I made it my practice to recite this surah every day during the second sequence of the dawn prayer. During the first, I would recite the whole of the surah: «Have We not opened out your breast?»[135] because I had heard something similar about it.

After a few months, God preserved me from my enemy, destroying him without any action on my part. Power and strength come from God alone! To this day I continue to recite the verses when I perform the dawn prayer.

What I had heard about «Have We not opened out your breast?» was this. 19.1
Abū Bakr ibn Shujāʿ, the Baghdadi Qurʾan scholar, who was my deputy when I was inspector of the mint at Sūq al-Ahwāz in 346 [957–58][136] and who was also treasurer of the local Friday Mosque, was a noble old gentleman and a reliable traditionist, one of the legal trustees of Judge al-Aḥnaf "the Lame" (that is to say, Muḥammad ibn ʿAbd Allāh ibn ʿAlī ibn Muḥammad Ibn Abī l-Shawārib). He transmitted to us the following, with his own chain of authorities, which I do not remember, any more than I remember the exact wording of the report, which I am unable to trace back to its source, but which I have made every effort to approximate, although my version may be longer or shorter:

Grief, anxiety, and poverty had reduced a God-fearing man almost to despair. One day as he walked along he declaimed:

When a man has been brought low,
it seems to me that death is best.

فهتف به هاتف يسمع صوته ولا يرى شخصه أو أُري في النوم أنا الشاكّ كأنّ قائلاً يقول [وافر]

أَلَا يَا أَيُّهَا ٱلْمَرْءُ ٱلَّذِي ٱلْهَمُّ بِهِ بَرَّحْ
إِذَا ضَاقَ بِكَ ٱلْأَمْرُ فَفَكِّرْ فِي ﴿أَلَمْ نَشْرَحْ﴾

قال فواصلتُ قراءتها في صلاتي فشرح الله صدري وأزال همّي وكربي سهّل أمري أو كما قال . ٢،١٩

وحدّثني غيره بهذا الخبر على قريب من هذا وزادني في الشعر [وافر] ٣،١٩

فَإِنَّ ٱلْعُسْرَ مَقْرُونٌ بِيُسْرَيْنِ فَلَا تَبْرَحْ

وقد ذكر القاضي أبو الحسين في كتابه كتاب الفرج بعد الشدّة البيتين المتّصلين فقط وقال في الآخر منهما إِذَا أَعْضَلَكَ ٱلْأَمْرُ ولم يذكر لهما خبرًا ويروى أيضًا إِذَا لَجَّ بِكَ ٱلْأَمْرُ وروى غيره البيتين الأوّلين لأبي العتاهية في غير حديث له .

A disembodied voice, which could be heard but not seen, called out to him—or else (I'm not sure which) he dreamed that someone said to him—

O you who are
  beset by care,
In your anguish, think on this:
  «Have We not opened out your breast?»[137]

The man said, "Thereafter, I recited this verse of the Qur'an whenever I said the ritual prayers, and God opened out my breast, took away my grief and affliction, and restored my fortunes"—or words to this effect. 19.2

Someone else transmitted this account to me in similar form but with an extra line of poetry: 19.3

Stand firm! for «hardship»'s paired
  with «ease» twice over![138]

In his book of *Deliverance following Adversity*, Judge Abū l-Ḥusayn mentions the first couplet, with the variant "When sore perplexed" and without the narrative. Another variant is "In times of torment." The couplet is attributed to Abū l-ʿAtāhiyah, with no context.

الباب الثاني

ما جاء في الآثار من ذكر الفرج بعد اللأواء وما يتوصّل به إلى كشف نازل الشدّة والبلاء

أخبرني القاضي أبو القاسم عليّ بن محمّد بن أبي الفهم التنوخيّ أبي رحمه الله تعالى قال حدّثنا محمّد بن إبراهيم الصِلحيّ قال حدّثنا بشر بن معاذ قال حدّثنا حمّاد بن واقد وحدّثنا عليّ بن أبي الطيّب قال حدّثنا ابن الجرّاح قال حدّثنا ابن أبي الدنيا قال حدّثنا محمّد بن عبد الله الأزديّ قال حدّثنا حمّاد بن واقد قال حدّثنا إسرائيل بن يونس[1] عن أبي إسحاق الهمذانيّ[2] عن أبي الأحوص عن عبد الله بن مسعود[3] قال ١،٢٠

قال رسول الله صلّى الله عليه وسلّم

سلوا الله عزّ وجلّ من فضله فإنّ الله يحبّ أن يُسأل وأفضل العبادة انتظار الفرج من الله تعالى.

أخبرني أبي قال حدّثنا الفضل بن محمّد العطّار الأنطاكيّ قال حدّثنا سليمان بن سلمة قال حدّثنا بقيّة عن مالك عن الزهريّ عن أنس عن النبيّ صلّى الله عليه وسلّم أنّه قال ٢،٢٠

انتظار الفرج من الله تعالى عبادة.

١ بن يونس: الزيادة من ش. ٢ الهمذانيّ: الزيادة من ش. ٣ الزيادة من ش. وفي م، ل: عبد الله بن عبّاس.

Chapter Two

What Tradition relates of deliverance following desolation and how one may be rescued from sore adversity and tribulation

I cite Judge Abū l-Qāsim ʿAlī ibn Muḥammad ibn al-Fahm al-Tanūkhī, my late father, God Exalted have mercy on him, citing Muḥammad ibn Ibrāhīm of Fam al-Ṣilḥ, citing Bishr ibn Muʿādh, citing Ḥammād ibn Wāqid; 20.1

I also cite ʿAlī ibn al-Ḥasan, citing Ibn al-Jarrāḥ, citing Ibn Abī l-Dunyā, citing Muḥammad ibn ʿAbd Allāh al-Azdī, citing Ḥammād ibn Wāqid, citing Isrāʾīl, citing Abū Isḥāq, quoting Abū l-Aḥwaṣ, quoting ʿAbd Allāh ibn Masʿūd, who said:

The Prophet, God bless and keep him, said:

Supplicate God of His bounty, for God, Mighty and Glorious, loves to be supplicated, and the most meritorious act of worship is to look forward to deliverance by God Exalted.

I cite my father, citing al-Faḍl ibn Muḥammad the Druggist of Antioch, citing Sulaymān ibn Salamah, citing Baqiyyah, quoting Mālik ibn Anas quoting al-Zuhrī, quoting Anas ibn Mālik, quoting the Prophet, God bless and keep him, who said: 20.2

To look forward to deliverance by God Exalted is an act of worship.

٣،٢٠ أخبرني أبي قال حدّثنا إسحاق بن إبراهيم الكوفيّ قال حدّثنا حسين بن حسن عن سفيان بن إبراهيم عن حنظلة المكّيّ عن مجاهد عن ابن عبّاس قال قال رسول الله صلّى الله عليه وسلّم

انتظار الفرج عبادة.

٤،٢٠ حدّثني أبي قال حدّثنا عبد الله بن أحمد بن عامر الطائيّ قال حدّثني أبي قال حدّثني عليّ بن موسى الرضا قال حدّثني أبي موسى قال حدّثني أبي جعفر قال حدّثنى أبي محمّد قال حدّثني أبي عليّ قال حدّثني أبي الحسين قال حدّثني أبي عليّ بن أبي طالب رضي الله عنهم قال قال رسول الله صلّى الله عليه وسلّم

أفضل أعمال أمّتي انتظار الفرج من الله عزّ وجلّ.

٥،٢٠ أخبرني أبي قال حدّثني أحمد بن عبد الله بن النعمان قال حدّثني محمّد بن يعقوب بن إسحاق الأعرج قال حدّثنا عبد الله بن محمّد عن سعدويه قال حدّثنا أحمد بن محمّد بن بكر قال حدّثنا عبد العزيز ابن عبد الله عن عليّ بن أبي عليّ عن جعفر بن محمّد عن أبيه عن جدّه عن عليّ رضي الله عنه أنّ رسول الله صلّى الله عليه وسلّم قال لعليّ عليه السلام في حديث ذكره

واعلم أنّ النصر مع الصبر والفرج مع الكرب ﴿إِنَّ مَعَ ٱلْعُسْرِ يُسْرًا﴾.

١،٢١ أخبرني أبي قال كتب إليّ عبد الله بن مبشّر حدّثنا أبو الأشعث قال حدّثنا أميّة بن خالد عن الحسين بن عبد الله بن ضميرة عن أبيه عن جدّه عن عليّ بن أبي طالب رضي الله عنه قال قال رسول الله صلّى الله عليه وسلّم

اشتدّي أزمة تنفرجي.

I cite my father, citing Isḥāq ibn Ibrāhīm of Kufa, citing Ḥusayn ibn Ḥasan, quoting Sufyān ibn Ibrāhīm, quoting Ḥanẓalah of Mecca, quoting Mujāhid, quoting Ibn ʿAbbās, who said: 20.3

To look forward to deliverance is an act of worship.

I cite my father, citing ʿAbd Allāh ibn Aḥmad ibn ʿĀmir al-Ṭāʾī, citing his own father, citing ʿAlī al-Riḍā, the son of Mūsā al-Kāẓim, citing his father, Mūsā, citing his father, Jaʿfar al-Ṣādiq, citing his father, Muḥammad al-Bāqir, citing his father, ʿAlī, citing his father, al-Ḥusayn, citing his father, ʿAlī ibn Abī Ṭālib, may God be pleased with all of them, who said: The Messenger of God, God bless and keep him, said: 20.4

The most meritorious of my community's works is to look forward to deliverance by God Exalted.

I cite my father, citing Aḥmad ibn ʿAbd Allāh ibn al-Nuʿmān, citing Muḥammad ibn Yaʿqūb ibn Isḥāq the Lame, citing ʿAbd Allāh ibn Muḥammad,[139] quoting Saʿdawayh, citing Aḥmad ibn Muḥammad ibn Bakr, citing ʿAbd al-ʿAzīz ibn ʿAbd Allāh, quoting ʿAlī ibn Abī ʿAlī, quoting Jaʿfar al-Ṣādiq, son of Muḥammad al-Bāqir, quoting his father, quoting his grandfather, quoting ʿAlī ibn Abī Ṭālib, God be pleased with him, saying that the Messenger of God, God bless and keep him, said to ʿAlī, peace on him, during a conversation which he reported: 20.5

Know that acceptance brings help and affliction deliverance, and that «the hardship shall bring ease.»[140]

I cite my father, who said: ʿAbd Allāh ibn Mubashshir wrote to me,[141] citing Abū l-Ashʿath, citing Umayyah ibn Khālid, quoting al-Ḥusayn ibn ʿAbd Allāh son of Ḍumayrah, citing his father, citing his grandfather, Ḍumayrah ibn Saʿīd, citing ʿAlī ibn Abī Ṭālib, God be pleased with him, who said: The Messenger of God, God bless and keep him, said: 21.1

The greater the disaster, the greater the deliverance.[142]

حدّثنا عليّ بن أبي الطيّب قال حدّثنا ابن الجرّاح قال حدّثنا ابن أبي الدنيا قال حدّثني عليّ بن الجعد قال أخبرني شعبة عن عمرو بن مرّة قال سمعت أبا وائل يحدّث عن كردوس بن عمرو وكان ممّن قرأ الكتب أنّ ٢،٢١

الله عزّ وجلّ[١] يبتلي العبد وهو يحبّه ليسمع تضرّعه.

حدّثنا عليّ بن أبي الطيّب قال حدّثنا ابن الجرّاح قال حدّثنا ابن أبي الدنيا قال حدّثنا أبو سعيد المديني قال حدّثني أبو بكر بن أبي شيبة الحزاميّ[٢] قال حدّثني محمّد بن إبراهيم ابن المطّلب بن أبي وداعة السهميّ قال حدّثنا زهرة بن عمرو التيميّ عن أبي حازم عن سهل بن[٣] سعد الساعديّ أنّ رسول الله صلّى الله عليه وسلّم قال لعبد الله بن عبّاس ٢٢

ألا أعلّمك كلمات تنتفع بهنّ قال بلى يا رسول الله قال احفظ الله يحفظك احفظ الله تجده أمامك تعرّف إلى الله في الرخاء يعرفك في الشدّة فإذا سألتَ فسَل الله وإذا استعنتَ فاستعن بالله جفّ القلم بما كان وما هو كائن فلو جهد العبّاد أن ينفعوك بشيء لم يكتبه الله عزّ وجلّ لك لم يقدروا عليه فإن استطعت أن تعمل لله بالصدق واليقين فافعل فإن لم تستطع فإنّ في الصبر على ما تكره خيرًا كثيرًا واعلم أنّ النصر مع الصبر وأنّ الفرج مع الكرب وأنّ ﴿مَعَ ٱلْعُسْرِ يُسْرًا﴾ .

أخبرني أبي قال حدّثت عن إسحاق بن الضيف قال حدّثنا داود ابن المحبّر قال حدّثنا عبد الله بن أبي رزين عن فراس بن يحيى[٤] عن ثابت عن أنس قال قال رسول الله صلّى الله عليه وسلّم ٢٣

إنّ المعونة من الله عزّ وجلّ تأتي العبد على قدر المؤونة وإنّ الصبر يأتي على قدر شدّة البلاء وربّما قال إنّ الفرج يأتي من الله تعالى على قدر شدّة البلاء.

١ عزّ وجلّ: من ش، بن، ل. ٢ كذا في م. ٣ سهل بن: الزيادة من ش. ٤ يحيى: التصحيح من ش.

I cite ʿAlī ibn al-Ḥasan, citing Ibn al-Jarrāḥ, citing Ibn Abī l-Dunyā, citing ʿAlī ibn al-Jaʿd, citing Shuʿbah, quoting ʿAmr ibn Murrah, who said: I heard Abū Wāʾil cite Kurdūs ibn ʿAmr, who had read the scriptures:[143] 21.2

When God, Mighty and Exalted, loves His servant, He tries him, in order to hear his entreaty.

I cite ʿAlī ibn al-Ḥasan, citing Ibn al-Jarrāḥ, citing Ibn Abī l-Dunyā, citing Abū Saʿīd of Medina, citing Abū Bakr Ibn Abī Shaybah,[144] citing Muḥammad ibn Ibrāhīm ibn al-Muṭṭalib ibn Abī Wadāʿah al-Sahmī,[145] citing Zuhrah Ibn ʿAmr al-Taymī,[146] quoting Sahl ibn Saʿd al-Sāʿidī: 22

The Messenger of God, God bless and keep him, said to ʿAbd Allāh ibn ʿAbbās: "Let me teach you some words that you will find profitable."

"Gladly," he replied.

He said, "Remember God, that He may remember you. Remember God, and He will be present to you. Make yourself known to God in prosperity, and He will know you in adversity. If you must beg, then supplicate God. When you ask for help, ask it of God—whom no pen can describe! Should people strive to bring you profit in any way that God, Mighty and Exalted, has not foreordained, it would not be in their power to do so. Serve God with sure and certain hope if you can; if you cannot, then there is much good in bearing injury with acceptance; and know that acceptance brings help and affliction deliverance, and that «the hardship shall bring ease.»"[147]

I cite my father, citing Isḥāq ibn al-Ḍayf, citing Dāwud ibn al-Muḥabbar, citing ʿAbd Allāh ibn Abī Razīn, quoting Firās ibn Yaḥyā, quoting Thābit, quoting Anas ibn Mālik, who said: The Messenger of God, God bless and keep him, said: 23

God, Mighty and Exalted, sends provision in proportion to His servant's needs, and acceptance in proportion to the severity of his tribulation.

(Or perhaps his words were: God, Mighty and Exalted, sends deliverance, in proportion to the severity of the tribulation.)

٢٤ حـدّثنا أبو محمّد وهب بن يحيى بن عبد الوهّاب المازنيّ لفظًا من حفظه في داره بالبصرة ببني سدوس الباطنة بحضرة قبر مجاشع ومجالد السلميّ صاحبي رسول الله صلّى الله عليه وسلّم بالقرب من بني يشكر قال حدّثنا نصر بن عليّ الجهضميّ قال أنبأنا محمّد بن بكر البرسانيّ عن ابن جريج عن ابن المنكدر عن أبي أيّوب عن مسلمة بن مخلّد قال قال النبيّ صلّى الله عليه وسلّم

من ستر مسلمًا ستره الله في الدنيا والآخرة ومن فكّ عن مكروب فكّ الله عنه كربة من كرب يوم القيامة ومن كان في حاجة أخيه كان الله في حاجته.

١،٢٥ أخـبرني أبي قال حدّثنا أبو عقيل الخولانيّ قال حدّثنا مؤمّل بن إهاب قال حدّثنا مالك بن سُعَيْر عن الأعمش وأنبأنا نصر بن القاسم قال حدّثنا الوكيعيّ قال حدّثنا أبو معاوية عن الأعمش قال أبي وأنبأنا ابن بنت[١] منيع من طريق آخر واللفظ له قال حدّثنا عبد الأعلى بن حمّاد قال حدّثنا حمّاد عن محمّد بن واسع وأبي سَورة عن الأعمش عن أبي صالح عن أبي هريرة قال قال رسول الله صلّى الله عليه وسلّم

من ستر أخاه المسلم ستره الله يوم القيامة ومن نفّس عن أخيه كربة من كرب الدنيا نفّس الله عنه كربة من كرب يوم القيامة وإنّ الله في عون العبد ما كان العبد في عون أخيه.

٢،٢٥ أخبرني أبي قال حدّثنا محمّد بن محمّد قال حدّثنا محمّد بن عبد الملك بن مغيث قال أخبرني أبي عن جدّي قال حدّثنا عقيل بن شهاب أنّ سالم بن عبد الله بن عمر أخبره أنّ ابن عمر أخبره أنّ رسول الله صلّى الله عليه وسلّم قال

من كان في حاجة أخيه كان الله تعالى في حاجته ومن فرّج عن مسلم كربة فرّج الله عنه بها كربة من كرب يوم القيامة ومن ستر مسلمًا ستره الله يوم القيامة.

---

١ بنت: الزيادة من ش.

We cite word for word what Abū Muḥammad Wahb ibn Yaḥyā ibn ʿAbd al-Wahhāb al-Māzinī recited from memory in his house in Basra, situated in the inner quarter of the Banū Sadūs sector by the tomb of Mujāshiʿ and Mujālid al-Sulamī, Companions of the Messenger of God, God bless and keep him, in the vicinity of the Banū Yashkur sector. He cited Naṣr ibn ʿAlī al-Jahḍamī, saying, We quote Muḥammad ibn Bakr of Bursān, quoting Ibn Jurayj, quoting Ibn al-Munkadir, quoting Abū Ayyūb, quoting Maslamah ibn Mukhallad, who said, The Prophet, God bless and keep him, said: 24

Whoever refuses to condemn a fellow Muslim will be spared condemnation by God in this world and the next. Whoever ransoms the afflicted will be ransomed by God from one of the afflictions of Judgment Day. God will care for whoever cares for his brother.

I cite my father, citing Abū ʿAqīl al-Khawlānī, citing Muʾammal ibn Ihāb, citing Mālik ibn Suʿayr, citing al-Aʿmash; 25.1

I also quote Naṣr ibn al-Qāsim, citing al-Wakīʿī, citing Abū Muʿāwiyah, quoting al-Aʿmash;

My father also said, We quote Abū l-Qāsim Ibn Bint Manīʿ, with a different line of transmission and reproducing his own wording. He cites ʿAbd al-Aʿlā ibn Ḥammād ibn Naṣr, citing Ḥammād, quoting Muḥammad ibn Wāsiʿ and Abū Sawrah, quoting al-Aʿmash, quoting Abū Ṣāliḥ, quoting Abū Hurayrah, who said, The Messenger of God, God bless and keep him, said:

Whoever refuses to condemn his brother Muslim will be spared condemnation by God on Judgment Day. Whoever comforts his brother for an affliction of this world will be comforted by God for one of the afflictions of Judgment Day. God will help His servant as long as His servant helps his brother.

I cite my father, citing Muḥammad ibn Muḥammad, citing Muḥammad ibn ʿAbd al-Malik ibn Mughīth,[148] citing his father, citing his grandfather, citing ʿAqīl ibn Shihāb, who told him that Sālim ibn ʿAbd Allāh ibn ʿUmar related to him that Ibn ʿUmar told him that the Messenger of God, God bless and keep him, said: 25.2

Whoever cares for his brother, God Exalted will care for him. God will repay whoever delivers a fellow Muslim from affliction by delivering him from one of the afflictions of Judgment Day; and whoever refuses to condemn a fellow Muslim will be spared condemnation by God on Judgment Day.

هذا حديث مشهور جاء به أبو داود في كتاب السنن الذي حدّثنا به عنه محمّد بن بكر ابن داسه باختلاف في اللفظ. وليس غرضي جمع طرقه وألفاظه فآتي بها مستقصاة.

١،٢٦ حـدّثنا أحمد بن عبد الله بن أحمد الورّاق قال حدّثنا أبو حامد محمّد ابن هارون الحضرميّ قال حدّثنا محمّد بن صالح النطّاح قال حدّثنا المنذر بن زياد الطائيّ قال حدّثنا عبد الله بن حسن بن حسن بن عليّ بن أبي طالب عن أبيه عن جدّه رضي الله عنهم عن النبيّ صلّى الله عليه وسلّم أنّه قال

من أكثر الاستغفار جعل الله له من كلّ همّ فرجًا ومن كلّ ضيق مخرجًا ورزقه ﴿مِنْ حَيْثُ لَا يَحْتَسِبُ﴾.

٢،٢٦ حدّثنا عليّ قال حدّثنا ابن الجرّاح قال حدّثنا ابن أبي الدنيا قال حدّثنا خالد بن خداش قال حدّثنا عبد الرزّاق عن بشر بن رافع الحارثيّ عن محمّد بن عجلان عن أبيه عن أبي هريرة قال قال رسول الله صلّى الله عليه وسلّم

قول لا حول ولا قوّة إلّا بالله دواء من تسعة وتسعين داء أيسرها الهمّ.

٣،٢٦ أخبرنا أبو محمّد الحسن بن خلّاد الرامهرمزيّ خليفة أبي على القضاء بها قال أخبرنا وكيع أنّ القاسم بن إسماعيل أبا المنذر السوريّ حدّثه قال حدّثنا نصر بن زياد قال كنت عند جعفر بن محمّد فأتاه سفيان بن سعيد الثوريّ فقال يا ابن رسول الله حدّثني قال

يا سفيان إذا استبطأت الرزق فأكثر من الاستغفار وإذا ورد عليك أمر تكرهه فأكثر من لا حول ولا قوّة إلّا بالله وإذا أنعم الله عليك فأكثر من الحمد لله.

١،٢٧ حـدّثنا محمّد بن جعفر بن صالح الصالحيّ أبو الفرج من ولد عليّ بن صالح صاحب المصلّى قال حدّثنا أبو الجهم أحمد بن الحسين بن طلّاب المشغرائيّ من قرية من قرى

This is a famous report, which Abū Dā'ūd cites in his *Sound Traditions* and which Muḥammad ibn Bakr ibn Dāsah transmitted to me with some differences in wording. It is not my purpose, however, to collect every single line of transmission and variant.

We cite Aḥmad ibn ʿAbd Allāh ibn Aḥmad the Stationer–Copyist, citing Abū Ḥāmid Muḥammad ibn Hārūn al-Ḥaḍramī, citing Muḥammad ibn Ṣāliḥ al-Naṭṭāḥ, citing al-Mundhir ibn Ziyād al-Ṭā'ī, citing ʿAbd Allāh ibn Ḥasan ibn Ḥasan ibn ʿAlī ibn Abī Ṭālib, quoting his father, quoting his grandfather, God be pleased with them, quoting the Prophet, God bless and keep him, as saying: **26.1**

Whoever pleads much for forgiveness will be granted deliverance from every sorrow by God, and relief from every constraint, «and He will give him provision whence he least expects it.»[149]

We cite ʿAlī ibn al-Ḥasan, citing Ibn al-Jarrāḥ, citing Ibn Abī l-Dunyā, citing Khālid ibn Khidāsh, citing ʿAbd al-Razzāq, quoting Bishr ibn Rāfiʿ al-Ḥārithī, quoting Muḥammad ibn ʿAjlān, quoting his father, ʿAjlān, quoting Abū Hurayrah, who said, The Messenger of God, God bless and keep him, said: **26.2**

The words "There is no might nor power save in God" are the cure for ninety-nine ailments, of which the easiest to bear is sorrow.

We cite Abū Muḥammad al-Ḥasan Ibn Khallād of Rāmhurmuz, my father's deputy there as judge, citing Judge Wakīʿ, who related that al-Qāsim ibn Ismāʿīl Abū l-Mundhir al-Sawramī cited Naṣr ibn Ziyād, who said: **26.3**

I was with Jaʿfar al-Ṣādiq when Sufyān ibn Saʿīd al-Thawrī came to him and said, "Son of the Messenger of God, give me a precept."

He said, "Sufyān, if provision is slow in reaching you, plead much for forgiveness. If injury befalls you, say, over and over, 'There is no might or power save in God'; and if God bestows blessings on you, praise Him over and over."

We cite Abū l-Faraj Muḥammad ibn Jaʿfar ibn Ṣāliḥ al-Ṣāliḥī, a descendant of ʿAlī ibn Ṣāliḥ, owner of the Prophet's prayer mat, citing Abū l-Jahm Aḥmad ibn al-Ḥusayn ibn Ṭallāb of Mashghrā (that is, from the village of Mashghrā in **27.1**

غوطة دمشق يقال لها مشغرا قال حدّثنا محمّد بن عبد الرحمٰن الجعفيّ قال حدّثنا أبو أسامة قال حدّثنا عبيد الله بن عمر عن سالم عن ابن عمر عن النبيّ صلّى الله عليه وسلّم أنّه قال

بينما ثلاثة رهط من بني إسرائيل يسيرون إذ أخذهم المطر فأَوَوا إلى غار فانطبقت عليهم صخرة فسدّت الغار فقالوا تعالوا فليسأل الله تعالى كلّ رجل منّا بأفضل عمله.

٢،٢٧ فقال أحدهم اللّٰهمّ إن كنت تعلم[١] أنّه كانت لي ابنة عمّ جميلة وكنت أهواها فدفعتُ إليها مائة دينار فلمّا جلستُ منها مجلس الرجل من المرأة قالت اتق الله يا ابن عمّ ولا تفضّ الخاتم إلاّ بحقّه فقمت عنها وتركت المائة دينار اللّٰهمّ إن كنت تعلم أنّي فعلت هذا خشية منك وابتغاء ما عندك فأفرج عنّا فانفرج عنهم ثلث الصخرة.

٣،٢٧ وقال الآخر اللّٰهمّ إن كنت تعلم أنّه كان لي أبوان شيخان كبيران وكنت أغدو عليهما بصبوحهما وأروح عليهما بغبوقهما فغدوت عليهما يوماً فوجدتهما نائمين فكرهت أن أوقظهما وكرهت أن أنصرف عنهما فيفقدا غداءهما فوقفت حتّى استيقظا فدفعت إليهما غداءهما اللّٰهمّ إن كنت تعلم أنّي إنّما فعلت ذلك ابتغاء ما عندك وخشية منك فأفرج عنّا فانفرج الثلث الثاني.

٤،٢٧ وقال الثالث اللّٰهمّ إن كنت تعلم أنّي استأجرت أجيرًا فلمّا دفعت إليه أجره قال عملي بأكثر من هذا فترك عليّ أجره وقال بيني وبينك يوم يُؤخذ فيه للمظلوم من الظالم ومضى فابتعت له بأجره غنمًا ولم أزل أنميها وأرعاها وهي تزيد وتكثر فلمّا كان بعد مدّة أتاني فقال لي يا هذا إنّ لي عندك أجرًا عملت كذا وكذا في وقت كذا و كذا فقلت خذ هذه الغنم فهي لك فقال تمنعني من أجري وتهزأ بي فقلت خذها فهي لك فأخذها ودعا لي اللّٰهمّ إن كنت تعلم أنّي فعلت هذا خشية منك وابتغاء ما عندك فأفرج عنّا فانفرج عنهم باقي الصخرة وخرجوا يمشون.

وذكر الحديث كذا.

---

١ إن كنت تعلم: الزيادة من س، ل.

the oasis of Damascus), citing Muḥammad ibn ʿAbd al-Raḥmān al-Juʿfī, citing Abū Usāmah, citing ʿUbayd Allāh ibn ʿUmar, quoting Sālim ibn ʿAbd Allāh ibn ʿUmar, quoting Ibn ʿUmar, quoting the Prophet, God bless and keep him, as having said:

Three Israelites were journeying one night when they were caught in the rain. They took shelter in a cave, but a rock fell and blocked the entrance. "Come," they said, "let each of us supplicate God in the name of the most meritorious thing he has done."

"O God!" said one of them. "If You know that I had a pretty cousin, that I 27.2
desired her, and gave her a hundred gold pieces, but when I was about to lie with her, she said, 'Cousin, for God's sake beware! Do not break the seal unlawfully,' and I let her be, and let her keep the hundred gold pieces—O God! If You know that this I did only for fear of You and in hope of Your reward, deliver us!"

As soon as he said this, a third of the rock split open.

"O God!" said the second man. "If You know that I had two aged parents 27.3
and brought them fresh milk to drink every morning and evening, and that one day I found them still asleep and, because I did not like either to wake them or to go away and leave them without food, I stayed there until they woke and I could give them their meal—O God, if You know that this I did only in hope of Your reward and for fear of You, deliver us!"

As soon as he said this, another third of the rock split open.

"O God!" said the third. "If You know that I hired a laborer, and when I 27.4
paid him, he said, 'I have earned more than this,' and refused to take his wage, saying, as he left, 'The day will come for you and me when the unjust man shall be made to pay the man he wronged'; that with the money he refused I bought some sheep for him, which grew and bred as I fattened and grazed them; and that when, a while later, the man returned and said, 'Here, you: You owe me wages for the work I did for you at such and such a time,' I said, 'Take these sheep, they are yours,' and he said, 'You deny me my wages and mock me!' and I repeated, 'Take them, they belong to you!' and he took them, and blessed me—O God! If You know that this I did only for fear of You and in hope of Your reward, deliver us!"

As soon as he said this, the last third of the rock split open, and they went on their way.

This is the version of Abū l-Faraj al-Ṣāliḥī.

٥،٢٧ قال مؤلّف هذا الكتاب: هذا الحديث مشهور رواه عن النبيّ صلّى الله عليه وسلّم عليّ بن أبي طالب وعبد الله بن عبّاس وعبد الله بن عمر وعبد الله بن أبي أوفى والنعمان بن بشير الأنصاريّ وغيرهم وعن كلّ واحد منهم عدّة طرق وقد اختلف في ألفاظه والمعنى واحد وليس غرضي هنا جمع طرقه وألفاظه فأستقصي ما رُوي من ذلك إلاّ أنّ في هذه الرواية غلطاً لا بدّ من تبيينه وهو أنّه رُوي من غير طريق عن أبي أسامة عن عمر بن حمزة العمريّ عن سالم عن ابن عمر ليس فيه عبيد الله والمشهور أنّه عن عبيد الله عن نافع عن ابن عمر.

٦،٢٧ وجاء من طريق أخرى أبين من هذا ووقع لنا بعلوّ فحدّثني أبو العبّاس محمّد بن أحمد الأثرم المقرئ البغداديّ بالبصرة سنة خمس وثلاثين وثلثمائة قال حدّثنا إبراهيم بن الهيثم البلديّ قال حدّثنا أبو اليمان الحكم بن نافع قال أنبأنا شعيب عن الزهريّ قال أخبرني سالم بن عبد الله بن عمر أنّ عبد الله بن عمر قال سمعت النبيّ صلّى الله عليه وسلّم يقول

انطلق ثلاثة رهط ممّن كان قبلكم حتّى أواهم المبيت إلى غار فدخلوا فانحدرت عليهم صخرة من الجبل فسدّت عليهم الغار. وذكر الحديث إلى نحو الرواية الأولى.

٢٨ حدّثنا عليّ بن الحسن قال حدّثنا ابن الجرّاح قال حدّثنا ابن أبي الدّنيا قال حدّثنا هارون بن سفيان قال حدّثنا عبيد بن محمّد عن محمّد بن مهاجر قال حدّثنا إبراهيم بن محمّد ابن سعد عن أبيه عن جدّه قال كنّا جلوساً عند رسول الله صلّى الله عليه وسلّم فقال

ألا أخبركم وأحدّثكم بشيء إذا نزل برجل منكم كرب أو بلاء من الدنيا ودعا به فرّج الله عنه فقيل له بلى قال دعاء ذي النون ﴿لَآ إِلَٰهَ إِلَّآ أَنتَ سُبۡحَٰنَكَ إِنِّي كُنتُ مِنَ ٱلظَّٰلِمِينَ﴾.

The author of this book observes: This report is famous. It was transmitted from the Prophet—God bless and keep him—by ʿAlī ibn Abī Ṭālib, ʿAbd Allāh ibn ʿAbbās, ʿAbd Allāh ibn ʿUmar, ʿAbd Allāh ibn Abī Awfā, al-Nuʿmān ibn Bashīr al-Anṣārī, and others. From each of these sources, there are several lines of transmission and differences of wording, although the meaning is the same. Here, however, it is not my purpose to collect every single line of transmission and variants and give an exhaustive account of the different versions, although I must point out that there is a mistake in a line of transmission that goes back from Abū Usāmah to ʿUmar ibn Ḥamzah al-ʿUmarī, citing Sālim ibn ʿAbd Allāh ibn ʿUmar, citing Ibn ʿUmar, and omitting ʿUbayd Allāh ibn ʿUmar, whereas it is well known that that line of transmission is: ʿUbayd Allāh citing Nāfiʿ citing Ibn ʿUmar. 27.5

There is another line of transmission that is clearer than the above, and that came to me with a chain of long-lived transmitters:[150] Abū l-ʿAbbās Muḥammad ibn Aḥmad the Gap-Toothed, the Baghdadi Qurʾan scholar, cited to me, in Basra in the year 335 [946],[151] Ibrāhīm ibn al-Haytham al-Baladī,[152] citing Abū l-Yamān al-Ḥakam ibn Nāfiʿ, who said, We quote Shuʿayb ibn Abī Ḥamzah, quoting al-Zuhrī, who was informed by Sālim ibn ʿAbd Allāh ibn ʿUmar that ʿAbd Allāh ibn ʿUmar said, I heard the Prophet, God bless and keep him, say: 27.6

Three men of former times set out on a journey and retired into a cave for the night, but once they were inside, a rock tumbled down the mountainside and blocked the entrance,

and then the narrative continues much as in the first version.

We cite ʿAlī ibn al-Ḥasan, citing Ibn al-Jarrāḥ, citing Ibn Abī l-Dunyā, citing Hārūn ibn Sufyān, citing ʿUbayd ibn Muḥammad, quoting Muḥammad ibn Muhājir, quoting Ibrāhīm ibn Muḥammad, quoting his father, Muḥammad ibn Saʿd, quoting his own father, Saʿd ibn Abī Waqqāṣ, who said: 28

We were sitting with the Messenger of God, God bless and keep him, when he said:

"Let me tell you this for you to pass on to others. Any of you may use it as a prayer when worldly affliction or tribulation befalls him, and God will deliver him."

"Please do," we said.

He said, "It is this: «There is no god but You. Glory to You! I am unjust,» the prayer of Dhū l-Nūn."[153]

١،٢٩ وجدت في كتاب ألّفه محمّد بن جرير الطبريّ وسمّاه كتاب الآداب الحميدة والأخلاق النفيسة حدّثنا ابن بشّار قال حدّثنا ابن أبي عديّ عن حُميد بن عبد الرحمٰن الحميريّ قال كان بأبي الحصاة فكان يلقى من شدّة ما به البلاء قال حُميد فانطلقت إلى بيت المقدس فلقيت أبا العوّام فشكوت إليه الذي بأبي وأخبرته خبره.

فقال مُره فليدع بهذه الدعوة ربّنا الذي في السماء عرشه ربّنا الذي في السماء تقدّس اسمه أمرك ماضٍ في السماء والأرض وكما رحمتك في السّماء فاجعلها في الأرض اغفر لنا ذنوبنا وخطايانا إنّك أنت الغفور الرحيم اللّٰهمّ أنزل رحمة من رحمتك وشفاء من شفائك على ما بفلان من وجع

٢،٢٩ قال فدعا به فأذهبه الله تعالى عنه.

٣٠ حدّثنا عليّ بن الحسن قال حدّثنا ابن الجرّاح قال حدّثنا ابن أبي الدنيا قال حدّثنا أبو خيثمة قال حدّثنا يزيد بن هارون عن سعيد بن أبي عروبة عن قتادة عن أبي العالية عن ابن عبّاس عن النبيّ صلّى الله عليه وسلّم قال

كلمات الفرج لا إله إلاّ الله الحليم الكريم لا إله إلاّ الله العليّ العظيم لا إله إلاّ الله ﴿رَبُّ ٱلسَّمَٰوَٰتِ ٱلسَّبۡعِ﴾ وربّ الأرضين السبع و﴿رَبُّ ٱلۡعَرۡشِ ٱلۡعَظِيمِ﴾.

١،٣١ حدّثنا عليّ بن الحسن قال حدّثنا ابن الجرّاح قال حدّثنا ابن أبي الدنيا قال حدّثنا زيد بن أخزم الطائيّ قال حدّثنا عبد الملك بن عمرو أبو عامر قال حدّثنا عبد الجليل ابن عطيّة عن جعفر بن ميمون قال حدّثني عبد الرحمٰن بن أبي بكرة عن أبيه عن النبيّ صلّى الله عليه وسلّم قال

دعوات المكروب اللّٰهمّ رحمتَك أَرجو فلا تكلني إلى نفسي طرفة عين وأصلح لي شأني كلّه لا إله إلاّ أنت.

I read in a book by Muḥammad ibn Jarīr al-Ṭabarī entitled *The Book of Praiseworthy Behavior and Valuable Principles*: We cite Ibn Bashshār, citing Ibn Abī ʿUdayy, quoting Ḥumayd ibn ʿAbd al-Raḥmān al-Ḥimyarī, who said: 29.1

When my father was suffering from gallstones, the pain of which was a severe trial, I went to Jerusalem, where I met Abū l-ʿAwwām. I told him about my father's illness and the pain he was in.

He said, "Tell him to say this prayer: Our Lord, Whose throne is in heaven; our Lord, Who are in heaven, hallowed be Your name. Your will is done in heaven and on earth. Just as You are compassionate in heaven, show Your compassion on earth. Forgive us our misdeeds and our sins, for You are forgiving and compassionate. O God! Send down an instance of Your compassion and Your healing on this person's pain. "

My father said the prayer, and God Exalted took away his gallstones. 29.2

We cite ʿAlī ibn al-Ḥasan, citing Ibn al-Jarrāḥ, citing Ibn Abī l-Dunyā, citing Abū Khaythamah, citing Yazīd ibn Hārūn, quoting Saʿīd ibn Abī ʿUrūbah, quoting Qatādah, quoting Abū l-ʿĀliyah, quoting Ibn ʿAbbās, quoting the Prophet, God bless and keep him, who said: 30

The words of deliverance are: "There is no god but God, Patient and Kind. There is no god but God, Exalted, Almighty. There is no god but God, Lord of the seven heavens, Lord of the seven earths, «Lord of the mighty throne»."[154]

We cite ʿAlī ibn al-Ḥasan, citing Ibn al-Jarrāḥ, citing Ibn Abī l-Dunyā, citing Zayd ibn Akhzam al-Ṭāʾī, citing Abū ʿĀmir ʿAbd al-Malik ibn ʿAmr, citing ʿAbd al-Jalīl ibn ʿAṭiyyah, quoting Jaʿfar ibn Maymūn, citing ʿAbd al-Raḥmān ibn Abī Bakrah, quoting his father, Abū Bakrah Nufayʿ, quoting the Prophet, God bless and keep him, who said: 31.1

The supplications of the afflicted are: "O God! In Your compassion is all my hope. Do not abandon me for a single moment to my own devices, but make all things well with me. There is no God but You!"

٢،٣١ أخبرني أبو بكر مكرّم بن أحمد بن عبد الوهّاب بن مكرّم القاضي قال حدّثنا ابن الأزهر[١] محمّد بن جعفر قال حدّثنا أبو نُعيم قال حدّثنا عبد العزيز بن عمر بن عبد العزيز عن هلال مولى عمر[٢] عن عمر بن عبد العزيز عن عبد الله بن جعفر قال

علّمتني أمّي أسماء بنت عميس شيئاً أمرها رسول الله صلّى الله عليه وسلّم أن تقوله عند الكرب

الله ربّي لا أشرك به شيئاً.

٣،٣١ أخبرني مكرّم بن أحمد القاضي قال حدّثنا محمّد بن إسماعيل السلميّ قال أنبأنا ابن أبي مريم قال حدّثني يحيى بن أيّوب قال حدّثني عبد العزيز بن عمر بن عبد العزيز عن هلال مولى عمر[٣] عن عمر بن عبد العزيز عن عبد الله بن جعفر أنّ رسول الله صلّى الله عليه وسلّم كان يقول عند الكرب

الله ربّي لا أشرك به شيئاً.

٤،٣١ حدّثنا بالموصل في مجلس عضد الدولة وهو يسمع إبراهيم بن محمّد الأنصاريّ المعروف بالثمديّ وهو يخلفني يومئذ في جملة من أعمالي على القضاء بجزيرة ابن عمر وسنّه أكثر من تسعين سنة وكان عضد الدولة استدعاه منها لعلوّ إسناده وعمل له مجلساً بحضرته حدّث فيه وأحضرني وجماعة مخصوصين من أهل العلم حتّى سمع منه وسمعنا معه قال حدّثنا عبد الله بن محمّد بن قريعة الأزديّ وأبو العبّاس محمّد بن حسّان البصريّان قالا حدّثنا عفّان بن مسلم قال حدّثنا حمّاد بن سلمة عن أسامة بن زيد عن محمّد بن كعب القرظيّ عن عبد الله بن شدّاد بن الهادّ عن عبد الله بن جعفر عن عليّ عليه السلام قال علّمني رسول الله صلّى الله عليه وسلّم إذا نزل بي كرب أو شدّة أن أقول

١ ابن: التصحيح من ش. ٢ ش: غفرة. ٣ ش: غفرة.

We cite Judge Abū Bakr Mukarram ibn Aḥmad ibn ʿAbd al-Wahhāb ibn Mukarram, citing Ibn al-Azhar Muḥammad ibn Jaʿfar, citing Abū Nuʿaym, citing ʿAbd al-ʿAzīz ibn ʿUmar ibn ʿAbd al-ʿAzīz, quoting Hilāl, the freedman of ʿUmar ibn ʿAbd al-ʿAzīz, quoting the caliph ʿUmar ibn ʿAbd al-ʿAzīz, quoting ʿAbd Allāh ibn Jaʿfar ibn Abī Ṭālib, who said: 31.2

My mother, Asmāʾ bint ʿUmays, taught me what the Messenger of God, God bless and keep him, had commanded her to say in any affliction:

God is my lord, and He alone is Lord.

I cite Judge Mukarram ibn Aḥmad, citing Muḥammad ibn Ismāʿīl al-Sulamī, who said, We quote Ibn Abī Maryam, citing Yaḥyā ibn Ayyūb, citing ʿAbd al-ʿAzīz ibn ʿUmar ibn ʿAbd al-ʿAzīz, quoting Hilāl, the freedman of ʿUmar ibn ʿAbd al-ʿAzīz, quoting ʿUmar ibn ʿAbd al-ʿAzīz, quoting ʿAbd Allāh ibn Jaʿfar ibn Abī Ṭālib, who said that the Messenger of God, God bless and keep him, used to say: 31.3

God is my lord, and He alone is Lord.

Ibrāhīm ibn Muḥammad al-Anṣārī, known as the Eye-Salve Merchant, who at that time was my deputy in a number of my judicial appointments in Jazīrat Ibn ʿUmar and was over ninety years old, was summoned thence to Mosul by ʿAḍud al-Dawlah becaue of the longevity of the transmitters in his chains of transmission for an audience in the prince's hearing.[155] ʿAḍud al-Dawlah held the audience especially for him to recite Prophetic reports in his presence. I and a number of favored religious scholars were invited to attend and listen too, and he said as follows:[156] We cite ʿAbd Allāh ibn Muḥammad ibn Qarīʿah al-Azdī and Abū l-ʿAbbās Muḥammad ibn Ḥassān, both of Basra, citing ʿAffān ibn Muslim, citing Ḥammād ibn Salamah, quoting Usāmah ibn Zayd, quoting Muḥammad ibn Kaʿb al-Quraẓī, quoting ʿAbd Allāh ibn Shaddād ibn al-Hādd, quoting ʿAbd Allāh ibn Jaʿfar ibn Abī Ṭālib, quoting ʿAlī ibn Abī Ṭālib, peace on him, who said: 31.4

لا إله إلاّ الله الحليم الكريم عزّ الله وتبارك الله ربّ العرش العظيم و﴿ٱلْحَمْدُ لِلَّهِ رَبِّ ٱلْعَالَمِينَ﴾.

٥،٣١ وأخبرني القاضي أبو الحسن عليّ بن إبراهيم بن حمّاد قال حدّثنا محمّد بن يونس الكُديميّ قال حدّثنا رَوح بن عبادة قال حدّثنا أسامة بن زيد فذكر بإسناده مثله. وأخبرني القاضي عليّ بن إبراهيم قال حدّثنا الكُديميّ قال حدّثني سعيد بن منصور البلخيّ قال حدّثنا يعقوب بن عبد الرحمٰن عن محمّد بن عجلان عن محمّد بن كعب القرظيّ فذكر بإسناده مثله.

٦،٣١ حدّثنا عليّ بن الحسن قال حدّثنا ابن الجرّاح قال حدّثنا ابن أبي الدنيا قال حدّثنا محمّد بن عبّاد بن موسى قال حدّثني رَوح بن عبادة عن أسامة بن زيد عن محمّد بن كعب القرظيّ عن عبد الله بن شدّاد عن عبد الله بن جعفر عن عليّ بن أبي طالب رضي الله عنه قال علّمني رسول الله صلّى الله عليه وسلّم إذا نزل بي كرب أن أقول.

لا إله إلاّ الله الحليم الكريم سبحان الله وتبارك الله ربّ العرش العظيم والحمد الله ربّ العالمين.

٧،٣١ حدّثنا عليّ بن الحسن قال حدّثنا ابن الجرّاح قال حدّثنا ابن أبي الدنيا قال حدّثنا أبو خيثمة قال حدّثنا عفّان بن مسلم عن عبد الواحد ابن زياد قال حدّثنا مجمّع بن يحيى قال حدّثنا أبو العيوف صعب أو صعيب العنزيّ عن أسماء بنت عميس قالت سمعت رسول الله صلّى الله عليه وسلّم يقول

من أصابه همّ أو غمّ أو سقم أو شدّة أو ذلّ أو لأواء فقال الله ربّي لا شريك له كشف الله ذلك عنه.

٨،٣١ حدّثنا عليّ بن الحسن قال حدّثنا ابن الجرّاح قال حدّثنا ابن أبي الدنيا قال حدّثني سعيد بن سليمان قال حدّثنا فضيل بن مرزوق قال حدّثنا أبو سلمة الجهنيّ عن

The Messenger of God, God bless and keep him, taught me to say, if affliction or adversity befell me: "There is no god but God, Patient and Kind. Mighty is God, Blessed is God, «Lord of the mighty throne».[157] «Praise be to God, Lord of all.»"[158]

For the same report, I cite Judge Abū l-Ḥasan ʿAlī ibn Ibrāhīm ibn Ḥammād, citing Muḥammad ibn Yūnus al-Kudaymī, citing Rawḥ ibn ʿUbādah, citing Usāmah ibn Zayd and the rest of the chain of transmitters given above. I also cite Judge ʿAlī ibn Ibrāhīm, citing al-Kudaymī, citing Saʿīd ibn Manṣūr of Balkh, citing Yaʿqūb ibn ʿAbd al-Raḥmān, quoting Muḥammad ibn ʿAjlān, quoting Muḥammad ibn Kaʿb al-Quraẓī and the rest of the chain of transmitters. 31.5

We cite ʿAlī ibn al-Ḥasan, citing Ibn al-Jarrāḥ, citing Ibn Abī l-Dunyā, citing Muḥammad ibn ʿAbbād ibn Mūsā, citing Rawḥ ibn ʿUbādah, quoting Usāmah ibn Zayd, quoting Muḥammad ibn Kaʿb al-Quraẓī, quoting ʿAbd Allāh ibn Shaddād, quoting ʿAbd Allāh ibn Jaʿfar ibn Abī Ṭālib, quoting ʿAlī ibn Abī Ṭālib, peace on him, who said: 31.6

The Messenger of God, God bless and keep him, taught me to say, if affliction or adversity befell me: "There is no god but God, Patient and Kind. Glory to God, Blessed is God, «Lord of the mighty throne.» «Praise be to God, Lord of all»."

We cite ʿAlī ibn al-Ḥasan, citing Ibn al-Jarrāḥ, citing Ibn Abī l-Dunyā, citing Abū Khaythamah, citing ʿAffān ibn Muslim, citing ʿAbd al-Wāḥid ibn Ziyād, citing Mujammiʿ ibn Yaḥyā, citing Abū l-ʿUyūf Ṣaʿb or Ṣuʿayb al-ʿAnazī, quoting Asmāʾ bint ʿUmays, who said, I heard the Messenger of God, God bless and keep him, say: 31.7

Whoever suffers sorrow or care, sickness or adversity; whoever is brought low or made desolate, will be rescued by God if he says, "God is my lord, and He alone is Lord."

We cite ʿAlī ibn al-Ḥasan, citing Ibn al-Jarrāḥ, citing Ibn Abī l-Dunyā, citing Saʿīd ibn Sulaymān,[159] citing Fuḍayl ibn Marzūq, citing Abū Salamah al-Juhanī, quoting al-Qāsim ibn ʿAbd al-Raḥmān, quoting his father, ʿAbd al-Raḥmān ibn ʿAbd Allāh ibn Masʿūd, who said: 31.8

The Messenger of God, God bless and keep him, said:

القاسم بن عبد الرحمٰن عن أبيه قال قال عبد الله بن مسعود[1] قال رسول الله صلّى الله عليه وسلّم

ما أصاب مسلماً قطّ همّ أو حزن فقال اللّٰهمّ إنّي عبدك وابن أمتك ناصيتي في يدك ماضٍ فيّ حكمك عدل فيّ قضاؤك أسألك بكلّ اسم هو لك سمّيت به نفسك أو أنزلته في كتابك أو علّمته أحداً من خلقك أو استأثرت به في علم الغيب عندك أن تجعل القرآن ربيع قلبي وجلاء حزني وذهاب همّي إلاّ أذهب الله عنه كربه وأبدله مكان حزنه فرحاً قالوا يا رسول الله أفلا نتعلّم هذه الكلمات قال بلى ينبغي لمن سمعهنّ أن يتعلّمهنّ.

٩،٣١ حدّثنا عليّ بن الحسن قال حدّثنا ابن الجرّاح قال حدّثنا ابن أبي الدنيا قال حدّثنا أبو حفص الصفّار أحمد بن حميد قال حدّثنا جعفر بن سليمان قال حدّثنا الخليل بن مرّة عن فقيه من أهل الأردن قال

بلغنا أنّ رسول الله صلّى الله عليه وسلّم كان إذا أصابه غمّ أو كرب يقول حسبي الربّ من العباد حسبي الخالق من المخلوق حسبي الرازق من المرزوق حسبي الله الذي هو حسبي حسبي الله ونعم الوكيل ﴿حَسْبِيَ ٱللَّهُ لَآ إِلَٰهَ إِلَّا هُوَ عَلَيْهِ تَوَكَّلْتُ وَهُوَ رَبُّ ٱلْعَرْشِ ٱلْعَظِيمِ﴾.

١٠،٣١ حدّثنا عليّ بن الحسن قال حدّثنا ابن الجرّاح قال حدّثنا ابن أبي الدنيا قال حدّثنا القاسم ابن هاشم قال حدّثني الخطّاب بن عثمان قال حدّثني ابن أبي فديك قال حدّثنا سعد بن سعيد قال حدّثنا أبو إسماعيل ابن أبي فديك قال قال رسول الله صلّى الله عليه وسلّم

ما كربني أمر إلاّ تمثّل لي جبريل عليه السّلام فقال يا محمّد قل توكّلت على الحيّ الذي لا يموت و ﴿وَقُلِ ٱلْحَمْدُ لِلَّهِ ٱلَّذِى لَمْ يَتَّخِذْ وَلَدًا وَلَمْ يَكُن لَّهُۥ شَرِيكٌ فِى ٱلْمُلْكِ﴾ إلى آخر الآية.

[1] قال عبد الله بن مسعود: الزيادة من ش.

"No Muslim who says, 'O God! I am Your servant; I am of Your community; my governance is in Your hand;[160] subject am I to Your ruling, just is Your decree concerning me; I supplicate You by all the names that belong to You, by which You have named Yourself or that You have sent down in Your Book or taught to any of Your creatures, and by that name which is hidden from us and known only to Yourself, to make the Qur'an the pasture of my heart, and to dispel my sorrow and take away my grief'—no Muslim who says this ever suffers sorrow or grief without God taking away his affliction and giving him joy in exchange for grief."

Those present asked, "Should we then learn these words, Messenger of God?"

"Indeed you should," he replied. "Everyone who hears them should learn them."

We cite ʿAlī ibn al-Ḥasan, citing Ibn al-Jarrāḥ, citing Ibn Abī l-Dunyā, citing 31.9
Abū Ḥafṣ Aḥmad ibn Ḥamīd the Coppersmith, citing Jaʿfar ibn Sulaymān, citing al-Khalīl ibn Murrah, quoting a jurist of al-Urdunn, who said, We have heard that:

Whenever care or affliction befell the Messenger of God, God bless and keep him, he would say, "With the Lord, I have no need of His servants; with the Creator, I have no need of His creatures; with the Provider, I have no need of provision. I have no need except of God, and I need nothing else; God, the best of guardians, is all I need.[161] «I have no need but of God, other than Whom there is no god. In Him I place all my trust; He is Lord of the mighty throne.»"[162]

We cite ʿAlī ibn al-Ḥasan, citing Ibn al-Jarrāḥ, citing Ibn Abī l-Dunyā, citing 31.10
al-Qāsim ibn Hāshim, citing al-Khaṭṭāb ibn ʿUthmān, citing Ibn Abī Fudayk, citing Saʿd ibn Saʿīd, citing Abū Ismāʿīl ibn Abī Fudayk,[163] who said, The Messenger of God, God bless and keep him, said:

I have never suffered an affliction without Gabriel, peace on him, appearing to me and saying, "Muḥammad! Say: 'I have placed all my trust in the Living One, Who never dies'; and the whole of the verse «Praise be to God, Who has taken to Himself no son, Who has no partner in His kingship . . .»[164] and so on."

حدّثنا عليّ بن الحسن قال حدّثني ابن الجرّاح قال حدّثنا ابن أبي الدنيا قال حدّثنا إسحاق بن إبراهيم قال حدّثنا النضر بن إسماعيل البجليّ عن عبد الرحمٰن بن إسحاق عن القاسم بن عبد الرحمٰن عن عبد الله قال كان رسول الله صلّى الله عليه وسلّم إذا نزل به همّ أو غمّ قال ١١،٣١

يا حيّ يا قيّوم برحمتك أستغيث.

حدّثنا جعفر بن أبي طالب بن أبي جعفر بن البهلول التنوخيّ القاضي قال حدّثنا أبو القاسم عبد الوهّاب بن أبي حيّة قال حدّثنا إسحاق ابن أبي إسرائيل قال حدّثني النضر بن إسماعيل عن عبد الرحمٰن بن إسحاق عن القاسم بن عبد الرحمٰن قال حدّثنا عبد الله بن مسعود قال كان رسول الله صلّى الله عليه وسلّم إذا نزل به غمّ أو كرب قال ١٢،٣١

يا حيّ يا قيّوم برحمتك أستغيث.

حدّثنا عليّ بن الحسن قال حدّثنا ابن الجرّاح قال حدّثنا ابن أبي الدنيا قال حدّثنا هارون بن سفيان قال حدّثني عبد الله بن محمّد القرشيّ عن نعيم بن مورّع عن جويبر عن الضحّاك قال ١٣،٣١

دعاء موسى حين توجّه إلى فرعون ودعاء رسول الله صلّى الله عليه وسلّم يوم حُنين ودعاء كلّ مكروب: كنتَ وتكون حيًّا لا تموت تنام العيون وتنكدر النجوم وأنت حيّ قيّوم لا تأخذك سِنة ولا نوم يا حيّ يا قيّوم.

دعاء الفرج أعطانيه أبو الحمد داود بن الناصر لدين الله واسمه أحمد بن الهادي للحقّ يحيى بن الحسين بن القاسم بن إبراهيم المعروف بطباطبا بن إسماعيل بن إبراهيم بن الحسن بن الحسن بن عليّ بن أبي طالب وقال لي إنّ أهله يتوارثونه وهو عن أمير المؤمنين عليه السلام ٣٢

We cite ʿAlī ibn al-Ḥasan, citing Ibn al-Jarrāḥ, citing Ibn Abī l-Dunyā, citing Isḥāq ibn Ibrāhīm, citing al-Naḍr ibn Ismāʿīl al-Bajlī, quoting ʿAbd al-Raḥmān ibn Isḥāq, quoting al-Qāsim ibn ʿAbd al-Raḥmān, quoting ʿAbd Allāh ibn Masʿūd, who said: 31.11

Whenever the Messenger of God, God bless and keep him, was beset with sorrow or care, he would say, "O Living One, O Eternal One,[165] I seek succor in Your compassion."

We cite Judge Jaʿfar ibn Abī Ṭālib ibn Abī Jaʿfar Ibn al-Buhlūl al-Tanūkhī, citing Abū l-Qāsim ʿAbd al-Wahhāb ibn Abī Ḥayyah, citing Isḥāq ibn Abī Isrāʾīl, citing al-Naḍr ibn Ismāʿīl al-Bajlī, quoting ʿAbd al-Raḥmān ibn Isḥāq, quoting al-Qāsim ibn ʿAbd al-Raḥmān, citing ʿAbd Allāh ibn Masʿūd, who said: 31.12

Whenever the Messenger of God, God bless and keep him, was beset with care or affliction, he would say, "O Living One, O Eternal One, I seek succor in Your compassion."

We cite ʿAlī ibn al-Ḥasan, citing Ibn al-Jarrāḥ, citing Ibn Abī l-Dunyā, citing Hārūn ibn Sufyān, citing ʿAbd Allāh ibn Muḥammad al-Qurashī,[166] quoting Nuʿaym ibn Muwarriʿ, quoting Juwaybir ibn Saʿīd, quoting al-Ḍaḥḥāk, who said: 31.13

The prayer said by the Messenger of God, God bless and keep him, at the Battle of Ḥunayn, and a prayer for anyone suffering affliction, is the prayer that Moses said when he was sent to Pharaoh: "You were, and You shall be, Living, Immortal. Eyes will close and stars will fall,[167] and still You shall live, Eternal, seized neither by slumber nor sleep,[168] O Living One, O Eternal One."

Here is a prayer of deliverance that was given to me by Abū l-Ḥamd Dāwūd ibn al-Nāṣir li-Dīn Allāh Aḥmad ibn al-Hādī li-l-Ḥaqq Yaḥyā ibn al-Ḥusayn ibn al-Qāsim ibn Ibrāhīm—known as Ṭabāṭabā—ibn Ismāʿīl ibn Ibrāhīm ibn al-Ḥasan ibn al-Ḥasan ibn ʿAlī ibn Abī Ṭālib. He told me that the members of his family hand it down among themselves, and that it comes from ʿAlī ibn Abī Ṭālib, Commander of the Faithful. 32

يا من تحلّ به عقد المكاره ويفلّ حدّ الشدائد ويا من يلتمس به المخرج ويُطلب منه رَوح الفرج أنت المدعوّ في المهمّات والمفزع في الملمّات لا يندفع منها إلاّ ما دفعت ولا ينكشف منها إلاّ ما كشفت. قد نزل بي ما قد علمت وقد كادني ثقله وألمّ بي ما بهظني حمله وبقدرتك أوردته عليّ وبسلطانك وجّهته إليّ ولا مصدر لما أوردت ولا كاشف لما وجّهت ولا فاتح لما أغلقت ولا ميسّر لما عسّرت ولا معسّر لما يسّرت فصلّ اللّهمّ على محمّد وعلى آل محمّد وافتح لي باب الفرج بطولك واحبس عنّي سلطان الهمّ بحولك وأنلني حسن النظر فيما شكوت وأذقني حلاوة الصنع فيما سألت وهبّ لي من لدنك فرجاً هنيّاً عاجلاً وصلاحاً في جميع أمري سنيّاً شاملاً واجعل لي من عندك فرجاً قريباً ومخرجاً رحباً ولا تشغلني بالاهتمام عن تعاهد فروضك واستعمال سنّتك فقد ضقت ذرعاً بما عراني وتحيّرت فيما نزل بي ودهاني وضعفت عن حمل ما قد أثقلني همّاً وتبدّلت بما أنا فيه قلقاً وغمّاً وأنت القادر على كشف ما قد وقعتُ فيه ودفع ما منيت به فافعل بي ذلك يا سيّدي ومولاي وإن لم أستحقّه وأجبني إليه وإن لم أستوجبه يا ذا العرش العظيم ثلاث مرّات.

وأعطاني دعاء آخر للفرج وقال لي إنّ أهله بصعدة يتوارثونه عن أهل البيت عليهم ٣٣
السلام

لا إله إلاّ الله حقّاً حقّاً لا إله إلاّ الله تعبّداً ورقّاً لا إله إلاّ الله إيماناً وصدقاً يا منزل الرحمة من معادنها ومنشئ البركة من أماكنها أسألك أن تصلّي على محمّد عبدك ونبيّك وخيرتك من خلقك وصفيّك وعلى آله مصابيح الدجى وأئمّة الهدى وأن تفرّج عنّي فرجاً عاجلاً وتنيلني صلاحاً لجميع أمري شاملاً وتفعل بي في ديني ودنياي ما أنت أهله يا كاشف الكرب يا غافر الذنب يا الله يا ربّ.

O You by Whom the knots of calamity are loosed, Who blunt the sharp edge of misfortune, to Whom we look for relief, from Whom we entreat the repose of deliverance: To You we pray in time of need. You are our refuge in our troubles, against which there is no defense but what You send and which only You can remove.

You know my plight. The weight of it trammels me; I sink under the burden of what has befallen me. It is Your power that has brought me to this, Your sovereignty that has visited it upon me. From the well to which you drive us we needs must drink. There is none to remove the misfortunes You send, no key to what You have locked, none to ease what You have made hard

Nor is there any to make hard what You have made easy: Bless, therefore, O God, Muḥammad and the House of Muḥammad; and by Your strength open to me the door of deliverance, and by Your might hold back from me the dominion of sorrow. Let me see the good in what I complain of; let me taste the sweetness of Your workings in what I have begged You for. Grant me speedy and salutary deliverance, and let things turn out wholly and gloriously for the best. Grant me swift deliverance and ample relief. Weary though I am with suffering, perplexed at what has beset and stricken me, and unable to bear the sorrow that weighs on me now that my former lot is exchanged for care and dismay, let not anxieties distract me from observing Your injunctions and applying Your laws. You have power to remove what has befallen me, to deflect what has struck me: Do so, my Liege and Master! unworthy though I am; heed my undeserving prayer, O «Lord of the mighty throne»![169]

This is to be said three times.

Here is another prayer of deliverance given me by Abū l-Ḥamd Dāwud, which 33
he told me his family in Ṣaʿdah hand down among themselves from the House of the Prophet, peace on them.

Truly, truly, there is no god but God. There is no god but God, sovereign and to be worshiped. There is no god but God, deserving of our faith and sincerity. O You who send down compassion from its fount and make blessing rise from its abodes: I beg you to bless Muhammad, Your servant and prophet, Your elect and chosen one, and his family, lights of our darkness, who lead us aright. I pray that that You will deliver me speedily and grant that matters turn out wholly to my good, and that You will deal with me body and soul as befits You, O Remover of affliction, O Forgiver of misdeeds, O God, O Lord.

١،٣٤ حدّثني أيّوب بن العبّاس بن الحسن الذي كان وزير المكتفي ولقيت أيّوب بالأهواز في حدود سنة خمسين وثلثمائة من حفظه قال حدّثني عليّ بن همّام بإسناد لست أحفظه

أنّ أعرابيّاً شكى إلى أمير المؤمنين عليّ بن أبي طالب عليه السلام شدّة لحقته وضيقاً في الحال وكثرة من العيال فقال له عليك بالاستغفار فإنّ الله تعالى يقول ﴿اسْتَغْفِرُوا رَبَّكُمْ إِنَّهُ كَانَ غَفَّارًا﴾ الآيات.

فعاد إليه وقال يا أمير المؤمنين قد استغفرت كثيرًا وما أرى فرجًا ممّا أنا فيه قال لعلّك لا تحسن أن تستغفر قال علّمني.

٢،٣٤ قال أخلص نيّتك وأطع ربّك وقل اللّهمّ إنّي أستغفرك من كلّ ذنب قوي عليه بدني بعافيتك أو نالته يدي بفضل نعمتك أو بسطت إليه يدي بسابغ رزقك أو اتّكلت فيه عند خوفي منه على أناتك أو وثقت فيه بحلمك أو عوّلت فيه على كرم عفوك اللّهمّ إنّي أستغفرك من كلّ ذنب خنت فيه أمانتي أو بخست فيه نفسي أو قدّمت فيه لذّتي أو آثرت فيه شهوتي أو سعيت فيه لغيري أو استغويت فيه من تبعني أو غلبت فيه بفضل حيلتي. أو أحلتُ فيه عليك يا مولاي فلم تؤاخذني على فعلي إذ كنتَ سبحانك كارهاً لمعصيتي لكن سبق علمك فيّ باختياري واستعمالي مرادي وإيثاري فحلُمت عنّي لم تدخلني فيه جبرًا ولم تحملني عليه قهرًا ولم تظلمني شيئاً. يا أرحم الراحمين يا صاحبي عند شدّتي يا مؤنسي في وحدتي ويا حافظي عند غربتي يا وليّي في نعمتي ويا كاشف كربتي ويا سامع دعوتي ويا راحم عبرتي ويا مقيل عثرتي يا إلهي بالتحقيق يا ركني الوثيق يا رجائي في الضيق يا مولاي الشفيق ويا ربّ البيت العتيق

أخرجني من حلق المضيق إلى سعة الطريق وفرج من عندك قريب وثيق واكشف عنّي كلّ شدّة وضيق واكفني ما أطيق وما لا أطيق اللّهمّ فرّج عنّي كلّ

I cite Ayyūb son of al-ʿAbbās ibn al-Ḥasan, who had been vizier to the caliph al-Muktafī; I met him in Ahwaz around the year 350 [961]. From memory, he cited ʿAlī ibn Hammām, and a chain of transmitters, which I did not memorize: 34.1

A Bedouin once complained to ʿAlī ibn Abī Ṭālib, Commander of the Faithful, that adversity had befallen him, leaving him in straitened circumstances with numerous dependents.

ʿAlī responded, "You must beg God's forgiveness, for God—Exalted—says, «Beg forgiveness of your Lord; He is ever-forgiving . . .»[170] and so on."

The Bedouin came back to ʿAlī and said, "Commander of the Faithful, I have begged God's forgiveness over and over, but I see no sign of deliverance."

"Perhaps," said ʿAlī, "you are not asking properly."

"Teach me how," said the Bedouin.

ʿAlī said, "Make sincere your intent, bend yourself to the will of your Lord, 34.2
and say, 'God! I ask Your forgiveness for every misdeed which Your gift of health has given my body strength to perpetrate, or which Your abundant blessings have empowered my hand to commit, or toward which the liberality of Your provision has encouraged me to stretch forth my hand, or in which, despite my fear of its consequences, I have put my faith in Your longsuffering or trusted in Your forbearance or relied on Your generous indulgence. God! I ask Your forgiveness for every misdeed by which I have betrayed my trust, or wronged myself, or put my own pleasures first, or preferred my own desires, or sought to harm others, or led others astray, or gained my ends by cunning, or tried to deceive You, dear Master.

"'You have not punished me for my misdeeds, for, glory to You! though You hate my disobedience, yet have You known for all eternity what actions I would choose and how I would employ my own free will and choice. Patiently, You did not intervene, and neither foreordained nor compelled me to sin. In nothing have You used me unjustly, most Compassionate One, my friend in adversity, my companion in solitude, my guardian in exile, my patron in prosperity, remover of my affliction, hearer of my supplication, pitier of my weeping, You Who pardon my errors, most truly my God, my sure support, my hope in every strait, my tender Master, Lord of the Kaaba.

"'Bring me from straitened places to broad ways, to Your sure and imminent deliverance. Rescue me from every adversity and constraint, and preserve me both from what I can and what I cannot bear. God! deliver me from every sorrow and affliction; lead me out of every care and grief, You Who dispel

همّ وكرب وأخرجني من كلّ غمّ وحزن يا فارج الهمّ ويا كاشف الغمّ ويا منزل القطر[1] ويا مجيب دعوة المضطرّ يا رحمٰن الدنيا والآخرة ورحيمها صلّ على خيرتك محمّد النبيّ وعلى آله الطيّبين الطاهرين وفرّج عنّي ما ضاق به صدري وعيل معه صبري وقلّت فيه حيلتي وضعفت له قوّتي يا كاشف كلّ ضرّ وبليّة ويا عالم كلّ سرّ وخفيّة يا أرحم الراحمين و ﴿فَسَتَذْكُرُونَ مَآ أَقُولُ لَكُمْ وَأُفَوِّضُ أَمْرِىٓ إِلَى ٱللَّهِ إِنَّ ٱللَّهَ بَصِيرٌۢ بِٱلْعِبَادِ﴾ و ﴿وَمَا تَوْفِيقِىٓ إِلَّا بِٱللَّهِ عَلَيْهِ تَوَكَّلْتُ وَهُوَ رَبُّ ٱلْعَرْشِ ٱلْعَظِيمِ﴾.

٣،٣٤ قال الأعرابيّ فاستغفرت بذلك مراراً فكشف الله عزّ وجلّ عنّي الغمّ والضيق ووسع عليّ في الرزق وأزال عنّي المحنة.

٠

١،٣٥ حدّثنا عليّ بن الحسن قال حدّثنا ابن الجرّاح قال حدّثنا ابن أبي الدنيا قال حدّثني عليّ ابن الجعد وإسحاق بن إسماعيل قالا حدّثنا سفيان ابن عيينة عن أبي السوداء عن أبي مجلز[2] قال قال عمر بن الخطّاب رضي الله عنه

ما أبالي على أيّ حالة أصبحت على ما أُحبّ أو على ما أكره وذلك أنّي لا أدري الخير فيما أُحبّ أو فيما أكره.

٢،٣٥ حدّثنا عليّ بن الحسن قال حدّثنا ابن الجرّاح قال حدّثنا ابن أبي الدنيا قال حدّثنا إبراهيم ابن سعيد قال حدّثنا أبو أسامة عن الأعمش عن إبراهيم قال

إن لم يكن لنا خير فيما نكره لم يكن لنا خير فيما نحبّ.

---

١ يلي هذه الكلمات في ل: ياكاشف السوء يا واسع العطايا يا سامع الدعاء يا عالم بما يرى وما لا يرى فإنّه إن يكن من عمرك تخلصت منه وإنلم يكن من عمرك أتاك الله فيه محبّتك واعلم أنّك إن تكسب شيئا سوى قوتك كنت فيه خازنا لغيرك بعد موتك. انظر ١١،٤٧. ٢ مجلز: التصحيح من ش.

care and remove sadness, sender of the rain,[171] answerer of the hard-pressed sufferer's supplication, You Who show compassion and pity to this world and the next.

"'Bless Your elect, the Prophet Muḥammad, and his pure and noble kin, and deliver me from the woes that oppress me; make me stray from acceptance; perplex and debilitate me, Remover of every hurt and tribulation, Knower of all secrets and hidden things, most supremely Compassionate.

"'«I commit myself to God, for God sees His servants»;[172] «nor can I succeed except through Him,»[173] and «in Him I place all my trust; He is the Lord of the mighty throne».'"[174]

The Bedouin said, "I used this prayer several times to ask God's forgiveness, and, Mighty and Glorious, He took away my grief and poverty, gave me ample provision, and released me from my ordeal." 34.3

We cite ʿAlī ibn al-Ḥasan, citing Ibn al-Jarrāḥ, citing Ibn Abī l-Dunyā, citing ʿAlī ibn al-Jaʿd and Isḥāq ibn Ismāʿīl, who both cite Sufyān ibn ʿUyaynah, quoting Abū l-Sawdāʾ, quoting Abū Mujliz, who said, ʿUmar ibn al-Khaṭṭāb, God be pleased with him, said: 35.1

I care not how I wake each day, whether to happiness or to suffering, because I know not in which of the two my good may lie.

We cite ʿAlī ibn al-Ḥasan, citing Ibn al-Jarrāḥ, citing Ibn Abī l-Dunyā, citing Ibrāhīm ibn Saʿīd citing Abū Usāmah, citing al-Aʿmash, citing Ibrāhīm,[175] who said: 35.2

If suffering does us no good, then neither will happiness!

حدّثنا عليّ بن الحسن قال حدّثنا ابن الجرّاح قال حدّثنا ابن أبي الدنيا قال حدّثنا عبد الرحمٰن بن صالح الأزديّ قال حدّثنا أبو رَوح رجل من أهل مرو عن سفيان بن عيينة قال ٣،٣٥

مرّ محمّد بن عليّ على محمّد بن المنكدر فقال ما لي أراك مغموماً فقال أبو حازم ذلك لدَين فدحه قال محمّد بن عليّ أَفُتِح له في الدعاء قال نعم قال لقد بورك لعبد في حاجة أكثر فيها دعاء ربّه كانت ما كانت.

حدّثنا عليّ بن الحسن قال حدّثنا ابن الجرّاح قال حدّثنا ابن أبي الدنيا قال حدّثنا عبد الرحمٰن بن صالح الأزديّ قال حدّثنا أبو رَوح قال قال ابن عيينة ٤،٣٥

ما يكره العبد خير له ممّا يحبّ لأنّ ما يكره يهيجه على الدعاء وما يحبّ يلهيه عنه.

قال ابن أبي الدنيا قال حدّثنا أبو نصر التمّار قال حدّثنا سعيد بن عبد العزيز التنوخيّ قال قال داود عليه السلام ٣٦

سبحان الله مستخرج الدعاء بالبلاء سبحان الله مستخرج الشكر بالرخاء.

حدّثنا عليّ بن الحسن قال حدّثنا ابن الجرّاح قال حدّثنا ابن أبي الدنيا قال حدّثنا أحمد ابن إبراهيم العبديّ قال حدّثنا العلاء بن عبد الجبّار العطّار قال حدّثنا أبو عبد الصمد العمّيّ قال سمعت مالك بن دينار يقول في مرضه وهو من آخر كلام سمعته يتكلّم به ٣٧

ما أقرب النعيم من البؤس يعقبان ويوشكان زوالاً.

حدّثنا عليّ بن الحسن قال حدّثنا ابن الجرّاح قال حدّثنا ابن أبي الدنيا قال حدّثنا محمّد بن الحسين قال حدّثني عبد الله بن محمّد التميميّ قال حدّثنا شيخ مولى لعبد القيس عن طاووس قال ١،٣٨

We cite ʿAlī ibn al-Ḥasan, citing Ibn al-Jarrāḥ, citing Ibn Abī l-Dunyā, citing ʿAbd al-Raḥmān ibn Ṣāliḥ al-Azdī, citing Abū Rawḥ, a man from Marw, quoting Sufyān ibn ʿUyaynah, who said: 35.3

Upon meeting Muḥammad ibn al-Munkadir, Muḥammad al-Bāqir asked, "Why do you look so careworn?"

He replied that he was heavily in debt. Muḥammad al-Bāqir asked him whether he had been able to pray.[176]

"Yes," he replied, and Muḥammad al-Bāqir said, "Anything, whatever it may be, that makes a man pray earnestly to his Lord, is a blessing."

We cite ʿAlī ibn al-Ḥasan, citing Ibn al-Jarrāḥ, citing Ibn Abī l-Dunyā, citing ʿAbd al-Raḥmān ibn Ṣāliḥ al-Azdī, citing Abū Rawḥ, who said: 35.4

Sufyān ibn ʿUyaynah said, "Suffering is better for a man than happiness, because suffering moves him to prayer, whereas happiness distracts him from it."

Ibn Abī l-Dunyā cites Abū Naṣr the Date Merchant, citing Saʿīd ibn ʿAbd al-ʿAzīz al-Tanūkhī, who said: 36

David, peace on him, said, "Glory to God, Who makes tribulation produce prayer! Glory to God, Who makes prosperity produce thankfulness!"

We cite ʿAlī ibn al-Ḥasan, citing Ibn al-Jarrāḥ, citing Ibn Abī l-Dunyā, citing Aḥmad ibn Ibrāhīm al-ʿAbdī, citing al-ʿAlāʾ ibn ʿAbd al-Jabbār the Druggist, citing Abū ʿAbd al-Ṣamad al-ʿAmmī, who said: 37

When he was ill, I heard Mālik ibn Dīnār say (and these are the last words I ever heard him utter): "How close are happiness and suffering! They alternate, and both are ephemeral."

We cite ʿAlī ibn al-Ḥasan, citing Ibn al-Jarrāḥ, citing Ibn Abī l-Dunyā, citing Muḥammad ibn al-Ḥusayn of Burjulān, citing ʿAbd Allāh ibn Muḥammad al-Tamīmī, citing a traditionist who was a client of the tribe of ʿAbd al-Qays, citing Ṭāwūs,[177] who said: 38.1

إنّي لفي الحِجْر ذات ليلة إذ دخل عليّ بن الحسين عليهما السلام فقلت رجل صالح من أهل بيت الخير لأستمعنّ إلى دعائه الليلة فصلّى ثمّ سجد فأصغيت بسمعي إليه فسمعته يقول عُبيدك بفنائك مسكينك بفنائك فقيرك بفنائك سائلك بفنائك

قال طاووس فحفظتهنّ فما دعوت بهنّ في كرب إلاّ فرّج الله عنّي. ٢،٣٨

١،٣٩ حدّثنا إبراهيم بن محمّد الأنصاريّ بالموصل بحضرة عضد الدولة قال أنبأنا أبو خليفة الفضل بن الحباب الجمحيّ القاضي وأبو جعفر محمّد بن محمّد بن حبّان الأنصاريّ البصريّان قالا حدّثنا موسى بن إسماعيل التبوذكيّ قال حدّثني حمّاد بن سلمة قال حدّثنا أبو عمران الجوفيّ عن نوف البكاليّ

أنّ نبيّاً أو صدّيقاً ذبح عجلاً بين يدي أمّه فخبل فبينما هو كذلك ذات يوم تحت شجرة فيها وكر طير إذ وقع فرخ طائر في الأرض وتغبّر في التراب فأتاه الطائر فجعل يطير فوق رأسه فأخذ النبيّ أو الصدّيق الفرخ فمسحه من التراب وأعاده في وكره

فردّ الله عزّ وجلّ عليه عقله. ٢،٣٩

٤٠ أخبرني أبي قال حدّثنا حرميّ بن أبي العلاء قال حدّثنا الزبير بن بكّار قال وحدّثني أحمد بن عبد الله بن أحمد الورّاق قال حدّثنا أحمد بن سليمان الطوسيّ قال حدّثنا الزبير بن بكّار قال أخبرني عثمان بن سليمان قال

قال عمر بن الخطّاب رضي الله عنه يوماً لجلسائه وفيهم عمرو بن العاص ما أحسن شيء فقال كلّ رجل برأيه وعمرو ساكت فقال ما تقول يا عمرو قال [رجز]

One night, when I was in the enclosure of the Kaaba, I was joined by ʿAlī ibn al-Ḥusayn, peace on them both. I said to myself, "A God-fearing member of the holy family—I will listen to his prayer tonight."

He performed the ritual prayer, then prostrated himself. I listened carefully, and heard him say, "Your poor servant is in Your courtyard; Your beggar is in Your courtyard; Your mendicant is in Your courtyard; Your supplicant is in Your courtyard."

Ṭāwūs said: 38.2

I memorized these words, and whenever I prayed with them in any affliction, God delivered me.

We cite Ibrāhīm ibn Muḥammad al-Anṣārī, who quoted to us, in Mosul, in 39.1
the presence of ʿAḍud al-Dawlah,[178] Judge Abū Khalīfah al-Faḍl ibn al-Ḥubāb al-Jumaḥī and Abū Jaʿfar Muḥammad ibn Muḥammad ibn Ḥibbān al-Anṣārī, both of Basra, who cited Mūsā ibn Ismāʿīl the Manure Seller, citing Ḥammād ibn Salamah, citing Abū ʿImrān al-Jawfī, quoting Nawf al-Bikālī:

A prophet (or a confessor) once slaughtered a calf in front of its mother and went mad.

One day during his madness, he found himself under a tree with a bird's nest in it. A fledgling fell out on to the ground and was covered in dust. The parent bird came and flew around above the head of the prophet (or confessor), who picked up the fledgling, brushed the dirt from it, and returned it to its nest.

Thereupon God, Mighty and Glorious, gave him back his wits. 39.2

I cite my father, citing Ḥaramī ibn Abī l-ʿAlāʾ, citing al-Zubayr ibn Bakkār; 40
my father also cited Aḥmad ibn ʿAbd Allāh ibn Aḥmad the Stationer-Copyist, citing Aḥmad ibn Sulaymān of Ṭūs, citing al-Zubayr ibn Bakkār, who said, I cite ʿUthmān ibn Sulaymān, who said:

ʿUmar ibn al-Khaṭṭāb, God be pleased with him, said one day to his companions, among whom was ʿAmr ibn al-Āṣ, "What is best of all?"

Each had his say, but ʿAmr said nothing.

"ʿAmr, what do you think?" asked ʿUmar.

He replied:

الغَمَرَاتُ ثُمَّ يَنْجَلِينَ

كتب سعيد بن حميد إلى عبيد الله بن عبد الله بن طاهر كتاباً من الاستتار قال فيه ٤١

وأرجو أن يكشف الله بالأمير أعزّه الله هذه الغمّة الطويل مداها البعيد منتهاها فإنّ طولها قد أطمع في انقضائها وتراخي أيّامها قد سهّل سبيل الأمل لفنائها.

قال مؤلّف هذا الكتاب ولحقتني محنة غليظة من السلطان فكتب إليّ أبو الفرج ١،٤٢
عبد الواحد بن نصر بن محمّد المخزوميّ الكاتب الشاعر النصيبيّ المعروف بالببّغاء رقعة يتوجّع لي فيها نسختها

بسم الله الرحمٰن الرحيم مُدد النعم أطال الله بقاء سيّدنا القاضي بغفلات المسارّ وإن طالت أحلام وساعات المحن وإن قصرت بشوائب الهمّ أعوام وأحظانا بالمواهب من ارتبطها بالشكر وأنهضنا بأعباء المصائب من قاومها بعدد الصبر إذ كان أوّلها بالعظة مذكّراً وآخرها بمضمون الفرج مبشّراً وإنّما يتعسّف ظلم الفتنة ويتمسّك بتفريط العجز ضالّ الحكمة من كان بسِنة الغفلة مغموراً وبضعف المُنّة والرأي مقهوراً وفي انتهاز فرص الحزم مفرّطاً ولمرضيّ ما اختاره الله تعالى فيه متسخّطاً.

٢،٤٢ وسيّدنا القاضي أدام الله تأييده أنور بصيرةً وأطهر سريرةً وأكمل حزماً وأنفذ مضاءً وعزماً من أن يتسلّط الشكّ على يقينه أو يقدح اعتراض الشبه في مروءته ودينه فيلقى ما اعتمده الله من طارق القضاء المحتوم بغير واجبة من فرض الرضا والتسليم ومع ذلك فإنّما تعظم المحنة إذا تجاوزت وضعف التنبيه من الله جلّ ذكره إلى واجب العقوبة ويصير مجيء السّلطان أدام الله عزّه بها وجوب الحجّة وشغلت

A sea of troubles, but it withdraws.[179]

When Saʿīd ibn Ḥumayd was in hiding, he wrote a letter to ʿUbayd Allāh ibn ʿAbd Allāh ibn Ṭāhir, which contained this passage: 41

I am confident that Your Excellency will be the means of God's removing this extended and extensive insecurity. Its very length raises expectation of its passing. That it has dragged on so long the more easily gives grounds to hope for its cessation.

The author of this book says, When I was subjected to a harsh ordeal by the sovereign, I was sent a letter of commiseration by Abū l-Faraj ʿAbd al-Wāḥid ibn Naṣr ibn Muḥammad al-Makhzūmī of Naṣībīn, the state scribe and poet, known as the Parrot,[180] of which this is the text: 42.1

In the name of God, full of compassion, ever compassionate. May God prolong the life of Your Excellency the judge. Periods of blessing, however long they last, are dreams, such is the heedlessness of joy; and times of trial, however short, are years, because they are marred by sorrow.

We are favored with gifts by One Who has bound them to thankfulness, and burdened with misfortunes by One Who has matched with them the resources of acceptance. Their beginning should be a warning to us, while their end gives good tidings of assured deliverance. Therefore only those whose wisdom has gone astray, who are sunk in the slumber of heedlessness and are feeble-minded and soft, will persist, perversely, in unjust rebelliousness and weak apathy, being too idle to seize the opportunity to show resolution and too peevish to assent to the will of God Exalted.

Your Excellency the Judge, may God ever sustain you, has a discernment too enlightened, is too pure-hearted, too perfectly resolute, and has too lively a strength of purpose for doubt to get the better of your assurance or niggling uncertainties to impair your manly honor and faith and prevent you from meeting with the requisite consent and resignation the ineluctable decree that God has determined shall come to pass. 42.2

Nevertheless, if an ordeal is lengthy, it is felt to be excessive, and God's warning of the necessity of chastisement, glorious is His name, loses its force. Should the ordeal, moreover, proceed from the sovereign, whom God

الألسن عن محمود الثناء منها بمذموم اللائمة فإذا خلت من هذه الصفات المليمة والشوائب المذمومة كانت وإن راع ظاهرها بصفات النعم أولى وبأسماء المنح أحقّ وأحرى.

٣،٤٢ ومتى أعمل ذو الفهم الثاقب والفكر الصائب مثله أعزّه الله بكامل عقله وزائد فضله فيما يسامح به الدنيا من مرتجع هباتها وتمدّ له من خدع لذّاتها علم أنّ أسعد أهلها فيها ببلوغ الآمال أقربهم فيما خوّله من التغيّر والانتقال فصفاؤها مشوب بالكدر وأمنها مروع بالحذر لأنّ انتهاء الشيء إلى حدّه ناقل له عمّا كان عليه إلى ضدّه فتكاد المحنة بهذه القاعدة لاقترانها من الفرج بفسيح الرجاء وانتهاء الشدّة منها إلى مستجدّ الرخاء أن تكون أحقّ بأسماء النعم وأدخل في أسباب المواهب والقسم وبالحقيقة فكلّ وارد من الله تعالى على العبد وإن جهل مواقع الحِكَم منه وساءه استتار عواقب الخيرة بمفارقة ما نقل عنه غير خالٍ من مصلحة بتقديم عاجل وادّخار آجل.

٤،٤٢ وهذا وصف ما ذكر الله به سيّدنا القاضي أدام الله تأييده إذ كان للمثوبة مفيدًا وللفرج ضامنًا وبالحظّ مبشّرًا وإلى المسرّة مؤدّيًا وبأفضل ما عوّده الله جلّ اسمه عائدًا.

٥،٤٢ وهو أدام الله كفايته يتنجّز ذلك بمستحكم الثقة ووجاهة الدعاء والرغبة ووسائط الصبر والمعونة ولعلّه أن يكون إليه أقرب من ورود رقعتي هذه عليه بقدرة الله ومشيئته.

٦،٤٢ ولولا الخوف من الإطالة والتعرّض للإضجار والملالة بإخراج هذه الرقعة عن مذهب الرقاع وإدخالها بذكر ما نطق به نصّ الكتاب من ضمان اليسر بعد العسر وما وردت به في هذا المعنى الأمثال السائرة والأشعار المتناقلة في جمّة الرسائل وحيّز المصنّفات لأودعتها نبذًا من ذلك لكنّي آثرت أن لا أعدل عمّا افتتحتها به

preserve, people demand reasons, and their tongues, instead of praising him as they should, are reprehensibly critical.

If, however, these blameworthy and censurable lapses are avoided, then the ordeal, however fearsome it may appear, should rather be seen as a blessing, and, if anything, deserves to be called a benefaction.

When a man of penetrating understanding and a just reasoner such as your- 42.3
self, God preserve you, applies his undivided intelligence and superior powers to considering how many of this world's impermanent gifts have been granted him, how many of its deceptive delights have been afforded him, he will recognize that those fortunate enough to have their wishes come true are closest to losing these gifts to mutability and transience. The pleasure they afford is always sullied and clouded, and their safe enjoyment tempered by fear and caution, for as soon as anything reaches its fullest extent, it changes into its opposite.

According to this principle, however, any ordeal should really rather be called a blessing and classed as a boon and a portion, because ample hope couples it with deliverance, and because adversity must needs end in renewed prosperity. And, in truth, nothing that God, Exalted, sends to His servants is devoid of benefit, ignorant though they may be of its wisdom or blinded to its good consequences by the evils of an altered situation, for it makes them accumulate merit in this world and lay up treasure for the next.

It is this that God wished your Excellency the Judge to reflect upon, may 42.4
God always sustain you, for doing so will bring requital, ensure deliverance, give good tidings of good fortune, lead to gladness, and bring about the best things that God, glorious is His name, has taught us to expect.

Your Excellency, may God ever protect you, will effect this outcome 42.5
through your own inveterate confidence in God, the assiduity of your prayers and fervent supplications, and by means both of divine aid and of your own acceptance of your ordeal. Indeed, if the Almighty so wills, deliverance may reach you before this letter does.

Did I not fear to expatiate and run the risk of being irksome and boring— 42.6
making this unlike the usual kind of letter and turning it instead into something more like an essay or a kind of composition—a theme I would have touched upon is what Scripture tells us about how ease is sure to follow hardship, and I would have cited well-known sayings and oft-quoted poetry to this effect. But I prefer to keep to the point with which I began this letter and to which I have devoted it, for I am assured that your Excellency the Judge, may God always

واستخدمتها له مقتصراً على استغناء سيّدنا القاضي أدام الله تأييده عن ذلك بمرشد حفظه ووفور فضله ومأثور نباهته ونبله.

والله يبلغه ويبلغنا فيه نهاية الآمال ولا يخليه في طول البقاء من موادّ السعادة والإقبال إن شاء الله تعالى وهو حسبنا ونعم الوكيل. ٧،٤٢

قال بعض الصالحين ٤٣

استعمل في كلّ بليّة تطرقك حسن الظنّ بالله عزّ وجلّ في كشفها فإنّ ذلك أقرب بك إلى الفرج.

وروي عن عليّ بن أبي طالب عليه السلام أنّه قال ١،٤٤

أفضل عمل الممتحنين انتظار الفرج من الله عزّ وجلّ والصبر على قدر البلاء.

وعنه الصبر كفيل بالنجاح والمتوكّل لا يخيب ظنّه. ٢،٤٤

وكان يقال ١،٤٥

العاقل لا يذلّ بأوّل نكبة ولا يفرح بأوّل نعمة فربّما أقلع المحبوب عمّا يضرّ وأجلى المكروه عمّا يسرّ.

شكا عبد الله بن طاهر إلى سليمان بن يحيى بن معاذ كاتبه بلاءً خافه وتوقّعه فقال له أيّها الأمير لا يغلبنّ على قلبك إذا اغتممت ما تكره دون ما تحبّ فلعلّ العاقبة تكون بما تحبّ وتوقّي ما تكره فتكون كمن يستسلف الغمّ والخوف قال أما إنّك قد فرّجت عنّي ما أنا فيه. ٢،٤٥

sustain you, has no need of such a hint, thanks to your own mindfulness, the abundance of your merits, and the distinction and nobility for which you are celebrated.

If God Exalted so wills, may He grant Your Excellency, and us with you, all that you wish for, and give you, however long you live, continual increase of happiness and good fortune, for He «is all we need, the best of guardians».[181] 42.7

A God-fearing man once said: 43

In every tribulation that may strike you, have full confidence that God, Mighty and Glorious, will remove it, for this is the quickest way to deliverance.

It is related of ʿAlī ibn Abī Ṭālib, peace on him, that he said: 44.1

To look forward to deliverance by God, Mighty and Glorious, is the best work of the sufferer. The greater his tribulation, the worthier his acceptance of it.

He also said: 44.2

Acceptance guarantees success, and he who puts all his trust in God will not be disappointed.

There is a saying: 45.1

The reasonable man is not cast down by the first calamity, nor does he rejoice at the first blessing, for sometimes good things give place to harm and bad ones make way for happiness.

ʿAbd Allāh ibn Ṭāhir told his secretary Sulaymān ibn Yaḥyā ibn Muʿādh that he went in fear of an impending ordeal. 45.2

Sulaymān replied, "General, when you are worried, you must not let feelings of despondency gain the upper hand. Should things turn out for the best rather than the worst, you will, as it were, have borrowed grief and fear."

The general said, "You have delivered me from my fears."

٤٦ بلغني أنّ الناس قحطوا بالمدينة في سنة من خلافة عمر بن الخطّاب فخرج بهم مستسقياً فكان أكثر قوله الاستغفار فقيل له يا أمير المؤمنين لو دعوت فقال أما سمعتم قوله عزّ وجلّ ﴿ ٱسْتَغْفِرُوا۟ رَبَّكُمْ إِنَّهُۥ كَانَ غَفَّارًا يُرْسِلِ ٱلسَّمَآءَ عَلَيْكُم مِّدْرَارًا وَيُمْدِدْكُم بِأَمْوَٰلٍ وَبَنِينَ وَيَجْعَل لَّكُمْ جَنَّٰتٍ وَيَجْعَل لَّكُمْ أَنْهَٰرًا ﴾ فصار الاستكثار من الاستغفار في الاستسقاء سنّة إلى اليوم.

١،٤٧ يُحكى عن أنوشروان أنّه قال جميع المكاره في الدنيا تنقسم على ضربين فضرب فيه حيلة فالاضطراب دواؤه وضرب لا حيلة فيه فالاصطبار شفاؤه.

٢،٤٧ كان بعض الحكماء يقول الحيلة فيما لا حيلة فيه الصبر.

٣،٤٧ وكان يقال من اتّبع الصبر اتّبعه النصر.

٤،٤٧ ومن الأمثال السائرة الصبر مفتاح الفرج. مَن صبر قدر. ثمرة الصبر الظفر. عند اشتداد البلاء يأتي الرخاء.

٥،٤٧ وكان يقال تضايقي تنفرجي.

٦،٤٧ وكان يقال إذا اشتدّ الخناق انقطع.

٧،٤٧ وكان يقال خِف المضارّ من خلل المسارّ وارجُ النفع من موضع المنع واحرص على الحياة بطلب الموت فكم من بقاء سببه استدعاء الفناء ومن فناء سببه إيثار البقاء وأكثر ما يأتي الأمن من قبل الفزع.

I have heard that: 46

One year during the caliphate of 'Umar ibn al-Khaṭṭāb, there was a drought in Medina. The caliph went out with the people to pray for rain, but asked mostly for forgiveness. They said to him, "Commander of the Faithful, be pleased to pray for rain!"

He replied, "Have you not heard what God, Mighty and Glorious, has said? «Beg forgiveness of your Lord; He is ever-forgiving. He sends down rain on you from the sky in streams. He supports you with cattle and offspring. He makes for you gardens. He makes for you watercourses»."[182]

To this day, it is the custom to beg forgiveness when praying for rain.

We are told that Anūshirwān said: 47.1

All the ills of this world fall into two categories: those about which something can be done, whose remedy is action, and those about which nothing can be done, whose cure is acceptance.

A certain sage used to say: 47.2

What can't be cured must be accepted.

There is a saying: 47.3

Accept your situation and help will follow.

Common sayings are: 47.4

Acceptance is the key to deliverance. Acceptance empowers. Success is the fruit of acceptance. When tribulation is at its worst, good times will follow.

Another saying is: 47.5

The harder the pass, the greater the deliverance.[183]

Another is: 47.6

The noose snaps when at its tightest.

Other sayings are: 47.7

Beware lest hurt come through happiness. Where there's lack, expect gain. Safeguard your life by seeking out death: Many a life is saved by courting destruction, many a death comes from trying to preserve life. What you dread will often keep you safe.[184]

٨،٤٧ والعرب تقول إنّ في الشرّ خياراً وقال الأصمعيّ معناه أنّ بعض الشرّ أهون من بعض وقال أبو عبيدة معناه إذا أصابتك مصيبة فاعلم أنّه قد يكون أجلّ منها فلتهن عليك مصيبتك.

٩،٤٧ قال بعض الحكماء عواقب الأمور تتشابه في الغيوب فرُبّ محبوب في مكروه ومكروه في محبوب وكم مغبوط بنعمة هي داؤه ومرحوم من داء هو شفاؤه.

١٠،٤٧ وكان يقال رُبّ خير من شرّ ونفع من ضرّ.

١١،٤٧ وروي أنّ أمير المؤمنين عليّاً قال يا ابن آدم لا تحمل همّ يومك الذي لم يأت على يومك الذي أتى فإنّه إن يكن في عمرك يأتك الله فيه بمجبّتك واعلم أنّك لن تكسب شيئاً سوى قوتك إلاّ كنت فيه خازناً لغيرك بعد موتك.

١٢،٤٧ وقال وداعة السهميّ في كلام له اصبر على الشرّ إن قدحك فربّما أجلى عمّا يفرحك وتحت الرغوة اللبن الصريح.

٤٨ قال شريح

إنّي لأصاب بالمصيبة فأحمد الله عزّ وجلّ عليها أربع مرّات أحمده إذ لم تكن أعظم ممّا هي وأحمده إذ رزقني الصبر عليها وأحمده إذ وفّقني للاسترجاع لما أرجو فيه من الثواب وأحمده إذ لم يجعلها في ديني.

١،٤٩ ويشبه هذا ما روي عن بزرجمهر بن البختكان الحكيم الذي كان وزير أنوشروان فإنّه حبسه عند غضبه في بيت كالقبر ظلمةً وضيقاً وصفّده بالحديد وألبسه الخشن من الصوف وأمر أن لا يزاد في كلّ يوم على قرصين خبزاً شعيراً وكفّ ملح جريش ودورق ماء وأن تحصى ألفاظه فتُنقل إليه

The Arabs say: 47.8

Some ills are good.

Al-Aṣmaʿī explained this as meaning that not all ills are equally bad, while Abū ʿUbaydah said it means: Should you suffer a misfortune, be aware that it could have been worse, and make light of it.

A certain sage said: 47.9

Until they emerge, the outcomes of events cannot be told apart: There is good in many an evil, and evil in many a boon. A person is often envied for a blessing that proves to be a bane, and pitied for a bane that is a cure.

Another saying is: 47.10

There is often good in evil, and profit in loss.

It is related that the Commander of the Faithful ʿAlī ibn Abī Ṭālib said: 47.11

O Son of Adam! Do not anticipate tomorrow's sorrow today, for if it is to be, God will make it bring you good. Know too that, of anything you gain beyond your subsistence, you are only the custodian for others who will come after your death.

Wadāʿah al-Sahmī said, as part of a longer adage: 47.12

If you labor under an evil, accept it, for it may give way to happiness: Fresh milk lies beneath the froth.

Judge Shurayḥ said: 48

In misfortune, I praise God for it four times, Mighty and Glorious is He. I praise Him that it is no worse than it is. I praise Him for affording me acceptance of it. I praise Him for granting me a return on it, in my hope of reward for it; and I praise Him for not letting it impair my faith.

This resembles what is related of the sage Buzurjmihr ibn al-Bakhtakān, vizier 49.1 to Anūshirwān, who imprisoned him in anger in a cell as dark and narrow as the grave, loaded him with chains, and made him wear rough wool. He commanded that his daily ration be no more than two flaps of barley bread with a handful of coarse salt and a pannikin of water, and that his words should be counted and reported back to him.

٢،٤٩ فأقام بـزرجمهر شهورًا لا تسمع له لفظة فقال أنوشروان أدخلوا إليه أصحابه ومُروهم أن يسألوه ويفاتحوه في الكلام واسمعوا ما يجري بينهم وعرّفونيه.

٣،٤٩ فدخل إليه جماعة من المختصّين كانوا به فقالوا له أيّها الحكيم نراك في هذا الضيق والحديد والصوف والشدّة التي وقعت فيها ومع هذا فإنّ سحنة وجهك وصحّة جسمك على حالهما لم تتغيّرا فما السبب في ذلك.

٤،٤٩ فقال إنّي عملت جوارشًا من ستّة أخلاط آخذ منه كلّ يوم شيئًا فهو الذي أبقاني على ما ترون قالوا فصِفْه لنا فعسى أن نبتلى بمثل بلواك أو أحد من إخواننا فنستعمله ونَصفه له قال الخلط الأوّل الثقة بالله عزّ وجلّ والخلط الثاني علمي بأنّ كلّ مقدّر كائن والخلط الثالث الصبر خير ما استعمله الممتحنون والخلط الرابع إن لم أصبر أنا فأيّ شيء أعمل ولِمَ أعين على نفسي بالجزع والخلط الخامس قد يمكن أن أكون في شرّ ممّا أنا فيه والخلط السادس من ساعة إلى ساعة فرج.

٥،٤٩ قال فبلغ كسرى كلامه فعفا عنه.

١،٥٠ فـصلٌ لبعض كتّاب زماننا وهو عليّ بن نصر بن عليّ الطبيب

وكما أنّ الله جلّ و علا يأتي بالمحبوب من الوجه الذي قدّر ورود المكروه منه ويفتح بفرج عند انقطاع الأمل واستبهام وجوه الحيل ليحضّ سائر خلقه بما يريهم من تمام قدرته على صرف الرجاء إليه وإخلاص آمالهم في التوكّل عليه وأن لا يزووا وجوههم في وقت من الأوقات عن توقّع الرَوح منه فلا يعدلوا بآمالهم على أيّ حال من الحالات عن انتظار فرج يصدر عنه وكذلك أيضًا يسرّهم فيما ساءهم بأن كفاهم بمحنة يسيرة ما هو أعظم منها وافتداهم بملمّة سهلة ممّا كان أنكى فيهم لو لحقهم.

For several months, Buzurjmihr was not heard to utter a word. 49.2

Then Anūshirwān said, "Send his friends to him. Let them question him and lead him into conversation. Listen to what passes between them and inform me of it."

Several of his former close associates visited him, and said to him, "Sage! 49.3 We see you in confinement, in chains, clothed in wool, and fallen into this adversity; yet your face is as serene, your body as sound as ever. What is the reason that they remain unchanged?"[185]

He replied, "What has preserved me is an aid to digestion, which I have 49.4 made from six ingredients. I take a little every day."

"Give us the prescription," they said, "so that we may share it, if we or any of our comrades suffer a tribulation like yours."

He said, "The first ingredient is trust in God, Mighty and Glorious. The second is my realization that whatever has been decreed will come to pass. The third is knowing that it is best to accept one's trials. The fourth is: What is there for me but acceptance? Do I wish to be known as a faint-heart? The fifth is: Things could be worse; and the sixth: Deliverance may come at any moment."

When Chosroes[186] Anūshirwān heard what he had said, he pardoned him. 49.5

An aphoristic passage composed by a contemporary state scribe, ʿAlī ibn Naṣr 50.1 ibn ʿAlī the Physician:[187]

Just as God, Glorious and Sublime, brings good to pass from the very place whence He has decreed evil should come, and grants deliverance at the very moment when hope is gone and no recourse can be descried, thereby favoring all of His creation by showing them the completeness of His power when hope is directed toward Him alone and when they wholeheartedly hope and place their complete trust in Him, that they may never turn their faces from anticipation of His sending them comfort, nor in any manner let their expectations swerve from looking forward to the deliverance that will emanate from Him, so also He causes their woes to bring them rejoicing, inasmuch as He saves them by means of a lesser trial from a greater, and ransoms them by means of a light misfortune from what would have caused them greater injury had it befallen them.

قال إسحاق[1] العابد ٢،٥٠

ربّما امتحن الله العبد بمحنة يخلّصه بها من الهلكة فتكون تلك المحنة أجلّ نعمة.

قال سمعون[2] ٣،٥٠

إنّ من احتمل المحنة ورضي بتدبير الله تعالى في النكبة وصبر على الشدّة كشف له عن منفعتها حتّى يقف على المستور عنه من مصلحتها.

وقال عبد الله بن المعتزّ ما أوطأ راحلة الواثق بالله وآنس مثوى المطيع لله. ٤،٥٠

حكى بعض النصارى أنّ بعض الأنبياء عليهم السلام قال ٥،٥٠

المحن تأديب من الله والأدب لا يدوم فطوبى لمن تصبّر على التأديب وتثبّت عند المحنة فيجب له لبس إكليل الغلبة وتاج الفلاح الذي وعد الله به محبّيه وأهل طاعته.

قال إسحاق ٦،٥٠

احذر الضجر إذا أصابتك أسنّة المحن وأعراض الفتن فإنّ الطريق المؤدّي إلى النجاة صعب المسلك.

قال بزرجمهر ٧،٥٠

انتظار الفرج بالصبر يعقب الاغتباط.

فصل آخر لبعض كتّاب زماننا وهو عليّ بن نصر بن بشر الطبيب ١،٥١

كما أنّ الرجاء مادّة الصبر والمعين عليه فكذلك علّة الرجاء ومادّته حسن الظنّ بالله الذي لا يجوز أن يخيب فإنّا قد نستقري الكرماء فنجدهم يرفعون مَن أحسن ظنّه

---

١ س: إسماعيل. ٢ التصحيح من ل. ش: وسمعت. س: اسماعيل العابد.

The holy man Isaac[188] said: 50.2

Sometimes, by testing a servant through an ordeal that delivers him from death, God turns the ordeal into a glorious blessing.

Simeon[189] said: 50.3

Whoever bears an ordeal and is content in calamity with God's disposal, Exalted is He, and shows acceptance in adversity, to him will He reveal its utility, so that he understands the benefits it concealed.

ʿAbd Allāh ibn al-Muʿtazz[190] said: 50.4

How sure-footed is the mount of one who puts his confidence in God! How pleasant the dwelling of one who obeys God!

As related by a Christian, one of the prophets, peace on them, said: 50.5

Trials are God's discipline. The disciplining is of short duration. Blessed are they who bear it with acceptance and persevere through their trials, for they shall wear the crown of victory and the diadem of salvation, which God has promised those who love and obey Him.

Isaac the holy man said: 50.6

Be not dismayed if the shafts of trial and blades of temptation strike you, for the path that leads to salvation is hard to tread.

Buzurjmihr said: 50.7

Rejoicing will follow when deliverance is looked forward to with acceptance.

Here is another aphoristic passage composed by our contemporary, the state 51.1
scribe ʿAlī ibn Naṣr ibn Bishr the Physician:[191]

Just as hope is the substance and vehicle of acceptance and its helper, so the instrument and substance of hope is confidence in God, which cannot be disappointed.

We seek the hospitality of generous men, and find that they raise up those who have confidence in them. They avoid the sin of disappointing their

بهم ويتحوّبون من تخييب أمله فيهم ويتحرّجون من إخفاق رجاء من قصدهم فكيف بأكرم الأكرمين الذي لا يعوزه أن يمنح مؤمّليه ما يزيد على أمانيهم فيه.

٢،٥١ وأعدل الشواهد بمحبّة الله جلّ ذكره لتمسّك عبده برجابه وانتظار الروح من ظلّه ومآبه أنّ الإنسان لا يأتيه الفرج ولا تدركه النجاة إلاّ بعد إخفاق أمله في كلّ ما كان يتوجّه نحوه بآماله ورغبته وعند انغلاق مطالبه وعجز حيلته وتناهي ضرّه ومحنته ليكون ذلك باعثاً له على صرف رجائه أبداً إلى الله عزّ وجلّ وزاجراً له على تجاوز حسن ظنّه به.

١،٥٢ وروي عن عبد الله بن مسعود

الفرج والرَوح في اليقين والرضا والهمّ والحزن في الشكّ والسخط.

٢،٥٢ وكان يقول الصبور يدرك أحمد الأمور.

٣،٥٢ قال أبان بن تغلب سمعتُ أعرابياً يقول

من أفضل آداب الرجال أنّه إذا نزلت بأحدهم جائحة استعمل الصبر عليها وألهم نفسه الرجاء لزوالها حتّى كأنّه لصبره يعاين الخلاص منها والغناء توكّلاً على الله عزّ وجلّ وحسن ظنّ به فمتى لزم هذه الصفة لم يلبث أن يقضي الله حاجته ويزيل كربته وينجح طلبته ومعه دينه وعرضه ومروءته.

١،٥٣ روى الأصمعيّ عن أعرابيّ أنّه قال

خِف الشرّ من موضع الخير وارجُ الخير من موضع الشرّ فرُبّ حياة سببها طلب الموت وموت سببه طلب الحياة وأكثر ما يأتي الأمن من ناحية الخوف.

expectations and refrain from dashing the hopes of those who seek them out. How much more so the One Who is most generous of all, and has no difficulty exceeding the expectations of any who put their hope in Him!

The truest witness that God, glorious is His name, delights in His servants' 51.2
frequenting His courts and expecting to find repose in His shadow and abode, is that deliverance and salvation come to no one until they have met with disappointment from every other to whom they have brought their expectations and desires. Only when the door has been barred to requests and there is no more that they can do, and their pain and suffering are extreme, are they moved to direct their hopes ever and always toward God, Mighty and Glorious, and deflected from relinquishing their confidence in Him.

52.1
ʿAbd Allāh ibn Masʿūd is reported to have said:

Deliverance and serenity come from firm faith and resignation, sorrow and grief from doubt and anger.

He also used to say: 52.2

Those who accept what God sends achieve the worthiest ends.

Abān ibn Taghlib said, I heard a Bedouin say: 52.3

When catastrophe befalls any man, his best practice is to counter it with acceptance and inspire his soul with hope of its cessation. Then he will all but descry his release from it and the peace of mind that comes through relying wholly on God, Mighty and Glorious, and through confidence in Him. This done, God will lose no time in granting his wishes, putting an end to his affliction, and vindicating not only his request but also his faith, honor, and manhood.

Al-Aṣmaʿī reports that a Bedouin said: 53.1

Fear evil where good is, and hope for good where there is evil. Many a life comes from seeking death, and many a death is caused by seeking life. What you fear will often keep you safe.

قال مؤلّف هذا الكتاب ما أقرب هذا الكلام من قول قطريّ بن الفجاءة الخارجيّ ذكره أبو تمّام الطائيّ في كتابه المعروف بالحماسة [كامل] ٢٫٥٣

لَا يَرْكُنَنْ أَحَدٌ إِلَى ٱلْإِحْجَامِ يَوْمَ ٱلْوَغَى مُتَخَوِّفًا لِحِمَامِ
فَلَقَدْ أَرَانِي لِلرِّمَاحِ دَرِيئَةً مِنْ عَنْ يَمِينِي مَرَّةً وَأَمَامِي
حَتَّى خَضَبْتُ بِمَا تَحَدَّرَ مِنْ دَمِي أَحْنَاءَ سَرْجِي أَوْ عِنَانَ لِجَامِي
ثُمَّ ٱنْصَرَفْتُ وَقَدْ أَصَبْتُ وَلَمْ أُصَبْ جَذَعَ ٱلْبَصِيرَةِ قَارِحَ ٱلْإِقْدَامِ

فهذا مَن أحبّ الموت طلباً لحياة الذكر.

وقد أفصح بهذا الحصين بن الحمام المرّيّ حيث يقول [طويل] ٣٫٥٣

تَأَخَّرْتُ أَسْتَبْقِي ٱلْحَيَاةَ فَلَمْ أَجِدْ لِنَفْسِي حَيَاةً مِثْلَ أَنْ أَتَقَدَّمَا

وهذا كثير متّسع وليس هو ممّا نحن فيه بسبيل فنستوعبه ونستوفيه ولكنّ الحديث ذو شجون والشيء بالشيء يُذكر ونعود إلى ما كنّا فيه.

قال بعض عقلاء التجّار ما أصغر المصيبة بالأرباح إذا عادت بسلامة الأرواح. ١٫٥٤

وكأنّه من قول العرب إن تسلم الجلّة فالسخل هدر. ٢٫٥٤

ومن كلامهم لا تيأس أرض من عمران وإن جفاها الزمان. ٣٫٥٤

والعامّة تقول نهر جرى فيه الماء لا بدّ أن يعود إليه. ٤٫٥٤

The author of this book observes: This is very similar to a poem by the Kharijite Qaṭarī ibn al-Fujā'ah, which Abū Tammām quotes in his book *Valor*: 53.2

If you fear death in war,
don't seek safety in flight.
I'm the target of spears
from in front, from the right;
My gore drenches my pommel,
my cantle, my reins.
I strike down my enemy, and I survive him,
In mettle a yearling, a lion in daring.

This is an example of someone who wishes to die so that his name will live on.

The same idea is expressed elegantly by al-Ḥuṣayn ibn al-Ḥumām al-Murrī in the line: 53.3

I hung back to prolong my life,
but found I gained it by advancing.

The theme is very common, but as it has nothing to do with our topic, there is no reason to pursue or indeed include it. "Conversation tends to drift," however, and "one thing calls another to mind."[192]

Let us return to the matter in hand.

A sensible merchant said: 54.1

Getting home safely is worth more than turning a profit.

This is like the Bedouin saying: 54.2

It's worth losing a lamb to save a sheep.

Another saying is: 54.3

Exhausted fields may yet bear crops.

The common people say: 54.4

A river that has flowed once will flow again.

وقال تيمسطوس ٥،٥٤

لم يتفاضل أهل العقول والدين إلاّ في استعمال الفضل في حال القدرة والنعمة وابتذال الصبر في حال الشدّة والمحنة.

وقال بعض الحكماء ٦،٥٤

العاقل يتعزّى فيما نزل به من المكروه بأمرين أحدهما السرور بما بقي له والآخر رجاء الفرج مما نزل به والجاهل يجزع في محنته بأمرين أحدهما استكثار ما أدّي إليه والآخر تخوّفه ممّا هو أشدّ منه.

١،٥٥ وكان يقال المحن آداب الله عزّ وجلّ لخلقه وتأديب الله يفتح القلوب والأسماع والأبصار.

ووصف الحسن بن سهل المحن فقال فيها ٢،٥٥

تمحيص من الذنب وتنبيه من الغفلة وتعرّض للثواب بالصبر وتذكير بالنعمة واستدعاء للمثوبة وفي نظر الله عزّ وجلّ وقضائه الخيار.

٣،٥٥ وبلغني هذا الخبر على وجه آخر قرئ على أبي بكر الصوليّ وأنا حاضر أسمع بالبصرة في سنة خمس وثلاثين وثلثمائة في كتابه كتاب الوزراء حدّثكم أبو ذكوان القاسم بن إسماعيل قال

سمعت أبا إسحاق إبراهيم بن العبّاس بن محمّد بن صول الكاتب يصف الفضل بن سهل ويذكر تقدّمه وعلمه وكرمه وكان ممّا حدّثني به أنّه برئ من علّة كان فيها فجلس للناس وهنّوه بالعافية فلمّا فرغ الناس من كلامهم قال الفضل

إنّ في العلل لنعماً لا ينبغي للعاقل أن يجهلها تمحيص للذنب وتعرّض لثواب الصبر

Themistius said: 54.5

Philosophers and divines[193] are superior only insofar as they are virtuous in good fortune and practice acceptance in misfortune.

A certain sage said: 54.6

Two things console the rational man for the ills that befall him: first, he takes pleasure in whatever remains to him; second, he hopes for deliverance from his plight.

The fool, in his time of trial, is made wretched by two things: first, his plight, which he exaggerates; second, his fear of worse to come.

As the saying goes: 55.1

Trials are the lessons that God, Mighty and Glorious, teaches humankind. God's schooling opens up their hearts, hearing, and sight.

Al-Ḥasan ibn Sahl said, of trials: 55.2

They cleanse us of sin; they rouse us from heedlessness; they give occasion for divine reward through the exercise of acceptance; they remind us of our blessings; they call forth divine recompense. Whatever God rules and decrees is for the best, Mighty and Glorious is He.

The same report has also reached me in a different form. In Basra in the year 335 [946], in my presence and hearing, this passage from Abū Bakr al-Ṣūlī's *Book of Viziers*[194] was read back to him for verification: You cite[195] Abū Dhakwān al-Qāsim ibn Ismāʿīl saying: 55.3

I heard Abū Isḥāq Ibrāhīm ibn al-ʿAbbās ibn Muḥammad ibn Ṣūl, the state scribe,[196] describe the eminence, learning, and generosity of al-Faḍl ibn Sahl. One of the things he related to me was that, on recovering from an illness, he held audience for people to congratulate him on regaining his health.[197] When they had finished paying their compliments, al-Faḍl said:

Sicknesses bring blessings no rational person should ignore. They cleanse sin, are an occasion for acceptance to be rewarded, awaken us from heedlessness, and remind us what a blessing health is. They call forth divine

وإيقاظ من الغفلة وإذكار بالنعمة في حال الصحّة واستدعاء للمثوبة وحضّ على الصدقة وفي قضاء الله وقدره بعدُ[1] الخيار.

وكتب محمّد بن الحنفيّة إلى عبد الله بن عبّاس حين سيّره ابن الزبير عن مكّة إلى الطائف ٥٦

أمّا بعد فإنّه بلغني أنّ ابن الزبير سيّرك إلى الطائف فأحدث الله عزّ وجلّ لك بذلك أجرًا وحطّ به عنك وزرًا يا ابن عمّ إنّما يبتلى الصالحون وتعدّ الكرامة للأخيار ولو لم تؤجر إلاّ فيما تحبّ لقلّ الأجر وقد قال الله تعالى ﴿وَعَسَىٰٓ أَن تَكۡرَهُواْ شَيۡـٔٗا وَهُوَ خَيۡرٞ لَّكُمۡۖ وَعَسَىٰٓ أَن تُحِبُّواْ شَيۡـٔٗا وَهُوَ شَرّٞ لَّكُمۡ﴾ عزم الله لنا ولك بالصبر على البلاء والشكر على النعماء ولا أشمت بنا وبك الأعداء والسلام.

وكتب بعض الكتّاب إلى صديق له في محنة لحقته ٥٧

إنّ الله تعالى ليمتحن العبد ليكثر التواضع له والاستعانة به ويجدّد الشكر على ما يوليه من كفايته ويأخذ بيده في شدّته لأنّ دوام النعم والعافية يبطران الإنسان حتّى يعجب بنفسه ويعدل عن ذكر ربّه وقد قال الشاعر [بسيط]

لَا يَتْرُكُ اللهُ عَبْدًا لَيْسَ يَذْكُرُهُ　　مِمَّنْ يُؤَدِّبُهُ أَوْ مَنْ يُؤَنِّبُهُ
أَوْ نِعْمَةٍ تَقْتَضِي شُكْرًا يَدُومُ لَهُ　　أَوْ نِقْمَةٍ حِينَ يَنْسَى الشُّكْرَ تَنْكُبُهُ

وقال الحسن البصريّ ١،٥٨

الخير الذي لا شرّ فيه هو الشكر مع العافية والصبر عند المحنة فكم من منعم عليه غير شاكر وكم مبتلى بمحنة وهو غير صابر.

١ عبدُ: ساقط من ل.

recompense. They encourage acts of charity. What God ordains and decrees is indeed for the best.

When Ibn al-Zubayr made ʿAbd Allāh ibn ʿAbbās leave Mecca and go to Taif, 56
Muḥammad ibn al-Ḥanafiyyah wrote to him:

Now I come to what I have to say.[198] I have been told that Ibn al-Zubayr has made you go to Taif. Cousin, may this be the occasion for God, Mighty and Glorious, to reward you and relieve you of a burden. Only the God-fearing are made to suffer tribulation and only the virtuous are held in esteem. Few would be rewarded were we rewarded only for what is agreeable. God, Exalted, says, «You may dislike what is good for you and like what is bad for you.»[199] His will is that both you and I should accept our tribulations and be thankful for His favor. May our enemies never rejoice in our discomfiture! Farewell!

A state scribe wrote to a friend in time of trial: 57

God, exalted is He, tries His servants in order to make them more humble and dependent, so that they will once more thank Him for His protection and for standing by them in adversity; for uninterrupted prosperity and well-being make men insolent, vain, and forgetful of their Lord. As the poet[200] says:

> By teaching or by reprimand,
> God makes His servants mindful of Him:
> His blessings demand ceaseless thanks,
> His wrath pursues the thankless.

Ḥasan of Basra said: 58.1

There is one good that is unmixed with any evil. It is thankfulness in well-being and acceptance of one's trials. How many are ungrateful for their blessings, and how many are unable to accept tribulation!

وقال أبو الحسن المدائنيّ في كتابه كتاب الفرج بعد الشدّة والضيقة ٢،٥٨

كان ابن شبرمة إذا نزلت به شدّة يقول سحابة ثمّ تنقشع.

وقال في كتابه هذا عن جعفر بن سليمان الهاشميّ قال قال بعض الحكماء ٣،٥٨

آخر الهمّ أوّل الفرج.

وكان جعفر يقول قد وجدناه كذلك.

وقد ذكر هذا الخبر القاضي أبو الحسين في كتابه كتاب الفرج بعد الشدّة عن المدائنيّ ٤،٥٨
هكذا.

وذكر أبو الحسين القاضي في كتابه كتاب الفرج بعد الشدّة فقال حدّثني بعض أصحابنا قال حدّثني الحسن بن مكرّم قال حدّثني ابن أبي عديّ عن شعبة عن قتادة عن زرارة بن أوفى عن أبي هريرة قال

سمعت النبيّ صلّى الله عليه وسلّم يقول لَأنْ أكون في شدّة أتوقّع بعدها رخاء أحبّ إليّ من أن أكون في رخاء أتوقّع بعده شدّة.

وذُكر عن النبيّ صلّى الله عليه وسلّم بغير إسناد أنّه قال ١،٥٩

لو كان العسر في كوّة لجاء يسران فأخرجاه.

قال مؤلّف هذا الكتاب ٢،٥٩

كان لي في هذا الحديث خبر طريف وذلك أنّي كنت قد لجأتُ إلى البطيحة هاربًا من نكبة لحقتني واعتصمت بأميرها معين الدولة أبي الحسين عمران بن شاهين السلميّ على ما كان يقول رحمه الله فألفيت هناك جماعة من معارفي بالبصرة وواسط خائفين

Al-Madāʾinī says, in his book *Deliverance following Adversity and Hardship*: 58.2

Whenever adversity befell Ibn Shubrumah, he would say, "It is but a cloud and will soon disperse."

In the same book, al-Madāʾinī quotes Jaʿfar ibn Sulaymān al-Hāshimī as saying: 58.3
A certain sage has said:

The end of sorrow is the beginning of deliverance,

and adds:

Jaʿfar used to say, "We have found this to be true."

Judge Abū l-Ḥusayn quotes this report in the same form in his *Book of Deliverance following Adversity*, where he also says: 58.4

I cite a colleague, citing al-Ḥasan ibn Mukarram, citing Ibn Abī ʿUdayy, quoting Shuʿbah, quoting Qatādah, quoting Zurārah ibn Awfā, quoting Abū Hurayrah, who said:

I heard the Prophet, God bless and keep him, say, "I would rather anticipate prosperity in adversity than adversity in prosperity."

It has been reported, with no chain of transmitters, that the Prophet, God bless and keep him, said: 59.1

Were hardship in a loophole, ease twice over[201] would come and dislodge it.

The author of this book observes: 59.2

In connection with this report, a curious thing once happened to me. Fleeing a calamity, I had taken refuge in the Marshes, putting myself under the protection of the Lord of the Marshes, Muʿīn al-Dawlah Abū l-Ḥusayn ʿImrān ibn Shāhīn (a member of the tribe of Sulaym, or so he used to claim, God rest his soul).

على نفوسهم قد هربوا من ابن بقيّة الذي كان في ذلك الوقت وزيرًا ولجأوا إلى البطيحة فكنّا نجتمع في المسجد الجامع بشقّشى الذي بناه معزّ الدولة أبو الحسين فنتشاكى أحوالنا ونتمنّى الفرج ممّا نحن فيه من الخوف والشدّة والشقاء.

٣،٥٩ فقال لي أبو الحسن محمّد بن عبد الله بن جيشان الصِلحيّ التاجر وكان هذا في يوم الجمعة لتسع ليال خلون من جمادى الأولى سنة خمس وستّين وثلثمائة حدّثني في هذا اليوم أبو محمّد الحسن بن محمّد بن عثمان بن قنيف وكان أحد خلفاء الحجّاب في دار المقتدر بالله وهو شيخ مشهور ملازم الآن خدمة معين الدولة قال حدّثنا أبو القاسم ابن بنت منيع قال حدّثنا أبو نصر التمّار قال حدّثنا حمّاد بن سلمة عن ثابت البنانيّ عن أنس بن مالك قال

قال رسول الله صلّى الله عليه وسلّم لو دخل العسر كوّة جاء يسران فأخرجاه.

فلمّا سمعت ذلك قلت بديهًا [منسرح]

إِنَّا رُوِينَا عَنِ ٱلنَّبِيِّ رَسُولِ الـ ـلَّهِ فِيمَا أُفِيدَ مِنْ أَدَبِهِ
لَوْ دَخَلَ ٱلْعُسْرُ كُوَّةً لَأَتَى يُسْـ ـرَانِ فَاسْتَخْرَجَاهُ مِنْ ثَقْبِهِ

٤،٥٩ فما مضى على هذا المجلس إلاّ أربعة أشهر حتّى فرّج الله تعالى عنّي وعن كثير ممّن حضر ذلك المجلس من الممتحنين وردّنا إلى عوائده عندنا فله الحمد والشكر.

٥،٥٩ وجدت هذا الخبر على غير هذا فقد حدّثنا به من أصل كتابه جعفر بن أبي طالب ابن البهلول قال حدّثنا أبو القاسم عبد الله بن محمّد البغويّ قال حدّثني عليّ بن الجعد قال أنبأنا شعبة عن معاوية بن قرّة عمّن حدّثه عن عبد الله بن مسعود قال

لو أنّ العسر دخل في جحر لجاء اليسر حتّى يدخل معه قال الله تعالى ﴿فَإِنَّ مَعَ ٱلْعُسْرِ يُسْرًا إِنَّ مَعَ ٱلْعُسْرِ يُسْرًا﴾.

There I found several of my acquaintances from Basra and Wāsiṭ who, fleeing in fear of their lives from Ibn Baqiyyah, who was then vizier, had also sought refuge in the Marshes. We used to meet in the Friday Mosque that Muʿizz al-Dawlah had built at Shaqshā to bemoan our situation and hope and pray for deliverance from our wretched and fearful plight.

It was in these circumstances that the merchant Abū l-Ḥasan Muḥammad 59.3
ibn ʿAbd Allāh ibn Jayshān of Fam al-Ṣilḥ said to me, on Friday 9 Jumada I in the year 365 [14 January 976]:

Today a saying of the Prophet was related to me by Abū Muḥammad al-Ḥasan ibn Muḥammad ibn ʿUthmān ibn Qanīf, who used to be a deputy chamberlain in the palace of the caliph al-Muqtadir and is a well-known transmitter of Prophetic traditions, now in the service of Muʿīn al-Dawlah. He said: We cite Abū l-Qāsim Ibn Bint Manīʿ, citing Abū Naṣr the Date Merchant, citing Ḥammād ibn Salamah, quoting Thābit al-Banānī, citing Anas ibn Mālik, who said:

The Messenger of God, God bless and keep him, said, "Were hardship to wedge itself in a loophole, ease twice over would come and dislodge it."

On hearing this, I immediately extemporized a couplet:[202]

From God's Apostle come words of wisdom
  that we have just been told:
Were Hardship wedged tight, Ease Twice Over
  would flush it from its hole.

Only four months after this gathering, God Exalted delivered me and many 59.4
of the sufferers who had been present there, restoring to us the way of life to which He had accustomed us, praise and thanks be to Him.

I have read this hadith in a different version: We cite Jaʿfar ibn Abī Ṭālib 59.5
Ibn al-Buhlūl, who read it out to us from his notebook, saying: We cite Abū l-Qāsim Ibn Bint Manīʿ of Baghshūr, citing ʿAlī ibn al-Jaʿd, who said: We quote Shuʿbah, quoting Muʿāwiyah ibn Qurrah, quoting an unnamed transmitter, quoting ʿAbd Allāh ibn Masʿūd, who said:

Were hardship to enter a stone, ease would enter it at the same time. God has said, «So, the hardship shall bring ease. The hardship shall bring ease».[203]

وحدّثنا عليّ بن الحسن قال حدّثنا ابن الجرّاح قال حدّثنا ابن أبي الدنيا قال حدّثنا عليّ بن الجعد فذكر نحوه بإسناده.

٦،٥٩ وأخبرني أبي[١] قال قال جعفر بن محمّد بن عيينة حدّثنا محمّد بن معمّر قال حدّثنا حُميد بن حمّاد قال حدّثنا عائذ بن شريح قال سمعت أنس بن مالك قال كان رسول الله صلّى الله عليه وسلّم ينظر إلى جحر بحيال وجهه فقال

لو جاءت العسرة حتّى تدخل تحت هذا الجحر لجاءت اليسرة حتّى تخرجها فأنزل الله تعالى ﴿فَإِنَّ مَعَ ٱلْعُسْرِ يُسْرًا إِنَّ مَعَ ٱلْعُسْرِ يُسْرًا﴾.

١،٦٠ وذكر القاضي أبو الحسين في كتابه كتاب الفرج بعد الشدّة بغير إسناد أنّ عليّاً عليه السلام قال

عند تناهي الشدّة تكون الفرجة وعند تضايق البلاء يكون الرخاء ومع العسر يكون اليسر.

٢،٦٠ وذكر عنه عليه السلام أنّه قال

ما أبالي بالعسر رُميت أو باليسر لأنّ حقّ الله تعالى في العسر الرضا والصبر وفي اليسر الحمد والشكر.

٣،٦٠ قال مؤلّف هذا الكتاب حدّثني بعض الشيعة بغير إسناد قال

قصد أعرابيّ أمير المؤمنين عليّاً عليه السلام فقال إنّي ممتحن فعلّمني شيئاً أنتفع به.

٤،٦٠ فقال يا أعرابيّ إنّ للمحن أوقاتاً ولها غايات فاجتهاد العبد في محنته قبل إزالة الله تعالى إيّاها زيادة فيها يقول الله عزّ وجلّ ﴿إِنْ أَرَادَنِىَ ٱللَّهُ بِضُرٍّ هَلْ هُنَّ كَـٰشِفَـٰتُ ضُرِّهِۦٓ

١ ل: وأخبرني أبي بإسناد لا أقوم عليه.

We also cite ʿAlī ibn al-Ḥasan, citing Ibn al-Jarrāḥ, citing Ibn Abī l-Dunyā, citing ʿAlī ibn al-Jaʿd, who cites this in similar form with the same chain of transmitters.

My father told me: Jaʿfar ibn Muḥammad ibn ʿUyaynah said: We cite Muḥammad ibn Muʿammar, citing Ḥumayd ibn Ḥammād, citing ʿĀʾidh ibn Shurayḥ, who said: I heard Anas ibn Mālik say: **59.6**

Contemplating a stone that lay before him, the Messenger of God, God bless and keep him, said, "Were hardship to squeeze beneath this stone, ease would be sure to come and dislodge it."

God Exalted then sent down the verses: «So, the hardship shall bring ease. The hardship shall bring ease».

In his *Book of Deliverance following Adversity*, Judge Abū l-Ḥusayn reports, **60.1**
with no chain of transmitters, that ʿAlī ibn Abī Ṭālib, peace on him, said:

When adversity is at its worst, then comes relief. When tribulation grips tightest, then comes release; and with hardship comes ease.

He is also reported to have said, peace on him: **60.2**

What care I whether I endure hardship or enjoy ease, for in hardship we owe God Exalted resignation and acceptance and in ease, praise and thankfulness.

The author of this book says: A Shiʿi told me, with no chain of transmitters: **60.3**

A Bedouin sought out the Commander of the Faithful, ʿAlī, and said, "I am in a predicament. Teach me something that will help."

ʿAlī said, "Bedouin, each trial has its time and purpose. If a man struggles **60.4**
against his ordeal before God Exalted chooses to remove it, he will only make it worse. God, Mighty and Exalted, says, «If God means to hurt me, can they take away His hurt? Or if He means to show me compassion, can they hold back His compassion? Say: God is all I need; on Him those who trust in Him

أَوْ أَرَادَنِي بِرَحْمَةٍ هَلْ هُنَّ مُمْسِكَٰتُ رَحْمَتِهِۦ قُلْ حَسْبِيَ ٱللَّهُ عَلَيْهِ يَتَوَكَّلُ ٱلْمُتَوَكِّلُونَ﴾ ولكن استعن بالله واصبر وأكثر من الاستغفار فإنّ الله عزّ وجلّ وعد الصابرين خيرًا وقال ﴿ٱسْتَغْفِرُوا۟ رَبَّكُمْ إِنَّهُۥ كَانَ غَفَّارًا يُرْسِلِ ٱلسَّمَآءَ عَلَيْكُم مِّدْرَارًا وَيُمْدِدْكُم بِأَمْوَٰلٍ وَبَنِينَ وَيَجْعَل لَّكُمْ جَنَّٰتٍ وَيَجْعَل لَّكُمْ أَنْهَٰرًا﴾.

فانصرف الرجل فقال أمير المؤمنين عليه السلام [طويل] ٥،٦٠

إِذَا لَمْ يَكُنْ عَوْنٌ مِنَ اللهِ لِلْفَتَى فَأَوَّلُ مَا يَجْنِي عَلَيْهِ ٱجْتِهَادُهُ

حدّثنا أبو محمّد الحسن بن محمّد المهلّبيّ في وزارته قال ٦١

كنت في وقت من الأوقات يعني في أوّل أمره قد دُفعت إلى شدّة شديدة وخوف عظيم لا حلية لي فيهما فأقمت يومي قلقًا وهجم الليل فلم أعرف الغمض فلجأت إلى الصلاة والدعاء وأقبلت على البكاء في سجودي والتضرّع ومسألة الله عزّ وجلّ تعجيل الفرج لي وأصبحت من غد على قريب من حالي إلّا أنّي قد سكنت قليلًا فلم ينسلخ اليوم حتّى جاءني الغياث من الله تعالى وفرّج عنّي ما كنت فيه على أفضل ما أردت فقلت [طويل]

بَعَثْتُ إِلَى رَبِّ ٱلْعَطَايَا رِسَالَةً تَوَسَّلَ لِي فِيهَا دُعَاءٌ مُنَاصِحُ
فَجَاءَ جَوَابٌ بِالْإِجَابَةِ وَٱنْجَلَتْ بِهَا كُرَبٌ ضَاقَتْ بِهِنَّ ٱلْجَوَانِحُ

أخبرنا أبو عبيد الله محمّد بن عمران بن موسى قال حدّثنا ابن دريد قال أخبرنا السكن بن سعيد عن محمّد بن عبّاد عن ابن الكلبيّ عن أبيه قال كان عمرو بن أحيحة الأوسيّ يقول ٦٢

عند تناهي الشدّة تكون الفرجة وعند تضايق البلاء يكون الرخاء ولا أبالي أيّ الأمرين نزل بي عسر أم يسر لأنّ كلّ واحد منهما يزول بصاحبه.

place all their trust».[204] Therefore, seek God's help, show acceptance, and pray much for forgiveness, for God, Mighty and Glorious, has promised good things to those who show acceptance, saying, «Beg forgiveness of your Lord; He is ever-forgiving. He sends down rain on you from the sky in streams. He supports you with cattle and offspring. He makes for you gardens. He makes for you watercourses».”[205]

As the man went on his way, the Commander of the Faithful said: 60.5

A man's first sin is to struggle
when he gets no help from God.

61 We cite Abū Muḥammad al-Ḥasan ibn Muḥammad al-Muhallabī, who told us, when he was vizier:[206]

Once upon a time (that is, at the start of his career) I found myself helpless in dire and terrifying straits. A whole day passed in agitation, and when night fell I knew no rest. I turned to prayer and supplication, weeping, begging, and imploring God, Mighty and Glorious, to hasten my deliverance as I prostrated myself.

The next morning, I was almost as distraught, if a little less agitated; but hardly had the day passed before succor came to me from God Exalted, and I was delivered in a way that met my dearest wishes. As a result, I composed this poem:

I sent a message to the Lord of Gifts,
a prayer to be my friend and plead for me.
The answer He returned granted my plea,
and from the grip of anguish set me free.

62 Abū ʿUbayd Allāh Muḥammad ibn ʿImrān al-Marzubānī informed us, citing Ibn Durayd as saying: Al-Sakan ibn Saʿīd related to us, quoting Muḥammad ibn ʿAbbād, quoting Hishām ibn Muḥammad Ibn al-Kalbī, quoting his father, that ʿAmr ibn Uḥyaḥah al-Awsī used to say:

When adversity is at its worst, then comes relief. When tribulation grips tightest, then comes release;[207] I do not care whether I suffer hardship or enjoy ease, for each removes the other.

١،٦٣ أخبرني أبو محمّد الحسن بن عبد الرحمن بن خلّاد الرامهرمزيّ خليفة أبي على القضاء بها قال حدّثنا محمّد بن العبّاس اليزيديّ قال حدّثني عمّي الفضل بن محمّد اليزيديّ قال

أراد جعفر بن محمّد الحجّ فمنعه المنصور.

٢،٦٣ فقال الحمد لله الكافي سبحان الله الأعلى حسبي الله وكفى ليس من الله منجى ماشاء الله قضى ليس وراء الله منتهى ﴿إِنِّي تَوَكَّلْتُ عَلَى ٱللَّهِ رَبِّي وَرَبِّكُمْ مَّا مِن دَآبَّةٍ إِلَّا هُوَ ءَاخِذٌ بِنَاصِيَتِهَآ إِنَّ رَبِّي عَلَىٰ صِرَٰطٍ مُّسْتَقِيمٍ﴾.

اللّٰهمّ إنّ هذا عبد من عبيدك خلقته كما خلقتني ليس له عليّ فضل إلاّ ما فضلته عليّ به فاكفني شرّه وارزقني خيره واقدح لي في قلبه المحبّة واصرف عنّي أذاه لا إله إلاّ أنت سبحان الله ﴿رَبُّ ٱلْعَرْشِ ٱلْعَظِيمِ﴾ وصلّى الله على محمّد النبيّ وعلى آله وسلّم كثيراً.

٣،٦٣ قال فأذن له المنصور في الحجّ.

I was informed by Abū Muḥammad al-Ḥasan Ibn Khallād of Rāmhurmuz, my father's deputy there as judge,[208] citing Muḥammad ibn al-ʿAbbās al-Yazīdī, citing his paternal uncle, al-Faḍl ibn Muḥammad al-Yazīdī: 63.1

Jaʿfar al-Ṣādiq wished to perform the Pilgrimage, but the caliph al-Manṣūr would not permit it.[209]

Jaʿfar said: "Praise be to God, the Sufficient. Glory be to God, the Sublime. 63.2 God is all I need, He suffices me. There is nowhere to escape from God. What God wills is decreed. God is infinite. I «have placed all my trust in God, my Lord and your Lord. There is no creature whose governance is not in His hand. The path of my Lord is straight».[210]

"O God! This man is one of Your servants; You created him as You created me; he has no superiority to me other than what You have allowed him. Therefore preserve me from his malice and grant me his good will, kindle love for me in his heart and let him not harm me. There is no god but You. Glory to God, «Lord of the mighty Throne».[211] Much may God bless, and may He keep, Muḥammad the Prophet and his kin."

After this, al-Manṣūr allowed him to perform the Pilgrimage. 63.3

الباب الثالث

من بُشّر بفرج من نطق فال
ونجا من محنة بقول أو دعاء أو ابتهال

أخبرني أبو بكر محمّد بن يحيى الصوليّ بالبصرة سنة خمس وثلاثين وثلثمائة قراءة عليه وأنا أسمع عن البرقيّ قال ١،٦٤

رأيت امرأة بالبادية وقد جاء البَرَد فذهب بزرع كان لها فجاء الناس يعزّونها فرفعت طرفها الى السماء وقالت اللّهمّ أنت المأمول لأحسن الخلف وبيدك التعويض عمّا تلف فافعل بنا ما أنت أهله فإنّ أرزاقنا عليك وآمالنا مصروفة إليك.

قال فلم أبرح حتّى جاء رجل من مياسير أهل البلد[1] فحُدّث بما كان فوهب لها خمسمائة دينار. ٢،٦٤

وحدّثني أبي في المذاكرة من لفظه وحفظه ولم أكتبه عنه في الحال وعلق بحفظي والمعنى واحد ولعلّ اللفظ يزيد أو ينقص عن أبي محمّد عبد الله بن أحمد بن حمدون لا أظنّ إلّا أنّه هو سمعه منه أو حدّثه من سمعه من عبد الله بن أحمد بن حمدون نديم المعتضد بالله عن المعتضد أنّه قال ١،٦٥

لمّا ضرّب إسماعيل بن بلبل بيني وبين أبي الموفّق فأوحشه منّي حتّى حبسني الحبسة المشهورة وكنت أتخوّف القتل صباحاً ومساءً ولا آمن أن يرفع إسماعيل عنّي ما يزيد

١ كذا في ل، وفي ش: رجل من الأجلاء.

Chapter Three

Presages bringing tidings of delivery to those saved from trials by speech, prayer, or entreaty

I cite al-Barqī, on the authority of Abū Bakr Muḥammad ibn Yaḥyā al-Ṣūlī,[212] 64.1
to whom I heard this was read back for verification in Basra in the year 335 [946]:

I saw a woman out in the countryside after hail had fallen and destroyed all her crops. People came to commiserate; she responded by raising her eyes heavenward and saying, "O God! You are our hope of ample restitution; You have power to compensate for what has been destroyed. Deal with us as befits You: On You we rely for our provision; all our hopes are placed in You."

No sooner had she said this than a wealthy local appeared and, on being told 64.2
what had happened, made her a gift of five hundred dinars.

The following is something my father transmitted to me in the course of con- 65.1
versation, in his own words, from memory. Although I did not write it down at once, it stuck in my recollection; there may be a few words more or less, but the sense is the same. He cited Abū Muḥammad ʿAbd Allāh ibn Aḥmad Ibn Ḥamdūn, the court companion of the caliph al-Muʿtaḍid. To the best of my knowledge, his source was Ibn Ḥamdūn, viva voce, or else he transmitted al-Muʿtaḍid's own words as told him viva voce by Ibn Ḥamdūn.

Ibn Ḥamdūn said: When he was caliph, al-Muʿtaḍid told me:

Ismāʿīl ibn Bulbul stirred up trouble between my father al-Muwaffaq and me, and drove us apart. This led to the famous incident in which my father imprisoned me. Day and night I lived in fear of death, convinced that Ismāʿīl would report whatever I said to him and make him so angry that he would

في غيظ الموفّق عليّ فيأمر بقتلي فكنت كذلك حتّى خرج الموفّق الى الجبل فازداد خوفي وأشفقت أن يكاتبه[1] عنّي إسماعيل بكذب فيجعل غيبته طريقاً إليه فلا يكشفه ويأمر بقتلي فأقبلت على الدعاء والتضرّع إلى الله والابتهال في تخليصي.

٢،٦٥ وكان إسماعيل يجيئني في كلّ يوم مراعياً خبري ويريني أنّ ذلك خدمة لي فدخل إليّ يوماً وبيدي المصحف وأنا أقرأ فتركته وأخذت أحادثه فقال أيّها الأمير أعطني المصحف لأتفاءل لك به فلم أجبه بشيء.

٣،٦٥ فأخذ المصحف ففتحه فكان في أوّل سطر منه ﴿عَسَىٰ رَبُّكُمْ أَن يُهْلِكَ عَدُوَّكُمْ وَيَسْتَخْلِفَكُمْ فِى ٱلْأَرْضِ فَيَنظُرَ كَيْفَ تَعْمَلُونَ﴾ فاسودّ وجهه واربدّ. وخلط الورق وفتحه الثانية وخرج ﴿وَنُرِيدُ أَن نَّمُنَّ عَلَى ٱلَّذِينَ ٱسْتُضْعِفُوا۟ فِى ٱلْأَرْضِ وَنَجْعَلَهُمْ أَئِمَّةً وَنَجْعَلَهُمُ ٱلْوَٰرِثِينَ﴾ إلى قوله ﴿يَحْذَرُونَ﴾ فازداد قلقاً واضطراباً.

وفتحه الثالثة فخرج ﴿وَعَدَ ٱللَّهُ ٱلَّذِينَ ءَامَنُوا۟ مِنكُمْ وَعَمِلُوا۟ ٱلصَّٰلِحَٰتِ لَيَسْتَخْلِفَنَّهُمْ فِى ٱلْأَرْضِ كَمَا ٱسْتَخْلَفَ ٱلَّذِينَ مِن قَبْلِهِمْ﴾ فوضع المصحف من يده وقال أيّها الأمير أنت والله الخليفة بغير شكّ فما حقّ بشارتي.

٤،٦٥ فقلت الله الله في أمري احقن دمي أسأل الله أن يبقي أمير المؤمنين والأمير الناصر وما أنا وهذا ومثلك في عقلك لا يطلق مثل هذا القول بمثل هذا الاتّفاق.

٥،٦٥ فأمسك عنّي وما زال يحدّثني ويخرجني من حديث ويدخلني في غيره إلى أن جرى حديث ما بيني وبين أبي فأقبل يحلف لي بأيمان غليظة أنّه لم يكن له في أمري صنع ولا سعاية بمكروه فصدّقته ولم أزل أخاطبه بما تطيب به نفسه خوفاً من أن تزيد وحشته فيسرع في التدبير لتلفي إلى أن انصرف. ثمّ صار إليّ بعد ذلك وأخذ في التنصّل والاعتذار وأنا أظهر له التصديق والقبول حتّى سكن ولم يشكّ أنّي معترف ببراءة ساحته.

---

[1] كذا في بن، س، ل. وفي ش: يحدّثه.

order my execution. This continued until al-Muwaffaq set off for al-Jabal on campaign,[213] when I grew even more frightened, fearing that Ismāʿīl would use his absence to manipulate him into having me executed by writing him lies about me that would go unquestioned. I fell to praying, beseeching, and entreating God for my release.

Now, every day Ismāʿīl would call on me so as to keep watch on me—though he pretended that he came to pay his respects. One day he found me holding a Qurʾan, which I laid aside to speak to him. 65.2

"Prince," he said, "give me your Qurʾan and I'll predict your future from it."

I refused flatly.

But he took it and opened it, and the first line he encountered was: «It may be that your Lord will destroy your enemy and make you caliph[214] in the land and scrutinize how you act then!» 65.3

His face darkened; he glowered. He riffled the pages and opened the Qurʾan again. This time it said: «Yet We will favor those that are deemed powerless. We shall make them leaders;[215] We shall make them the inheritors . . . and make them make Pharaoh and Haman and their hosts see what they dreaded.»[216]

Increasingly uneasy and agitated, he opened the volume for the third time. It said: «God has promised those of you who show faith and act righteously to make you caliph in the land as he made those before you.»[217]

At this, he put down the Qurʾan and said, "Prince! You will be caliph. There is no doubt about it, I swear. What will you give me in return for giving you the good tidings?"

I replied: "Unhappy me! Spare my life! I beseech God to preserve both the caliph and Prince al-Nāṣir.[218] What have I to do with being caliph? A man of your intelligence has no business saying such things because of a coincidence." 65.4

Ismāʿīl let the subject drop and resumed the conversation, leading it from one thing to another until it touched on the bad relations between my father and me. He swore heartily that they were nothing to do with his meddling and slander—which I pretended to believe. So as not to alienate him any further, lest he hasten my destruction, I was all conciliation until he left. 65.5

Subsequently he came to me full of excuses and apologies, which, to reassure him, I made a show of believing and accepting, leaving him convinced that I thought him innocent.

٦،٦٥ فما كان بأسرع من أن جاء الموفّق من الجبل وقد اشتدّت علّته ومات فأخرجني الغلمان من الحبس فصيّروني مكانه وفرّج الله عنّي وفاجأني[١] الخلافة ومكّنني من عدوّي وعدوّ الله[٢] إسماعيل بن بلبل فأنفذت حكم الله فيه.

١،٦٦ وحدّثني عليّ بن هشام الكاتب قال سمعت أبا عبد الله الباقطائيّ يقول سمعت عبيد الله بن سليمان يقول في وزارته قال لي أبي

كنت يوماً في حبس محمّد بن عبد الملك الزيّات في خلافة الواثق آيس ما كنت من الفرج وأشدّ محنة وغمّاً حتّى وردت عليّ رقعة أخي الحسن بن وهب وفيها شعر له [كامل]

مِحَنٌ أَبَا أَيُّوبَ أَنْتَ مَحَلُّهَا ... فَإِذَا جَزِعْتَ مِنَ ٱلْخُطُوبِ فَمَنْ لَهَا
إِنَّ ٱلَّذِي عَقَدَ ٱلَّذِي انْعَقَدَتْ بِهِ ... عُقَدُ ٱلْمَكَارِهِ فِيكَ يُحْسِنُ حَلَّهَا
فَٱصْبِرْ فَإِنَّ اللهَ يُعْقِبُ فُرْجَةً ... وَلَعَلَّهَا أَنْ تَنْجَلِي وَلَعَلَّهَا
وَعَسَى تَكُونُ قَرِيبَةً مِنْ حَيْثُ لَا ... تَرْجُو وَتَمْحُو عَنْ جَدِيدِكَ ذُلَّهَا

قال فتفاءلت بذلك وقويت نفسي فكتبت إليه [كامل]

صَبَّرْتَنِي وَوَعَظْتَنِي وَأَنَا لَهَا ... وَسَتَنْجَلِي بَلْ لَا أَقُولُ لَعَلَّهَا
وَيَحُلُّهَا مَنْ كَانَ صَاحِبَ عَقْدِهَا ... ثِقَةً بِهِ إِذْ كَانَ يَمْلِكُ حَلَّهَا

٢،٦٦ قال فلم أصلّ العتمة ذلك اليوم حتّى أطلقت فصلّيتها في داري.[٣]

٣،٦٦ وروي أنّ هاتين الرقعتين وقعتا بيد الواثق الرسالة والجواب فأمر بإطلاق سليمان

١ كذا في بن، س. وفي ش: وقاد الخلافة إليّ. ٢ كذا في بن، س. وفي ش: من عدوّي. ٣ كذا في بن. يلي هذه الجملة في ب، ل، ش: ولم يمض يومي ذاك حتّى فرّج الله عنّي وأطلقت من حبسي.

Al-Muwaffaq returned from al-Jabal gravely ill, and died. The Turkish troops lost no time in taking me from prison and setting me in his place. God delivered me, making me heir to the caliphate unexpectedly, and giving into my hands Ismāʿīl ibn Bulbul, God's enemy and mine, on whom I executed God's judgment.[219] 65.6

I cite ʿAlī ibn Hishām, the state scribe, who said I heard Abū ʿAbd Allāh of Bā Qaṭāyā say I heard ʿUbayd Allāh ibn Sulaymān ibn Wahb say, when he was vizier My father Abū Ayyūb Sulaymān ibn Wahb told me: 66.1

During the caliphate of al-Wāthiq, I was imprisoned by Ibn al-Zayyāt,[220] and was laboring under the grief of the ordeal in utter despair of deliverance, when I received a note from my brother al-Ḥasan ibn Wahb with a poem that he had composed:

Abū Ayyūb! Ordeals have befallen you.
If you let misfortunes grieve you, who shall withstand them?
He Who has let the knots of calamity bind you,
Well can He loose them!
Who knows, who knows but that they may dissolve?
Therefore accept them, for God will make joy follow:
It may be near, from whence you do not hope,[221]
And it will wipe the stain from your young life.

I took this as a prediction. My spirits rose, and I wrote in reply:

Your exhortation to accept I follow.
I know the knot of woe will be dissolved;
That He who tied the knot can loosen it,
And He alone. In Him I put my trust.

And indeed I was released from my imprisonment before the bedtime prayer,[222] which I performed in my own house. 66.2

It is related that both notes—the letter and the reply—fell into the hands of al-Wāthiq, who ordered Sulaymān's release, saying, "By God! I will leave no 66.3

وقال والله لا تركتُ في حبسي من يرجو الفرج ولا سيّما من خدمني فأطلقه على كره من ابن الزيّات لذلك.

١،٦٧ وحدّثني بعض شيوخنا بإسناد ذهب عنّي حفظه وبلغني عن صالح بن مسمار فجمعت بين الخبرين

أنّ الحسن البصريّ دخل على الحجّاج بواسط فلمّا رأى بناءه قال الحمد لله أنّ هؤلاء الملوك ليرون في أنفسهم عبرًا وأنّا لنرى فيهم عبرًا يعمد أحدهم إلى قصر فيشيّده وإلى فرش فيتّخذه وقد حفّ به غلمانه[١] ثمّ يقول ألا فانظروا ما صنعت فقد رأينا يا عدوّ الله ما صنعت فماذا يا أفسق الفسقة ويا أفجر الفجرة أمّا أهل السماء فلعنوك وأمّا أهل الأرض فمقتوك.

٢،٦٧ ثمّ خرج وهو يقول إنّما أخذ الله الميثاق على العلماء ليبيّننّه للنّاس ولا يكتمونه.

فاغتاظ الحجّاج غيظًا شديدًا ثمّ قال يا أهل الشام هذا عُبيد أهل البصرة يشتمني في وجهي فلا ينكر عليه أحد عليّ به وآلله لأقتلنّه.

٣،٦٧ فمضى أهل الشام فأحضروه وقد أعلم بما قال فكان في طريقه يحرّك شفتيه بما لا يسمع.

فلمّا دخل على الحجّاج رأى السيف والنطع بين يديه وهو متغيّظ فلمّا وقعت عليه عين الحجّاج كلّمه بكلام غليظ. ورفق به الحسن ووعظه فأمر الحجّاج بالسيف والنطع فرفعا ثمّ لم يزل الحسن يمرّ في كلامه إلى أن دعا الحجّاج بالطعام فأكلا وبالوضوء فتوضّآ وبالغالية فغلّفه[٢] بيده ثمّ صرفه مكرّمًا.

٤،٦٧ وقال صالح بن مسمار قيل للحسن بن أبي الحسن بم كنت تحرّك شفتيك.

قال قلت يا غياثي عند دعوتي ويا عدّتي في ملمّتي ويا ربّي عند كربتي ويا صاحبي في

---

١ غلمانه: كذا في ب، ل. وفي ش: ذباب طمع وفراش نار. ٢ كذا.

one in my prison who puts his hope in deliverance, especially one who has served me." He had Sulaymān released despite Ibn al-Zayyāt's objections.

I cite one of our teachers, on a chain of authorities that I do not recall. I also have this from Ṣāliḥ ibn Mismār, and have merged the two accounts: 67.1

Ḥasan of Basra paid a visit to al-Ḥajjāj in Wāsiṭ. When he saw what he had built for himself, he exclaimed, "Praise be to God! These grandees think of themselves as examples, but we see them as warnings. One will build himself a mighty palace[223] and fill it with furnishings; his attendants cluster round him,[224] and he cries out, 'Will you not look upon my works?' Aye, enemy of God, we have looked on them! And what are they, you vilest of sinners and filthiest of fornicators? In heaven you are cursed, and on earth you are detested!"

With this, he departed, saying, "God made a covenant with the doctors of religion that they should disclose these things to the people, not conceal them." 67.2

Furious, al-Ḥajjāj exclaimed, "Syrians![225] This sanctimonious Basran insults me to my face and no one gainsays him. Fetch him back! By God, I'll kill him!"

The Syrians went after him and brought him back; but he had been told what al-Ḥajjāj had said, and as he walked, he moved his lips soundlessly. 67.3

When he came before al-Ḥajjāj, he saw his anger, and the sword and the executioner's leather mat that had been laid before him; and al-Ḥajjāj raved at him when first his eye fell upon him. But Ḥasan answered him gently and admonished him, and al-Ḥajjāj had the sword and mat removed. Ḥasan continued to speak, and al-Ḥajjāj sent for food, water, and perfumed unguent. The two men ate, and rinsed their hands together; then al-Ḥajjāj pressed the perfume into Ḥasan's hand and sent him away with every mark of honor.[226]

Ṣāliḥ ibn Mismār said: 67.4

Ḥasan was asked, "What was it you said under your breath?"

He replied: "I said, O You my succor in my supplications, my resource in emergencies, my Lord in my affliction, my companion in adversity and

شدّتي ويا وليّي في نعمتي ويا إلهي وإله إبراهيم وإسماعيل وإسحاق ويعقوب والأسباط وموسى وعيسى ويا ربّ النبيّين كلّهم أجمعين ويا ربّ كهيعص وطه وطس ويس وربّ القرآن الحكيم يا كافي موسى فرعون ويا كافي محمّد الأحزاب صلّ على محمّد وآله الطيّبين الطاهرين الأخيار وارزقني مودّة عبدك الحجّاج وخيره ومعروفه واصرف عنّي أذاه وشرّه ومكروهه ومعرّته.

٥،٦٧ فكفاه الله تعالى شرّه بمنّه وكرمه. قال صالح فما دعونا بها في شدّة إلاّ فرج عنّا.

١،٦٨ وجدت في بعض الكتب بغير إسناد

كتب الوليد بن عبد الملك بن مروان إلى صالح بن عبد الله المزنيّ عامله على المدينة أن أنزل الحسن بن الحسن بن عليّ بن أبي طالب رضي الله عنهم فاضربه في مسجد رسول الله صلّى الله عليه وسلّم خمسمائة سوط.

٢،٦٨ قال فأخرجه صالح إلى المسجد ليقرأ عليهم كتاب الوليد بن عبد الملك ثمّ ينزل فيضرب الحسن فبينما هو يقرأ الكتاب إذ جاء عليّ بن الحسين عليهما السلام مبادراً يريد الحسن فدخل والناس معه الى المسجد واجتمع الناس حتّى انتهى إلى الحسن فقال له يا ابن عمّ ادع بدعاء الكرب فقال وما هو يا ابن عمّ.

٣،٦٨ قال قل لا إله إلّا الله الحليم الكريم لا إله إلّا الله العليّ العظيم سبحان الله ربّ السماوات السبع ﴿وَهُوَ رَبُّ ٱلْعَرْشِ ٱلْعَظِيمِ﴾ و﴿ٱلْحَمْدُ لِلَّهِ رَبِّ ٱلْعَالَمِينَ﴾.

٤،٦٨ قال وانصرف عليّ وأقبل الحسن يكرّرها دفعات كثيرة فلمّا فرغ صالح من قراءة الكتاب ونزل عن المنبر قال للنّاس أرى سحنة رجل مظلوم أخّروا أمره حتّى أراجع أمير المؤمنين وأكتب في أمره ففعل ذلك ولم يزل يكاتب حتّى أطلق.

٥،٦٨ قال وكان النّاس يدعون ويكرّرون هذا الدعاء وحفظوه قال فما دعونا بهذا الدّعاء في شدّة إلّا فرجها الله عنّا بمنّه.

friend in prosperity; my God, God of Abraham, Ishmael, and Isaac, of Jacob, of the Tribes of Israel, of Moses and of Jesus; O Lord of all the prophets, of *kāf-hā'-yā'-'ayn-ṣād*, of *ṭā'-hā'*, of *ṭā'-sīn*, of *yā'-sīn*,[227] and of the Wise Qur'an; O preserver of Moses from Pharaoh, of Muḥammad from the factions, bless Muḥammad and his noble kin, pure and elect; make the love, good will, and beneficence of Your servant al-Ḥajjāj my provision, and keep from me his harm, evil, injury, and perfidy."

God's favor and goodness preserved him; and, Ṣāliḥ said, "Whenever we use this prayer in adversity, we are delivered." 67.5

I read in a book, with no chain of transmitters: 68.1

The caliph al-Walīd ibn 'Abd al-Malik ibn Marwān wrote to his governor of Medina, Ṣāliḥ ibn 'Abd Allāh al-Muzanī, with the instruction: "Arrest al-Ḥasan ibn al-Ḥasan ibn 'Alī ibn Abī Ṭālib"—God be pleased with them—"and administer five hundred lashes to him in the mosque of the Messenger of God"—God bless and keep him.

Ṣāliḥ brought al-Ḥasan to the mosque in order to read out the caliph's 68.2 sentence publicly before flogging him; but he was interrupted when 'Alī ibn al-Ḥusayn, peace on both of them, burst into the mosque, surrounded by a crowd, which followed him as he hurried up to al-Ḥasan and cried, "Cousin! Say the prayer of affliction!"

"What prayer is that, cousin?"

'Alī replied, "Say: There is no god but God, Patient and Kind. There is no 68.3 god but God, Exalted, Almighty. Glory be to God, Lord of the seven heavens, «Lord of the mighty throne».[228] «Praise be to God, Lord of all»."[229]

Then 'Alī left, and al-Ḥasan fell to repeating the prayer over and over; and 68.4 when Ṣāliḥ had finished reading out the letter and come down from the pulpit, he said to his henchmen, "I can see from his appearance that this man has been wronged.[230] Do not carry out the sentence until I have written to consult the caliph," and he sent letter after letter until al-Ḥasan was released.

People memorized this prayer, and repeated it in their own devotions; and 68.5 whenever we[231] have used it in adversity, we have been delivered, by God's favor.

حدّثنا عليّ بن أبي الطيّب قال حدّثنا ابن الجرّاح قال حدثنا ابن أبي الدنيا قال حدّثني محمّد بن الحسين قال حدّثني محمّد بن سعيد قال حدّثنا شريك عن عبد الملك بن عمير قال ٦،٦٨

كتب الوليد بن عبد الملك إلى عثمان بن حيّان المرّيّ خذ الحسن بن الحسن فاجلده مائة جلدة وقفه للناس يوماً ولا أراني إلّا قاتله قال فبعث إليه فجيء به وبالخصوم بين يديه فقام إليه عليّ بن الحسين عليه السلام فقال يا أخي تكلّم بكلمات الفرج يفرّج الله عنك قال ما هنّ.

قال قل لا إله إلّا الله الحكيم الكريم لا إله إلّا الله العليّ العظيم سبحان الله ربّ السموات السبع ﴿وَهُوَ رَبُّ ٱلْعَرْشِ ٱلْعَظِيمِ﴾ و﴿ٱلْحَمْدُ لِلَّهِ رَبِّ ٱلْعَالَمِينَ﴾. ٧،٦٨

قال فقالها فأنفذ فردّه وقال أنا أكاتب أمير المؤمنين بعذره فإنّ الشاهد يرى ما لا يرى الغائب. ٨،٦٨

ووجدت هذا الخبر بأعلى وأثبت من هذين الطريقين حدّثنا أبو العبّاس محمّد بن أحمد الأثرم المقرئ قال حدّثنا أحمد بن الربيع اللجميّ الخزّاز[١] الكوفيّ قال حدّثنا الحسين بن عليّ يعني الجعفيّ عن والده عن قدامة عن عبد الملك بن عمير قال حدّثني أبو مصعب قال ٩،٦٨

كتب عبد الملك إلى عامله بالمدينة هشام بن إسماعيل أنّ حسن بن حسن كاتب أهل العراق فإذا جاءك كتابي هذا فابعث إليه الشرط فليأتوا به.

قال فأتي به فسأله عن شيء فقام إليه عليّ بن الحسين عليهما السلام فقال يا ابن عمّ قل كلمات الفرج لا إله إلّا الله ربّ السّموات السّبع و﴿وَهُوَ رَبُّ ٱلْعَرْشِ ٱلْعَظِيمِ﴾ و﴿ٱلْحَمْدُ لِلَّهِ رَبِّ ٱلْعَالَمِينَ﴾. ١٠،٦٨

قال فقالها ثمّ إنّ الأمير نظر إلى وجهه فقال أرى وجهاً قد قرف بكذبة خلّوا سبيله فلأراجعنّ أمير المؤمنين فيه. ١١،٦٨

---

١ الخزّاز: التصحيح من ش.

We cite ʿAlī ibn al-Ḥasan, citing Ibn al-Jarrāḥ, citing Ibn Abī l-Dunyā, who cites Muḥammad ibn al-Ḥusayn, citing Muḥammad ibn Saʿīd, citing Sharīk, citing ʿAbd al-Malik ibn ʿUmayr, who said: 68.6

Al-Walīd ibn ʿAbd al-Malik wrote to ʿUthmān ibn Ḥayyān al-Murrī: "Seize al-Ḥasan ibn al-Ḥasan; give him a hundred lashes, and put him on public display for a whole day. I want him to die of his treatment."

ʿUthmān had al-Ḥasan brought before him, along with some people prepared to swear against him. But ʿAlī son of al-Ḥusayn, peace on him, went to him and said, "Brother! Say the words of deliverance, and God will deliver you."

"What are they?" al-Ḥasan asked.

ʿAlī said, "Say: There is no god but God, Patient and Kind. There is no god but God, Exalted, Almighty. Glory be to God, Lord of the seven heavens, «Lord of the mighty throne». «Praise be to God, Lord of all»." 68.7

Al-Ḥasan repeated the words, and ʿUthmān disregarded his instructions and released him, saying, "I will write to the caliph to have him pardoned. Eyewitnesses see what those who are not present cannot see." 68.8

I have read the same account with an older and more reliable chain of transmission. We cite the Qurʾan scholar, Abū l-ʿAbbās Muḥammad ibn Aḥmad the Gap-Toothed, citing Aḥmad ibn al-Rabīʿ al-Lakhmī the Silk Merchant of Kufa, citing al-Ḥusayn ibn ʿAlī (al-Juʿfī, that is), quoting his father, quoting Qudāmah, quoting ʿAbd al-Malik ibn ʿUmayr, who said: I cite Abū Muṣʿab, who said: 68.9

Caliph ʿAbd al-Malik wrote to his governor of Medina, Hishām ibn Ismāʿīl: "Al-Ḥasan son of al-Ḥasan is in correspondence with the Iraqis. When you receive this letter, have the police fetch him in."

They brought him to Hishām, who was questioning him when up came ʿAlī ibn al-Ḥusayn, peace on them both, and said, "Cousin! Say the words of deliverance: There is no god but God, Lord of the seven heavens, «Lord of the mighty throne». «Praise be to God, Lord of all»." 68.10

When al-Ḥasan had repeated these words, the governor studied his face, and said, "I see in his face that he has been falsely accused. Let him go. I shall take up his case with the caliph." 68.11

حدّثني عليّ بن أبي الطيّب قال حدّثني ابن الجرّاح قال حدّثنا ابن أبي الدنيا عن الفضل ابن يعقوب قال حدّثنا الفريابيّ[1] قال ١،٦٩

لمّا أخذ أبو جعفر إسماعيل بن أميّة أمر به إلى الحبس فرأى في طريقة على حائط مكتوبًا يا وليّي في نعمتي ويا صاحبي في وحدتي ويا عدّتي في كربتي.

٢،٦٩ قال فلم يزل يكرّرها حتّى خلّى سبيله فاجتاز بذلك الحائط فإذا ليس عليه شيء مكتوب.

١،٧٠ وروى أنّ حيّة استجارت برجل من العبّاد من رجل يريد قتلها قال فرفع ذيله وقال ادخلي فتطوّقت على بطنه.

٢،٧٠ وجاء رجل بسيف وقال له يا رجل حيّة هربت منّي الساعة أردت قتلها فهل رأيتها قال ما أرى شيئًا.

٣،٧٠ فلمّا أجارها وانصرف من يريد قتلها قالت له الحيّة لا بدّ من قتلك فقال لها الرجل ليس غنى عن هذا قالت لا قال فأمهليني حتّى آتي سفح جبل فأصلّي ركعتين وأدعو الله تعالى وأحفر لنفسي قبرًا فإذا نزلته فافعلي ما بدا لك قالت افعل.

٤،٧٠ فلمّا صلّى ودعا أوحى الله إليه إنّي قد رحمتك فاقبض على الحيّة فإنّها تموت في يدك ولا تضرّك.

٥،٧٠ ففعل ذلك وعاد إلى موضعه وتشاغل بعبادة ربّه.

٦،٧٠ وروى هذا الخبر جعفر العابد برامهرمز على غير هذه السياقة إلّا أنّ المعنى متقارب فأوردت ما بلغني من ذلك فقال

١ حدّثنا الفريابيّ: الزيادة من س.

I cite ʿAlī ibn al-Ḥasan, citing Ibn al-Jarrāḥ, citing Ibn Abī l-Dunyā from al-Faḍl ibn Yaʿqūb, who said: We cite al-Faryābī: 69.1

The caliph al-Manṣūr had Ismāʿīl ibn Umayyah seized and ordered him to be taken to prison; but on his way there, he saw written on a wall: "O my friend in prosperity, my companion in solitude, my resource in affliction!"

He repeated the words over and over, and was eventually released. Later, he passed the wall again, but there was nothing there. 69.2

It is related that a snake sought refuge with a holy man from someone who was trying to kill it. The holy man lifted the hem of his garment, said, "In here!" and the snake wrapped itself round his waist. 70.1

Up came a man with a sword and said to the holy man: 70.2

"You there, a snake I was trying to kill has just escaped me. Have you seen it?"

"I see nothing," he replied.

Once its would-be killer had gone, the snake said to its protector, "I must slay you." 70.3

"Must you?"

"Indeed I must."

"Then," said the holy man, "give me time to go up on to the mountain and say two prayer sequences, make supplication to God Exalted, and dig my grave. When I have laid myself in my grave, do as you wish."

"Very well," said the snake.

When the man had prayed and made supplication, God said to him: 70.4

"I am moved with compassion for you. Take hold of the snake: it will die in your hand without harming you."

He did so, returned whence he had come, and devoted himself to worshiping his Lord. 70.5

In Rāmhurmuz, Jaʿfar the holy man told the same story differently, although the gist is similar. Here is what I know of his version: 70.6

قرأت في كتب الأوائل أنّ حيّة أفلتت من يد طالب لها ليقتلها وأنّها سألت الرجل أن يخبأها فخبأها في فمه وأنكرها للطالب لها.

٧،٧٠ وحدّثني[1] عبد الله بن الحارث بن السرّاج الواسطيّ قال حدّثني بعض أصحاب أبي محمّد سهل بن عبد الله التستريّ عنه قال

كان في بني إسرائيل رجل في صحراء قريبة من جبل يعبد الله تعالى إذ مثلت له حيّة فقالت له قد أرهقني من يريد قتلي فأجرني أجارك الله في ظلّه يوم لا ظلّ إلّا ظلّه قال لها وممّن أجيرك قالت من عدوّ يريد قتلي قال وممّن انت قالت من أهل لا إله إلّا الله قال فأين أخبيك قالت في جوفك إن كنت تريد المعروف.

٨،٧٠ ففتح فاه وقال ادخلي ففعلت فلمّا جاء الطالب قال له رأيتَ حيّة تسعى فقال العابد ما أرى شيئاً وصدق في ذلك فقال له الطالب الله فقال الله فتركه ومضى ثمّ قال لها اخرجي الآن فقالت إنّي من قوم لا يكافئون على الجميل إلّا بقبيح.

ثمّ ساق الحديث على قريب ممّا تقدّم.

٩،٧٠ ووقع إليّ الخبر بقريب من هذا المعنى على خلاف هذه السياقة قرئ على أبي العبّاس الأثرم المقرئ البغداديّ وهو محمّد بن أحمد بن حمّاد بن إبراهيم بن ثعلب في منزله بالبصرة في جمادى الأولى سنة خمس وثلاثين وثلثمائة وأنا حاضر أسمع حدّثكم عليّ ابن حرب الطائيّ الموصليّ قال حدّثنا جعفر بن المنذر الطائيّ العابد بمهروبان قال

١ ب: وقرأت في بعض الكتب أنّ عابدًا من بني إسرائيل بينا هو يعبد الله الخ. ل: وقرأت . . . أنّ عابدا من بني إسرائيل يعبد الله الخ.

I have read in the books of the Ancients that a snake slipped from the grasp of a would-be killer and asked this holy man to hide it. He hid it in his mouth and feigned ignorance of it to its pursuer.

I cite ʿAbd Allāh ibn al-Ḥārith ibn al-Sarrāj of Wāsiṭ, citing Abū Muḥammad Sahl ibn ʿAbd Allāh of Tustar[232] as quoted by a follower of his: 70.7

Among the Children of Israel, there was a man living in a wilderness near a mountain, worshiping God Exalted. A snake suddenly appeared to him, saying:

"One who would kill me is in hot pursuit. Protect me, and may God's shadow protect you on that Day when there shall be no shadow but His!"

"Who is this person?" the man asked.

"A murderous enemy!" the snake cried.

"What is your tribe?" asked the man.

"The tribe of those who declare there is no god but God."

"Where shall I hide you?"

The snake said, "Be so benevolent as to hide me in your belly."

The man opened his mouth and said, "Get in!" so that when the snake's pursuer appeared and asked, "Have you seen a snake heading this way?" the holy man was able to declare truthfully: "I see nothing at all." 70.8

"Honest to God?"

"Honest to God."

When the pursuer had gone away, the holy man said, "You can come out now."

But the snake said, "My people return only evil for good."

My source then told the rest of the story in much the same way as the previous versions.

I have also heard the story told differently, though with the same meaning, as read back for verification to the Baghdadi Qur'an scholar, Abū l-ʿAbbās the Gap-Toothed, whose name is Muḥammad ibn Aḥmad ibn Ḥammād ibn Ibrāhīm ibn Thaʿlab, in his house in Basra in Jumada I 335 [December 946][233] in my presence and hearing, as follows: You cite ʿAlī ibn Ḥarb al-Ṭāʾī of Mosul, who heard it from Jaʿfar ibn Mundhir al-Ṭāʾī the holy man[234] in Mahrūbān, who said: I was with Sufyān ibn ʿUyaynah when he turned to a Hadith scholar who was present and said, "Tell us the story of the snake!" The man said, citing ʿAbd al-Jabbār: 70.9

كنت عند سفيان بن عيينة فالتفت إلى شيخ حاضر فقال له حدّث القوم بحديث الحيّة فقال الرجل حدّثني عبد الجبّار أنّ حُميد بن عبد الله خرج إلى متعبّده فمثلت بين يديه حيّة وقالت له أجرني أجارك الله في ظلّه قال وممّن أجيرك قالت من عدوّ يريد قتلي قال فأين أخبئك قالت في جوفك.

١٠،٧٠ ففتح فاه فما استقرّت حتّى وافاه رجل بسيف مجرّد فقال له يا حميد أين الحيّة قال ما أرى شيئاً فذهب الرجل فأطلعت الحيّة رأسها وقالت يا حميد أتحسّ الرجل فقال لا قد ذهب فاخرجي قالت اختر منّي إحدى خصلتين إمّا أن أنكتك نكتةً فأقتلك أو أفرث كبدك فترميه من دبرك قطعاً فقال والله ما كافيتني فقالت قد عرفتَ العداوة التي بيني وبين أبيك آدم قديماً وليس معي مال فأعطيك ولا دابّة فأحملك عليها فقال امهليني حتّى آتي سفح الجبل وأجفر لنفسي قبراً.

١١،٧٠ قالت له افعل فبينا هو يسير إذ لقيه فتى حسن الوجه طيّب الريح حسن الثياب فقال له يا شيخ ما لي أراك مستسلماً للموت آيساً من الحياة قال من عدوّ في جوفي يريد هلاكي فاستخرج من كمّه شيئاً فدفعه إليه وقال كله

١٢،٧٠ قال ففعلت ذلك فوجدت مغصاً شديداً ثمّ ناولني شيئاً آخر فإذا بالحيّة سقطت من جوفي قطعاً.

فقلت له من أنت يرحمك الله فما أحد أعظم عليّ منّة منك فقال أنا المعروف إنّ أهل السماء رأوا غدر هذه الحيّة بك فسألوا الله عزّ وجلّ أن يعيذك فقال لي الله

Ḥumayd ibn ʿAbd Allāh had gone to the place where he practiced his devotions, when suddenly a snake appeared and said to him, "Protect me, and may God's shadow protect you!"

"From whom am I to protect you?" he asked.

"From a murderous enemy," the snake replied.

"Where shall I hide you?"

"In your belly."

He opened his mouth, and no sooner had the snake slipped inside than up came a man with a drawn sword, saying: 70.10

"Ḥumayd! Where's the snake?"

Ḥumayd replied, "I see nothing," and the man went away again.

The snake poked out its head and asked, "Is he still there?"

Ḥumayd said, "No, he's gone. You can come out."

The snake said, "I give you a choice. I can either kill you by felling you with a single bite, or I can pierce your liver and make you excrete it in little bits."

Ḥumayd said, "By God, that's not a fair exchange!"

The snake replied, "You well know the old enmity that is between me and your father, Adam.[235] And in any case, I've no money to press on you or horses to reward you with."[236]

Ḥumayd said, "Give me time to go up on to the mountain and dig my grave."

"Very well," said the snake; and Ḥumayd set off; but on the way he was met by a comely youth, sweetly perfumed and handsomely dressed. 70.11

"Old man!" said the youth. "Why do you despair of life and yield yourself up to death?"

Ḥumayd said, "Because there is an enemy in my belly who means to destroy me."

The youth took something from his sleeve and gave it to Ḥumayd, saying, "Swallow this."

Ḥumayd takes up the narrative: 70.12

I took it, and my bowels churned. Then the youth gave me something else to take, and I vomited up the snake from my belly in little bits.

"Who are you?" I asked the youth. "May God keep you in His mercy! Never was I so deeply indebted to anyone."

The youth said, "I am Benevolence. In heaven they saw how treacherously this snake treated you, and supplicated God, Mighty and Glorious, to keep you

تعالى يا معروف أدركْ عبدي فإيّاي أراد بما صنع.

١،٧١ بلغني أنّه جنى رجل جناية على عهد عبد الملك بن مروان فأهدر دمه ودم من يؤويه وأمر بطلبه فتحاماه الناس كلّهم فكان يسيح في الجبال والبراري ولا يذكر اسمه فيضاف اليوم واليومين فإذا عُرف طرد ولم يدع أن يستقر.

٢،٧١ قال الرجل فكنت أسيح يوماً في بطن واد فإذا بشيخ أبيض الرأس واللحية عليه ثياب بياض وهو قائم يصلّي فقمت إلى جنبه فلمّا سلّم انفتل إليّ وقال لي من أنت قلت رجل أخافني السلطان وقد تحاماني الناس فلم يجرني أحد من خلق الله تعالى فأنا أسيح في هذه البراري خائفاً على نفسي قال فأين أنت عن السبع قلت وأيّ سبع.

٣،٧١ قال تقول سبحان الله الإله الواحد الذي ليس غيره أحد سبحان الدائم الذي ليس يعادله شيء سبحان الدائم القديم الذي لا ندّ له ولا عديل سبحان الذي يحيي ويميت سبحان الذي هو كلّ يوم في شأن سبحان الذي خلق ما يرى وما لا يرى سبحان الذي علم كلّ شيء بغير تعليم اللّٰهمّ إنّي أسألك بحقّ هذه الكلمات وحرمتهنّ أن تفعل بي كذا وكذا وأعادهنّ عليّ فحفظتهنّ.

٤،٧١ قال الرجل وفقدت صاحبي فألقى الله تعالى الأمن في قلبي وخرجت من وقتي متوجّهاً إلى عبد الملك فوقفت ببابه واستأذنت عليه فلمّا دخلت عليه قال أتعلّمت السحر قلت لا يا أمير المؤمنين ولكن كان من شأني كذا وكذا وقصصت عليه القصّة.

٥،٧١ فأمّنني وأحسن إليّ.

from harm. God Exalted said to me: Benevolence, go to My servant; for what he did, he did for My sake."[237]

I have heard that: 71.1

When ʿAbd al-Malik ibn Marwān was caliph, a man committed a crime and ʿAbd al-Malik declared his blood lawful as well as that of anyone who sheltered him. He ordered him to be hunted down, and everyone shunned him. He roamed over hill and dale, concealing his name so as to obtain hospitality for a day or two; but as soon as he was recognized he would be expelled, and could not settle anywhere.

The outlaw takes up the narrative: 71.2

One day as I was crossing a valley floor, I came upon an old man with white hair and beard, clothed all in white. He was performing the ritual prayer, and when I took my place beside him, he turned to greet me, asking, "Who are you?"

I answered, "A man in fear of the authorities, shunned by everyone. No creature of God Exalted will give me refuge, and I roam these wastelands in fear of my life."

The old man said, "Have you tried the seven?"

"What seven?" I asked.

He replied, "You should say, 'Glory be to God, the sole god than Whom 71.3
there is no other. Glory to Him Who will exist for all eternity and is unequaled. Glory to the Eternal Who has existed from all eternity and has no match or peer. Glory to Him who gives life and death. Glory to Him Who «every day» has «some great task».[238] Glory to the Creator of what is visible and what is invisible. Glory to Him Who knows all things of His own knowledge. O God! I supplicate You by these sacred words to do thus and thus for me.'"

I memorized the words, which the old man made me repeat to him.

Then he vanished. But God Exalted cast peace into my heart, and I set off at 71.4
once to find ʿAbd al-Malik. I begged admittance at his door, and the moment I appeared before him, he exclaimed:

"Are you a magician?"[239]

"No sire," I replied. "This is what happened," and I told him my story.

The caliph pardoned me and treated me generously. 71.5

٧٢ وأخبرني صديق لي أنّ بعض أصحابنا من الكتّاب دُفع إلى محنة صعبة فكان من دعائه يا كاشف الضر بك استغاث من اضطرّ قال وقد رأيته نقش ذلك على خاتمه وكان يردّد الدعاء به فكشف الله محنته عن قريب.

١،٧٣ حدّثني عليّ بن هشام قال سمعت أبا عبد الله حمْد بن محمّد القنّائي ابن أخت الحسن ابن مخلد قال مؤلّف هذا الكتاب قال لي أبو القاسم عيسى بن عليّ بن عيسى في كلام جرى بيننا غير هذا طويل كان حمد بن محمّد هذا ابن عمّة الحسن بن مخلد وكان أبي عرّفني أنّه أشار على المقتدر بالله وقد استشاره فيمن يقلّده الوزارة قال فأسميتُ له حمد بن محمّد هذا وأبا عيسى أخا أبي صخرة وأبا زنبور ومحمّد بن عليّ المادرائيّين قال سمعت عبيد الله بن سليمان بن وهب يقول كان المتوكّل أغيظ الناس على إيتاخ وذكر حديثاً طويلاً وصف فيه كيف قبض المتوكّل على إيتاخ وابنيه ببغداد لمّا رجع من الحجّ بيد إسحاق بن إبراهيم بن مصعب

٢،٧٣ قال فيه قال سليمان بن وهب ساعة قُبض على إيتاخ ببغداد قبض عليّ بسرّ من رأى وسلّمت إلى عبيد الله بن يحيى.

٣،٧٣ وكتب المتوكّل إلى إسحاق بن إبراهيم بدخول سرّ من رأى ليتقوّى به على الأتراك لأنّه كان معه بضعة عشر ألفاً ولكثرة الطاهريّة بخراسان وشدّة شوكتهم.

٤،٧٣ فلمّا دخل إسحاق سامراء أمر المتوكّل بتسليمي إليه وقال هذا عدوّي ففصّل لحمه عن عظمه هذا كان يلقاني في أيّام المعتصم فلا يبدأني بالسلام فأبدأه به لحاجتي إليه فيردّ عليّ كما يردّ المولى على عبده وكلّ ما دبّره إيتاخ فمن رأيه.

٥،٧٣ فأخذني إسحاق وقيّدني بقيد ثقيل وألبسني جبّة صوف وحبسني في كنيف وأغلق عليّ خمسة أبواب فكنت لا أعرف الليل من النهار فأقمت على ذلك عشرين يوماً لا يُفتح عليّ الباب إلّا دفعة واحدة في كلّ يوم وليلة يُدفع إليّ فيها خبز وملح

72 A friend of mine told me that an associate of ours, a state scribe, under the compulsion of a severe ordeal, prayed: "From You, Remover of hurts, the hard-pressed seek succor!"—a phrase which I noticed he had had engraved on his signet ring. He said this prayer over and over, and before long God rescued him from his ordeal.

73.1 I cite ʿAlī ibn Hishām, who said: I heard Abū ʿAbd Allāh Ḥamd ibn Muḥammad of Dayr Qunnā, the son of al-Ḥasan ibn Makhlad's sister, say:

(The author of this book observes: Abū l-Qāsim ʿĪsā, son of ʿAlī ibn ʿĪsā,[240] told me, in the course of a long conversation—not the one in which I heard this anecdote—that Ḥamd ibn Muḥammad was in fact the son of the *paternal aunt* of al-Ḥasan ibn Makhlad. He added: "My father informed me that when the caliph al-Muqtadir asked him whom he should make vizier, he nominated Ḥamd ibn Muḥammad, Abū ʿĪsā the brother of Abū Ṣakhr, Abū Zunbūr, and Muḥammad ibn ʿAlī. The latter two belonged to the Mādharāʾī family.")[241]

I heard ʿUbayd Allāh ibn Sulaymān ibn Wahb say:

The caliph al-Mutawakkil was extremely angry with Ītākh—and he related a long anecdote describing how, when Ītākh returned from the Pilgrimage, al-Mutawakkil had him and his two sons arrested in Baghdad by Isḥāq ibn Ibrāhīm ibn Muṣʿab.

73.2 In the course of this anecdote, ʿUbayd Allāh said: Sulaymān ibn Wahb said:

At the very moment Ītākh was arrested in Baghdad, I was arrested in Samarra and handed over to ʿUbayd Allāh ibn Yaḥyā ibn Khāqān.[242]

73.3 Al-Mutawakkil sent written orders to Isḥāq ibn Ibrāhīm ibn Muṣʿab, who had some ten thousand men, to enter Samarra and strengthen the caliph's position there against the Turks. The Ṭāhirid forces were numerous, and they were all-powerful in Khurasan.[243]

73.4 As soon as Isḥāq ibn Ibrāhīm arrived in Samarra, al-Mutawakkil had me transferred into his custody, saying, "This is my enemy. Strip the flesh from his bones! When al-Muʿtaṣim was caliph, he would never be first to greet me when we met. Because I had need of him, I would greet him, and he would return my salutation in the manner of a master acknowledging his slave. He is the brains behind all Ītākh's plotting."

73.5 Isḥāq took charge of me and loaded me with heavy chains. He made me wear a woolen shift and imprisoned me in a privy, where I could not tell night

جريش وماء حارّ فكنت آنس بالخنافس وبنات وردان وأتمنّى الموت من شدّة ما أنا فيه.

٦،٧٣ فعرض لي ليلة من الليالي أن أطلت الصلاة وسجدت فتضرّعت إلى الله تعالى ودعوته بالفرج وقلت في دعائي اللّهمّ إن كنت تعلم أنّه كان لي في دم نجاح بن سلمة صنع فلا تخلّصني ممّا أنا فيه وإن كنت تعلم أنّه لا صنع لي فيه ولا في الدماء التي سفكت ففرّج عني.

٧،٧٣ فما استتممت الدعاء حتّى سمعت صوت الأقفال تفتح فلم أشكّ أنّه القتل ففتحت الأبواب وجيء بالشمع وحملني الفرّاشون لثقل حديدي فقلت لحاجبه سألتك بالله اصدقني عن أمري

فقال ما أكل الأمير اليوم شيئاً لأنّه أغلظ عليه في أمرك وذلك أنّ أمير المؤمنين وبّخه بسببك وقال سلّمت إليك سليمان بن وهب تسمنه أو تستخرج ماله فقال الأمير أنا صاحب سيف ولا أعرف المناظرة على الأموال ووجوهها ولو قرّر أمره على شيء لطالبته به فأمر أمير المؤمنين الكتّاب بالاجتماع عند الأمير لمناظرتك وإلزامك مالاً يؤخذ به خطّك وتطالب به وقد اجتمعوا واستدعيت لهذا.

٨،٧٣ قال فحملت إلى المجلس فإذا فيه موسى بن عبد الملك صاحب ديوان الخراج والحسن ابن مخلد صاحب ديوان الضياع وأحمد بن إسرائيل الكاتب وأبو نوح عيسى بن إبراهيم كاتب الفتح بن خاقان وداود بن الجرّاح صاحب الزمام فطرحت في آخر المجلس.

٩،٧٣ فشتمني إسحاق أقبح شتم وقال يا فاعل يا صانع تعرّضني لاستبطاء أمير المؤمنين والله لأفرّقنّ بين لحمك وعظمك ولأجعلنّ بطن الأرض أحبّ إليك من ظهرها أين الأموال فاحتججت بنكبة ابن الزيّات لي فبدرني الحسن بن مخلد فقال أخذت من

from day, behind five locked doors. For twenty days, my door was opened only once a day for me to be given bread, coarse salt, and tepid water. My companions were dung beetles and cockroaches. My suffering was such that I longed for death.

It so happened that one night I prolonged my ritual prayers, prostrating myself and entreating God Exalted as I prayed for deliverance: "O God! If, to Your knowledge, I had any part in the death of Najāḥ ibn Salamah,[244] then do not release me from my plight! But if You know that I had no part in his death, nor in any other blood that was shed, deliver me!" 73.6

No sooner had I finished this prayer than I heard the sound of the bolts being drawn. I was sure that this meant death. The doors were opened, torches were brought, and house servants hoisted me up (my chains were too heavy for me to walk). 73.7

"I implore you in God's name, tell me truthfully what's going to happen to me," I begged Isḥāq's chamberlain.

This was his reply:

"The general Isḥāq ibn Ibrāhīm ibn Muṣʿab has been so harassed on your account that he has not eaten all day, for the caliph has taken him to task regarding you, and they had this exchange. The caliph said, 'Did I give you charge of Sulaymān ibn Wahb for you to fatten him up, or to extract money from him?' To which the general replied, 'I'm a man of the sword. I don't know how to conduct cross-examinations about money and financial matters. If Your Majesty will only give me something to go on, I'll make him pay up.'

"As a consequence, the caliph has commanded the state scribes to assemble in the general's house to cross-examine you. You are to be made to pledge yourself to pay over the sum that they will demand. They are all here, and you have been summoned to appear before them."

I was carried into the meeting, at which were present: Mūsā ibn ʿAbd al-Malik, head of the Bureau of Land Tax;[245] al-Ḥasan ibn Makhlad, in charge of Estates; the state scribe Aḥmad ibn Isrāʾīl; Abū Nuḥ ʿĪsā ibn Ibrāhīm, secretary to al-Fatḥ ibn Khāqān; and Dāwud ibn al-Jarrāḥ, head of Bureaucratic Supervision. I was flung down at the back of the room. 73.8

Isḥāq began by yelling abuse at me. "You scoundrel! You blackguard! It's on your account that the Commander of the Faithful accuses me of dragging my feet! I'll split your flesh from your bones, by God! I'll make you wish you were dead and buried! Where's the money?" 73.9

الناس أضعاف ما أدّيت وعادت يدك إلى كبّة إيتاخ فأخذت ضياع السلطان واقتطعتها لنفسك وحزتها سرقةً إليك وأنت تغلّها ألفي ألف درهم وتتزيّا بزيّ الوزراء وقد بقيت عليك من تلك المصادرة جملة لم تؤدّها وأخذت الجماعة تواجهني بكلّ قبيح إلّا موسى بن عبد الملك فإنّه كان ساكتاً لصداقة كانت بيني وبينه.

١٠،٧٣ فأقبل من بينهم على إسحاق وقال يا سيّدي أتأذن لي في الخلوة به لأفصل أمره قال افعل فاستدناني فخلت إليه فسارّني وقال عزيز عليّ يا أخي حالك وبالله لو كان خلاصك بنصف ما أملكه لفديتك به ولكن صورتك قبيحة وما أملك إلّا الرأي فإن قبلت منّي رجوت خلاصك وإن خالفتني فأنت والله هالك قال فقلت لا أخالفك فقال الرأي أن تكتب خطّك بعشرة آلاف ألف درهم تؤدّيها في عشرة أشهر عند انقضاء كلّ شهر ألف ألف درهم وتترفّه عاجلاً ممّا أنت فيه.

١١،٧٣ فسكتّ سكوت مبهوت فقال لي ما لك فقلت له والله ما أرجع إلى ربعها إلّا بعد بيع عقاري ومن يشتري منّي وأنا منكوب وكيف يتوفّر لي الثمن وأنا على هذه الحالة فقال أنا أعلم أنّك صادق ولكن احرس نفسك عاجلاً بعظم ما تبذله ويطمع فيه من جهتك وأنا من وراء الحيلة لك في شيء أميل به رأي الخليفة من جهتك يعود إلى صلاحك والله المعين ومن ساعة إلى ساعة فرج ولا تتعجّل الموت ولو لم تستفد إلّا الراحة ممّا أنت فيه يوماً واحداً لكفى قال فقلت لست أتّهم ودّك ولا رأيك وأنا أفعل ما تقول.

١٢،٧٣ فأقبل على الجماعة وقال يا سادتي إنّي قد أشرت عليه أن يكتب خطّه بشيء لا يطيقه فضلاً عمّا هو أكثر منه ورجوت أن نعاونه بأموالنا وجاهنا ليمشي أمره وقد وافقته ليكتب بكذا وكذا فقالوا الصواب له أن يفعل هذا.

I pleaded that Ibn al-Zayyāt had stripped me of office.[246]

Al-Ḥasan ibn Makhlad interrupted, "You took twice as much as you paid up. You controlled Ītākh's scribes. You annexed state properties, assigned them to yourself, and took criminal possession of them. They bring in two million dirhams! And you dress like a vizier even though you still haven't paid over everything that was confiscated!"

At this, they all began to hurl abuse at me, with the exception of Mūsā ibn ʿAbd al-Malik, who kept silent because we were friends.

Instead, he turned to Isḥāq and said, "Sir, may I see him privately and get to the bottom of this?" 73.10

With Isḥāq's consent, he motioned for me to be brought to his side, and whispered, "It grieves me to see you in this situation, brother. I swear to God I'd give half of all I have to get you out of it. But things look bad for you, and I have nothing but my ingenuity. If you'll be guided by it, I think I can have you released, but unless you do as I tell you, you're a dead man, I swear to God."

"I'll do whatever you say," I said.

"Then here's what you must do. Sign a pledge that you'll pay ten million dirhams over ten months, in installments of one million at the end of each month. That'll buy you easy terms immediately."

I was stunned into silence. 73.11

"What's the matter?" Mūsā asked.

"God! I couldn't find a quarter of that amount unless I sold my properties, and who would buy them? I've been stripped of office! How would I get paid when my income's forfeit?"

Mūsā said, "I know. Of course. The thing is to buy safety for now by raising these people's expectations and making them greedy. Meanwhile, I've a plan to win the caliph over to your side. With God's help, it'll work. Deliverance can come at any moment! No need to meet death halfway! It'll be worth it even if you only gain one day's respite."

I said, "Your love and advice are unimpeachable. I'll do as you say."

Mūsā ibn ʿAbd al-Malik now turned to the others and addressed them. 73.12 "Gentlemen," he said, "I have advised him to put his signature to a sum that is more than he can afford, let alone any greater amount. May I ask that we use our own money and position to help him out and make the arrangement work? This is the sum I've said we'll back him for."

"Fair enough," they said.

١٣،٧٣ فدعا لي بدواة وقرطاس وأخذ خطّي بالمال على نجومه فلمّا أخذه قام قائماً وقال لإسحاق يا سيّدي هذا رجل قد صار عليه للسلطان أعزّه الله مال وسبيله أن يرفّه وتحرس نفسه وينقل من هذه الحال ويغيّر زيّه ويردّ جاهه بإنزاله داراً كبيرة وإخدامه بفرش وآلة حسنة وإخدامه خدّاماً بين يديه ويمكّن من لقاء من يؤثّر لقاءه من معامليه ومن يحبّ لقاءه من أهله وولده وحاشيته ليجدّ في حمل المال الحالّ عليه قبل محلّه ونعينه نحن ويبيع أملاكه ويرتجع ودائعه ممّن هي عنده فقال إسحاق الساعة أفعل ذلك وأبلغه جميع ما ذكرت وأمكّنه منه ونهضت الجماعة.

١٤،٧٣ فأمر إسحاق بفكّ حديدي وإدخالي الحمّام وجاءني بخلعة حسنة وطيب وبخور فاستعملته واستدعاني فلمّا دخلت عليه نهض إليّ ولم يكن في مجلسه أحد واعتذر إليّ ممّا خاطبني به وقال أنا صاحب سيف ومأمور وقد ألحقني اليوم من أجلك سماع كلّ مكروه حتّى امتنعت عن الطعام غمّاً بأن أبتلى بقتلك أو يعتب الخليفة عليّ من أجلك وإنّما خاطبتك بذلك إقامة عذر عند هؤلاء الأشرار ليبلغوا الخليفة ذلك وجعلته وقاية لك من الضرب والعذاب فشكرته وقلت ما حضرني من الكلام.

١٥،٧٣ فلمّا كان من الغد حوّلني إلى دار كبيرة واسعة حسنة مفروشة ووكّل بي فيها على إحسان وإجلال[١] عشرة فاستدعيت كلّ من أريده وتسامع بي أصحابي فجاؤوني.

١٦،٧٣ وفرّج الله عنّي ومضت سبعة وعشرون يوماً وقد أعددت ألف ألف درهم مال النجم الأوّل وأنا أتوقّع أن يحلّ فأطالب فأؤدّيه فإذا بموسى بن عبد الملك قد دخل إليّ فقمت إليه فقال أبشر فقلت ما الخبر يا سيّدي.

١٧،٧٣ فقال ورد كتاب عامل مصر بمبلغ مال مصر لهذه السنة مجملاً في مبلغ الحمل والنفقات إلى أن ينفذ حسابه مفصّلاً فقرأ عبيد الله ذلك على المتوكّل فوقّع إلى ديواني

١ كذا في بن، س. ش: على إحسان عشرة وإجلال.

So Mūsā sent for inkwell and paper,[247] and made me put my signature to the payments. Then he rose to his feet and addressed Isḥāq: "Sir, here is a man who owes money to our revered caliph's government, which should secure his person by granting him easy terms. Let him be taken from custody and his clothes changed, and let him be restored to his proper status and lodged in spacious quarters with servants, fine furnishings, and personal attendants. Let him be free to meet with whichever of his associates he wants, and with any wife, children, or household members he likes, so that he will do his best to get the money he owes before it falls due. We will help him. Let him sell his possessions, and let all his deposits be called in from their consignees." 73.13

"I'll have this done at once," said Isḥāq. "I'll tell him what you said and give him a free hand."

With this, the meeting broke up.

On Isḥāq's orders, my shackles were struck off and I was taken to the bathhouse. He had them bring me a handsome robe of honor, and scents and incense to perfume my clothes. Then he sent for me. He rose as I entered; we were alone. 73.14

He apologized for having been rude to me: "I'm a man of the sword and I obey orders. I've had an earful on your account today, and I was put off my food worrying that I might actually have to execute you to avoid the caliph's displeasure. I said what I did to cover myself in front of those villains so they'd report it to the caliph and I wouldn't have to have you flogged and tortured."

I thanked him as best I could.

The next morning, he had me moved to large, handsome, spacious, furnished quarters, and as a mark of kindness and respect provided me with ten servants. I could invite whatever visitors I wanted. Word reached my friends, who rallied round. 73.15

Then God delivered me: for when twenty-seven days had passed, I had raised a million dirhams, the amount of the first installment. I was just waiting for it to fall due, and to pay off the demand, when Mūsā ibn ʿAbd al-Malik was shown in. 73.16

I rose to greet him and he cried, "Rejoice!"

"What news, sir?" I asked.

He replied, "The comptrollor of Egypt has sent in his provisional financial statement for this year, surplus and expenditure combined, with a detailed statement to follow. ʿUbayd Allāh ibn Yaḥyā ibn Khāqān read it out 73.17

بإخراج العبرة لمصر ليعرف أثر العامل فأخرجت ذلك من ديوان الخراج والضياع لأنّ مصر تجري في ديوان الخراج والضياع وينفذ حسابها إلى الديوانين كما قد علمت وجعلت سنتك التي تولّيت فيها عمالة مصر مصدّرة وأوردت بعدها السنين الناقصة عن سنتك تلطّفاً في خلاصك وجعلت أقول النقصان في سنة كذا عن سنة كذا وكذا التي صدّرناها كذا وكذا ألفاً فلمّا قرأ عبيد الله العمل على المتوكّل قال فهذه السنة الوافرة من كان يتولّى عمالتها فقلت أنا سليمان بن وهب يا أمير المؤمنين فقال المتوكّل فلم لا يُردّ إليها فقلت وأين سليمان بن وهب ذاك مقتول بالمطالبة قد استصفي وافتقر.

١٨،٧٣ فقال تزال عنه المطالبة ويعان بمائة ألف درهم ويعجّل إخراجه فقلت وتردّ ضياعه يا أمير المؤمنين ليرجع جاهه قال ويفعل ذلك وقد تقدّم إلى عبيد الله بهذا واستأذنته في إخراجك فأذن لي فقم بنا إلى الوزير قال وكان قد أرسل إلى إسحاق برسالة الخليفة تأذنه له في إطلاقي[1] فخرجت من وقتي ولم أؤدّ من مال النجم الأوّل حبّة واحدة ورددته إلى موضعه وجئت إلى عبيد الله فوقّع لي بمائة ألف درهم معونة على سفري ودفع إليّ عهدي على مصر فخرجت إليها.

١،٧٤ حدّثني أبو بكر محمّد بن إسحاق الأهوازيّ أحد شهود أبي بها عن مسرور بن عبد الله الأستاديّ قال

حزبني أمر ضقت به ذرعاً فأتيت يحيى بن خالد الأزرق وكان مستجاب الدعوة فرآني مكروباً قلقاً فقال لي ما شأنك فقلت دُفعت إلى كيت وكيت فقال لي استعن بالصبر فإنّ الله وعد الصابرين خيراً فقلت له ادع لي.

[1] كذا في س. ش: وقد كان دخل إلى اسحاق برسالة الخليفة بإطلاقي.

to al-Mutawakkil, who authorized my office[248] to draw up Egypt's adjusted averages, so as to see how the comptroller has performed. I took the figures from the offices of land tax and estates, since Egypt comes under both and its accounts go through both offices, as you know. To help persuade them to release you, I put down the year when you were comptroller of Egypt at the top, followed by the years that were in deficit by comparison, and explained to them:

"'The deficit in the year such and such, as compared to the year so and so, at the top, is X thousand.'

"When 'Ubayd Allāh read out the arithmetic to al-Mutawakkil, he asked, 'The bumper year—who was comptroller then?'

"I said, 'Sulaymān ibn Wahb, sire.'

"'Then why wasn't he reappointed?'

"'Where is Sulaymān ibn Wahb to be found? Fined to death! A pauper, his fortune confiscated!'

"'Cancel the fine,' said the caliph. 'Give him a hundred thousand dirhams 73.18
for his expenses and send him to Egypt with all speed!'

"'And may his estates be returned to him, sire, to restore his standing?'

"'That too!'

"'Ubayd Allāh ibn Yaḥyā ibn Khāqān had already agreed to this, and I've got his authorization for your appointment, so off with us to the vizier!"

The caliph's written order for my release had been forwarded to Isḥāq, enabling me to set off on the instant—without my having paid a jot of the first installment, which I gave back. 'Ubayd Allāh wrote me a draft for a hundred thousand dirhams for travel expenses and handed me my letter of appointment, and I set out for Egypt.[249]

I cite Abū Bakr Muḥammad ibn Isḥāq of Ahwaz, who acted as a legal witness 74.1
there for my father, quoting Masrūr ibn 'Abd Allāh al-Ustādī:

Vexed by an intolerable situation, I went to see Yaḥyā ibn Khālid the Blue-Eyed, for he was a person whose prayers were answered. Seeing me afflicted and troubled, he asked, "What is the matter?"

I told him my plight.

He replied, "Call acceptance to your aid, for God has promised good things to those who show acceptance."

فحرّك شفتيه بشيء لا أعلم ما هو فانصرفت على جملتي من القلق فلمّا أصبحت أتاني الفرج بإذن الله تعالى. ٢،٧٤

قال مؤلّف هذا الكتاب ويحيى بن خالد هذا هو جدّ عبد الله بن محمّد بن يحيى الأهوازيّ الكاتب وعبد الله هذا جدّي لأمّي.

حدّثني عبد الله بن أحمد بن داسه البصريّ قال ١،٧٥

اعتللت علّة شديدة أيست فيها من نفسي على شدّة كنت فيها فعادني بعض أصحاب أبي محمّد سهل بن عبد الله التستريّ فقال كان أبو محمّد سهل يدعو الله في علله بدعاء ما دعا به أحد إلّا عوفي فقلت وما هو فقال قل اللّهمّ اشفني بشفائك وداوني بدوائك وعافني من بلائك.

قال فواصلت الدعاء بذلك فعوفيت. ٢،٧٥

حدّثني أبو الحسن أحمد بن يوسف الأزرق بن يعقوب بن إسحاق ابن البهلول التنوخيّ عن أبي الحسين بن البوّاب المقرئ قال ١،٧٦

كان يصحبنا على القرآن رجل مستور صالح يكنى أبا أحمد وكان يكتب كتب العطف للناس فحدّثني يوماً قال

بقيت يوماً بلا شيء وأنا جالس في دكّاني وقد دعوت الله أن يسهّل قوتي فما استتممت الدعاء حتّى فتح باب دكّاني غلام أمرد حسن الوجه جدّاً فسلّم عليّ وجلس فقلت له ما حاجتك فقال أنا عبد مملوك وقد طردني مولاي وغضب عليّ وقال انصرف عنّي إلى حيث شئت. وما أعددت لنفسي من أطرحها عليه في مثل هذا الوقت ولا أعرف من أقصده وقد بقيت متحيّرًا في أمري وقيل لي إنّك تكتب كتب العطف فاكتب لي كتاباً

"Pray for me!" I said.

74.2 His lips moved, but I could not make out the words, and went away just as troubled as before; but the very next morning brought me deliverance from God, exalted is He.

(The author of this book observes: This Yaḥyā ibn Khālid was the grandfather of ʿAbd Allāh ibn Muḥammad ibn Yaḥyā of Ahwaz, the state scribe, who was my own maternal forebear.)[250]

75.1 I cite ʿAbd Allāh ibn Aḥmad ibn Dāsah of Basra, who said:

I suffered an adversity that made me so ill I despaired of my life. I received a visit from a follower of Abū Muḥammad Sahl ibn ʿAbd Allāh of Tustar, who told me:

"Whenever al-Tustarī was ill, he would say a prayer to God, which always healed whoever said it."

"What was it?" I asked.

"Say: O God! Give me Your remedy; treat me with Your medicine, and cure me of the tribulation You have sent."

75.2 I said the prayer over and over, and was cured.

76.1 I cite Abū l-Ḥasan Aḥmad ibn Yūsuf the Blue-Eyed, son of Yaʿqūb ibn Isḥāq ibn al-Buhlūl al-Tanūkhī, quoting the Qur'an scholar Abū l-Ḥusayn, son of the Doorman, who said: An upright man whose courtesy name was Abū Aḥmad used to study the Qur'an with us. He wrote charms to reconcile people who had quarreled, and told me:

One day I was sitting in my shop, and because no business had come my way, I made a prayer to God to let me earn my bread. Before my prayer was done, my shop door was opened by an extremely good-looking beardless boy,[251] who greeted me and sat down.

"What can I do for you?" I asked.

He said, "I'm a slave. My master is angry with me and has thrown me out. 'Leave me and go where you like!' he said. But I've no one to turn to in an emergency, and I don't know what to do because I've no one to go to. But someone told me you write charms for people who have fallen out. Write one for me!"

فكتبت له الكتاب الذي كنت أكتبه وهو ﴿ بِسْمِ ٱللَّهِ ٱلرَّحْمَٰنِ ٱلرَّحِيمِ ٱلْحَمْدُ لِلَّهِ رَبِّ ٱلْعَٰلَمِينَ ﴾ إلى آخر السورة والمعوّذتين وسورة الإخلاص وآية الكرسي و ﴿ لَوْ أَنزَلْنَا هَٰذَا ٱلْقُرْءَانَ عَلَىٰ جَبَلٍ لَّرَأَيْتَهُۥ خَٰشِعًا مُّتَصَدِّعًا مِّنْ خَشْيَةِ ٱللَّهِ وَتِلْكَ ٱلْأَمْثَٰلُ نَضْرِبُهَا لِلنَّاسِ لَعَلَّهُمْ يَتَفَكَّرُونَ ﴾ إلى آخر السورة وكتبت آيات العطف وهي ﴿ لَوْ أَنفَقْتَ مَا فِى ٱلْأَرْضِ جَمِيعًا مَّآ أَلَّفْتَ بَيْنَ قُلُوبِهِمْ وَلَٰكِنَّ ٱللَّهَ أَلَّفَ بَيْنَهُمْ ﴾ الآية ﴿ وَمِنْ ءَايَٰتِهِۦٓ أَنْ خَلَقَ لَكُم مِّنْ أَنفُسِكُمْ أَزْوَٰجًا لِّتَسْكُنُوٓا۟ إِلَيْهَا وَجَعَلَ بَيْنَكُم مَّوَدَّةً وَرَحْمَةً ﴾ إلى آخر الآية ﴿ وَٱذْكُرُوا۟ نِعْمَتَ ٱللَّهِ عَلَيْكُمْ إِذْ كُنتُمْ أَعْدَآءً فَأَلَّفَ بَيْنَ قُلُوبِكُمْ فَأَصْبَحْتُم بِنِعْمَتِهِۦٓ إِخْوَٰنًا ﴾ إلى آخر الآية. ٢،٧٦

وقلت له خذ هذه الرقعة فشدّها على عضدك الأيمن ولا تعلّقها عليك إلّا وأنت طاهر فأخذها وقام وهو يبكي وطرح بين يديّ دينارًا عينًا فداخلتني له رحمة فصلّيت ركعتين ودعوت له أن ينفعه الله بالكتاب ويردّ عليه قلب مولاه. ٣،٧٦

وجلست فما مضت إلّا ساعاتان وإذا بأبي الجود خليفة عجيب غلام نازوك وكان خليفته على الشرطة قد جاءني فقال لي أجب الأمير نازوك فارتعت فقال لا بأس عليك وأركبني بغلاً وجاء بي إلى دار نازوك فتركني في الدهليز ودخل فلمّا كان بعد ساعة أدخلت. ٤،٧٦

فإذا نازوك جالس في دست عظيم وبين يديه الغلمان قيامًا سماطين نحو ثلثمائة غلام وأكثر وكاتبه الحسين جالس بين يديه ورجل آخر لا أعرفه فارتعت وأهويت لأقبّل الأرض فقال مه عافاك الله لا تفعل هذا من سنن الجبّارين وما نريد نحن هذا اجلس يا شيخ ولا تخف فجلست فقال لي جاءك اليوم غلام أمرد فكتبت له كتابًا للعطف قلت نعم قال اصدقني عمّا جرى بينكما حرفًا حرفًا. ٥،٧٦

فأعدته عليه حتّى لم أدع كلمة وتلوت عليه الآيات التي كتبتها فلمّا بلغت إلى قول الغلام أنا عبد مملوك وما أعددت لنفسي من أقصده في هذه الحال ولا أعرف أحدًا ٦،٧٦

So I wrote him my standard charm: the whole of the first surah, «In the name of God, full of compassion, ever compassionate: Praise be to God, Lord of all . . .»;[252] the two refuge surahs;[253] Ikhlāṣ;[254] the Throne Verse;[255] the end of Ḥashr: «Had We made this Qur'an come down upon a mountain, you would have seen it flatten and split for fear of God; these parables We strike for men, to make them reflect . . .»;[256] and I wrote the conciliation verses:[257] the whole of the verse «. . . had you expended everything on earth, you could not have reconciled their hearts; but God has reconciled them . . .»;[258] the whole of the verse «And one of His signs is that He made you spouses from your own selves to live with in peace, and set love and compassion between you . . .»;[259] and the whole of the verse «. . . and remember God's blessing on you, that you were enemies, and He reconciled your hearts, and by His blessing you became brothers . . .».[260] 76.2

Then I said to him, "Take this and bind it on your right arm, making sure you're in a state of ritual purity." 76.3

He took it and got to his feet, weeping, and threw me a solid-gold dinar.

I felt so sorry for him that I said a prayer of two sequences for God to make the charm work for him and give him back his master's heart.

Not two hours later, I was sitting in my shop when Abū l-Jūd, the lieutenant of ʿAjīb, Nāzūk's henchman, who was his deputy in charge of the police, came in and terrified me by saying, "General Nāzūk wants you.[261] It's nothing to worry about," he added, and put me on a mule, took me to Nāzūk's mansion, and left me in the antechamber. After a while, I was told to enter. 76.4

There was Nāzūk, seated on a great throne, with soldiers drawn up in two ranks in front of him, three hundred of them or more, his secretary Abū l-Qāsim seated beside him, and another man I did not recognize. 76.5

I threw myself down in terror and made to kiss the ground.

"Whoa! Stop, bless you!" said Nāzūk. "That's for tyrants; it's not our way. Sit down, sir, and don't be afraid."

I sat, and he continued: "Today, a beardless boy came to see you, and you wrote him a reconciliation charm."

"Yes," I said.

"Tell me truthfully what passed between you, every single syllable."

I repeated what had happened without leaving out one word, and recited the verses that I had written down. When I came to the part where the boy said, "I'm a slave, and I've no one to go to in an emergency. There's no one to 76.6

ألجأ إليه وقد طردني مولاي بكيت لما تداخلني من رحمة له وأريته الدينار الذي أعطانيه.

فدمعت عينا نازوك وتجلّد واستوفى الحديث وقال قم يا شيخ بارك الله عليك ومهما عرضت لك من حاجة أو لجار لك أو صديق فسلْنا إيّاها فإنّا نقضيها وأكثر عندنا وانبسط في هذه الدار فإنّك غير محجوب عنها. ٧،٧٦

فدعوت له وخرجت فلمّا صرت خارج باب المجلس إذا بغلام قد أعطاني قرطاساً فيه ثلثمائة درهم فأخذته وخرجت فلمّا صرت في الدهليز إذا بالفتى فعدل بي إلى موضع وأجلسني فقلت ما خبرك فقال أنا غلام الأمير وكان قد طردني وغضب عليّ فلمّا جلست عندك[١] طلبني فرجعت مع رسله فقال لي أين كنت فصدقت الحديث فلم يصدّقني وأمر بإحضارك فلمّا اتّفقنا في الحديث وخرجت الساعة أحضرني وقال يا بنيّ أنت الساعة من أجلّ غلماني عندي وأمكنهم من قلبي وأخصّهم بي إذ كنت لمّا غضبت عليك ما غيّرك ذلك عن محبّتي والرغبة في خدمتي وطلب الحيل في الرجوع إليّ وانكشف لي أنّك ما أعددت لنفسك بعد الله سواي ولا عرفت وجهاً تلجأ إليه في الدنيا غيري فما ترى بعد هذا إلّا كلّ ما تحبّ وسأعلي منزلتك وأبلغ بك أعلى مراتب نظرائك ولعلّ الله سبحانه استجاب فيك دعاء هذا الرجل الصالح ونفعك بالآيات فبأيّ شيئ كافأت الرجل فقلت ما أعطيته غير ذلك الدينار. ٨،٧٦

فقال سبحان الله قم إلى الخزانة فخذ منها ما تريد وأعطه فأخذت منها هذا القرطاس وجئتك به فخذه وأعطاني أيضاً خمسمائة درهم وقال لي الزمني فإنّي أحسن إليك ٩،٧٦

فجئته بعد مديدة فإذا هو قائد جليل وقد بلغ به نازوك تلك المنزلة فوصلني بصلة جليلة وصار لي عدّةً على الدهر وذخيرةً. ١٠،٧٦

[١] س: جئتك جلست عندك. ب، ش: فلمّا أن جئتك واحتبست عندك.

give me a home now my master has thrown me out," I burst into tears of pity, and showed Nāzūk the gold coin the boy had given me.

Nāzūk wept. Then he mastered himself, and when he had heard me out, he said, "That will do, sir. God bless you. Whenever there is anything you need—you, or any neighbor or friend of yours—come to us, and we will take care of it. And come here often; make yourself at home; to you, our door is never barred." 76.7

I thanked him and left. Outside the audience chamber, a soldier gave me a receipt for three hundred dirhams. 76.8

I was on my way out through the antechamber when I suddenly saw my young man. He took me aside and sat me down.

"What's going on?" I asked.

He said, "My master, who lost his temper and threw me out, is the general. While I was with you, he sent messengers to look for me. I went back with them and he asked me, 'Where have you been?' I told him, but he didn't believe me and sent for you. Just now, when our two accounts tallied, just after you left him, he called me in and said:

"'Child, from now on, I shall think more of you than of any of my other men, and I will love and trust you more than any of them, for even when I was angry with you, you didn't stop loving me and wanting to serve me and trying to find a way to get me to take you back. I realize now that, God excepted, I am your sole support and you have no one else in the world to turn to. From now on, you shall always be well treated. I will promote you and pay you the highest salary your peers receive. It seems to me that God, glory to Him, has answered that good man's prayers on your behalf and made the verses work for you. How have you repaid him?'

"'I only gave him the one dinar,' I said.

"'Good heavens!' he said. 'Go to the treasury, take as much as you want and give it to him!' So I took this voucher. Here!" he said, giving me another receipt for five hundred dirhams. "Stick to me and I'll look after you." 76.9

Shortly after, I went to see him, and found that Nāzūk had made him a high-ranking officer. He gave me a large sum of money, and became my insurance against vicissitude. 76.10

١،٧٧ حدّثني محمّد بن محمّد المعروف بابن[1] المهندس قال حدّثني أبو مروان الجامديّ قال

لمّا ظلم الناس بواسط أحمد بن سعيد الكوفيّ وهو إذ ذاك يتقلّدها لناصر الدولة وقد أمره الإمرة ببغداد كنت أحد من ظلم[2] وأخذ من ضيعتي بالجامدة نيّفاً وأربعين كرّاً أرزّاً بالنصف من حقّ الرقبة بغير تأويل ولا شبهة سوى ما أخذه بحقّ بيت المال وظلم فيه أيضاً فتظلّمت إليه وكلّمته فلم ينفعني معه شيء وكان الكرّ الأرزّ بالنصف إذ ذاك بثلاثين ديناراً.

٢،٧٧ فقلت له قد أخذ منّي سيّدي ما أخذ ووالله ما أهتدي أنا وعيالي إلى ما سوى ذلك وما لي ما أقوتهم به باقي سنتي ولا ما أعمّر به ضيعتي وقد طابت نفسي أن تطلق لي من جملته عشرة أكرار وجعلتك من الباقي في حلّ فقال ما إلى هذا سبيل فقلت فخمسة أكرار فقال لا أفعل فبكيت وقبّلت يده ورقّقته وقلت هب لي ثلاثة أكرار وتصدّق عليّ بها وأنت من الجميع في حلّ فقال لا والله ولا أرزة واحدة فتحيّرت وقلت فإنّي أتظلّم منك إلى الله تعالى فقال لي كن على الظلامة يكرّرها دفعات ويكسر الميم بلسان أهل الكوفة.

٣،٧٧ فانصرفت منكسر القلب منقطع الرجاء فجمعت عيالي وما زلنا ندعو عليه ليالي كثيرة.

٤،٧٧ فهرب من واسط في الليلة الحادية عشرة من أخذه الأرزّ فجئت إلى البيدر والأرزّ مطروح فأخذته وحملته إلى منزلي وما عاد الكوفيّ بعدها إلى واسط ولا أفلح.

١،٧٨ وحدّثني غير واحد من الكتّاب عمّن سمع أبا عليّ بن مقلة لمّا عاد من فارس وزيراً يحدّث قال

من طريف ما اتّفق لي في نكبتي هذه التي أدّتني إلى الوزارة أنّي أصبحت وأنا محبوس مقيّد في حجرة من دار ياقوت أمير فارس وقد لحقني من اليأس من الفرج

[1] المعروف بابن: الزيادة من بن. [2] كذا في س. ش: ظلمني أحمد بن علي بن سعيد الكوفيّ وهو يتقلّد واسط لناصر الدولة وقد تقلّد إمرة الأمراء ببغداد وكنت أحد من ظلم فظلمني.

I cite Muḥammad ibn Muḥammad, known as the Son of the Geometer, who said: Abū Marwān of Jāmidah told me: 77.1

When Aḥmad ibn ʿAlī ibn Saʿīd of Kufa was perverting the course of justice in Wāsiṭ, of which he had been appointed governor by Nāṣir al-Dawlah at the same time as he was supreme commander in Baghdad,[262] I was one of his victims. He unjustly took from my estate in Jāmidah some forty half-bushels of rice in dues,[263] for which he gave no explanation or excuse, in addition to what he levied in tax, which he also assessed unfairly.

I went and lodged an official complaint, and reasoned with him, but it was no use.

At that time, the value of a half-bushel of rice was thirty dinars.

"I swear to God that what Your Excellency has taken from me is all that I and my dependents have to live on," I told him. "I have nothing left to feed them on for the rest of the year, and nothing to keep the farm going. If you give me back ten bushels, I'm happy for the rest to be legally yours." 77.2

"Impossible."

"Five bushels, then."

"Certainly not."

I wept and kissed his hand and wheedled: "Give me three bushels as charity, and all the rest is yours by law!"

"No, by God, not one grain!"

Confounded, I exclaimed, "I'll lodge an official complaint against you with the Almighty!"

"Go right ahead with your compl*int*," he said, repeating the word several times and distorting it, as Kufan speakers do.

I went away heartbroken and desperate, and gathered my household, and together we cursed him for several days running. 77.3

On the eleventh night after he stole the rice, he fled Wāsiṭ. I went to the threshing floor where the rice lay, loaded it up, and took it home. The Kufan never returned to Wāsiṭ—nor did he prosper.[264] 77.4

Several state scribes have told me what they heard Ibn Muqlah relate, after he returned from Fars as vizier:[265] 78.1

A curious thing happened to me during the disgrace that brought me to the vizierate. I was imprisoned and lay in chains in a suite in the palace of

وضيق الصدر ما أقنطني وكاد يذهب بعقلي وكنّا أنا وفلان محبوسين مقيّدين في بيت واحد من الحجرة إلّا أنّا على سبيل ترفيه وإكرام فدخل علينا كاتب لياقوت وكان كثيرًا ما يجيئنا برسالته فقال الأمير يقرئكما السلام ويتعرّف أخباركما ويعرض عليكما قضاء حاجة إن كانت لكما.

٢،٧٨ فقلت له تقرأ عليه السلام وتقول له قد والله ضاق صدري واشتهيت أن أشرب على غناء طيّب فإن جاز أن يسامحنا بذلك سرًّا ويتّخذ به منّة عليّ ويدًا تفضّل بذلك فقال له المحبوس الذي كان معي يا هذا ما في قلوبنا فضل لذلك فقلت للكاتب أدِّ عنّي ما قلت لك قال السمع والطاعة.

٣،٧٨ ومضى وعاد فقال الأمير يقول لك نعم وكرامة وعزازة أيّ وقت شئت فقلت الساعة فلم تمض إلّا ساعة حتّى جاءوا بالطعام فأكلنا وبالمشامّ والفواكه والنبيذ وصفّ المجلس فجلست أنا والمحبوس الذي معي في القيدين وقلت له تعال حتّى نشرب ونتفاءل بأوّل صوت تغنّيه المغنّية في سرعة الفرج ممّا نحن فيه فلعلّه يصحّ الفأل فقال أمّا أنا فلا أشرب فلم أزل أرفق به حتّى شرب.

٤،٧٨ فكان أوّل صوت غنّته المغنّية [طويل]

تَوَاعَدَ لِلْبَيْنِ ٱلْخَلِيطُ لِيَنْبَتُّوا وَقَالُوا لِرَاعِي الذَّوْدِ مَوْعِدُكَ السَّبْتُ
وَلَٰكِنَّهُمْ بَانُوا وَلَمْ أَدْرِ بَغْتَةً وَأَفْظَعُ شَيْءٍ حِينَ يَفْجُؤكَ ٱلْبَغْتُ

قال أبو عليّ ذكر المبرّد في كتابه المعروف بالكامل البيت الأوّل ورواه لمحمّد بن يسير.[1]

فقال لي ما هذا ممّا يتفاءل به وأيّ معنى فيه ممّا يدلّ على فرجنا فقلت ما هو إلّا فأل مبارك وأنا أرجو أن يفرّق الله بيننا وبين هذه الحالة التي نحن عليها

١ كذا والصحيح: محمّد بن نمير، أي النميريّ.

Yāqūt, the military governor of Fars. Depression and despair of deliverance had sapped my morale and almost deprived me of my reason. I and another man, both of us in chains, occupied a single room in the suite. It was, however, luxurious, and we were treated with deference.

One morning, Yāqūt's secretary, who often came on errands from him, entered, saying, "The governor sends you his greetings and inquires after your health. If there is anything you want, he is at your service."

"Return his greetings," I said, "and tell him how very depressed I am. I long to drink wine and listen to good singing. Would he be so kind as allow us to do so in private, if he feels he may, as a favor for which I would be much obliged?" 78.2

"We haven't the heart for it, friend," said the other prisoner.

"Convey my message," I told the secretary.

"To hear is to obey," he said.

He went off and returned, announcing, "The governor says, with the deepest respect: Yes, you may, whenever you please." 78.3

"This instant!" I said.

In no time, we were brought perfumes, fruit, and date wine, and were served a meal. The singer took her place,[266] as did I and my fellow prisoner in our chains.

"Come," I said to him, "let's drink. The first song the woman sings we'll use to tell our fortune and see how long it will be before we're delivered. It may come true."

"No wine for me," said my companion; but eventually I coaxed him to have some.

The first song the woman sang was this: 78.4

My lover's tribe resolved to part.
They told the herdsman, "Load the beasts
On Saturday." But suddenly
they left, and I all unawares. How dire it is to be surprised!

(Ibn Muqlah observed: Al-Mubarrad quotes the first verse in his *Comprehensive Corpus* and says that it is by Muḥammad ibn Yasīr.)[267]

"You can't tell your fortune from that," my companion objected, "and what's in it to show we'll be delivered?"

وبين الفرج والصلاح يوم السبت قال وأخذنا في شربنا يومنا وسكرنا وانصرفت المغنّية.

ومضت الأيّام فلمّا كان يوم السبت وقد مضى من النهار ساعتان إذا بياقوت قد دخل علينا فارتعنا وقمت إليه فقال أيّها الوزير الله الله في أمري وأقبل إليّ مسرعًا وعانقني وأجلسني وأخذ يهنّيني بالوزارة فبهتّ ولم يكن عندي علم بشيء من الأمر ولا مقدّمة له. ٥،٧٨

فأخرج إليّ كتابًا ورد عليه من القاهر بالله يعلمه فيه بما جرى من قتل المقتدر[1] ومبايعة الناس له بالخلافة ويأمره بأخذ البيعة على من بفارس من الأولياء وفيه تقليده إيّاي الوزارة ويأمره بطاعتي وسلّم إليّ أيضًا كتابًا من القاهر يأمرني فيه بالنظر في أموال فارس والأولياء بها واستصحاب ما يمكنني من المال وتدبير أمر البلد بما أراه والبدار إلى حضرته وأنّه استخلف لي إلى أن أحضر الكلوذانيّ. ٦،٧٨

فحمدت الله كثيرًا وشكرته وإذا الحدّاد واقف فتقدّمت إليه بفكّ قيودي وقيود الرجل ودخلت الحمّام وأصلحت أمري وأمر الرجل وخرجت فنظرت في الأعمال والأموال وجمعت مالًا جليلًا في أيّام يسيرة وقرّرت أمور البلد وسرت واستصحبت الرجل معي إلى الحضرة حتّى جلست هذا المجلس وفرّج الله عنّا. ٧،٧٨

قال محمّد بن عبدوس في كتابه كتاب الوزراء: وجدت بخطّ أبي عليّ أحمد بن إسماعيل الكاتب حدّثني أحمد بن أبي الأصبغ قال ١،٧٩

وجّهني عبيد الله بن يحيى إلى أبي أيّوب ابن أخت أبي الوزير أيّام تقلّد أبي صالح عبد الله بن محمّد بن يزداد الوزارة وكان ابن يزداد يقصد أبا أيّوب ويعاديه فقال لي عبيد الله الْقه وسهّل عليه الأمر وقل له أرجو أن يكفيك الله شرّه فوصلت إليه وهو يصلّي وقد علّق في محرابه رقعة فأنكرتها وأدّيت إليه الرسالة فقال لي قل له جُعلت

[1] كذا في بن، س. ش: بما جرى على المقتدر.

"On the contrary," I cried, "it's a blessed presage! I'm sure it says that God will *part* us from our painful situation and make plain our deliverance and happiness this *Saturday*!"

The singing woman left, and we spent the rest of the day getting drunk.

The days passed, and on Saturday, two hours after noon, Yāqūt startled us 78.5
by bursting in. As I rose to greet him, he rushed up and embraced me, forcing me to take my seat again, and exclaimed:

"My lord vizier! For God's sake forgive me!" And he started congratulating me on becoming vizier, which amazed me, for I knew nothing about it and had had no warning of it.

Yāqūt then produced a letter sent to him by al-Qāhir telling him that al- 78.6
Muqtadir had been murdered and that he had been sworn in as caliph. The letter ordered Yāqūt to administer the oath of allegiance to al-Qāhir's supporters in Fars, appointed me vizier, and commanded him to obey me. Yāqūt gave me another letter in which the new caliph ordered me to take stock of the finances of Fars and of his supporters in the province, and bring as much money with me as I could, to organize local affairs as I saw fit, and hasten to Baghdad, where al-Kalwadhānī would act as my deputy until my arrival.

The smith appeared as I was pouring out praise and thanks to God. I told 78.7
him to strike off my fetters and those of my fellow prisoner. Afterward I had a bath, put us both to rights, and went off to inspect districts and finances. In a few days I had collected a large amount of money and reorganized local government. Then I traveled to Baghdad, taking my fellow prisoner with me; and now I'm vizier, and God has delivered us both![268]

In his *Book of Viziers*, Muḥammad ibn ʿAbdūs al-Jahshiyārī says: I have read, in 79.1
the handwriting of Abū ʿAlī Aḥmad ibn Ismāʿīl the state scribe: I cite Aḥmad ibn Abī l-Aṣbagh, who said:

ʿUbayd Allāh ibn Yaḥyā ibn Khāqān sent me to see Abū Ayyūb, the maternal nephew of Abū l-Wazīr, when Abū Ṣāliḥ ʿAbd Allāh ibn Muḥammad ibn Yazdād was vizier. Ibn Yazdād was Abū Ayyūb's enemy and sought to destroy him.

ʿUbayd Allāh said, "Go and see him: tell him things aren't so bad. I'm sure God will preserve you from the vizier."

فداك لست أغتمّ بشيء لأنّ أمره قريب وقد رفعت فيه إلى الله تعالى قصّة إذ أعجزني المخلوقون أما تراها معلّقة في القبلة فكاد يغلبني الضحك فضبطت نفسي وانصرفت إلى عبيد الله فحدّثته الحديث فضحك منه.

٢،٧٩ قال فوالله ما مضت بابن يزداد إلّا أيّام يسيرة حتّى سُخط عليه وصرف فاتّفق لأبي أيّوب الفرج ونزل بابن يزداد المكروه في مثل المدّة التي تخرج فيها التوقيعات في القصص.

١،٨٠ قال مؤلّف الكتاب وأنا شاهدت مثل هذا وذلك أنّ أبا الفرج محمّد بن العبّاس بن فسانجس لمّا ولي الوزارة أظهر من الشرّ على الناس والظلم لهم بخلاف ما كان يُقدّر فيه وكنت أحد من ظلمه فإنّه أخذ ضيعتي بالأهواز وأقطعها بالحقّين وأخرجها عن يدي فأصعدت الى بغداد متظلّماً إليه من الحال فما أنصفني على حرمات كانت بيني وبينه.

٢،٨٠ وكنت أتردّد إلى مجلسه فرأيت فيه شيخاً من شيوخ العمّال يعرف بأبي نصر محمّد ابن محمّد الواسطيّ أحد من كان يتصرّف في عمالات بنواحي الأهواز وكان صديقاً لي فسألته عن أمره فذكر أنّ الحسن بن بختيار أحد قوّاد الديلم ضمن أعمال الخراج والضياع بنهر تيرى وبها منزل أبي نصر هذا وأنّه طالبه بظلم لا يلزمه فبعد عن البلد فكبس داره وأخذ جميع ما كان فيها وكان فيما أخذ عُهَد ضياعه كلّها وأنّه حضر للوزير محمّد ابن العبّاس متظلّماً منه فلمّا عرف الحسن بن بختيار ذلك أنفذ بالعهد إلى الوزير وقال له قد أهديت إليك هذه الضياع فقبل الوزير منه ذلك وكتب إلى وكيله في ضيعته بالأهواز فأدخل يده في ضياعي وقد تظلّمت إليه فلم ينصفني.

٣،٨٠ فلمّا كان بعد أيّام دخلت المشهد بمقابر قريش فزرت موسى بن جعفر وعدلت إلى موضع الصلاة لأصلّي فإذا بقصّة معلّقة بخطّ أبي نصر هذا وقد كتبها إلى موسى بن

When I arrived, Abū Ayyūb was saying his prayers. In the prayer niche he had stuck an odd-looking piece of paper. I delivered the message, to which he responded:

"Tell ʿUbayd Allāh, with my thanks, that I'm not at all worried, as Ibn Yazdād's time is at hand. Since no earthly creature would help me, I have brought a suit against him with God Exalted. Look, it's up there in the prayer niche."

I nearly burst out laughing, but contained myself. When I reported back to ʿUbayd Allāh, he laughed out loud.

But I swear to God, only a few days later, Ibn Yazdād was disgraced and 79.2
dismissed. By coincidence, Abū Ayyūb was delivered and Ibn Yazdād ruined in pretty much the time that it takes for the depositions in a lawsuit to be processed.

The author of this book observes: I myself have witnessed something similar. 80.1
When Abū l-Faraj Muḥammad ibn al-ʿAbbās ibn Fasānjus became vizier,[269] he showed himself unexpectedly malicious and inequitable. I was one of his victims: he seized my estate in Ahwaz, impounded it for unpaid taxes and dues,[270] and expropriated me. I sailed up to Baghdad[271] to make an official complaint against him, but he denied me justice despite the ties of obligation that bound us.

On one of my many visits to his audience chamber, I noticed a senior admin- 80.2
istrative officer called Abū Naṣr Muḥammad ibn Muḥammad of Wāsiṭ, who had held office in the Ahwaz district and was friends with me. I asked what he was doing there. He said that a Daylamī commander, al-Ḥasan ibn Bakhtiyār, had been granted the farming of land tax and estates in Nahr Tīrā, where Abū Naṣr had his house. He made wholly extortionate demands on Abū Naṣr, and in Abū Naṣr's absence he occupied his house and seized its contents, including the title deeds to all his lands. Abū Naṣr had come to the vizier to make an official complaint, but when the commander heard about it, he sent the title deeds to the vizier, saying, "I make you a present of these estates." The vizier accepted his gift, and (said Abū Naṣr) "instructed the steward of his own estate in Ahwaz to take possession of mine! I have complained to him officially, but he has denied me justice."

Some days later, I went to the graveyard of Quraysh to visit the shrine of 80.3
Mūsā al-Kāẓim, and as I turned aside to pray, my eye was caught by a deposition

جعفر يتظلّم فيها من محمّد بن العبّاس ويشرح أمره ويتوسّل في القصّة بمحمّد وعليّ وفاطمة والحسن والحسين وباقي الأئمّة عليهم السلام أن يأخذ له بحقّه من محمّد بن العبّاس ويخلّص له ضياعه.

٤،٨٠ فلمّا قرأت الورقة عجبت من ذلك عجباً شديداً ووقع عليّ الضحك لأنّها قصّة إلى رجل ميّت وقد علّقها عند رأسه وكنت عرفت أبا نصر بمذهب الإماميّة الاثني عشريّة فظننت أنّه مع هذا الاعتقاد كان أكبر قصده أن يشنّع على الوزير بالقصّة فإنّه أمل أن تقع عين الوزير على القصّة عند دخوله إلى قبر موسى بن جعفر عليه السلام[١] وكان كثير الزيارة له أيّام وزارته وقبلها وبعدها ليعلم أنّ الرجل على مذهبه فيتذمّم من ظلمه ويرهب الدعاء في ذلك المكان.

٥،٨٠ فانصرفت فلمّا كان بعد أيّام كنت في المشهد وجاء الوزير فرأيته يلاحظ الرقعة فعلمت أنّه قد قرأها ومضى على هذا الحديث مدّة وما رهب القصّة ولا أنصف الرجل وامتدّت محنة الرجل شهوراً.

٦،٨٠ ورحل محمّد بن العبّاس إلى الأهواز للنظر في أبواب المال وتقرير أمر العمّال وأقمت أنا ببغداد لأنّه لم يكن أنصفني ولا طمعت في إنصافه إيّاي لو صحبته وانحدر أبو نصر في جملة من انحدر معه.

٧،٨٠ فلمّا صار بالمأمونيّة قرية حيال سوق الأهواز وهو يريد دخولها من غد ورد من بغداد كتاب إلى بختكين التركيّ مولى معزّ الدولة المعروف بآزاذرويه وكان يتقلّد الحرب والخراج بالأهواز وكورها فقبض عليه وقبض على أمواله وقيّده.

ومضى أبو نصر إلى ضياعه فأدخل يده فيها وكفي ما كان من أمر الوزير واستقرّت ضياعه في يده إلى الآن.

١ كذا في بن، س. ش: أن يشنّع على الوزير بالقصّة عند قبر موسى بن جعفر عليه السلام.

hanging there. It was in the writing of Abū Naṣr and was addressed to Mūsā al-Kāẓim. It was an official complaint against Ibn Fasānjus, explaining Abū Naṣr's case and imploring Muḥammad, ʿAlī, Fāṭimah, al-Ḥasan, al-Ḥusayn, and all the blessed imams to see that he got justice from Ibn Fasānjus and that his estate was given back to him.

Astounded by this document—addressed to a dead man, and suspended in his tomb!—I started to laugh. I knew that Abū Naṣr was a Twelver Shiʿi; nevertheless, I imagined that all he was hoping was that when Ibn Fasānjus entered the tomb of Mūsā al-Kāẓim, peace upon him, which he visited often both before, during, and after his vizierate, he would catch sight of the deposition, and realizing that he and Abū Naṣr were both of the same creed, be ashamed of his iniquity and afraid to pray in that place. 80.4

I left the shrine, but a few days later I was there when the vizier came. I saw him eye the piece of paper, so I knew that he had read it. Time passed, but the deposition failed to frighten him; nor did he give justice to Abū Naṣr, whose ordeal stretched to months. 80.5

Then the vizier journeyed to Ahwaz to inspect local finances and give orders to the district officers. I remained in Baghdad, for he had not given me justice, and I had no hope that he would do so even if I traveled with him. Abū Naṣr, however, went down to Ahwaz in his entourage. 80.6

But at the village of al-Maʾmūniyyah opposite Sūq al-Ahwāz, which the vizier had intended to visit the following day, a letter came from Baghdad for Bukhtakīn the Turk, known as Āzādhrawayh, the protégé of Muʿizz al-Dawlah, who was in charge of War and Land Tax in Ahwaz and its dependencies. He arrested the vizier, threw him in chains, and seized his property.[272] 80.7

Rid of the vizier, Abū Naṣr went to his estate, regained possession of it, and remains in possession to this day.

وأقمت أنا سنين أتظلّم من تلك المحنة التي ظلمني فيها محمّد بن العبّاس فما أنصفني أحد وأيست وخرجت تلك الضيعة من يدي فما عادت إلى الآن وصحّ لأبي نصر بقصّته ما لم يصحّ لي وكانت محنته ومحنتي واحدة ففاز هو بتعجيل الفرج بها من حيث لم يغلب على ظنّي أن أطلب الفرج منه. ٨،٨٠

قال محمّد بن عبدوس في كتاب الوزراء إنّ ابراهيم بن العباس الصوليّ قال ١،٨١

كنت أكتب لأحمد بن أبي خالد فدخلت عليه يوماً فرأيته مطرقاً مفكرّاً مغموماً فسألته عن الخبر فأخرج إليّ رقعة فإذا فيها أنّ حظيّة من أعزّ جواريه عنده يخالَف إليها وتوطئ فراشه غيره ويستشهد في الرقعة بخادمين كانا ثقتين عنده وقال لي دعوت الخادمين فسألتهما عن ذلك فأنكرا فتهدّدتهما فأقاما على الإنكار فضربتهما وأحضرت لهما آلة العذاب فاعترفا بكلّ ما في الرقعة على الجارية وإنّي لم أذق أمس ولا اليوم طعاماً وقد هممت بقتل الجارية.

٢،٨١ فوجدت بين يديه مصحفاً ففتحته لأتفاءل بما يخرج فيه فكان أوّل ما وقعت عيني عليه ﴿يَٰٓأَيُّهَا ٱلَّذِينَ ءَامَنُوٓاْ إِن جَآءَكُمۡ فَاسِقُۢ بِنَبَإٖ فَتَبَيَّنُوٓاْ﴾ الآية فشككت في صحّة الحديث ورأيته ما خرج به الفأل وقلت دعني أتلطّف في كشف هذا قال افعل.

٣،٨١ فخلوت بالخادمين منفردين ورفقت بأحدهما فقال النار ولا العار وذكر أنّ امرأة ابن أبي خالد أعطته ألف دينار وسألته الشهادة على الجارية وأحضرني الكيس مختوماً بخاتم المرأة وأمرته أن لا يذكر شيئاً إلّا بعد أن يوقع به المكروه ليكون أثبت للخبر ودعوت الآخر فاعترف بمثل ذلك أيضاً.

٤،٨١ فبادرت إلى أحمد بالبشارة فما وصلت إليه حتّى جاءته رقعة الحرّة تعلمه أنّ الرقعة الأولى كانت من فعلها غيرة عليه من الجارية وأنّ جميع ما فيها باطل وأنّها حملت

I, on the other hand, spent years seeking redress for the ordeal of the unfair dealing visited on me by Ibn Fasānjus and could get justice from no one. In the end I gave up and lost possession of my estate, which I have still not gotten back. Abū Naṣr, with his deposition, achieved what I could not achieve, although our predicaments were identical. He won early deliverance, whereas it never entered my mind to appeal for deliverance to a higher power! 80.8

In the *Book of Viziers*, Muḥammad ibn ʿAbdūs al-Jahshiyārī[273] says: Ibrāhīm ibn al-ʿAbbās al-Ṣūlī[274] says: 81.1

I was secretary to Aḥmad ibn Abī Khālid. When I came to him one day, I saw that he was grief-stricken, his head bowed in thought. I asked him what was the matter. In reply, he showed me a letter, which said that his concubine, one of his most beloved slaves, was deceiving him with another man. Two of his trusted eunuchs were cited as witnesses.

"I sent for them and questioned them," he told me. "They denied it; I threatened them. They still denied it, so I flogged them and threatened them with torture. Then they confessed to everything the letter said about the woman. No food has passed my lips for two days. I mean to kill her."

Now, there was a Qur'an lying there. I opened it in search of a presage, and the first passage my eye lighted on was: «Believers! If an evildoer brings you news, find out what it means . . .».[275] The allegation must be untrue, I thought, and I showed the passage to Aḥmad, saying, "Let me use persuasion to discover the truth." 81.2

"Very well," said he.

I interviewed the two eunuchs separately, in private. Because I was gentle with him, the first one said, "Better damned than dishonest," and told me that Aḥmad's wife had given him a thousand dinars to bear witness against the slave woman. He showed me the purse with her seal on it. To strengthen his evidence, she had ordered him to say nothing unless the worst came to the worst. I then called in the second eunuch, who made a similar confession. 81.3

I hurried to bring the good news to Aḥmad, but was forestalled by a letter from his wife telling him that the first letter was her doing. She was jealous of the slave woman, and everything it said was a lie. She had made the eunuchs bear false witness, and was truly sorry for this and for other things she had done. 81.4

الخادمين على ذلك وأنّها تائبة إلى الله تعالى من هذا الفعل وأمثاله فجاءته براءة الجارية من كلّ وجه فسرّ بذلك وزال عنه ما كان فيه وأحسن إلى الجارية.

١،٨٢ حدّثني أبو القاسم طلحة بن محمّد بن جعفر الشاهد المقرئ المعروف بغلام ابن مجاهد قال حدّثني أبو الحسين الخصيبيّ قال حدّثني أبو خازم القاضي قال حدّثني أبو الحسن أحمد بن محمّد بن المدبّر قال

كان بدء خروجي إلى الشام أنّ المتوكّل خرج يتنزّه بالمحمّديّة فخلا به الكتّاب هناك فأحكموا عليّ القصّة وأنا لا أعلم ثمّ بعثوا إليّ وأنا لا أدري فحضرت وهم مجتمعون فقالوا لي وكان المخاطب لي موسى بن عبد الملك. فقال لي قد جرت أسباب أوجبت أنّ أمير المؤمنين أمر أن تخرج إلى الرقّة فكم تحتاج لنفقتك فقلت أمّا خروجي فالسمع والطاعة لأمير المؤمنين وأمّا الذي أحتاج إليه للنفقة فهو ثلاثون ألف درهم فما برحت حتّى دفعت إليّ. وقالوا اخرج الساعة فقلت أودّع أمير المؤمنين فقالوا ما إلى ذلك سبيل فقلت أصلح من شأني فقالوا ولا هذا.

٢،٨٢ وأخذ موسى يعرّض لي أنّ السلطان قد سخط عليّ وأنّ الصواب الخروج وترك الخلاف وأقبل يقول إنّ السلطان إذا سخط على الرجل فالصواب لذلك الرجل أن ينتهي إلى أمره كلّه وأن لا يراجعه في شيء وينبغي أن يعلم أنّ التباعد عن السلطان له فيه الحظّ فقلت يكفي الله ويلطف.

فوكّلوا بي جماعة حتّى خرجت من البلد وأنا في حالة الأسر عندي أحسن منها وأطيب وحثّوا بي السير.

٣،٨٢ فلمّا قاربت الرقّة وأردت الدخول إليها أدركنا الليل فإذا بأعرابيّ في ناحية عنّي ومعه إبل يحدوها ويقول [رجز]

Aḥmad's gloom lifted now that he had proof from all sides of his slave woman's innocence. He rejoiced, and showed her every kindness.

I cite Abū l-Qāsim Ṭalḥah ibn Muḥammad ibn Jaʿfar, the legal witness and Qurʾan scholar, known as Ibn Mujāhid's Pupil, citing Abū l-Ḥusayn al-Khaṣībī, citing Judge Abū Khāzim, citing Abū l-Ḥasan Aḥmad ibn Muḥammad Ibn al-Mudabbir, who said: 82.1

This is how my posting to Syria came about. The caliph al-Mutawakkil went on an outing to al-Muḥammadiyyah.[276] There the state scribes took him aside and made a complaint against me of which I knew nothing, and sent for me while I was still in ignorance. When I arrived, there they all were, and they said—their spokesman was Mūsā ibn ʿAbd al-Malik:[277]

"Circumstances have arisen that oblige the Commander of the Faithful to order you to proceed to Raqqah. How much do you need for your travel expenses?"

I replied, "I will certainly proceed to Raqqah in obedience to the Commander of the Faithful. My expenses will be thirty thousand dirhams," and I refused to budge until the money was paid.

Then they said, "Proceed immediately."

I said, "I must first take leave of the Commander of the Faithful."

"Impossible!"

"I must put my affairs in order."

"On no account."

Mūsā ibn ʿAbd al-Malik represented to me that I had fallen from favor and ought to leave at once without arguing. "When a man has lost favor with the regime," he said, "that man ought to call it a day and not quibble. He should realize that it is in his best interest to remove himself from the scene." 82.2

"God's grace will suffice," I retorted.

Prison would have been less irksome than the way they kept me under observation and nagged me to leave.

Finally, as I neared Raqqah and was about to enter the city, night fell, and a Bedouin appeared, herding his camels and saying: 82.3

كَمْ مَرَّةٍ حَفَّتْ بِكَ ٱلْمَكَارِهُ   خَارَ لَكَ اللهُ وَأَنْتَ كَارِهُ

قال ولم يزل يكرّر ذلك فحفظته وتبرّكت بالفأل ودخلت الرقّة فلم أقم بها إلّا أيّاماً ٤،٨٢ يسيرة حتّى ورد كتاب أمير المؤمنين بالخروج إلى الشام للتعديل وأجرى عليّ مائة ألف درهم وذكر أنّ هذا عمل جليل كان المأمون خرج فيه بنفسه لجلالته وعظم خطره وأنّه رآني أهلاً له.

فخرجت فرأيت كلّ ما أحبّ حتّى لو بذلت لي العراق بأسرها على فراق تلك الناحية ٥،٨٢ ما سمحت نفساً بذلك فلله الحمد والمنّة.

وذكر هذا الخبر محمّد بن عبدوس في كتاب الوزراء فقال حدّثني أبو الحسين عبد الواحد ٦،٨٢ ابن محمّد الخصيبيّ قال حدّثني أبو خازم القاضي قال حدّثني جدّك أحمد بن محمّد بن مدبّر وكان جدّه لأمّه وحدّثني أنّه لم يره قطّ أنّ المتوكّل خرج إلى المحمّديّة سنة إحدى وأربعين ومائتين متنزّهاً فأتاني رسوله وأحضرني فحضرت فوجدت عبيد الله بن يحيى والحسن بن مخلد وأحمد بن الخصيب وجماعة من الكتّاب حضوراً فقال لي عبيد الله ابن يحيى إنّ أمير المؤمنين يقول لك قد فسد علينا أمر الرقّة.

ثمّ ذكر نحواً من الحديث الأوّل إلّا أنّه لم يكن فيه إطلاق ثلاثين ألف درهم بل قال ٧،٨٢

فخرجت وما أقدر على نفقة ففكّرت فيمن أقصده وأستعين بماله فما ذكرت غير المعلّى ابن أيّوب وكانت بيني وبينه وحشة فكتبت إليه رقعة حملت نفسي على الصعب فيها فوجّه إليّ خمسة آلاف دينار فتحمّلت بها.

ثمّ ذكر باقي الحديث على سياقة الخبر الأوّل إلّا أنّه قال إنّ الذي أجري عليه لمّا أمر ٨،٨٢ بالخروج للتعديل في كلّ شهر مائة ألف وعشرين ألف درهم قال فشخصت إليها ولو أعطيت الآن بقصري فيها سرّ من رأى كلّها ما سمحت نفساً بذلك.

Oft, when calamities surround you,
God has planned it for your good.

Again and again he said this, and I memorized it and took it for a blessed presage. And indeed, only a few days after my arrival in Raqqah, a letter came from the Commander of the Faithful saying that I was to be paid a hundred thousand dirhams to proceed to Syria and assess the harvest—a matter of such magnitude and extreme importance, he said, that the caliph al-Ma'mūn had undertaken it in person; but I, he said, was equal to the task. 82.4

To Syria therefore I proceeded, and everything went so well that, had I been offered the whole of the revenue of Iraq to leave the province, I would have turned it down. Praise to God for His favor![278] 82.5

Muḥammad ibn ʿAbdūs al-Jahshiyārī mentions this story in the *Book of Viziers*, citing Abū l-Ḥusayn ʿAbd al-Wāḥid ibn Muḥammad al-Khaṣībī, citing Judge Abū Khāzim, who said "your grandfather" Aḥmad ibn Muḥammad Ibn al-Mudabbir told me (that is, his grandfather on his mother's side, whom al-Khaṣībī said he had never met): 82.6

Al-Mutawakkil went on an outing to al-Muḥammadiyyah in 241 [855]. I was summoned to him by messenger, but instead found ʿUbayd Allāh ibn Yaḥyā ibn Khāqān, al-Ḥasan ibn Makhlad, Aḥmad ibn al-Khaṣīb, and a number of other state scribes waiting for me when I arrived.

ʿUbayd Allāh ibn Yaḥyā said, "The Commander of the Faithful says to you: 'Raqqah is being misgoverned.'"

The narrative that follows is similar to the one above, except that instead of being given thirty thousand dirhams, Ibn al-Mudabbir says: 82.7

I set off without the wherewithal to pay my expenses. I wondered who to turn to for money, and the only person I could think of was al-Muʿallā ibn Ayyūb,[279] with whom I had fallen out. I humbled myself to write to him, and he sent me five thousand dinars, with which I equipped myself for the journey.

The narrative then unfolds as above, except that Ibn al-Mudabbir says that what he was paid when he received the order to proceed to the assessment of the harvest was 120,000 dirhams per month; and he says: 82.8

And so I went to Syria; and if the whole of Samarra were offered to me now in return for my mansion there, I would turn it down.[280]

وكان قصره بالرملة وكان جليلاً.

١،٨٣ أخبرني أبو طالب محمّد بن أحمد بن إسحاق بن البهلول فيما أجاز لي روايته عنه بعد ما سمعته منه من حديث قال حدّثني أبو سعيد أحمد بن الصقر بن ثوبان مستملي بندار وكتبه لنا بخطّه ونقلته أنا من أصل أبي طالب الذي ذكر أنّه بخط أبي سعيد قال حدّثنا محمّد بن عبد الله الأنصاريّ قال حدّثنا محمّد بن عليّ بن الحسين ابن عليّ قال

بعث معاوية إلى الحسن بن عليّ أو الحسين بن عليّ عليهما السلام ودعا بضبارة سياط فوضعها بين يديه فلمّا دخل الحسن عليه السلام أخذ السياط فرمى بها ومدّ يده إليه وقال مرحباً بسيّد شباب قريش ودعا بعشرة آلاف دينار وقال استعن بها على زمانك.

٢،٨٣ فلمّا خرج تبعه الحاجب فقال له يا ابن رسول الله إنّا نخدم هذا السلطان ولسنا نأمن بادرته وقد رأيتك تحرّك شفتيك بشيء فما هو فقال أعلّمك على أن لا تعلّم أحداً من آل معاوية قال نعم.

٣،٨٣ قال إذا وقعت في شدّة أو مكروه أو خفت من سلطان فقل لا إله إلّا الله الحليم الكريم لا إله إلّا الله العليّ العظيم لا إله إلّا الله الكبير المتعال سبحان الله ربّ السماوات السبع و ﴿رَبُّ ٱلْعَرْشِ ٱلْعَظِيمِ﴾ و ﴿ٱلْحَمْدُ لِلَّهِ رَبِّ ٱلْعَالَمِينَ﴾ اللّهمّ جلّ ثناؤك وعزّ جارك[1] ولا إله غيرك اللّهمّ إنّي أعوذ بك من شرّ فلان وأتباعه وأشياعه من الجنّ والإنس أن يفرطوا عليّ أو أن يطغوا.

١،٨٤ أخبرني القاضي أبو طالب إجازة قال حدّثنا أبو سعيد قال حدّثني سهل بن محمّد

١ كذا. جارك ساقط من ب.

(His mansion was in Ramlah, and was indeed magnificent.)

I cite Abū Ṭālib Muḥammad ibn Aḥmad ibn Isḥāq ibn al-Buhlūl (this is part of the material that he authorized me to transmit from him after I had studied Tradition with him). He cited Abū Saʿīd Aḥmad ibn al-Ṣaqr ibn Thawbān, who was lecture-room assistant to Bundār.[281] Abū Ṭālib Muḥammad copied it down for us in his own hand, and I myself transcribed it from his original, which said that it was in the hand of Abū Saʿīd, who cites Muḥammad ibn ʿAbd Allāh al-Anṣārī, who cites Muḥammad, great-grandson of ʿAlī ibn Abī Ṭālib, who said: 83.1

The caliph Muʿāwiyah summoned either al-Ḥasan ibn ʿAlī or al-Ḥusayn ibn ʿAlī, peace on them both, first sending for a bundle of whips, which he had placed before him. But when al-Ḥasan, peace on him, entered, Muʿāwiyah took the whips and cast them aside, and held out his hand to him, saying, "Welcome to the sovereign youth of Quraysh!"

Then he sent for ten thousand dinars and said, "Accept this as a contribution to your living expenses."

When al-Ḥasan left, the chamberlain followed him and said, "Grandson of the Messenger of God, although we serve this ruler, we are not safe from his wrath. I observed your lips moving—what was it that you said?" 83.2

"I will tell you," said al-Ḥasan, "on condition that you never pass it on to any member of the House of Muʿāwiyah."

"I agree."

"When you experience adversity or injury, or are in fear of the powers that be, say: There is no god but God, Patient and Kind. There is no god but God, Exalted, Almighty. There is no god but God, Great, Sublime. Glory be to God, Lord of the seven heavens, «Lord of the mighty throne».[282] «Praise be to God, Lord of all».[283] O God! Glorious is Your praise and powerful Your protection, and there is no god beside You. O God! I seek refuge with You from the malice of so and so, his henchmen and faction, be they jinn or men, lest they wrong or oppress me." 83.3

I cite Judge Abū Ṭālib Muḥammad ibn Aḥmad ibn Isḥāq ibn al-Buhlūl, who authorized me to transmit this, and who cites Abū Saʿīd Aḥmad ibn al-Ṣaqr 84.1

قال حدّثنا أبو هشام الرفاعيّ قال حدّثنا وكيع قال حدّثنا مسعر عن أبي بكر بن حفص عن الحسن بن أبي الحسن

أنّ عبد الله بن جعفر لمّا أراد أن يهدي ابنته إلى زوجها خلا بها فقال لها إذا نزل بك أمر فظيع من أمور الدنيا أو الموت فاستقبليه بقول لا إله إلّا الله الحليم الكريم لا إله إلّا الله ﴿رَبُّ ٱلْعَرْشِ ٱلْعَظِيمِ﴾ و ﴿ٱلْحَمْدُ لِلَّهِ رَبِّ ٱلْعَالَمِينَ﴾.

٢،٨٤ قال الحسن فبعث إليّ الحجّاج فقلتهنّ فلمّا مثلتُ بين يديه قال لقد بعثت إليك وأنا أريد قتلك واليوم ما أحد أكرم عليّ منك فسلْ حوائجك.

١،٨٥ حدّثنا عليّ بن الحسن قال حدّثنا أحمد بن محمّد بن الجرّاح قال حدّثنا ابن أبي الدنيا قال حدّثني المثنّى بن عبد الكريم قال حدّثني زافر بن سليمان عن يحيى بن سليم قال

بلغني أنّ ملك الموت استأذن ربّه عزّ وجلّ أن يسلّم على يعقوب فأذن له فأتاه فسلّم عليه فقال له يعقوب بالذي خلقك أقبضت روح يوسف قال لا ولكنّي أعلّمك كلمات لا تسأل الله بها شيئاً إلّا أعطاك قال ما هي قال قل يا ذا المعروف الذي لا ينقطع أبداً ولا يحصيه غيره فقالها فما طلع الفجر من غده حتّى أتاه البشير بالقميص.

٢،٨٥ حدّثنا عليّ بن الحسن قال حدّثنا ابن الجرّاح قال حدّثنا ابن أبي الدنيا قال حدّثني الحسين بن عبد الرحمن قال حدّثني أبو غسّان مالك ابن ضيغم عن إبراهيم بن خلّاد الأزديّ قال

ibn Thawbān, citing Sahl ibn Muḥammad, citing Abū Hishām al-Rifāʿī, citing Wakīʿ, citing Misʿar, quoting Abū Bakr ibn Ḥafṣ, quoting Ḥasan of Basra:

When ʿAbd Allāh ibn Jaʿfar ibn Abī Ṭālib was about to give his daughter in marriage, he took her aside and said to her privately:

"Should any worldly abomination, or even death, befall you, meet it with the words: There is no god but God, Patient and Kind. There is no god but God, «Lord of the mighty throne».[284] «Praise be to God, Lord of all»."[285]

Ḥasan said: 84.2

I said these words when I was summoned by al-Ḥajjāj, and when I appeared before him, he said:

"I sent for you in order to kill you, but now there is no one I am more eager to honor. Only tell me what I may do for you."

We cite ʿAlī ibn al-Ḥasan, citing Ibn al-Jarrāḥ, citing Ibn Abī l-Dunyā, citing 85.1
al-Muthannā ibn ʿAbd al-Karīm, citing Ẓāfir ibn Sulaymān, quoting Yaḥyā ibn Sulaym, who said:

I have heard that the Angel of Death[286] asked leave of his Lord, Mighty and Glorious, to salute Jacob, and having God's permission, went and did so.

"By Him Who created you," said Jacob, "does this mean that you have claimed Joseph's soul?"[287]

"No!" said the angel. "I have come to teach you words by which to supplicate God so that He will grant you anything you ask."

"What are they?"

"Say: O You of Whose beneficence there is no end and which none but You can enumerate!"

Jacob repeated this, and no sooner had dawn risen the next day than the messenger brought him Joseph's shirt.

We cite ʿAlī ibn al-Ḥasan, citing Ibn al-Jarrāḥ, citing Ibn Abī l-Dunyā, citing 85.2
al-Ḥusayn ibn ʿAbd al-Raḥmān, citing Abū Ghassān Mālik ibn Ḍaygham, quoting Ibrāhīm ibn Khallād al-Azdī, who said:

Gabriel came down to Jacob, peace on him, who complained to him of his longing for Joseph.

نزل جبريل على يعقوب عليه السلام فشكى إليه ما هو عليه من الشوق إلى يوسف فقال ألا أعلّمك دعاء إن دعوت به فرّج الله عنك قال بلى قال قل يا من لا يعلم كيف هو إلّا هو ويا من لا يبلغ قدرته غيره فرّج عنّي فقالها فأتاه البشير بالقميص.

٣،٨٥ حدّثنا عليّ بن الحسن قال حدّثنا ابن الجرّاح قال حدّثنا ابن أبي الدنيا قال حدّثنا هارون ابن عبد الله قال حدّثنا سعيد بن عامر الضبعيّ عن المعمّر بن سليمان قال

لقي يعقوب رجل فقال له يا يعقوب ما لي لا أراك كما كنت قال طول الزمان وكثرة الأحزان قال قل اللّهمّ اجعل لي من كلّ همّ همّني وكربني من أمري في ديني ودنياي وآخرتي فرجاً ومخرجاً واغفر لي ذنوبي وثبّت رجاءك في قلبي واقطعه عمّن سواك حتّى لا يكون لي رجاء إلّا إيّاك.

٤،٨٥ قال داود بن رُشيد حدّثني الوليد بن مسلم عن خُليد بن دعلج عن الحسن بن أبي الحسن قال

لو عري من البلاء أحد لعري منه آل يعقوب مسّهم البلاء ثمانون سنة.[١]

٥،٨٥ حدّثنا علي بن الحسن قال حدّثني ابن الجرّاح قال حدّثنا ابن أبي الدنيا قال حدّثني مدلج ابن عبد العزيز عن شيخ من قريش

أنّ جبريل عليه السلام هبط على يعقوب صلّى الله عليه فقال له يا يعقوب تملّق إلى ربّك فقال يا جبريل كيف أقول فقال قل يا كثير الخير يا دائم المعروف فأوحى الله إليه لقد دعوتني بدعاء لو كان ابناك ميتين لأنشرتهما لك.

٦،٨٥ حدّثنا علي بن الحسن قال حدّثنا ابن الجرّاح قال حدّثنا ابن أبي الدنيا قال حدّثني الحسن بن عمرو بن محمد القرشيّ قال حدّثني أبي قال حدّثنا زافر بن سليمان عن يحيى

١ س: حلّ بهم البلاء ثمانية سنة. ب: جاسّهم البلاء الخ. ل: حاسبهم البلاء الخ.

Gabriel said, "Let me teach you to say a prayer by which God will deliver you."

"Gladly!" said Jacob.

The angel said, "Say: O You Who are known only to Yourself, O You whose power is unmatched, deliver me!"

Jacob said the prayer, and the messenger brought him Joseph's shirt.

We cite ʿAlī ibn al-Ḥasan, citing Ibn al-Jarrāḥ, citing Ibn Abī l-Dunyā, citing 85.3
Hārūn ibn ʿAbd Allāh, citing Saʿīd ibn ʿĀmir of Ḍabuʿ, quoting al-Muʿammar ibn Sulaymān, who said:

Jacob encountered a man who said to him:

"Jacob, why do you look so wretched?"[288]

"Another day, another grief," he replied.

The man said, "Say: O God, in every sorrow of mine that grieves or afflicts me in body, soul, or for the life to come, give me deliverance and relief. Forgive my misdeeds; make firm in my heart hope in You and sever it from all others, that I may have hope in You alone."

Dāwud ibn Rushayd said: I cite al-Walīd ibn Muslim, quoting Khulayd ibn 85.4
Diʿlaj, quoting al-Ḥasan of Basra, who said:

If anyone could have been spared further tribulation, it should have been the House of Jacob, after eighty years of it![289]

We cite ʿAlī ibn al-Ḥasan, citing Ibn al-Jarrāḥ, citing Ibn Abī l-Dunyā, citing 85.5
Mudlij ibn ʿAbd al-ʿAzīz, quoting an elder of Quraysh:

Gabriel, peace on him, went down to Jacob, may God bless him, and said:

"Jacob, woo your Lord!"

"How, Gabriel?"

"Say: Great is Your goodness, continual Your beneficence!"

And God said to Jacob, "This prayer is such that, were both your sons[290] dead, I would resurrect them for you."

We cite ʿAlī ibn al-Ḥasan, citing Ibn al-Jarrāḥ, citing Ibn Abī l-Dunyā, citing 85.6
al-Ḥasan ibn ʿAmr ibn Muḥammad al-Qurashī, citing his own father, citing Ẓāfir ibn Sulaymān, quoting Yaḥyā ibn ʿAbd al-Malik, quoting a certain man,

ابن عبد الملك عن رجل عن أنس بن مالك عن النبي صلّى الله عليه وسلّم قال

كان ليعقوب عليه السلام أخ مؤاخ في الله عزّ وجلّ فقال ليعقوب ما الذي أذهب بصرك وقوّس ظهرك.

فقال أمّا الذي قوّس ظهري فالحزن على بنيامين وأمّا الذي أذهب بصري فالبكاء على يوسف.

٨٥،٧ فأوحى الله تعالى إليه أما تستحي تشكوني إلى عبدي قال إنّما أشكو بثّي وحزني إلى الله ثمّ قال يا ربّ ارحم الشيخ الكبير أذهبت بصري وقوّست ظهري أردد عليّ ريحانتي يوسف أشمّه ثمّ افعل بي ما شئت.

٨٥،٨ فقال له جبريل عليه السلام إنّ ربّك يقرؤك السلام ويقول لك أبشر وليفرح قلبك فوعزّتي لو كانا ميتين لأنشرتهما لك فاصنع طعاماً للمساكين وادعهم إليه فإنّ أحبّ عبادي إليّ الأنبياء والمساكين وإنّ الذي ذهب ببصرك وقوّس ظهرك وسبّب صنع إخوة يوسف به ما صنعوا أنّكم ذبحتم شاة فأتاكم رجل صائم فلم تطعموه.

٨٥،٩ فكان يعقوب بعد ذلك إذا أراد الغداء أمر مناديه فنادى من كان يريد الغداء من المساكين فليتغدّ مع يعقوب وإن كان صائماً أمر مناديه فنادى من كان صائماً من المساكين فليفطر مع يعقوب.

٨٦،١ حدّثنا عليّ بن الحسن قال حدّثنا ابن الجرّاح قال حدّثنا ابن أبي الدنيا قال حدّثنا القاسم بن هاشم قال حدّثنا الخطّاب بن عثمان قال حدّثنا محمود بن عمر عن رجل من أهل الكوفة

أنّ جبريل عليه السلام دخل على يوسف السجن فقال له يا طيّب ما الذي أدخلك هاهنا قال أنت أعلم.

quoting Anas ibn Mālik, quoting the Prophet, God bless and keep him, who said:

Jacob, peace on him, had a brother in God, Mighty and Glorious, who asked him:

"What is it has taken away your sight and bowed your back?"

"My back is bowed with grief for Benjamin; my sight is gone with weeping for Joseph," he replied.

Then God, Exalted, said to Jacob, "Are you not ashamed to complain of Me to My servant?" and Jacob said: 85.7

"Rather, it is to God that I complain of my sadness and grief," and then: "O Lord! Show mercy to an aged man. My sight is gone; my back is bowed. Give me back Joseph, my scion and sweet-scented flower,[291] that I may smell his perfume.[292] Then do with me as You please."

Then Gabriel, peace on him, said to him, "Your Lord salutes you and says: Take cheer! Let your heart rejoice! By My might, were both sons dead, I would resurrect them for you. Make a meal for the poor and invite them to the feast, for the dearest to Me of My servants are prophets and the poor, and the reason why your sight is gone and your back is bowed, and why Joseph's brothers did what they did to him, is that once when your household slaughtered a sheep and a fasting man came to you, you gave him nothing to eat." 85.8

Thereafter, whenever Jacob was about to eat, he would send out a herald calling: "If any poor man wants to eat, let him eat with Jacob," and if he were fasting, the herald would cry: "If any poor man is fasting, let him break his fast with Jacob." 85.9

We cite ʿAlī ibn al-Ḥasan, citing Ibn al-Jarrāḥ, citing Ibn Abī l-Dunyā, citing al-Qāsim ibn Hāshim, citing al-Khaṭṭāb ibn ʿUthmān, citing Maḥmūd ibn ʿUmar, quoting a man from Kufa: 86.1

Gabriel, peace on him, came to Joseph in prison[293] and said:

"Sweet-scented one! What has brought you here?"

"You know better than I," replied Joseph.

"Do you wish to learn the words of deliverance?"

"Indeed I do."

قال أفلا أعلّمك كلمات الفرج قال بلى قال قل اللّٰهمّ يا شاهداً غير غائب ويا قريباً غير بعيد ويا غالباً غير مغلوب اجعل لي من أمري هذا فرجاً ومخرجاً وارزقني من حيث لا أحتسب.

٢،٨٦ حدّثنا عليّ بن الحسن قال حدّثنا ابن الجرّاح قال حدّثنا ابن أبي الدنيا قال حدّثني أزهر ابن مروان الرقّاشيّ قال حدّثني قزعة بن سويد عن أبي سعيد مؤذّن الطائف أنّ جبريل عليه السلام أتى يوسف فقال يا يوسف اشتدّ عليك الحبس قال نعم قال قل اللّٰهم اجعل لي من كلّ ما أهمّني وحزبني من أمر دنياي وآخرتي فرجاً ومخرجاً وارزقني من حيث لا أحتسب واغفر لي ذنوبي وثبّت رجاءك في قلبي واقطعه عمّن سواك حتّى لا أرجو أحداً غيرك.

٣،٨٦ حدّثنا عليّ بن الحسن قال حدّثنا ابن الجرّاح قال حدّثنا ابن أبي الدنيا قال حدّثني محمّد ابن عباد بن موسى قال حدّثني عبد العزيز القرشيّ عن جعفر بن سليمان عن غالب القطّان قال

لمّا اشتدّ كرب يوسف وطال سجنه واتّسخت ثيابه وشعث رأسه وجفاه الناس دعا عند ذلك فقال اللّٰهمّ إنّي أشكو إليك ما لقيت من ودّي وعدوّي أمّا ودّي فباعوني وأمّا عدوّي فحبسني اللّٰهمّ اجعل لي فرجاً ومخرجاً فأعطاه الله عزّ وجلّ ذلك.

١،٨٧ حدّثنا عليّ بن الحسن قال حدّثنا ابن الجرّاح قال حدّثنا ابن أبي الدنيا قال حدّثني الحسن ابن محبوب قال قال الفيض بن إسحاق قال الفضيل بن عياض قال إبراهيم التيميّ

قبض عليّ الحجّاج بن يوسف فأنقذني إلى سجنه المعروف بالديماس فحبسني فيه فدخلت[1] على أناس في قيد واحد ومكان ضيّق لا يجد الرجل إلّا موضع مجلسه وفيه يأكلون وفيه يتغوّطون وفيه يصلّون.

١ كذا في بن، س. ش، ب: لمّا حُبستُ الحبسة المشهورة أدخلت السجن فأنزلت الخ.

"Say: O God, ever present, never absent, ever near, never far, victorious, never vanquished, give me deliverance and relief, and grant me provision whence I least expect it."[294]

We cite ʿAlī ibn al-Ḥasan, citing Ibn al-Jarrāḥ, citing Ibn Abī l-Dunyā, citing Azhar ibn Marwān al-Raqqāshī, citing Qazʿah ibn Suwayd, quoting Abū Saʿīd, the muezzin of Taif: 86.2

Gabriel, peace on him, came to Joseph and said:

"Joseph, do you find prison hard to bear?"

"I do indeed," said Joseph.

"Then say: O God, from everything that grieves or vexes me in body or soul, give me deliverance and relief. Grant me provision whence I least expect it.[295] Forgive my misdeeds; make firm in my heart hope in You and sever it from all others, that I may hope in You alone."

We cite ʿAlī ibn al-Ḥasan, citing Ibn al-Jarrāḥ, citing Ibn Abī l-Dunyā, citing Muḥammad ibn ʿAbbād ibn Mūsā, citing ʿAbd al-ʿAzīz al-Qurashī, quoting Jaʿfar ibn Sulaymān, quoting Ghālib the Cotton Merchant: 86.3

When Joseph's affliction grew hard to bear and he had been long in prison, and his clothing was soiled and his hair matted and men shunned him, he prayed and said:

"O God! I complain to You of how friend and enemy have treated me. My friends have sold me, my enemies imprisoned me. O God! Give me deliverance and relief;" and God, Mighty and Glorious, did so.

We cite ʿAlī ibn al-Ḥasan, citing Ibn al-Jarrāḥ, citing Ibn Abī l-Dunyā, citing al-Ḥasan ibn Maḥbūb, who said, al-Fayḍ ibn Isḥāq said, al-Fuḍayl ibn ʿIyāḍ said, Ibrāhīm al-Taymī said: 87.1

Al-Ḥajjāj arrested me and sent me to his dungeon known as the Black Hole, where I was imprisoned. I was put in a cell with other prisoners, shackled together in a narrow space where there was no room for a man to sit down; and there all ate, defecated, and prayed together.

٢،٨٧ قال فجيء برجل من أهل البحرين فأدخل علينا فلم نجد مكانًا فجعلوا يتبرّمون به فقال اصبروا فإنّما هي الليلة.

٣،٨٧ فلمّا دخل الليل قام يصلّي فقال يا ربّ مننت عليّ بدينك وعلّمتني كتابك ثمّ سلّطت عليّ شرّ خلقك يا ربّ الليلة الليلة لا أصبح فيه.

٤،٨٧ فما أصبحنا حتّى ضربت أبواب السجن أين البحرانيّ أين البحرانيّ فقال كلّ منّا ما دعي الساعة إلّا ليقتل

٥،٨٧ فخلّي سبيله فجاء فقام على باب السجن فسلّم علينا وقال أطيعوا الله لا يضيعكم.

١،٨٨ حدّثنا عليّ بن الحسن قال حدّثنا ابن الجرّاح قال حدّثنا ابن أبي الدنيا قال حدّثني أبو نصر المؤدّب عن أبي عبد الرحمٰن الطائيّ قال أخبرنا أبو سعد البقّال قال

كنت محبوسًا في ديماس الحجّاج ومعنا إبراهيم التيميّ فبات في السجن فأتى رجل فقال له يا أبا إسحاق في أيّ شيء حبست فقال جاء العريف فتبرّأ منّي وقال إنّ هذا كثير الصوم والصلاة وأخاف أنّه يرى رأي الخوارج.

٢،٨٨ فإنّا لنتحدّث مع مغيب الشمس ومعنا إبراهيم التيميّ إذ دخل علينا رجل السجن فقلنا يا عبد الله ما قصّتك وأمرك فقال لا أدري ولكنّي أخذت في رأي الخوارج ووالله إنّه لرأي ما رأيته قطّ ولا أحببته ولا أحببت أهله يا هؤلاء ادعوا لي بوضوء.

٣،٨٨ فدعونا له به ثمّ قام فصلّى أربع ركعات ثمّ قال اللّٰهمّ إنّك تعلم أنّي كنت على إساءتي وظلمي وإسرافي على نفسي لم أجعل لك ولدًا ولا شريكًا ولا ندًّا ولا كفؤًا فإن تعذّب فعدل وإن تعفُ فإنّك أنت العزيز الحكيم اللّٰهمّ إنّي أسألك يا من لا تغلّطه المسائل ولا يشغله سمع عن سمع ويا من لا يبرمه إلحاح الملحّين أن تجعل لي في ساعتي هذه فرجًا ومخرجًا ممّا أنا فيه من حيث أرجو ومن حيث لا أرجو وخذ لي بقلب عبدك

A man from al-Baḥrayn was brought to share our cell. The prisoners grumbled that there was no room. 87.2

"Wait until tonight," the new prisoner said.

Night fell, and when he had performed the ritual prayer, he said: 87.3

"O Lord, You have favored me with Your faith; You have taught me Your scripture; You have given Your creatures power to do me mischief. O Lord, may I be free of it on the morrow of this very night!"

The first thing next morning, there came a knocking on the prison doors: "Where's the man from al-Baḥrayn? Where's the man from al-Baḥrayn?" 87.4

We said to one another, "They must have sent for him to execute him."

Instead, he was released. He came and stood at the prison door to take leave of us, and said, "Obey God and He will not suffer you to perish." 87.5

We cite ʿAlī ibn al-Ḥasan, citing Ibn al-Jarrāḥ, citing Ibn Abī l-Dunyā, citing Abū Naṣr the Tutor, quoting Abū ʿAbd al-Raḥmān al-Ṭāʾī, who said: I was informed by Abū Saʿd the Greengrocer: 88.1

I and others were prisoners in al-Ḥajjāj's Black Hole together with Ibrāhīm al-Taymī. After he had been a night in prison, another prisoner was brought. Ibrāhīm greeted him: "Abū Isḥāq! What are you in prison for?"

The man replied, "A sergeant came and declared me an outlaw, saying, 'This man fasts and prays a lot. I suspect him of being a Kharijite.'"

As we and Ibrāhīm al-Taymī were chatting at sunset, another man was brought to our cell. 88.2

"Whoever you are," we said, "tell us about yourself and why you're here."

"I have no idea," he said. "I was arrested for being a Kharijite, but I swear to God I was never a Kharijite and I have no love for them or their creed. Please ask for water so that I can wash and pray!"

We did as he asked, and he performed four prayer sequences. Then he said: 88.3

"O God! You know that, wicked, unjust, and profligate as I am, I have never attributed to You a son, a partner, a peer, or an equal. If You punish, it is justice; if You spare, You are the Mighty, the Wise One. O God! I supplicate You—You Whom no petition fails to reach, Who can hear one and all, Whom no amount of importuning vexes: Give me deliverance and relief from my plight this very instant, from whence I hope and whence I do not hope for it. Incline to me the heart, the hearing, the eye, the hand, the foot of Your servant

الحجّاج وسمعه وبصره ويده ورجله حتّى تخرجني في ساعتي هذه فإنّ قلبه وناصيته بيدك يا ربّ يا ربّ.

٤،٨٨ قال وأكثر فوالذي لا إله غيره ما انقطع دعاؤه حتّى ضرب باب السجن وقيل أين فلان فقام صاحبنا فقال يا هؤلاء إن تكن العافية فوالله لا أدع الدعاء لكم وإن تكن الأخرى فجمع الله بيننا وبينكم في مستقرّ رحمته.

٥،٨٨ قال فبلغنا من الغد أنّه خلّي سبيله.

٨٩ حدّثنا عليّ بن الحسن قال حدّثنا ابن الجرّاح قال حدّثنا ابن أبي الدنيا قال حدّثني محمّد ابن عباد بن موسى قال حدّثنا كثير بن هشام عن الحكم بن هشام الثقفيّ قال

أخبرت أنّ رجلًا أخذ أسيرًا فألقي في جبّ وألقي على رأس الجبّ صخرة فتُلقّن فيه قل سبحان الله الحيّ القدّوس سبحان الله وبحمده فأخرج من غير أن يكون أخرجه إنسان.

١،٩٠ قال مؤلّف هذا الكتاب وقد ذكر القاضي هذا الخبر في كتابه قال حدّثني إبراهيم بن سعيد قال حدّثنا أبو سفيان الحميريّ قال سمعت أبا بلج الفزاريّ قال

أتي الحجّاج بن يوسف برجل كان جعل على نفسه إن ظفر به أن يقتله قال فلمّا دخل عليه تكلّم بكلام فخلّى سبيله

٢،٩٠ فقيل له أيّ شيء قلت فقال قلت يا عزيز يا حميد يا ذا العرش المجيد اصرف عنّي ما أطيق وما لا أطيق واكفني شرّ كلّ جبّار عنيد.

٩١ حدّثنا عليّ بن الحسن قال حدّثنا ابن الجرّاح قال حدّثنا ابن أبي الدنيا قال حدّثنا أحمد بن عبد الأعلى الشيبانيّ قال حدّثنا أبو عبد الرحمٰن الكوفيّ عن صالح بن حسّان عن محمّد بن عليّ

al-Ḥajjāj that I may be freed at once, for his heart and governance are in Your hand, O Lord, O Lord."

He repeated this over and over, and—I swear by the Only God—no sooner had he finished praying than someone knocked on the prison door and cried: 88.4

"Where is so and so?"

The man got to his feet and said, "Friends, if I'm to be spared, then, I swear by God I shall pray for you continually. If I go to my death, then may God unite us all in Paradise."

The next day we heard that he had been released.[296] 88.5

We cite ʿAlī ibn al-Ḥasan, citing Ibn al-Jarrāḥ, citing Ibn Abī l-Dunyā, citing Muḥammad ibn ʿAbbād ibn Mūsā, citing Kathīr ibn Hishām, quoting al-Ḥakam ibn Hishām al-Thaqafī, who said: 89

I have been told that a man was taken prisoner and cast into a pit, and the mouth of the pit was stopped with a boulder. Something prompted him to say:

"Glory be to God, the Living One, the Holy One. Glory be to God!" and to recite His praises. Through no human agency, he was released.

The author of this book observes: This next item is taken from Judge Abū l-Ḥusayn's book. He says: I cite Ibrāhīm ibn Saʿid, citing Abū Sufyān al-Ḥimyarī, who says: I heard Abū Balj al-Fazārī say: 90.1

There was a man whom al-Ḥajjāj had promised himself to kill if he ever fell into his hands. When the man was brought before him, he muttered something, and al-Ḥajjāj set him free.

"What was it you said?" the man was asked. 90.2

He replied, "O Mighty and Praiseworthy, enthroned in glory! Avert from me both what I can and what I cannot endure, and preserve me from the malice of all obdurate oppressors."

We cite ʿAlī ibn al-Ḥasan, citing Ibn al-Jarrāḥ, citing Ibn Abī l-Dunyā, citing Aḥmad ibn ʿAbd al-Aʿlā al-Shaybānī, citing Abū ʿAbd al-Raḥmān of Kufa quoting Ṣāliḥ ibn Ḥassān, citing Muḥammad al-Bāqir: 91

أنّ النبيّ صلّى الله عليه وسلّم علّم عليّاً عليه السلام دعاء يدعو به في كلّ همّ وكان عليّ يعلّمه الناس وهو يا كائناً قبل كلّ شيء يا مكوّن كلّ شيء ويا كائناً بعد كلّ شيء افعل بي كذا وكذا.

١،٩٢ حدّثنا عليّ بن الحسن قال حدّثنا ابن الجرّاح قال حدّثنا ابن أبي الدنيا قال حدّثني إسحاق بن البهلول التنوخيّ قال حدّثني إسحاق ابن عيسى ابن بنت داود بن أبي هند عن الحارث البصريّ عن عمرو السرايا قال

كنت أغير في بلاد الروم وحدي فبينا أنا ذات يوم نائم إذ ورد عليّ علج فحرّكني برجله فانتبهت.

فقال لي يا عربيّ اختر إن شئت مسايفة وإن شئت مطاعنة وإن شئت مصارعة فقلت أمّا المسايفة والمطاعنة فلا بقيا لهما ولكن مصارعة فنزل فلم ينهنهني أن صرعني وجلس على صدري وقال أيّ قتلة تريد أن أقتلك.

٢،٩٢ فذكرت الدعاء فرفعت رأسي إلى السماء فقلت أشهد أنّ كلّ معبود ما دون عرشك إلى قرار الأرضين باطل غير وجهك الكريم فقد ترى ما أنا فيه ففرّج عنّي وأغمي عليّ فأفقت فرأيت الروميّ قتيلاً إلى جانبي.

٣،٩٢ قال إسحاق بن بنت داود فسألت الحارث البصريّ عن الدعاء فقال سألت عنه عمرو السرايا فقلت له بالله يا عمرو ما قلت قال قلت اللّهمّ ربّ إبراهيم وإسماعيل وإسحاق ويعقوب وربّ جبريل وميكائيل وإسرافيل ومنزل التوراة والإنجيل والزبور والقرآن العظيم ادرأ عنّي شرّه فدرأ عنّي شرّه.

٤،٩٢ قال إسحاق بن بنت داود فحفظته وقلت أعلّمه الناس فوجدته نافذاً وهو الإخلاص بعينه.

The Prophet, God bless and keep him, taught ʿAlī, peace on him, a prayer to use on all occasions of anxiety, which ʿAlī in turn taught to others. It was this:

"O You Who were before anything was, Who make all things come into being, Who will be when all has ceased to be, do this for me."

We cite ʿAlī ibn al-Ḥasan, citing Ibn al-Jarrāḥ, citing Ibn Abī l-Dunyā, citing Isḥāq ibn al-Buhlūl al-Tanūkhī, citing Isḥāq ibn ʿĪsā son of the daughter of Dāwūd ibn Abī Hind, quoting al-Ḥārith of Basra, quoting ʿAmr of the Squadrons, who said: 92.1

One day as I was journeying alone through Byzantine territory in search of battle, I lay down to sleep. A Byzantine barbarian came and kicked me awake, and said:

"Arab! How do you want to fight? With sword or spear, or shall we wrestle?"

"I have lost my sword and spear. Let us wrestle," I said.

He dismounted, threw me effortlessly, and sat on my chest.

"How do you want me to kill you?" he asked.

Then I remembered this prayer, looked heavenward, and said:

"I bear witness that all that is worshiped under Your throne, unto the foundations of the universe, is vain except Your gracious face.[297] You see my plight. Deliver me!" 92.2

Then I fainted, and when I regained consciousness, I found the Byzantine lying dead beside me.

Isḥāq ibn ʿĪsā, son of the daughter of Dāwūd ibn Abī Hind, said: I questioned al-Ḥārith of Basra about the prayer and he said: I questioned ʿAmr of the Squadrons about it and said, "In God's name, ʿAmr, tell me truly what you said." He said: 92.3

I said, "O God, Lord of Abraham, Ishmael, Isaac, and Jacob; Lord of Gabriel, Michael, Israfel, and Azrael; Who sent down the Torah, the Gospels, the Psalms,[298] and the Mighty Qur'an: ward off his malice!" And He did.

Isḥāq ibn ʿĪsā, son of the daughter of Dāwūd ibn Abī Hind, said: 92.4

I learnt this prayer and said to myself: I must teach it to other people, for I have found it efficacious, and nothing better expresses true belief.

حدّثنا عليّ بن الحسن قال حدّثنا ابن الجرّاح قال حدّثنا ابن أبي الدنيا قال حدّثنا إسحاق ابن إسماعيل قال حدّثنا جرير بن حفص عن الشعبيّ قال ١،٩٣

كنت جالساً عند زياد فأتي برجل يُحمل ما يشكّ في قتله فحرّك الرجل شفتيه بشيء ما ندري ما هو فخلّى سبيله فقلت للرجل ما قلت.

قال قلت اللّهمّ ربّ إبراهيم وإسماعيل وإسحاق ويعقوب وربّ جبريل وميكائيل وإسرافيل ومنزل التوراة والإنجيل والزبور والفرقان العظيم ادرأ عنّي شرّ زياد فدرأه عنّي. ٢،٩٣

أخبرني محمّد بن الحسن بن المظفّر قال أخبرني عيسى بن عبد العزيز الظاهريّ قال أخبرني أبو عبد الله قال ١،٩٤

أمر الرشيد بعض خدمه فقال إذا كان الليلة فصر إلى الحجرة الفلانيّة فافتحها وخذ من رأيت فيها فأت به موضع كذا وكذا من الصحراء الفلانيّة فإنّ ثَمّ قليباً محفوراً فارمِ به وطمّه بالتراب وليكن معك فلان الحاجب.

قال فجاء الغلام إلى باب الحجرة ففتحه فإذا فيها غلام كالشمس الطالعة فجذبناه جذباً عنيفاً. ٢،٩٤

فقال له اتّق الله فإنّي ابن رسول الله فالله الله أن تلقى الله بدمي فلم يلتفت إلى قوله وأخرجه إلى الموضع.

فلمّا أشرف الفتى على التلف وشاهد القليب قال له يا هذا إنّك على ردّ ما لم تفعل أقدر منك على ردّ ما فعلت فدعني أصلّي ركعتين وامضِ لما أُمرت به فقال له شأنك وما تريد. ٣،٩٤

فقام الفتى فصلّى ركعتين قال فيهما يا خفيّ اللطف أغثني في وقتي هذا والطف بي بلطفك الخفيّ. ٤،٩٤

We cite ʿAlī ibn al-Ḥasan, citing Ibn al-Jarrāḥ, citing Ibn Abī l-Dunyā, citing Isḥāq ibn Ismāʿīl, citing Jarīr ibn Ḥafṣ, quoting al-Shaʿbī, who said: 93.1

I was with Ziyād ibn Abīhi when a man was carried before him. I was certain that he would be executed, but his lips moved and he said something we could not make out and was released.

I asked him, "What was it you said?"

He replied, "O God, Lord of Abraham, Ishmael, Isaac, and Jacob; Lord 93.2
of Gabriel, Michael, and Israfel; Who sent down the Torah, the Gospels, the Psalms, and our mighty Scripture: ward off the malice of Ziyād!" And He did.

I cite Muḥammad ibn al-Ḥasan ibn al-Muẓaffar,[299] citing ʿĪsā ibn ʿAbd al-ʿAzīz 94.1
al-Ẓāhirī, citing Abū ʿAbd Allāh al-Ḥazunbal, who said:

The caliph Hārūn al-Rashīd commanded one of his servants: "Tonight, go to a certain prison cell. Open it. Seize the person you find there. Take him to a certain place outside the city, where a pit has been dug. Throw him in, and fill in the pit. So and so the chamberlain will go with you."

When the slave opened the cell door, he beheld a youth like the rising sun. 94.2
He grabbed him roughly.

The youth said, "Beware! I am descended from the Messenger of God. God help you if you face Him with my blood on your hands!"

The slave took no notice but dragged him off to the pit.

When the youth saw the pit and realized he was close to death, he said to 94.3
the slave:

"My friend, you will find it easier to take back what you have not done than what you have. Let me say two prayer sequences. Then carry out your orders."

"All right," said the slave.

As he prayed, the youth said, "O You Whose grace works unseen, succor me 94.4
now, and graciously grant me Your invisible grace."

فلا والله ما استتمّ دعاءه حتّى هبّت ريح وغبرة حتّى لم ير بعضهم بعضاً فوقعوا لوجوههم واشتغلوا بأنفسهم عن الفتى ثمّ سكنت الرّيح والغبرة وطلبنا الفتى فلم يوجد وقيوده مرميّة.

٥،٩٤ فقال الحاجب لمن معه هلكنا والله سيقع لأمير المؤمنين أنّا أطلقناه فماذا نقول له إن كذبناه لم نأمن أن يبلغه خبر الفتى فيقتلنا ولئن صدقناه ليعجّلنّ لنا المكروه فقال له الآخر يقول الحكيم إن كان الكذب ينجي فالصدق أرجى وأنجى.

٦،٩٤ فلمّا دخلوا عليه قال لهم ما فعلتم فيما تقدّمت به إليكم.

فقال له الحاجب يا أمير المؤمنين الصدق أولى ما اتّبع في جميع الأمور ومثلي لا يجترئ أن يكذب بحضرتك وإنّه كان من الخبر كيت وكيت.

فقال الرشيد لقد تداركه اللطف الخفيّ والله لأجعلنّها في مقدّمات دعائي امض لشأنك واكتم ما جرى.

١،٩٥ حدّثني محمّد بن الحسن قال حدّثني محمّد بن عمرو بن البختريّ الرزّاز[١] في جامع المنصور في سنة ثلاث وثلاثين وثلثمائة قال حدّثنا الفضل بن إسحاق الدوريّ عن محمّد بن الحسن عن أبي سلمة عبد الله بن منصور قال

حزن رجل حزناً شديداً على شيء لحقه وأمر أهمّه وأقلقه فألحّ في الدعاء فهتف به هاتف يا هذا قل يا سامع كلّ صوت ويا بارئ النفوس بعد الموت ويا من لا تغشاه الظلمات ويا من لا يشغله شيء عن شيء.

٢،٩٥ قال فدعا بها ففرّج الله عنه ولم يسأل الله تلك الليلة حاجة إلّا أعطاه.

---

١ الرزّاز: التصحيح من ش.

And by God! no sooner had he finished praying than a wind arose, and a dust that made them[300] invisible to each other. They fell on their faces and forgot about him. Then the wind and the dust dropped, and when we[301] looked for the youth, he was nowhere to be seen, but his chains were lying on the ground.

The chamberlain said to his companions: 94.5

"We're dead men. The caliph will think we've let him go. What are we to tell him? If we lie, he may well learn the truth and have us executed; and if we tell the truth, we'll die anyway, but sooner."

His companion rejoined, "The sage has said, 'Though lying saves, the truth is better, and safer in the end.'"

"And how have you acted on my suggestion?" asked the caliph, when they 94.6 reported back to him.

The chamberlain replied, "Commander of the Faithful, the truth is always best, and the likes of me could not make so bold as to lie to Your Majesty. This is what happened."

Hārūn al-Rashīd responded, "He has indeed met with unseen grace. I swear to God that from now on I will preface my own prayers with his. Now be off, and keep this secret."

I cite Muḥammad ibn al-Ḥasan ibn al-Muẓaffar, citing Muḥammad ibn ʿAmr 95.1 ibn al-Bakhtarī the Rice Merchant as having cited to him, in the mosque of al-Manṣūr, in the year 333 [944–45], al-Faḍl ibn Isḥāq al-Dūrī, quoting Muḥammad ibn al-Ḥasan, quoting Abū Salamah ʿAbd Allāh ibn Manṣūr, who said:

A certain man was much grieved by something that was causing him anxiety and dismay. He prayed insistently, and a disembodied voice called out to him:

"Friend, say: O You Who hear every voice, Who absolve the souls of the dead, Whom darkness cannot veil, Whom one thing cannot distract from another!"

He repeated the words, and God delivered him; and on that night, whatever 95.2 he asked of God He gave him.

حدّثنا عليّ بن أبي الطيّب قال حدّثنا ابن الجرّاح قال حدّثنا ابن أبي الدنيا قال حدّثني القاسم بن هاشم قال حدّثنا أبو اليمان قال حدّثنا صفوان بن عمرو عن أبي يحيى إسحاق العدوانيّ قال ١،٩٦

كنّا بإزاء آزرمهر[١] عند مدينة الكرج وقد زحف إلينا في ثمانين فيلاً فكادت تنقض الصفوف وتشتّت الخيول وكان أميرنا محمّد بن القاسم فنادى عمران بن النعمان أمير أهل حمص وأمراء الأجناد فنهضوا فما استطاعوا فلمّا أعيته الأمور نادى مراراً لا حول ولا قوّة إلّا بالله.

فكشف الله الفيلة وسلّط عليها الحرّ فأنضجها ففزعت إلى الماء فما استطاع سوّاسها ولا أصحابها حبسها وحملت خيلنا وكان الفتح بإذن الله تعالى. ٢،٩٦

حدّثنا علي بن الحسن قال حدّثنا ابن الجرّاح قال حدّثنا ابن أبي الدنيا قال حدّثنا القاسم ابن هاشم قال حدّثنا أبو اليمان قال حدّثنا صفوان بن عمرو عن الأشياخ أنّ حبيب بن مسلمة كان يستحبّ إذا لقي العدوّ أو ناهض حصناً أن يقول لا حول ولا قوّة إلّا بالله. ٣،٩٦

ثمّ إنّه ناهض يوماً حصناً فانهزم الروم وتحصّنوا في حصن آخر لهم أعجزه فقالها فانصدع الحصن.

حدّثنا عليّ بن أبي الطيّب قال حدّثنا ابن الجرّاح قال حدّثنا ابن أبي الدنيا قال حدّثني الحسين بن عبد الرحمٰن قال ١،٩٧

بلغني أنّ بعض الملوك نفى وزيراً له لموجدة وجدها عليه فاغتمّ لذلك غمّاً شديداً فبينا هو يسير إذ أنشده رجل هذين البيتين [رمل]

---

١ كذا.

We cite ʿAlī ibn al-Ḥasan, citing Ibn al-Jarrāḥ, citing Ibn Abī l-Dunyā, citing al-Qāsim ibn Hāshim, citing Abū l-Yamān, citing Ṣafwān ibn ʿAmr, citing Abū Yaḥyā Isḥāq al-ʿAdwānī, who said: 96.1

Our battle line was drawn up outside the city of al-Karaj opposite Āzarmihr,[302] who brought up eighty elephants. Our ranks were about to break and the cavalry was on the point of scattering. Our general was Muḥammad ibn al-Qāsim al-Thaqafī. He called on the commander of the Syrian divisions and ʿImrān ibn al-Nuʿmān, who commanded the troops from Ḥimṣ, to reinforce us. They tried and failed. Seeing there was nothing to be done, he cried out repeatedly, "There is no might nor power save in God."

Then God put the elephants to flight. They grew hot, poured with sweat, 96.2
and bolted uncontrollably toward the water with their mahouts and the men they carried. Our cavalry charged and victory was ours, by the leave of the Almighty.

We cite ʿAlī ibn al-Ḥasan, citing Ibn al-Jarrāḥ, citing Ibn Abī l-Dunyā, citing 96.3
al-Qāsim ibn Hāshim, citing Abū l-Yamān, citing Ṣafwān ibn ʿAmr, quoting various authorities:

Whenever Ḥabīb ibn Maslamah engaged the enemy or stormed a fortress, he thought it pleasing to God to say, "There is no might nor power save in God."

Once, when he stormed a Byzantine fortress, the garrison fled to another stronghold, which he could not take. He said, "There is no might nor power save in God," and it fell.

We cite ʿAlī ibn al-Ḥasan, citing Ibn al-Jarrāḥ, citing Ibn Abī l-Dunyā, citing 97.1
al-Ḥusayn ibn ʿAbd al-Raḥmān, who said:

Once upon a time, a king flew into a rage with his vizier and banished him. As he went on his way, grieving sorely, the vizier heard a man declaim this couplet:

أَحْسِنِ ٱلظَّنَّ بِـرَبٍّ عَوَّدَكْ   حَسَـنًا أَمْسِ وَسَوَّى أَوَدَكْ
إِنَّ رَبًّا كَانَ يَكْفِـيكَ ٱلَّذِي   كَانَ بِٱلْأَمْسِ سَيَكْفِيكَ غَدَكْ

فسُرّي عن الوزير وأمر له بعشرة آلاف درهم. ٢،٩٧

١،٩٨ حـدّثنا عليّ بن أبي الطيّب قال حدّثنا ابن السّراج قال حدّثنا ابن أبي الدنيا قال حدّثنا محمّد بن أبي رجاء مولى بني هاشم قال

أصابني همّ شديد لأمركنت فيه فرفعت مقعداً لي كنت جالساً عليه فإذا برقعة مكتوبة فنظرت فيها فإذا فيها مكتوب [بسيط]

يَا صَاحِبَ ٱلْهَمِّ إِنَّ ٱلْهَمَّ مُنْقَطِعٌ   لَا تَيْأَسَنَّ كَأَنْ قَدْ فَـرَّجَ ٱللهُ

قال فذهب عنّي ماكنت فيه من الغمّ ولم ألبث أن فرّج الله عنّي فلله الحمد والشكر. ٢،٩٨

٩٩ حـدّثني أبو بكر الثقفيّ قال

قال بعضهم أصابني همّ ضقت به ذرعاً فنمت فرأيت كأنّ قائلاً يقول [كامل]

كُنْ لِلْمَكَارِهِ بِالْعَزَاءِ مُقَـطِّعًا   فَلَعَـلَّ يَوْمًـا لَا تَـرَى مَا تَكْرَهُ
وَلَرُبَّمَا ٱبْتَسَمَ ٱلْوَقُورُ مِنَ ٱلْأَذَى   وَضَـمِيرُهُ مِنْ حَرِّهِ يَتَأَوَّهُ

١،١٠٠ حـدّثني أبو الحسن عليّ بن الحسن الشاهد المعروف بالجرّاحيّ من حفظه قال حدّثني أبو الحسن بن أبي الطاهر محمّد بن الحسن الكاتب صاحب الجيش قال

قبض عليّ أبو جعفر محمّد بن القاسم بن عبيد الله في أيّام وزارته للقاهر بالله وعلى أبي فحبسنا في حجرة ضيّقة وأجلسنا على التراب وشدّد علينا وكان يخرجنا في كلّ

Don't doubt a Lord who yesterday
was good to you and met your needs.
A Lord who kept you yesterday
will certainly keep you tomorrow.

The king relented, and presented the vizier with ten thousand dirhams. 97.2

We cite ʿAlī ibn al-Ḥasan, citing Ibn al-Sarrāj,[303] citing Ibn Abī l-Dunyā, citing Muḥammad ibn Abī Rajāʾ, a protégé of the Abbasids, who said: 98.1

Once, when something was causing me great anxiety, I lifted up what I was sitting on[304] and found a piece of paper underneath. When I examined it, this is what was written on it:

O anxious man! Anxiety will shortly cease to trouble you.
Do not despair! for God, it seems, already has delivered you.

My anxiety left me, and before long God did indeed deliver me. God be thanked! 98.2

I cite Abū Bakr al-Thaqafī, citing an anonymous source: 99

Once, when I was laboring under an intolerable anxiety, I went to sleep and dreamed of someone saying:

Through equanimity, give surcease to
adversity, and it may disappear.
A man of dignity, although inside
himself he burns and sighs, smiles at his woes.

I cite Abū l-Ḥasan ʿAlī ibn al-Ḥasan the legal witness, known as al-Jarrāḥī, citing, from memory, Abū l-Ḥasan ibn Abī l-Ṭāhir Muḥammad ibn al-Ḥasan, the state scribe in charge of the army,[305] who said: 100.1

When Muḥammad ibn al-Qāsim ibn ʿUbayd Allāh ibn Sulaymān ibn Wahb was vizier to the caliph al-Qāhir,[306] he arrested me and my father and imprisoned us in a narrow chamber where we had to sit on the bare ground. He treated us harshly every day he would fetch us out and demand forfeiture

يوم فيطالب أبي بمال المصادرة وأضرب أنا بحضرة أبي ولا يُضرب هو فلاقينا من ذلك أمرًا شديدًا صعبًا.

٢،١٠٠ فلمّا كان بعد أيّام قال لي أبي إنّ هؤلاء الموكّلين قد صارت لهم بنا حرمة فتوصّل إلى مكاتبة أبي بكر الصيرفيّ وكان صديقًا لأبي حتّى ينفذ إلينا بثلاثة آلاف درهم نفرّقها ففعلت ذلك فأنفذ إلينا بالمال من يومه فقلت للموكّلين في عشيّ ذلك اليوم قد وجبت لكم علينا حقوق فخذوا هذه الدراهم فانتفعوا بها فامتنعوا فقلت ما سبب امتناعكم فورّوا عن ذلك فقلت إمّا قبلتم وإمّا عرّفتمونا السبب الذي لأجله امتناعكم فقالوا نشفق عليكم ونستحي من ذلك فقال لهم أبي اذكروه على كلّ حال قالوا قد عزم الوزير على قتلكما الليلة ولا نستحسن أخذ شيء منكما مع هذا[١] وقلت لأبي ما أصنع بالدراهم فقال ردّها على أبي بكر فرددتها عليه.

٣،١٠٠ وكان أبي يصوم تلك الأيّام كلّها فلمّا غابت الشمس تطهّر وصلّى المغرب فصلّيت معه ولم يفطر ثمّ أقبل على الصلاة والدعاء إلى أن صلّى العشاء الآخرة ثمّ دعاني فقال اجلس يا بنيّ إلى جانبي جاثيًا على ركبتك ففعلت وجلس هو كذلك ثمّ رفع رأسه إلى السماء فقال يا ربّ محمّد بن القاسم ظلمني وحبسني على ما ترى وأنا بين يديك وقد استعديت إليك وأنت أحكم الحاكمين فاحكم بيننا لا يزيد عن ذلك ثمّ صاح بها إلى أن ارتفع صوته ولم يزل يكرّرها بصياح ونداء واستغاثة إلى أن ظننت أنّه قد مضى ربع الليل.

٤،١٠٠ فوالله ما قطعها حتّى سمعت الباب يدقّ فذهب عليّ أمري ولم أشكّ في أنّه القتل وفُتحت الأبواب فدخل قوم بشموع فتأمّلت وإذا فيهم سابور خادم القاهر فقال أين أبو طاهر فقام إليه أبي فقال ها أنذا فقال أين ابنك فقال هو ذا فقال انصرفا إلى منزلكما

---

١ في ش بعد هذه الجملة: فقلقت ودخلت إلى أبي بغير تلك الصورة فقال ما لك فأخبرته بالخبر.

payments from my father, and instead of flogging my father, tortured us cruelly by having me flogged in front of him.

When some days had passed, my father said to me, "The guards are on our side now. Bribe them to let you write to Abū Bakr al-Ṣayrafī"—a friend of my father's—"asking him to send us three thousand dirhams to distribute to them." 100.2

I did as he told me, and Abū Bakr sent the money at once.

That evening, I said to the guards, "We are much obliged to you. Please accept this money for yourselves," but they refused.

I insisted: "Either take it or tell us why you refuse."

"We're sorry for you, and we feel awkward about it."

"At any rate, explain why," said my father.

They said, "The vizier's going to execute you this evening. Under the circumstances, we don't like to be beholden to you."

"What shall I do with the money, then?" I asked my father.

"Give it back to Abū Bakr."

I duly returned it.

All the time we had been in prison, my father had been fasting. Now, when the sun went down, he performed the ablution, and the two of us said the sunset prayer. Without breaking his fast, my father continued his prayers and devotions until the time of the final night prayer, when he called to me and said: 100.3

"Come, child, get down on your knees beside me."

We both knelt. Then he raised his face to heaven and said:

"Lord! Muḥammad ibn al-Qāsim has imprisoned me unjustly, as you see. I am in Your hands. I appeal to You, for You are the best of judges. All I ask is that You judge between us!"

Lifting up his voice, he shouted the words, with yells and cries and screams for help, for what I reckoned must have been a quarter of the night.

I swear by God that he had no sooner ceased than I heard knocking on the door. Certain that this meant death, I was beside myself. The doors[307] opened, and in came a group of men holding candles. Among them I recognized Sābūr, al-Qāhir's eunuch. 100.4

"Where's Abū Ṭāhir?" he asked.

My father rose. "Here," he said.

"And where's your son?"

My father said, "There."

"Get out of here and go home," said Sābūr.

فخرجنا فإذا هو قد قبض على محمّد بن القاسم وحدره إلى دار القاهر. وعاش محمّد بن القاسم في الاعتقال ثلاثة أيّام ومات.

١،١٠١ لّما خرج طاهر بن الحسين إلى محاربة عليّ بن عيسى بن ماهان جعل ذات يوم في كمّه دراهم يفرّقها في الفقراء ثمّ سها عنها فأرسلها فتبدّدت فتطيّر بذلك واغتمّ غمّاً شديداً حتّى تبيّن في وجهه.

٢،١٠١ فأنشده شاعر كان في عسكره [كامل]

هَـذَا تَفَـرُّقُ جَمْعِهِـمْ لَا غَيْـرُهُ ... وَذَهَـابُهُ مِـنْكُمْ ذَهَـابُ ٱلْهَـمِّ
شَيْءٌ يَكُونُ ٱلْهَمُّ بَعْضَ حُرُوفِهِ ... لَا خَيْـرَ فِي إِمْسَاكِهِ فِي ٱلْكُمِّ

٣،١٠١ قال فسلا طاهر وأمر له بثلاثين ألف درهم.

١،١٠٢ انصـرف يحيى بن خالد البرمكيّ من عند الهادي وقد ناظره في تسهيل خلع العهد على هارون فحلف له يحيى أنّه فعل وجهد فيه فامتنع عليه هارون فقال له الهادي كذبت ووالله لأفعلنّ بك وأصنعنّ وتوعّده بكلّ عظيمة وصرفه.

٢،١٠٢ فجاء الى بيته فكلّم بعض غلمانه بشيء فأجابه بما غاظه فلطمه يحيى فانقطعت حلقة خاتمه وطاح الفصّ فاشتدّ ذلك على يحيى وتطيّر منه واغتمّ.

٣،١٠٢ فدخل عليه السياريّ الشاعر وقد أخبر بالقصّة فأنشده في الحال [كامل]

أَخَـلَاكَ مِنْ كُلِّ ٱلْهُمُومِ سُقُوطُهُ ... وَأَتَاكَ بِٱلْفَـرَجِ ٱنْفِـرَاجُ ٱلْخَـاتِـمِ
قَدْ كَانَ ضَاقَ فَفَكَّ حَلْقَةَ ضِيقِهِ ... فَاصْبِرْ فَمَا ضِيقُ ٱلزَّمَانِ بِدَائِـمِ

We did as we were told. It turned out that Sābūr had arrested Muḥammad ibn al-Qāsim and taken him away to the caliph's palace, where he lingered in detention for three days before dying.

One day, when Ṭāhir ibn al-Ḥusayn was at war with ʿAlī ibn ʿĪsā ibn Māhān,[308] he put some dirhams up his sleeve to give away to the poor, but forgot he had done so. When they fell out and scattered, he interpreted it as a bad omen and was very worried, as could be seen from his face. 101.1

In the ranks of his army, however, was a poet who declaimed: 101.2

It's no good keeping cash up your sleeve—
cash as good as spells care.[309]
This is how it was meant to be given away.
It's done—so now stop fretting!

Ṭāhir cheered up and gave the poet thirty thousand dirhams. 101.3

Yaḥyā ibn Khālid al-Barmakī had been with the caliph al-Hādī, who wanted to make him persuade Hārūn al-Rashīd to renounce his claim to the succession. Yaḥyā swore that he had done his utmost but Hārūn had refused. 102.1

"You lie!" yelled al-Hādī. "I swear to God you'll suffer for this."

He uttered terrible threats and dismissed him.

Yaḥyā went home, where he gave an order to a page,[310] whose answer angered him. He slapped him; his signet ring came apart and the stone fell out. Yaḥyā was dreadfully upset, interpreting this as a bad omen. 102.2

On hearing this, the poet al-Sayārī came to his audience chamber and extemporized: 102.3

The loss of the stone means your cares will cease.
The damaged ring means deliverance.
Too tight, it loosened: accept this means
the straits you're in won't last.

٤،١٠٢ قال فما أمسى حتّى ارتفعت الواعية بموت موسى الهادي وصار الأمر إلى هارون الرشيد فأعطاه مائة ألف درهم.

١،١٠٣ قـال أبو عليّ القنائيّ قال لي جدّي

بكّرت يوماً إلى موسى بن عبد الملك وحضر داود بن الجرّاح فوقف إلى جانبي فقال لي كان لي أمس خبر طريف انصرفت من عند موسى بن عبد الملك فوجدت في منزلي امرأة من شرائف النساء فشكته إليّ وقالت قد حاول أن يأخذ ضيعتي الفلانيّة وأنت تعلم أنّها عمدتي في معيشتي وأنّ في عنقي صبيةً أيتاماً فأيّ شيء تدبّر في أمري أو تشير عليّ فقلت من معك وراء الستر فقالت ما معي أحد فقلت أمّا التدبير في أمرك فما لي فيه حيلة وأمّا المشورة فقد قال النبطيّ لا تبعْ أرضك من إقدام الرجل السوء فإنّ الرجل السوء يموت والأرض تبقى فدعت لي وانصرفت.

٢،١٠٣ فما انقضى كلامه حتّى خرج موسى فقال لداود يا أبا سليمان لا تبعْ أرضك من إقدام الرجل الرديء فإنّه يموت والأرض تبقى فقال لي داود أسمعت هذا والله الموت أين أهرب أين أمضي ما آمنه والله على نفسي ولا على نعمتي فأشر عليّ بما أصنع قبل نفاذ طريقنا ونزولنا معه إلى الديوان فقلت والله ما أدري.

٣،١٠٣ فرفع يديه إلى السماء وقال اللّهمّ اكفني أمره وشرّه وضرّه فإنّك تعلم قصّتي وأنّي ما أردت بما قلت إلّا الخير واشتدّ قلقه وبكاؤه ودعاؤه.

٤،١٠٣ وقربنا من الديوان فقال موسى وهو على دابّته متى حدث هذا الجبل الأسود في طريقنا ومال على سرجه حتّى سقط وأسكت

٥،١٠٣ فحُمل إلى منزله وكان آخر العهد به.

That very evening, the wail went up for al-Hādī's passing. Hārūn succeeded him, and Yaḥyā gave the poet a hundred thousand dirhams. 102.4

Abū ʿAlī of Dayr Qunnā said: my grandfather told me: 103.1

One morning when I went on duty at Mūsā ibn ʿAbd al-Malik's,[311] Abū Sulaymān Dāwūd ibn al-Jarrāḥ came and stood beside me and said:

"A funny thing happened to me yesterday. When I got back from the office, I found a noblewoman at my house. She made a complaint to me about Mūsā ibn ʿAbd al-Malik, saying, 'He tried to seize my estate. You know that it's my prop and livelihood, and that I have fatherless children to take care of. Can you do anything, or advise me?'

"I asked, 'Who is with you behind the curtain?'[312]

"'No one,' she said.

"'There's nothing I can do for you,' I said. 'As for advice, I can only say what the peasants[313] say: Don't let a bad man make you sell your land. Bad men pass, land lasts.'

"She thanked me and went away."

The words were no sooner out of Dāwūd's mouth than Mūsā made his entrance and addressed him: "Abū Sulaymān," he said, "don't let a bad man make you sell your land. Bad men pass, land lasts." 103.2

"Did you hear that?" Dāwūd gabbled. "This means death for sure! Where can I run to, where can I go? Neither I nor my fortune is safe from him, by God. Tell me what to do, before we have to make our way down to the office with him!"

"Goodness!" I said. "I've no idea!"

Dāwūd lifted up his hands to heaven and said, "O God! Preserve me from him, from his wickedness and spite! You know what happened, and that I meant what I said for the best!" He wept and prayed frantically. 103.3

As we drew near the office, Mūsā, who was on horseback, exclaimed, "Where did that black mound in the road come from?" Then he lurched in the saddle and fell. He had had a stroke. 103.4

They carried him back to his house, and that was the end of him. 103.5

ذكر المدائنيّ في كتابه قال أبو سعيد وأنا أحسبه يعني الأصمعيّ ١،١٠٤

نزلت بحيّ من كلب مجدبين قد توالت عليهم السنون فماتت المواشي ومنعت الأرض من أخراج النبات وأمسكت السماء قطرها فجعلت أنظر إلى السحابة ترتفع من ناحية القبلة سوداء متقاربة حتّى تطبّق الأرض فيتشوّف لها أهل الحيّ ويرفعون أصواتهم بالتكبير ثمّ يعدلها الله عنهم مراراً.

فلمّا كثر ذلك خرجت عجوز منهم فعلت نشزاً من الأرض ثمّ نادت بأعلى صوتها يا ذا العرش اصنع كيف شئت فإنّ أرزاقنا عليك ٢،١٠٤

فما نزلت من موضعها حتّى تغيّمت السماء غيماً شديداً وأمطروا مطراً كاد أن يغرقهم وأنا حاضر. ٣،١٠٤

وذكر المدائنيّ في كتابه قال ١،١٠٥

وجّه سليمان بن عبد الملك حين ولي الخلافة محمّد بن يزيد إلى العراق فأطلق أهل السجون وقسم الأموال وضيّق على يزيد بن أبي مسلم كاتب الحجّاج فظفر به يزيد بأفريقية لمّا وليها في شهر رمضان عند المغرب وفي يده عنقود عنب.

فجعل محمّد يقول اللّهمّ احفظ لي إطلاقي الأسرى وإعطائي الفقراء فقال له يزيد حين دنا منه محمّد بن يزيد ما زلت أسأل الله أن يظفرني بك قال له وما زلت أسأل الله أن يجيرني منك قال والله ما أجارك ولا أعاذك منّي ووالله لأقتلنّك قبل أن آكل هذه الحبّة العنب ووالله لو رأيت ملك الموت يريد قبض روحك لسبقته إليها فأقيمت الصلاة فوضع يزيد الحبّة العنب من يده وتقدّم فصلّى بهم. ٢،١٠٥

وكان أهل أفريقية قد أجمعوا على قتله فلمّا ركع ضربه رجل منهم على رأسه بعمود حديد فقتله. ٣،١٠٥

وقيل لمحمّد اذهب حيث شئت فمضى سالماً.

This is from al-Madā'inī's book.[314] Abū Saʿīd (by whom I think he means al-Aṣmaʿī) said: 104.1

I visited a tribe of the Kalb confederation, that was suffering drought. They had had several dry years: their animals died, the soil bore no crops, and still the rain refused to fall. I looked at the clouds that had piled up, covering the whole earth toward the south, black and close-packed. The tribespeople scanned them and raised their voices in cries of "God is great!" but over and again, God drove the clouds away.

When this had happened many times, an old tribeswoman came and climbed on top of a piece of raised ground and cried at the top of her voice: "Lord of the Throne![315] Do as You will! You are our sole provider!" 104.2

Before she had even climbed down again, the sky filled with clouds and the rain came down in floods, as I saw for myself. 104.3

This is from al-Madā'inī's book. 105.1

When Sulaymān ibn ʿAbd al-Malik became caliph, he sent Muḥammad ibn Yazīd, client of the Anṣār, to Iraq, where he freed the prisoners and distributed the revenue equitably, but put Yazīd ibn Abī Muslim, al-Ḥajjāj's scribe, into prison. But when Yazīd became governor of North Africa, Muḥammad fell into his power. This was in the month of Ramadan, at the time of the sunset prayer, and Yazīd had a bunch of grapes in his hand.

Muḥammad began to pray. "O God!" he said. "Remember how I freed the prisoners and gave to the poor!" 105.2

Yazīd said, "Muḥammad ibn Yazīd! I've been begging God to throw you into my power."

"And I have begged Him to protect me from you," Muḥammad said.

Yazīd said, "He can't protect you now. He can't save you from me. By God, I'll have you executed before I've finished eating this bunch of grapes. If I saw the Angel of Death coming for you I'd get there first, I swear to God!"

As it was prayer time, Yazīd put down the grapes and joined the worshipers.

But the people of the province had agreed together to kill him, and when he bowed in prayer, one of them struck him on the head with an iron bar, and he died. 105.3

Muḥammad was told: "You're free to go," and he went on his way safe and sound.

ذكره القاضي أبو الحسين في كتابه بغير إسناد ولم يعزه إلى المدائنيّ وجاء به على خلاف هذا اللفظ والمعنى واحد إلّا أنّه جعل بدل محمّد بن يزيد وضّاحاً صاحب عمر بن عبد العزيز وبدلاً من سليمان بن عبد الملك عمر بن عبد العزيز ولم يذكر الدعاء في خبره. ٤،١٠٥

ووقع إليّ هذا الخبر على غير هذا حدّثنيه علي بن أبي الطيّب قال حدّثنا ابن الجرّاح قال حدّثنا ابن أبي الدنيا قال حدّثنا يعقوب بن إسحاق بن زياد قال حدّثنا أبو همّام الصلت بن محمّد الخاركيّ قال حدّثنا مسلمة بن علقمة عن داود بن أبي هند قال حدّثني محمّد بن يزيد قال ٥،١٠٥

إنّ سليمان بن عبد الملك[1] أنفذ محمّد بن يزيد إلى ديماس الحجّاج وفيه يزيد الرقاشيّ ويزيد الضبيّ وعابدة من أهل البصرة فأطلق كلّ من فيه غير يزيد بن أبي مسلم.

فلمّا مات سليمان قال محمّد كنت مستعملاً على أفريقية إذ قدم يزيد بن أبي مسلم أميراً في خلافة يزيد بن عبد الملك قال محمّد فعذّبني عذاباً شديداً حتّى كسر عظامي فأُتي بي يوماً في كساء أحمل عند المغرب. ٦،١٠٥

فقلت له ارحمني فقال التمس الرحمة من عند غيري ولو رأيت ملك الموت عند رأسك لبادرته إلى نفسك اذهب حتّى أصبح لك.

فدعوت الله وقلت اللّٰهمّ اذكر ما كان منّي في أهل الديماس اذكر يزيد الرقاشيّ وفلاناً وفلاناً واكفني شرّ يزيد بن أبي مسلم وسلّط عليه من لا يرحمه واجعل ذلك من قبل أن يرتدّ إليّ طرفي وجعلت أحبس طرفي رجاء الإجابة. ٧،١٠٥

فدخل عليه ناس من البربر فقتلوه ثمّ أطلقوني فقالوا لي اذهب حيث شئت فقلت لهم اذهبوا واتركوني فإنّي أخاف إن انصرفت أن يظنّ أنّ هذا من عملي فذهبوا وتركوني. ٨،١٠٥

---

١ بن: لمّا قام سليمان بن عبد الملك بن مروان بعثني إلى العراق إلى أهل الديماس الذين سجنهم الحجّاج فأخرجتهم وفيهم يزيد الرقاشيّ ويزيد الضبيّ وعابدة من أهل البصرة.

Judge Abū l-Ḥusayn reproduces this in his book with no chain of transmitters and without attributing it to al-Madāʾinī. The wording is different, but the gist is the same, except that his protagonist is Waḍḍāḥ, the appointee of the caliph ʿUmar ibn ʿAbd al-ʿAzīz instead of Muḥammad ibn Yazīd, and he substitutes ʿUmar ibn ʿAbd al-ʿAzīz for Sulaymān ibn ʿAbd al-Malik and omits the captive's prayer. 105.4

I have also come across a different version. I cite ʿAlī ibn al-Ḥasan, citing Ibn al-Jarrāḥ, citing Ibn Abī l-Dunyā, citing Yaʿqūb ibn Isḥāq ibn Ziyād, citing Abū Hammām al-Ṣalt ibn Muḥammad of Kharg, citing Maslamah ibn ʿAlqamah, quoting Dāwūd ibn Abī Hind, citing Muḥammad ibn Yazīd, who said that: 105.5

Sulaymān ibn ʿAbd al-Malik sent Muḥammad ibn Yazīd to Iraq to al-Ḥajjāj's Black Hole, where Yazīd al-Raqqāshī,[316] Yazīd al-Ḍabbī, and a holy woman of Basra were imprisoned. Muḥammad released everyone except Yazīd ibn Abī Muslim.[317]

After Sulaymān's death (said Muḥammad), when I was financial comptroller of North Africa in the caliphate of Yazīd ibn ʿAbd al-Malik, Yazīd ibn Abī Muslim arrived as military governor. He tortured me so severely that my bones were broken. One day, at the time of the sunset prayer, he had me carried in wrapped in nothing but a smock. 105.6

"Have pity on me!" I cried.

"Don't ask *me* for pity," he said. "If I saw the Angel of Death at your side, I'd get to you first. Away with you—I'll deal with you in the morning."

Then I prayed to God, saying: 105.7

"O God, remember how I freed the prisoners in the Black Hole. Remember Yazīd al-Raqqāshī and the others, and preserve me from the mischief Yazīd ibn Abī Muslim means to do me, and throw *him* into the power of someone who will show him no mercy; and let this happen in the twinkling of an eye!"—and I covered my own eyes in the hope that my prayer would be answered.

And so it was: A band of Berbers burst in on him and murdered him.[318] The Berbers released me, saying, "You're free to go," but I replied: 105.8

"You go, but let me stay here. I'm afraid that if I leave prison, this will be thought to be my doing." They did as I asked and left me behind.

٩،١٠٥ حدّثنا عليّ بن أبي الطيّب قال حدّثنا ابن الجرّاح قال حدّثنا ابن أبي الدنيا قال حدّثني عمر بن شبّة قال حدّثني محدّث عن أميّة بن خالد عن وضّاح بن خيثمة قال

أمرني عمر بن عبد العزيز بإخراج من في السجن فأخرجتهم إلّا يزيد بن أبي مسلم فنذر دمي.

١٠،١٠٥ فإنّي لَبإفريقية إذ قيل لي قد قدم يزيد ابن أبي مسلم فهربت منه فأرسل في طلبي فأخذت وأتي بي إليه فقال وضّاح قلت وضّاح فقال أما والله طالما سألت الله أن يمكّنني منك فقلت وأنا والله لطالما سألت الله أن يعيذني منك فقال والله ما أعاذك منّي ووالله لأَقتلنّك ولو سابقني إليك ملك الموت لسبقته.

١١،١٠٥ ثمّ استدعى بالسيف والنطع فجيء بهما وكتّفت وأقعدت فيه لتضرب عنقي وقام قائم على رأسي بالسيف مشهوراً.

فأقيمت الصلاة فخرج يزيد وصلّى بهم فلمّا خرّ ساجداً أخذته سيوف الجند وأطلقت.

١٢،١٠٥ حدّثني محمّد بن الحسن بن المظفّر قال أخبرني أحمد بن محمّد السرخسيّ أبو بكر قال أخبرنا أبو العبّاس ثعلب عن الزبير بن بكّار قال

كان وضّاح حاجباً لعمر بن عبد العزيز فلمّا حضرت عمر الوفاة أمر بإخراج كلّ من في الحبس إلّا يزيد بن أبي مسلم وذكر الحديث.

١،١٠٦ حـدّثني أبو طالب عبد العزيز بن أحمد بن محمّد بن الفضل بن أحمد بن محمّد بن حمّاد دنقش مولى المنصور وصاحب حرسه وكان محمّد بن حمّاد يحجب الرشيد والمعتصم وأحمد بن محمّد أحد القوّاد بسرّ من رأى مع صالح بن وصيف وولي الشرطة بها للمهتدي وأحمد بن محمّد بن الفضل يكنّى أبا عيسى وكان أحد أمناء القضاة ببغداد قال قال لي القاضي أبو القاسم عليّ بن محمّد التنوخيّ قال حدّثني القاضي أبو جعفر

I cite ʿAlī ibn al-Ḥasan, citing Ibn al-Jarrāḥ, citing Ibn Abī l-Dunyā, citing ʿUmar ibn Shabbah, citing an unnamed transmitter, quoting Umayyah ibn Khālid, quoting Waḍḍāḥ ibn Khaythamah, who said: 105.9

The caliph ʿUmar ibn ʿAbd al-ʿAzīz ordered me to release all prisoners. I released everyone except Yazīd ibn Abī Muslim, who swore revenge.

Then, in North Africa, I was told, "Yazīd ibn Abī Muslim has come." 105.10

I fled, but he had me pursued, and I was captured and brought before him.

"Are you Waḍḍāḥ?" he asked.

"I am," I replied.

He said, "I've been begging God for ages to let me get my hands on you."

"For ages I've been begging Him to save me from you."

"God can't save you now," he said. "By God, I'm going to execute you, and if it were a race, I'd beat the Angel of Death to it!"

He sent for the sword and execution mat. My arms were pinioned and I was thrust down onto the mat to have my head cut off. Sword aloft, a man stepped forward. 105.11

But it was prayer time, and Yazīd went and joined the worshipers; and when he prostrated himself, the soldiers fell on him with their swords, and I was released.

I cite Muḥammad ibn al-Ḥasan ibn al-Muẓaffar, citing Abū Bakr Aḥmad ibn Muḥammad of Sarakhs, citing Abū l-ʿAbbās Thaʿlab, quoting al-Zubayr ibn Bakkār, who said: 105.12

Waḍḍāḥ was ʿUmar ibn ʿAbd al-ʿAzīz's chamberlain. On his deathbed, ʿUmar ordered all prisoners except Yazīd ibn Abī Muslim to be released.

Al-Zubayr ibn Bakkār then told the story as above.

I cite Abū Ṭālib ʿAbd al-ʿAzīz ibn Aḥmad ibn Muḥammad ibn al-Faḍl ibn Aḥmad ibn Muḥammad ibn Ḥammād Danqash.[319] (Ḥammād Danqash was the freedman of the caliph al-Manṣūr and his captain of the guard.[320] Muḥammad ibn Ḥammād was chamberlain to the caliphs Hārūn al-Rashīd and al-Muʿtaṣim. Aḥmad, his son, was an army chief at Samarra together with Ṣāliḥ ibn Waṣīf, and chief of police at Samarra under the caliph al-Muhtadī. Aḥmad ibn Muḥammad ibn al-Faḍl, whose courtesy name was Abū ʿĪsā, was 106.1

أحمد بن إسحاق بن البهلول التنوخيّ الأنباريّ قال حدّثني أبو عبد الله بن أبي عوف البزوريّ قال

دخلت على أبي العبّاس بن ثوابة وكان محبوساً فقال لي احفظ عنّي قلت نعم فقال [طويل]

عَوَاقِبُ مَكْرُوهِ ٱلأُمُورِ خِيَارُ   وَأَيَّامُ سُوءٍ لَا تَدُومُ قِصَارُ
وَلَيْسَ بِبَاقٍ بُؤْسُهَا وَنَعِيمُهَا   إِذَا كَرَّ لَيْلٌ ثُمَّ كَرَّ نَهَارُ

قال فلم تمض إلّا أيّام يسيرة حتّى أطلق من حبسه. ٢،١٠٦

وقد ذكر أبو الحسين القاضي في كتابه هذين البيتين بغير إسناد ولم يذكر القصّة ولا سبب الشعر.

١،١٠٧ حدّثني أحمد بن عبد الله بن أحمد الورّاق قال حدّثني أبو بكر محمّد بن عبد الله العلّاف المعروف بالمستعينيّ قال حدّثنا عبد الله بن أبي سعد قال حدّثني محمّد بن الحسن الأنصاريّ قال حدّثني إبراهيم بن مسعود عن بعض تجّار المدينة قال

كنت أختلف إلى جعفر بن محمّد وكنت له خليطاً وكان يعرفني بحسن حال فتغيّرت حالي فأتيته فجعلت أشكو إليه فأنشأ يقول [وافر]

فَلَا تَجْزَعْ وَإِنْ أَعْسَرْتَ يَوْماً   فَقَدْ أَيْسَرْتَ فِي ٱلزَّمَنِ ٱلطَّوِيلِ

قال فخرجت من عنده وأنا أغنى الناس.

٢،١٠٧ حدّثني أحمد بن عبد الله بن أحمد الورّاق قال حدّثنا أبو الفضل أحمد بن سليمان القاضي قال حدّثنا طاهر بن يحيى بن الحسن بن جعفر بن عبد الله بن الحسين بن

a legal trustee in Baghdad.) Abū Ṭālib ʿAbd al-ʿAzīz cited Judge Abū l-Qāsim ʿAbū ibn Muḥammad al-Tanūkhī, citing Judge Abū Jaʿfar Aḥmad ibn Isḥāq ibn al-Buhlūl al-Tanūkhī of al-Anbār, citing Abū ʿAbd Allāh ibn Abī ʿAwf the Grain Merchant, who said:

I visited Abū l-ʿAbbās ibn Thawābah when he was in prison.

"Would you memorize what I tell you?" he asked.

"Willingly," I replied, and he said:

Dire events lead to good things.
Hard times are short: they pass.
Pain does not endure, but time
brings joy, and joy will last.

Only a few days later, he was released from prison. 106.2

Judge Abū l-Ḥusayn reproduces this couplet in his book, with no chain of transmitters and no narrative to explain the occasion that gave rise to the poetry.

107.1 I cite Aḥmad ibn ʿAbd Allāh ibn Aḥmad the Stationer–Copyist, citing Abū Bakr Muḥammad ibn ʿAbd Allāh the Fodder Merchant, known as al-Mustaʿīnī, citing ʿAbd Allāh ibn Abī Saʿd, citing Muḥammad ibn al-Ḥusayn al-Anṣārī, citing Ibrāhīm ibn Masʿūd, quoting a merchant of Medina, who said:

I was on close terms with Jaʿfar al-Ṣādiq and often visited him. When he first knew me, I was well off, but my circumstances changed. One day I went to see him and began to tell him my woes. He declaimed:

When you've had many years of ease,
do not repine if times are hard!

I went away feeling incomparably rich.

107.2 I cite Aḥmad ibn ʿAbd Allāh ibn Aḥmad the Stationer–Copyist, citing Judge Abū l-Faḍl Aḥmad ibn Sulaymān, citing Ṭāhir son of Yaḥyā son of al-Ḥasan son of Jaʿfar son of ʿAbd Allāh son of al-Ḥusayn ibn ʿAlī ibn Abī Ṭālib, peace on

عليّ بن أبي طالب عليهما السلام قال حدّثني أبي عن أبيه عن جدّه عن عليّ بن جعفر بن محمّد قال

جاء رجل إلى جعفر بن محمّد فشكا إليه الإضاقة فأنشده جعفر بن محمّد [وافر]

فَلَا تَجْزَعْ إِذَا أَعْسَرْتَ يَوْمًا   فَكَمْ أَرْضَاكَ بِٱلْيُسْرِ ٱلطَّوِيلِ
وَلَا تَيْأَسْ فَإِنَّ ٱلْيَأْسَ كُفْرٌ   لَعَلَّ اللهُ يُغْنِي عَنْ قَلِيلِ
وَلَا تَظُنَّنْ بِرَبِّكَ غَيْرَ خَيْرٍ   فَإِنَّ اللهَ أَوْلَى بِالْجَمِيلِ

قال الرجل فذهب عنّي ما كنت أجد.

وروى القاضي أبو الحسين في كتابه كتاب الفرج بعد الشدّة هذا الشعر بغير خبر ولا إسناد ونسبه إلى الحسين بن عليّ بن أبي طالب عليهما السلام وروى البيت الأوّل كما رواه ابن أبي سعد في الخبر الذي رويت قبل هذا وقال بعده [وافر] ٣،١٠٧

فَإِنَّ ٱلْعُسْرَ يَتْبَعُهُ يَسَارٌ   وَقِيلُ اللهِ أَصْدَقُ كُلِّ قِيلِ

ثمّ جاء بالبيتين الثاني والثالث كما جاءا في هذين الخبرين وزاد بعد ذلك بيتاً خامساً وهو [وافر]

وَلَوْ أَنَّ ٱلْعُقُولَ تَسُوقُ رِزْقًا   لَكَانَ ٱلْمَالُ عِنْدَ ذَوِي ٱلْعُقُولِ

وذكر القاضي أبو الحسين في كتابه أنّ المدائنيّ روى عن محمّد بن الزبير التميميّ ١،١٠٨

أنّ عبيد الله بن زياد أُتي برجل من القرّاء فشتمه وقال له أحروريّ أنت فقال الرجل لا والله ما أنا بحروريّ فقال والله لأفعلنّ بك ولأصنعنّ انطلقوا به إلى السجن فانطلقوا

them all, who said: I cite my father, quoting his father, quoting his grandfather, quoting ʿAlī son of Jaʿfar al-Ṣādiq son of Muḥammad al-Bāqir, who said:

A man went to Jaʿfar al-Ṣādiq complaining of reduced circumstances. Jaʿfar said:

When you've had many years of wealth,
do not repine when times are hard.
Despair is thankless, impious—
soon, God may make you rich again.
Never criticize your Lord:
God deserves your commendation!

The man said, "At this, all my sorrow left me."

In his book *Deliverance following Adversity*, Judge Abū l-Ḥusayn quotes this poem with no accompanying narrative and no chain of transmitters and attributes it to al-Ḥusayn ibn ʿAlī ibn Abī Ṭālib, peace on them both. He quotes the first verse in the form in which Ibn Abī Saʿd quoted it in the version I quoted above. He gives this as the next line: 107.3

Nothing is truer than God's Word:
after hardship, easefulness![321]

He then quotes the second and third verses, as above, and goes on to add a fifth:

If being wise could yield provision,
every wise man would be rich.

In his book, Judge Abū l-Ḥusayn reports al-Madāʾinī as quoting from Muḥammad ibn al-Zubayr al-Tamīmī: 108.1

A "Qurʾan reader"[322] was haled before ʿUbayd Allāh ibn Ziyād. ʿUbayd Allāh heaped abuse on him and asked, "Are you a Ḥarūrī?"

The man said, "I swear by God I'm no such thing!"

But ʿUbayd Allāh yelled, "By God, I'll make you suffer for it! Off with him to prison!"

به فسمعه ابن زياد يهمهم فردّه وقال له ما قلت فقال عنّ لي بيتان من الشعر قلتهما فقال إنّك لفارغ القلب أنت قلتهما أم شيء سمعته قال بل قلتهما وهما [طويل]

عَسَى فَرَجٌ يَأْتِي بِهِ اللهُ إِنَّهُ   لَهُ كُلَّ يَوْمٍ فِي خَلِيقَتِهِ أَمْرُ
إِذَا ٱشْتَدَّ عُسْرٌ فَارْجُ يُسْرًا فَإِنَّهُ   قَضَى ٱللهُ أَنَّ ٱلْعُسْرَ يَتْبَعُهُ يُسْرُ

٢،١٠٨ فسكت ابن زياد ساعة ثمّ قال قد أتاك الفرج خلّوا سبيله.

أخبرني محمّد بن الحسن بن المظفّر قال أخبرنا محمّد بن عبد الواحد قال أخبرني عليّ بن دبيس الكاتب عن أحمد بن الحارث الخرّاز عن عليّ بن محمّد المدائنيّ عن محمّد بن الزبير التميميّ فذكر نحوه.

١،١٠٩ وذكر القاضي أبو الحسين في كتابه قال حدّثني أبي قال حدّثني أبو يوسف يعقوب بن بيان قال حدّثني عليّ بن الحسين بن محمّد بن موسى بن الفرات قال

كنت أتولّى ماسبذان وكان صاحب البريد بها عليّ بن يزيد وكان قديمًا يكتب للعبّاس بن المأمون فحدّثني أنّ العبّاس غضب عليه وأخذ جميع ما كان يملكه حتّى إنّه بقي بسرّ من رأى لا يملك شيئًا إلّا برذونه بسرجه ولجامه ومبطّنة وطيلسانًا وقميصًا وشاشيّة وأنّه كان يركب في أوّل النهار فيلقى من يريد لقاءه ثمّ ينصرف فيبعث ببرذونه إلى الكراء فيكسب عليه ما يعلفه وما ينفقه هو وغلامه.

٢،١٠٩ فاتّفق في بعض الأيّام أنّ الدابّة لم تكسب شيئًا فبات هو وغلامه طاويين قال ونالنا من الغد مثل ذلك فقال غلامي يا مولاي نحن نصبر ولكن الشأن في الدابّة فإنّي أخاف أن تعطب قلت فأيّ شيء أعمل ليس إلا السرج واللجام وثيابي

As the man was dragged off, ʿUbayd Allāh heard him muttering. He called him back and demanded, "What's that you said?"

"Just a couple of lines of verse that came into my head."

"You're a cool one! Did you make them up, or are they by someone else?"

"I composed them myself. Listen:

God may yet bring deliverance,
  Who every day works for mankind.
Great hardship brings us hope of ease:
  ease after hardship God decrees!"[323]

ʿUbayd Allāh was momentarily lost for words. Then he said, "You have been delivered. Let him go." 108.2

I cite Muḥammad ibn al-Ḥasan ibn al-Muẓaffar, citing Muḥammad ibn ʿAbd al-Wāḥid, Thaʿlab's Pupil, citing ʿAlī ibn Dubays the state scribe, citing Aḥmad ibn al-Ḥārith the Cobbler, quoting al-Madāʾinī, quoting Muḥammad ibn al-Zubayr al-Tamīmī, for a similar version.

Judge Abū l-Ḥusayn, in his book, cites his father, Judge Abū ʿUmar Muḥammad, citing Abū Yūsuf Yaʿqūb ibn Bayān, citing ʿAlī ibn al-Ḥusayn ibn Muḥammad ibn Mūsā Ibn al-Furāt, who said: 109.1

When I was governor of Māsabadhān, the postmaster and intelligencer was ʿAlī ibn Yazīd, who had been secretary to al-ʿAbbās, the son of the caliph al-Maʾmūn. ʿAlī ibn Yazīd told me that:

He fell out of favor with Prince ʿAbbās, who seized everything he owned, leaving him in Samarra with nothing but his horse, its saddle and bridle, an under-jacket, a stole of office,[324] a shirt, and a turban. He would ride out first thing in the morning to meet whoever he had business with, and then go home and put his horse out to hire. This brought in enough to pay for the beast's fodder and to keep him and his servant boy.

It happened that, one day, the horse earned nothing, and he and his servant went hungry. 109.2

ʿAlī ibn Yazīd takes up the narrative:

The next day the same thing happened. My servant said, "Sir, you and I can put up with hunger. The problem is the horse—I don't think it can go on."

وإن بعت من ذلك شيئاً تعطّلت عن الحركة وطلب التصرّف قال فانظر في أمرك فنظرت فإذا بحصيري خلق ومخدّتي لبنة مغشّاة بخرقة أدعها تحت رأسي ومطهرة خزف للطهور فلم أجد غير منديل دبيقيّ خلق قد بقي منه الرسم فقلت للغلام خذ هذا المنديل فبعه واشتر علفاً للدابّة ولحماً بدرهم واشوِه وجئ به فقد قرمت إلى أكل اللحم.

٣،١٠٩ فأخذ المنديل ومضى وبقيت في الدار وحدي وفيها شاهمرج قد جاع لجوعنا فلم أشعر إلاّ بعصفور قد سقط في المطهرة التي فيها الماء للطهور عطشاً فشرب فنهض إليه الشاهمرج فناهضه فلضعفه ما قصر عنه وطار العصفور ثمّ عاد إلى المطهرة فتغسّل ونشر جناحيه فناهضه الشاهمرج ثانية فقبض عليه فصاح[1] فبكيت ورفعت رأسي إلى السماء وقلت اللّٰهمّ كما فرّجت عن هذا الشاهمرج فرّج عنّا وارزقنا من حيث لا نحتسب.

٤،١٠٩ فما رددت طرفي حتّى دقّ بابي فقلت من أنت قال أنا إبراهيم بن يوحنّا وكيل العبّاس ابن المأمون فقلت ادخل فدخل فلمّا نظر إلى صورتي قال مالي أراك على هذه الصورة فكتمته خبري فقال لي الأمير يقرأ عليك السلام وقد اصطبح[2] اليوم وذكرك وقد أمر لك بخمسمائة دينار وأخرج الكيس فوضعه بين يديّ.

٥،١٠٩ فحمدت الله تعالى ودعوت للعبّاس ثمّ شرحت له قصّتي وأطفته في داري وبيوتي وحدّثته بحديث الدابّة وما تقاسيه من الضرّ والمنديل والشاهمرج والدعاء فتوجّع لي وانصرف ولم يلبث أن عاد فقال لي صرت الى الأمير وحدّثته بحديثك كلّه فاغتمّ لذلك وأمر لك بخمسمائة دينار أخرى قال تأثّث بتلك وأنفق هذه إلى أن يفرج اللّٰه.

١ كذا في ل. ش: وطار العصفور ووقف الشاهمرج فعاد العصفور إلى المطهرة فبادره الشاهمرج فناهضه فأخذه بحميّة فابتلعه فلمّا صار في حوصلته عاد الخ. ٢ ب، س: أصبح.

"What are we to do?" I asked. "All we have is the saddle and bridle, and my clothes. If I sell any of those, I won't be able to go out and look for work."

"Think," the boy said.

I did, and realized I also had a worn reed mat, my pillow—a brick wrapped in rags that I put under my head—an earthenware washbowl that I used for washing before prayers, and, other than these, only a tattered Dabīqī kerchief held together by the embroidery.[325]

I told the boy, "Take the kerchief and sell it. Buy fodder for the horse, and a dirham's worth of meat. Have it roasted and bring it home[326]—I'm longing for some meat."

The boy went off with the kerchief, leaving me alone in the house where, 109.3
like us, the resident stork had gone without food. Suddenly, I saw a sparrow hop into the water in my washbasin to quench its thirst. The stork pounced on it, but was too weak to catch it. The sparrow flew off, and then flew back again, bathed, and spread its wings. Once again, the stork attacked, and this time it caught the sparrow, which let out a cry.

I wept and looked heavenward. "O God!" I said. "Deliver us as You have delivered this stork, and provide for us whence we least expect it!"[327]

No sooner had I lowered my eyes than there came a knock at the door. 109.4
"Who's there?" I called.

"Ibrāhīm ibn Yūḥannā, the steward of Prince ʿAbbās," was the reply.

"Come in!"

Taken aback by my appearance, the steward said, "You look dreadful!"

I did not explain, and he continued, drawing out a purse which he placed before me: "The Prince sends you his greetings. When he drank his wine this morning, he thought of you, and has sent you five hundred dinars."

I praised God Exalted and called down blessings on the prince; and then 109.5
I told Ibrāhīm ibn Yūḥannā everything. I showed him round the bare rooms; I told him about the horse and its sufferings, and about the kerchief, the stork, and my prayer. He took his leave, full of commiseration, and in no time he was back again, saying:

"I've just been with the prince. I told him all about you, and he was very upset. He's sent you another five hundred dinars, with the instructions to 'Get some furniture with the first lot, and use this to tide you over until God delivers you!'"

وعاد غلامي وقد باع المنديل واشترى منه ما أردته فأريته الدنانير وحدّثته الحديث ففرح حتّى كاد أن تنشقّ مرارته وما زال صنع الله يتعاهدنا.

١،١١٠ قال المدائنيّ في كتابه وجاء به القاضي أبو الحسين في كتابه عن المدائنيّ بغير إسناد واللفظان متقاربان

إنّ أعرابيّة كانت تخدم نساء النبيّ صلّى الله عليه وسلّم وكانت كثيرًا ما تمثّل [طويل]

وَيَوْمَ ٱلْوِشَاحِ مِنْ تَعَاجِيبِ رَبِّنَا أَلَا إِنَّهُ مِنْ ظُلْمَةِ ٱلْكُفْرِ نَجَّانِي

٢،١١٠ فقيل لها إنّك تكثرين من التمثّل بهذا البيت وإنّا نظنّه لأمر فما هو قالت أجل كنت عسيفة على قوم بالبادية قال مؤلّف هذا الكتاب العسيف الأجير فوضعت جارية منهم وشاحًا فمرّت عقاب فاختطفته ونحن لا ندري ففقدنه وقلن أين هو أنت صاحبته فحلفتُ واعتذرتُ فأبين قبول قولي وعذري واستعدين بالرجال فجاءوا ففتّشوني فلم يجدوا شيئًا فقال بعضهم احتملته في فَرْجها فأرادوا أن يفتّشوا فرجي فما ظنّكم بامرأة تخاف ذلك.

٣،١١٠ فلمّا خفت الشرّ رفعت رأسي إلى السماء فقلت يا ربّاه أغثني فمرّت العقاب فطرحته بيننا فندموا وقالوا ظلمنا المسكينة وجعلوا يعتذرون إليّ فما وقعت في كربة إلاّ ذكرت ذلك وهو يوم الوشاح فرجوت الفرج.

٤،١١٠ حدّثنا عليّ بن أبي الطيّب قال حدّثنا ابن الجرّاح قال حدّثنا ابن أبي الدنيا قال حدّثني محمّد بن الحجّاج الضبيّ قال حدّثنا أبو معاوية عن هشام بن عروة عن أبيه عن عائشة رضي الله عنها قالت كانت امرأة تغشانا تمثّل بهذا البيت [طويل]

My servant returned, having sold the kerchief and bought what I had told him. When I showed him the money and explained what had happened, he nearly burst for joy; and from then on, God took care of us.

Al-Madā'inī says in his book—and Judge Abū l-Ḥusayn reproduces this, quoting al-Madā'inī with no chain of transmission; the two versions are similar: 110.1

An Arab woman who waited on the wives of the Prophet, God bless and keep him, often used to recite:

> The Day of the Sash was a marvel of the Lord:
> He saved me from the shadow of the underworld.

They said, "There must be a reason why you say this so often. What is it?" 110.2

She replied:

You're right, there is. When I was hire-quean to a Bedouin tribe (the author of this book observes: a "hire-quean" is a paid servant), a young tribeswoman took off her sash and a passing eagle snatched it, but no one realized. When the women couldn't find it, they said, "Where is it? You took it!"

I vowed I hadn't and pleaded with them, but they wouldn't take my word, and set the men on me.

The men searched me but found nothing. "She must have put it up her vagina," said one of them.

They meant to search my vagina!—a woman's worst fear, as you can imagine.

In my terror, I lifted up my face to heaven and said, "O Lord! Send me succor!" and at that very moment the eagle flew by and dropped the sash. 110.3

Then they were sorry and said, "We did the poor woman an injustice," and apologized.

Whenever I'm afflicted, I remember what happened then, on "the Day of the Sash," and put my hope in deliverance.

We cite ʿAlī ibn al-Ḥasan, citing Ibn al-Jarrāḥ, citing Ibn Abī l-Dunyā, citing Muḥammad ibn al-Ḥajjāj al-Ḍabbī, citing Abū Muʿāwiyah, quoting Hishām ibn ʿUrwah, quoting his father, quoting ʿĀ'ishah, God be pleased with her, who said: 110.4

A woman who used to visit us was in the habit of reciting this line:

وَيَوْمَ ٱلسِّخَابِ مِنْ تَعَاجِيبِ رَبِّنَا   عَلَى أَنَّهُ مِنْ ظُـلْمَةِ ٱلْكُفْرِ نَجَّانِي

فقالت لها أمّ سلمة

٥،١١٠ وذكر نحو ذلك إلاّ أنّه قال فيه فقالت عجوز منهنّ لا رعة لها فتّشوا مالها أي فَرْجها فأشرفتُ على الفضيحة فرفعت رأسي إلى السماء فقلت يا غياث المستغيثين فما أتممتها حتّى جاء غراب فرمى السخاب بيننا فلو رأيتهم يا أمّ المؤمنين وهم حوالي يقولون اجعلينا في حلّ فنظمت ذلك في بيت فأنا أنشده لئلاّ أنسى النعمة فأترك شكرها.

١،١١١ ذكر القاضي أبو الحسين في كتابه قال حدّثني أبو الحسن محمّد بن عبد الله بن الحسين بن سعد عن أبيه عبد الله بن الحسين قال حدّثني الحسين ابن نمير الخزاعيّ قال

صار الفضل بن الربيع إلى الفضل بن يحيى بن خالد البرمكيّ في حاجة له فلم يرفع له رأساً ولا قضى حاجته فقام مغضباً فلم يدع بدابّته ولا اكترث له.

٢،١١١ ثمّ أتبعه رجلاً فقال انظر ما يقول فإنّ الرجل ينبئ عمّا في نفسه في ثلاثة مواضع إذا اضطجع على فراشه وإذا خلا بعرسه وإذا استوى على سرجه.

٣،١١١ قال الرجل فاتّبعته فلمّا استوى على سرجه عضّ على شفتيه وقال [طويل]

عَسَى وَعَسَى يُثْنِي ٱلزَّمَانُ عِنَانَهُ   بِدَوْرِ زَمَانٍ وَٱلزَّمَانُ يَدُورُ
فَيُعْقِبُ رَوْعَاتٍ سُرُوراً وَغِبْطَةً   وَتَحْدُثُ مِنْ بَعْدِ ٱلْأُمُورِ أُمُورُ

فلم يكن بين ذلك وبين أن سخط الرشيد على البرامكة واستوزر الفضل بن الربيع إلّا أيّاماً يسيرة.

The Day of the Necklace was a marvel of the Lord,
For He saved me from the shadow of the underworld.

Umm Salamah asked her . . .

The story then continues much as above, except that it says: 110.5

A shameless old crone said, "Search her privates!" (meaning her vagina). Just as I was about to be dishonored (the woman said), I lifted up my face to heaven and said, "O Savior of those who seek succor . . ." but before I could finish, a crow came along and dropped the necklace.

O Mother of the Faithful![328] I wish you could have seen them crowding round me begging, "Don't hold us to account!"

That's why I made up that line, and I recite it so as not to forget the blessing and stop being thankful for it.

Judge Abū l-Ḥusayn says in his book: I cite Abū l-Ḥasan Muḥammad ibn ʿAbd Allāh ibn al-Ḥusayn ibn Saʿd, quoting his father, ʿAbd Allāh ibn al-Ḥusayn, citing al-Ḥusayn ibn Numayr al-Khuzāʿī, who said: 111.1

Al-Faḍl ibn al-Rabīʿ called on al-Faḍl ibn Yaḥyā ibn Khālid al-Barmakī to ask him a favor. The latter did not so much as glance at him, nor did he grant the request. Angered, al-Faḍl ibn al-Rabīʿ got up to leave. Al-Faḍl ibn Yaḥyā did not tell his servants to bring round his horse, and took no notice of him.

Instead, he had someone follow him, with the instructions: 111.2

"Find out what he says. There are three places where a man reveals himself: in his bed, in his wife's arms, and in the saddle."

"I followed him," said the man, "and when he had swung himself into the saddle, he bit his lip and said: 111.3

Perhaps, perhaps Fate's course will change—
for Time turns without cease—
And joy and bliss will follow fear,
and everything be changed."

It was only a few days later that Hārūn al-Rashīd turned against the Barmakīs and made al-Faḍl ibn al-Rabīʿ vizier.

وحدّثني بهذا الخبر أبي على مثل هذا الإسناد ولم أحفظه لأنّي لم أكتبه عنه في الحال ٤،١١١
فقال في البيت الأوّل [طويل]

عَسَى وَعَسَى يُثْنِي ٱلزَّمَانُ عِنَانَهُ   بِعَشْرَةِ دَهْرٍ وَٱلزَّمَانُ عَثُورُ

وقال في البيت الثّاني [طويل]

فَتُدْرَكُ حَاجَاتٌ وَتُقْضَى مَآرِبُ   وَتَحْدُثُ مِنْ بَعْدِ ٱلأُمُورِ أُمُورُ

وزاد فيه أنّ الفضل بن يحي بن خالد ردّه فقضى حوائجه.

وأخبرنيه محمّد بن الحسن بن المظفّر قال حدّثني أبو بكر الصوليّ عن ميمون بن هارون ٥،١١١
قال حدّثني الحسين بن نمير الخزاعيّ وذكره وقد دخل فيما أجازه لي الصوليّ.

وقرئ على أبي بكر الصوليّ بالبصرة في كتابه كتاب الوزراء سنة خمس وثلاثين وثلثمائة وأنا حاضر أسمع قال حدّثنا أحمد بن يزيد بن محمّد يعني المهلّبيّ قال حدّثني أبي عن إسحاق قال

دخل الفضل بن الربيع على يحيى بن خالد فلم يوسّع له ولا هشّ به ثمّ قال ما جاء بك يا أبا العبّاس قال رقاع معي فردّه عن جميعها

فوثب الفضل وهو يقول [طويل] ٦،١١١

عَسَى وَعَسَى يُثْنِي ٱلزَّمَانُ عِنَانَهُ   بِعَشْرَةِ دَهْرٍ وَٱلزَّمَانُ عَثُورُ
فَتُدْرَكُ آمَالٌ وَتُحْوَى رَغَائِبُ   وَتَحْدُثُ مِنْ بَعْدِ ٱلأُمُورِ أُمُورُ

فردّه يحيي ووقّع له بجميع ما أراد.

My father related this story to me with a similar chain of transmitters, which I forgot because I failed to write it down immediately. His version of the first line of the poem was: 111.4

> Perhaps, perhaps Fate's course will swerve—
> for Time and Fate are chance—

and of the second line:

> Requests be granted, fears removed,
> and everything be changed,

and he added that al-Faḍl ibn Yaḥyā called back al-Faḍl ibn al-Rabīʿ and granted his request.

I also cite for this story Muḥammad ibn al-Ḥasan ibn al-Muẓaffar, citing Abū Bakr al-Ṣūlī, quoting Maymūn ibn Hārūn, citing al-Ḥusayn ibn Numayr al-Khuzāʿī, who transmitted it as part of the material that al-Ṣūlī had authorized him to transmit. 111.5

In addition, the following was read back to al-Ṣūlī for verification in my presence and hearing in Basra in the year 335 [946] as part of his *Book of Viziers*. He cited Aḥmad ibn Yazīd ibn Muḥammad (that is, al-Muhallabī), citing his father, quoting Isḥāq,[329] who said:

Al-Faḍl ibn al-Rabīʿ called on Yaḥyā ibn Khālid al-Barmakī, who showed him no kindness or courtesy, but merely asked, "What brings you here, Abū l-ʿAbbās?"

Al-Faḍl ibn al-Rabīʿ replied, "I have some petitions for you," but Yaḥyā ibn Khālid refused them all.

Al-Faḍl ibn al-Rabīʿ leapt to his feet and said: 111.6

> Perhaps, perhaps Fate's course will change—
> for Time and Fate are chance—
> And hopes and wishes all come true,
> and everything be changed,

whereupon Yaḥyā ibn Khālid called him back and countersigned everything.

وأخبـرني عليّ بن عبد الله الورّاق المعروف بابن أبي لؤلؤ قال حدّثنا محمّد بن جرير الطبريّ قال حدّثنا يونس بن عبد الأعلى قال حدّثنا ابن وهب قال أخبرني سعيد بن أبي أيّوب عن عبد الرحمٰن بن عليّ عن عبد الله بن جعفر ١١٢

أنّ رجلاً أصابه مرض شديد منعه من الطعام والشراب والنوم فبينا هو ذات ليلة ساهرًا إذ سمع وجبة شديدة في حجرته فراعه[١] فإذا هو كلام[٢] فوعاه فتكلّم به فبرأ مكانه وهو أللّٰهمّ أنا عبدك وبك أملي فاجعل الشفاء في جسدي واليقين في قلبي والنور في بصري والشكر في صدري وذكرك بالليل والنهار ما بقيت على لساني وارزقني منك رزقًا غير محظور ولا ممنوع.

١ فراعه: الزيادة من ل. ٢ ب، ل: فإذا هو كلام قائل يقول أنا عدبك.

I cite ʿAlī ibn ʿAbd Allāh the Stationer–Copyist known as Ibn Abī Luʾluʾ, citing Muḥammad ibn Jarīr al-Ṭabarī, citing Yūnus ibn ʿAbd al-Aʿlā, citing Ibn Wahb, citing Saʿīd ibn Abī Ayyūb, quoting ʿAbd al-Raḥmān ibn ʿAlī, quoting ʿAbd Allāh ibn Jaʿfar: 112

A certain man had a serious illness that prevented him from eating, drinking, or sleeping. As he lay awake one night, he was startled by a loud noise in his room. He made out these words,[330] which he repeated, and which cured him on the spot:

"O God! I am Your servant. In You is all my hope. Make my body sound and my heart untroubled. Illumine my eyes, and put thankfulness in my breast and remembrance of You on my tongue, night and day, as long as I live; and neither withhold nor deny, but grant me Your ample and ready provision."

Notes

1 Q Ṭā Hā 20:26.

2 The line is quoted again at §40 in its first version.

3 An allusion to Q Hūd 11:56.

4 An echo of Q Sharḥ 94:1 and anticipation of the opening passage of Chapter One.

5 My rendering follows Ghersetti's, *Il Sollievo*, 28.

6 Al-Shāljī has: "*following Adversity*," which is not found in all MSS. Its omission fits better with what al-Tanūkhī goes on to say at §0.8: "They were happy enough to borrow versions of the title of al-Madā'inī's book without reproducing it exactly."

7 Abū l-Ḥusayn ʿUmar al-Azdī, henceforth referred to by al-Tanūkhī as Judge Abū l-Ḥusayn.

8 Chapter Two reproduces a number of sayings based on the idea that "deliverance follows adversity," but nowhere does it cite these precise words or identify the source of the expression.

9 Q Sharḥ 94:1–8. The words are said to be addressed to the Prophet Muḥammad.

10 The Arabs of the desert were credited with an intuitive sense of linguistic correctness.

11 Q Ṭalāq 65:7.

12 Q Ṭalāq 65:2–3.

13 Q Baqarah 2:259.

14 Q Zumar 39:36.

15 Q Yūnus 10:12.

16 Q Yūnus 10:22–23.

17 Q Anʿām 6:63–64.

18 Q Ibrāhīm 14:13–14.

19 Q Qaṣaṣ 28:5–6.

20 Q Naml 27:62.

21 Q Ghāfir 40:60.

22 Q Baqarah 2:186.

23 Q Baqarah 2:155–57.

24 Q Āl ʿImrān 3:173–74.

25 See §§67.1–4.

26 Q Baqarah 2:155–57.

27 Q Āl ʿImrān 3:173–74.

28 The speaker is Moses.

29 Q Ghāfir 40:44–45.

30 Literally "the man of the fish" (Dhū l-Nūn). Jonah's story is told at §§8.1–5 and 13.8–11, and his prayer is referred to at §28.

31 See §§8.4–5 for this unusual interpretation of the verb.

32 Q Anbiyāʾ 21:87–88.

33 Q Āl ʿImrān 3:147–48.

34 Q Baqarah 2:31.

35 See Q Baqarah 2:34; Aʿrāf 7:11; Ḥijr 15:29; Isrāʾ 17:61; Kahf 18:50; Ṭā Hā 20:116; Ṣād 38:71.

36 See Q Aʿrāf 7:19–21; Ṭā Hā 20:120–21.

37 Q Ṭā Hā 20:121–22.

38 None of Adam's sons is named in the Qurʾan.

39 Q Ṣāffāt 37:77.

40 Al-Tanūkhī is referring to the great number of "tales of the prophets" that were in circulation. They were the stock-in-trade of popular preachers, but scholarly commentators also made use of them, as does al-Tanūkhī himself at §§7.1, 7.2, 11.1–3, 13.8–11, 85.1–9, and 86.1–3.

41 Q Hūd 11:43–45. The son decides out of unbelief to go to a mountaintop instead of entering the ark. One tradition says that the son took refuge on the mountain out of habit, not disobedience. See Wheeler, *Prophets in the Quran*, 58.

42 Q Hūd 11:42.

43 See Q Qaṣaṣ 28:6, cited at §1.7 above; but the allusion is to Q Hūd 11:48: «He was told, Noah, disembark in peace.»

44 Q Ṣāffāt 37:75–78; "peace" is added in the translation from Ṣāffāt 37:79.

45 Q Anbiyāʾ 21:76.

46 See Q Anbiyāʾ 21:52–58.

47 Q Anbiyāʾ 21:69.

48 Q Anbiyāʾ 21:51.

49 Q Anbiyāʾ 21:68–73.

50 Neither Sarah nor Hagar is named in the Qurʾan. *Hājara*, "emigrated," is a play on Hagar's name that draws attention to this prefiguration by Abraham of the Prophet Muḥammad's exodus. See §12.2.

51 Q Ibrāhīm 14:37. The verse continues: «near Your sacred house,» that is, the Kaaba.

52 This is not in the Qur'an. The commentators tell how, in response to Abraham's prayer, an angel dug the well of Zamzam to save Hagar and her son from dying of thirst after Abraham left them.

53 Q Ṣāffāt 37:101–8.

54 Q Ṣāffāt 37:112–13.

55 "Her": Sarah.

56 Q Hūd 11:71.

57 See Q Ḥijr 15:53; Dhāriyāt 51:28.

58 For the same reason (that a prophet may not doubt God), Jonah's incredulity is denied at §8.3.

59 At Q Hūd 11:78–79 and Ḥijr 15:68–71, Lot's people spurn his offer to give them his daughters in place of his guests.

60 The passages are Q Hūd 11:77–82, Ḥijr 15:61–74, Shuʿarāʾ 26:160–73, Naml 27:53–58, ʿAnkabūt 29:28–35.

61 Q 12, Sūrat Yūsuf.

62 Q Yūsuf 12:19.

63 Potiphar is not in fact named here, but is called by the title of "Great One," as in the Qur'an (Q Yūsuf 12:51).

64 Q Yūsuf 12:84.

65 Indirect quotation of Q Yūsuf 12:80.

66 Q Yūsuf 12:93–96.

67 The maggots are not mentioned in the Qur'an.

68 Q Nisāʾ 4:163; Anʿām 6:84; Anbiyāʾ 21:83–84; Ṣād 38:41–44.

69 Q Anbiyāʾ 21:83.

70 In 337/948–49, al-Tanūkhī was aged about ten.

71 The locusts of gold are not mentioned in the Qur'an.

72 Q Ṣāffāt 37:139–48.

73 Ibn ʿAbbās, Saʿīd, and Nawf represent a pietistic storytelling tradition, while al-Farrāʾ and Abū ʿUbaydah are founding fathers of scholarly Qur'anic lexicography.

74 Q Anbiyāʾ 21:87–88.

75 More usually interpreted as «We had no power over him.»

76 Q Ṭalāq 65:7.

77 Q Sabaʾ 34:39.

78 Q Qaṣaṣ 28:7–13.

79 Abū l-ʿAtāhiyah (d. 211/826), famous for his ascetic poetry.

80 Q Aʿrāf 7:179.

81 I have chosen to omit a passage absent from the Berlin, Paris, and Sülemaniye MSS that is found in only one of al-Shāljī's MSS and does not make narrative sense. The Sultan Ahmet MS reads: "For *the mother of* Moses, the outcome of the above misfortunes, and of a third series of misfortunes that will be related in due course, was that God made him a prophet . . ."

82 Q Qaṣaṣ 28:20–21.

83 Q Qaṣaṣ 28:22–24.

84 Q Qaṣaṣ 28:25.

85 Q Ṭā Hā 20:10, Naml 27:7, Qaṣaṣ 28:29.

86 Q Ṭā Hā 20:12–24, Naml 27:9–12, Qaṣaṣ 28:30–35, Nāzi'āt 79:15–19.

87 Indirect quotation of Q Qaṣaṣ 28:35.

88 Q A'rāf 7:127.

89 Q A'rāf 7:128–29.

90 Q A'rāf 7:137.

91 Q 85, Sūrat al-Burūj.

92 Q Tawbah 9:99; Fatḥ 48:6.

93 Hereafter 'Alī ibn al-Ḥasan, as al-Tanūkhī usually calls him.

94 Hereafter Ibn al-Jarrāḥ, as al-Tanūkhī usually calls him.

95 His companion was Abū Bakr; see §12.2.

96 Q Tawbah 9:40.

97 That is, the Meccans.

98 Q Fātiḥah 1:2.

99 After "verses," the Berlin MS inserts: "by means of which God has profited many," and the Leiden MS: "by means of which God has graciously profited and will continue to profit people."

100 Q Ṭalāq 65:2–3.

101 Presumably Sufyān ibn 'Uyaynah, from whom Isḥāq ibn Ismā'īl also transmits to Ibn Abī l-Dunyā at §35.1.

102 Q Ṭalāq 65:2 (end) and Q Ṭalāq 65:3 (beginning).

103 Or al-Qurashī. Added by al-Shāljī from his MS of Ibn Abī l-Dunyā, *al-Faraj ba'd al-shiddah.* This extra link is necessary because Isḥāq ibn Sulaymān died ca. 200, whereas Ibn Abī l-Dunyā was not born until 208/823–24.

104 Q Raḥmān 55:29.

105 Q Naml 27:62. It is not clear whether this is a human or a disembodied voice.

106 Q Āl 'Imrān 3:200, preceded by an echo of Q Sharḥ 94:5–6.

107 Q Anbiyā' 21:87.

108 Al-Shāljī adopts the more folkloric reading "went and hovered about the throne of God," which is also found in the Berlin MS.

109 Q Ṣāffāt 37:145.

110 The public treasury of Kufa, of which Ibn Masʿūd was in charge. There is a missing link in this chain of transmission, since Ibn Masʿūd died in 32/653, while ʿAmr ibn Maymūn died ca. 145/762. In Ibn Abī l-Dunyā, *al-Faraj baʿd al-shiddah*, 11, the link is supplied by Abū l-Aḥwaṣ, who died in the early second/eighth century and is cited at §20.1.

111 Q Anbiyāʾ 21:87.

112 Q Ṣāffāt 37:145.

113 Q 91, Sūrat al-Shams, which has fifteen verses.

114 Q 92, Sūrat al-Layl, which has twenty-one verses.

115 In the Berlin and Sülemaniye MSS the sum is not specified.

116 *The Book of Praiseworthy Behavior and Valuable Principles*, now lost, is cited again at §29.1.

117 Q Shams 91:1 and Layl 92:1. See §14.1.

118 Q Tīn 95:1. Surah 95 has eight verses.

119 The plant *Althaea officinalis.*

120 Al-Muʿtaṣim was a warrior, his son al-Wāthiq an intellectual, and the chief judge Aḥmad ibn Abī Duʾād and his son Abū l-Walīd upholders of rationalist Muʿtazilī theology, giving the ensuing story a rather surprising lineage. See Beaumont, "In the Second Degree," 128–30, for a translation and discussion of this story.

121 *Hātif.* A collection of reports about such voices by Ibn Abī l-Dunyā, *Kitāb al-Hawātif*, is still extant.

122 Q Ṭalāq 65:2–3.

123 In none of the texts consulted does the hero reveal his identity.

124 By contributing to a joint capital, the woman and her husband become trading partners.

125 This is a standard happy ending used to suggest that a story is true.

126 Al-Tanūkhī cites it again at §§79.1, 81.1 and 82.6.

127 This story is set early in the reign of al-Muʿtaṣim.

128 On a caliphal progress, when the ruler traveled about his domains, a skeleton bureaucracy went with him.

129 *Naffāṭah.* I am unable to find any information about this type of lamp.

130 Q Anʿām 6:63–64.

131 The voweling of the name is uncertain. He is usually described as al-Muʿtaṣim's chamberlain. For the sake of chronology, al-Shāljī has substituted his name for the reading "Ḥammād Danqash," who was captain of the guard in the previous century. See §106.1.

132 A pointed insult: by "peasants," Arabs of this period meant the native non-Arab population of Iraq. Al-Faḍl came from a native Christian family, like a significant proportion of the bureaucracy, and had bought land as soon as his career began to prosper. See Sourdel, "Vizirat," 247 and *EI2*, "al-Faḍl b. Marwān."

133 The Arabic word *kātib*, usually rendered as "state scribe," encompasses all levels of bureaucrat from the junior clerk to the private secretary up to the level of vizier.

134 Q 105, Sūrat al-Fīl has five verses. It describes how a great Ethiopian army with war elephants, seeking to seize Mecca, was annihilated by a flock of birds.

135 Q 94, Sūrat al-Sharḥ, which has eight verses.

136 Al-Tanūkhi would have been under twenty at this time.

137 Q Sharḥ 94:1.

138 See Q Sharḥ 94:5–6 and §§1.1–3.

139 Probably ʿAbd Allāh ibn Muḥammad Ibn Abī Shaybah (d. 235/849, see *EI2* "Ibn Abī S͟hayba"), cited at §22 as Abū Bakr ibn Abī Shaybah.

140 Q Sharḥ 94:6. See §1.1.

141 The preferred way of transmitting reports was face to face, whether from memory alone or from a written text. Transmission by correspondence is relatively rare, or rarely acknowledged.

142 This saying seems to be at the origin of the title *Deliverance Follows Adversity*. A similar saying is cited without attribution at §47.5.

143 Scriptures preceding and including the Qur'an.

144 Ibn Abī l-Dunyā, *al-Faraj baʿd al-shiddah*, 15, and the Leiden MS read: "Abū Bakr ibn Shaybah."

145 Al-Muṭṭalib was not the son but the grandson of Abū Wadāʿah al-Sahmī.

146 ʿAmr al-Taymī was not Zuhrah's father but his grandfather's great-grandfather.

147 Q Sharḥ 94:6.

148 Both this name (Mughīth is perhaps to be read Mughīrah) and the next (ʿAqīl, or ʿUqayl) are garbled and therefore conjectural.

149 Q Ṭalāq 65:3.

150 Here, as at §31.4, the longevity of the transmitters seems to be valued as giving a greater sense of closeness to the Prophet.

151 The year before the transmitter's death. Al-Tanūkhī would have been no more than eight years old at the time. See also §§55.3, 64.1, 70.9, 111.5 for teaching sessions that al-Tanūkhī attended in Basra in this year.

152 A Baghdadi traditionist who died ca. 277/890. He was famous for this report about the three men in a cave, and for another about the occasion, described at §12.2, when the Prophet and Abū Bakr concealed themselves in a cave.

153 "The Man of the Fish," i.e., Jonah, Q Anbiyā' 21:87. See §§1.10 and 8.4.

154 Q Tawbah 9:129, Mu'minūn 23:86, Naml 27:26. See §§31.4–6. For the "seven heavens," see Q Baqarah 2:29, Isrā' 17:44, Mu'minūn 23:86, Fuṣṣilat 41:12, Ṭalāq 65:12, Mulk 67:3 and Nūḥ 71:15; for the "seven earths," see Q Ṭalāq 65:12.

155 By "in the prince's hearing," al-Tanūkhī is formally identifying the Buyid ruler ʿAḍud al-Dawlah (r. 338–72/949–83) as a potential re-transmitter of the materials heard by him on this occasion.

156 Jazīrat Ibn ʿUmar lies north of Mosul, which ʿAḍud al-Dawlah occupied in 367/977. Al-Tanūkhī was a member of his court, and he bestowed judicial appointments on him as he progressed northward expanding his territories from his base in Fars and Khuzistan and his new capital, Baghdad. As was customary, al-Tanūkhī delegated whatever appointments he found it inconvenient to exercise in person.

157 Q Tawbah 9:129, Mu'minūn 23:86, Naml 27:26. See §31.9.

158 Q Fātiḥah 1:1.

159 Saʿdawayh, cited at §20.5.

160 A reference to Q Hūd 11:56. See §0.4.

161 A paraphrase of Q Ṭalāq 65:3 and Āl ʿImrān 3:173.

162 Q Tawbah 9:129.

163 Grandfather of the previous Ibn Abī Fudayk.

164 Q Isrā' 17:111.

165 An echo of Q Baqarah 2:255.

166 Ibn Abī l-Dunyā, *al-Faraj baʿd al-shiddah*, 49, reads "ʿUbayd Allāh ibn Muḥammad al-Qurashī," but neither individual is identifiable.

167 An allusion to Q Takwīr 81:2.

168 A paraphrase of part of Q Baqarah 2:255.

169 Q Tawbah 9:129, Mu'minūn 23:86, Naml 27:26.

170 Q Nūḥ 71:10. The passage is quoted in full at §46.

171 See §§46 and 60.4.

172 Q Ghāfir 40:44.

173 Q Hūd 11:88.

174 Q Tawbah 9:129.

175 Al-Shāljī identifies this Ibrāhīm as the ascetic Ibrāhīm ibn Yazīd al-Taymī, see §§87.1 and 88.1–2.

176 An unusual instance of indirect speech.

177 This chain of transmission does not make sense chronologically. For "'Abd Allāh," Ibn Abī l-Dunyā, *al-Faraj baʿd al-shiddah*, 49, reads "'Ubayd Allāh ibn Muḥammad al-Qurashī," probably Ibn 'Ā'ishah the younger, who died in 228/843.

178 See §31.4.

179 The first half of a line attributed to the early Muslim poet al-Aghlab al-ʿIjlī, d. 21/641, quoted by al-Tanūkhī at §0.3.

180 Cited at §16.1.

181 Q Āl ʿImrān 3:173.

182 Q Nūḥ 71:10–12.

183 At §21.1 a similar saying is attributed to the Prophet.

184 Compare §53.1.

185 This and the following exchange are an example of the longevity of the formats of wisdom literature, finding an echo as late as Robert Southey's "The Old Man's Comforts and How He Gained Them" (1799) and Lewis Carroll's parody "You Are Old, Father William." For Buzurjmihr as a wisdom figure in Sasanian lore and Arabic writings, see Marlow, *Counsel for Kings*, vol. 2, 52–53.

186 Anūshirwān's name, taken by the Arabs as a title.

187 The Paris MS calls him ʿAlī ibn Naṣr ibn ʿAlī ibn Bishr the Christian.

188 Unidentified.

189 Unidentified.

190 See Bray, "Ibn al-Muʿtazz and Politics," 115–17, for an overview of studies and discussions of his aphorisms (*fuṣūl qiṣār*).

191 The same as the ʿAlī ibn Naṣr ibn ʿAlī of §50.1.

192 These are proverbs.

193 Literally "people of reason and of religion."

194 This *Book of Viziers* is no longer extant. Al-Ṣūlī met a violent death in obscure circumstances shortly after the teaching session recorded here. See §§64.1 and 111.5 for other citations of al-Ṣūlī, the last also from his *Book of Viziers*.

195 Al-Ṣūlī's authorial "We cite" is changed to "You cite" when it is read back to him.

196 Cited again at §81.1.

197 Such occasions were important in early Abbasid court ceremonial and involved the presentation of gifts and poems by courtiers: see Bray, "Bleeding Poetry." This is a rare instance of the patient's contribution to the occasion.

198 In letters, the transition from the salutation is often marked by this phrase (which is also used at §0.3 to mark the start of al-Tanūkhī's introduction). It forms a pair with the valediction "Farewell!"

199 Q Baqarah 2:216.

200 Unidentified.

201 A reference to Q Sharḥ 94:5–6; see §§1.1–3.

202 Al-Tanūkhī is speaking.

203 Q Sharḥ 94:5–6.

204 Q Zumar 39:38.

205 Q Nūḥ 71:10–12.

206 He was appointed chief secretary to the Buyid ruler of Iraq, Muʿizz al-Dawlah, in 339/950; the title of vizier was granted him in 345/956. It is not certain which period is referred to here. See *EI2*, "al-Muhallabī."

207 Identical with the beginning of §60.1.

208 Also cited at §26.3.

209 The caliph was afraid that his presence in Mecca would lead to an anti-Abbasid uprising.

210 Q Hūd 11:56.

211 Q Tawbah 9:129, Mu'minūn 23:86, Naml 27:26.

212 See §55.3; he is cited again twice at §111.5.

213 I.e., al-Jibāl. See Sourdel, *Vizirat*, 324 and *EI2*, "al-Muwaffaḳ."

214 Q Aʿrāf 7:129. In context, the word means "successors." See §9.8 for a literal rendering.

215 Literally *imāms*. In ʿAbbasid times, this was another word for caliph.

216 Q Qaṣaṣ 28:5–6; only the last word of verse six is given in the Arabic. It is quoted in full at §1.7.

217 Q Nūr 24:55.

218 Al-Muwaffaq was also called al-Nāṣir, "the Helper" or "the Victorious."

219 See Sourdel, *Vizirat*, 325–26. Accounts of how Ismāʿīl ibn Bulbul was put to death agree that he was subjected to lingering and humiliating torture.

220 See Sourdel, *Vizirat*, 262–65 for this episode.

221 An allusion to Q Ṭalāq 65:3.

222 The term used is *al-ʿatamah*, which refers to the first third of the night. See Souag, "Archaic and Innovative Islamic Prayer Names," 351–60.

223 An allusion to Q Ḥajj 22:45.

224 Al-Shāljī follows the reading: "he is encompassed by the flies of avarice and the couches of hellfire."

225 Al-Ḥajjāj's power as governor of Iraq for the Umayyads rested on his Syrian troops.

226 On Ḥasan of Basra's image as a man who spoke truth to power, see Mourad, *Early Islam between Myth and History*. On al-Ḥajjāj's mixed image as a brutal autocrat and a great statesman, see Périer, *Vie d'al-Hadjdjâdj* and Dietrich, "al-Ḥadjdjādj b. Yūsuf."

227 *Kāf-hā'-yā'-'ayn-ṣād* are the opening letters of Q 19, Sūrat Maryam. Twenty-nine surahs open with discrete letters whose significance has never been resolved. *Ṭā'-hā'* are the opening letters of Q 20, Sūrat Ṭā Hā, one of the four surahs that take their name from their opening letters. *Ṭā'-sīn* are the opening letters of Q 27, Sūrat al-Naml. *Yā'-sīn* are the opening letters of Q 36, Sūrat Yā Sīn.

228 See Q Tawbah 9:129 and §31.9.

229 Q Fātiḥah 1:1.

230 Ṣāliḥ is using the art of physiognomy, *qiyāfah* or *firāsah*. 'Uthmān ibn Ḥayyān does the same at §68.11. See Fahd, *La divination*, 370–87.

231 The unidentified narrator is speaking.

232 The mystic Sahl al-Tustarī.

233 See §27.6 for this date, al-Tanūkhī's age at the time, and the other sessions he attended during this year that are cited in chapters two and three.

234 Al-Shāljī thinks that this Ja'far and the Ja'far of §70.6 are the same, but the dates of the transmitters in this version make it unlikely, if al-Tanūkhī met the first Ja'far as he perhaps implies.

235 In the Qur'an, Adam is tempted not by the serpent but by the Devil, Q Ṭā Hā 20:120; see §2.2.

236 The usual rewards from dignitaries to those who have served them.

237 The origins and diffusion of these versions of the tale of the man and the snake are discussed by Ghersetti, "La 'storia del uomo e del serpente' nell'opera di al-Tanū<u>kh</u>ī."

238 An adaptation of Q Raḥmān 55:29.

239 Either the caliph is astonished that the outlaw has survived or, by providential coincidence, he had been intending to send for him at the very moment he appeared.

240 See Bowen, *The Life and Times of 'Alí ibn 'Ísà*, for this important political figure. His grandfather, Dāwud ibn al-Jarrāḥ, appears later in this story as head of Bureaucratic Supervision at §73.8, and in §§103.1–3. For his son 'Īsā, see Bowen, *The Life and Times of 'Alí ibn 'Ísà*, 34, 397–98.

241 On Abū Zunbūr and Muḥammad ibn 'Alī al-Mādharā'ī, see Bowen, *The Life and Times of 'Alí ibn 'Ísà*, 168–71, 254.

242 Aged about twenty-eight at this time (ca. 236/850), 'Ubayd Allāh ibn Yaḥyā ibn Khāqān had just become al-Mutawakkil's vizier. See Sourdel, *Vizirat*, 274.

243 The Ṭāhirids were Isḥāq ibn Ibrāhīm ibn Muṣʿab's kin. The eastern province of Khurasan, which they governed, was a loyalist stronghold. The Turks were the Turkic slave troops (who eventually murdered al-Mutawakkil in 247/861).

244 See Sourdel, *Vizirat*, 280–81 for this incident.

245 Mūsā ibn ʿAbd al-Malik appears again at §§82.1 and 103.1–4, both times as an oppressor.

246 When a bureaucrat was stripped of office, any assets he had been unable to hide were liable to confiscation by the state.

247 Or papyrus.

248 The Bureau of Land Tax, see §73.8.

249 On Sulaymān ibn Wahb's tenure in Egypt: see Sourdel, *Vizirat*, 301. Despite this happy turn of events, he later fell foul of the regent al-Muwaffaq and died in prison in 272/885, see Sourdel, *Vizirat*, 311–12 and *EI2*, "Wahb, Banū."

250 For this branch of al-Tanūkhī's maternal ancestry, see Bray, "Place and Self-Image: The Buhlūlids," 63.

251 The "beardless boy" is the standard beloved of homoerotic romance.

252 Q 1, Sūrat al-Fātiḥah.

253 Q 113, Sūrat al-Falaq and Q 114, Sūrat al-Nās. They both begin "Say: I seek refuge" and are quoted for protection.

254 Q 112, Sūrat al-Ikhlāṣ.

255 Q Baqarah 2:255.

256 Q Ḥashr 59:21.

257 The keywords of these verses are "reconciliation" and "love."

258 Q Anfāl 8:63.

259 Q Rūm 30:21.

260 Q Āl ʿImrān 3:103.

261 On Nāzūk, see Bowen, *The Life and Times of ʿAlí ibn ʿĪsà*, 217, 243–44, 268–70, 281–86, and Kennedy, *The Court of the Caliphs*, 156–57.

262 In 330/941–42. See Kennedy, *The Prophet and the Age of the Caliphates*, 272.

263 "In dues" is a speculative translation of *min ḥaqq al-raqabah*, which looks like an official term but is not mentioned in Donohue, *The Buwayhid Dynasty*, 253–54. The version of this story in al-Tanūkhī's *Nishwār* (vol. 8, 158) has the phrase *min ḥaqq raqabatī*. My translation seems to be supported by §80.1 where al-Tanūkhī's estates are seized *bi l-ḥaqqayn*, literally "on both counts," neither of them specified.

264 Margoliouth translated the *Nishwār* version of this story, al-Tanūkhī, "Table Talk," (*Islamic Culture*, 4 (1932), 235–36), dating it to 331/942–43. It is discussed by Canard, "Le riz," 116–17.

265 This was the second of Ibn Muqlah's three vizierates, 320–21/932–33.

266 The singer is not referred to explicitly in the impersonal expression *ṣuffa al-majlis*.

267 This is a misreading for Muḥammad ibn Numayr, known as al-Numayrī, a love poet who died ca. 90/708. See al-Mubarrad, *Kāmil*, 318. The poem begins conventionally with the motif of the lovers' tribes parting to seek fresh grazing, leaving them bereft, but is unusual in that it names the day of parting.

268 These events took place in 320/932.

269 In 359/970. See Donohue, *The Buwayhid Dynasty*, 144.

270 A speculative translation of *aqṭaʿahā bi l-ḥaqqayn*. Compare §77.1.

271 Most travel in Iraq was by boat. As well as the Tigris and Euphrates, there were numerous canals.

272 See Donohue, *The Buwayhid Dynasty*, 151, 237 for what lay behind these events.

273 See §§17.1, 79.1, and 82.6.

274 See §55.3.

275 Q Ḥujurāt 49:6.

276 In the version of these events in Sourdel, *Vizirat*, 278–79, al-Mutawakkil is in Rayy. Neither version explains why Ibn al-Mudabbir is instructed to go to Raqqah.

277 In §§73.8–18 he plays the role of a benefactor; in §§103.1–4, as here, he appears as an oppressor.

278 This event took place ca. 240/854.

279 For al-Muʿallā ibn Ayyūb's own earlier tribulations, see §§17.1–4.

280 These and other versions are discussed by Sourdel, *Vizirat*, 278–79. The events they relate took place in 240/854 or 241/855–56. For more detail, and surviving harvest assessment documents written on papyrus, see Abbott, "Arabic Papyri of the Reign of Ǧaʿfar al-Mutawakkil."

281 Bundār was the nickname of Ibn Bashshār, cited at §29.1 by al-Ṭabarī.

282 Q Tawbah 9:129.

283 Q Fātiḥah 1:1.

284 Q Tawbah 9:129.

285 Q Fātiḥah 1:1.

286 The Angel of Death is mentioned in Q Sajdah 32:11.

287 After Joseph's brothers cast him in the pit (see §6), they said he had been devoured by a wolf, but Jacob, though accepting his loss, hoped that he was still alive and lived in fear of his death, Q Yūsuf 12:16–18, 85–87. This story and those that follow are given in various forms from a variety of sources in al-Thaʿlabī, *Lives of the Prophets*, 192–229.

288 Compare §85.6.

289 The Quranic prophets were long-lived. Thus "eighty years passed from the time Joseph left his father until the day he saw him again, during which Jacob's eyes were never dry from tears," al-Thaʿlabī, *Lives of the Prophets*, 223.

290 Joseph and Benjamin.

291 Basil or myrtle.

292 See Q Yūsuf 12:94.

293 See §6 for Joseph's imprisonment.

294 A paraphrase of Q Ṭalāq 65:3.

295 A paraphrase of Q Ṭalāq 65:3.

296 "Governance" is a reference to Q Hūd 11:56. This story may not have ended happily for everyone in it, since Ibrāhīm al-Taymī was done to death by al-Ḥajjāj in 94/712–13.

297 An anti-Trinitarian prayer.

298 The Torah is the scripture of the Jews. The Gospels are the scripture given to Jesus. The psalms are the scripture given to David, Q Nisāʾ 4:163; Isrāʾ 17:55.

299 See §§13.5, 105.12, 108.2, and 111.5.

300 The slave, the chamberlain, and his henchmen.

301 There has been a change of narrator, and in the next passage, there is confusion as to the number of protagonists.

302 Al-Karaj seems to have been a city in Sind elsewhere called al-Kīrāj. The Arab invasion of Sind took place in 93/711. Āzarmihr is an unidentified, presumably Persian, general.

303 Sic; presumably Ibn al-Jarrāḥ is intended.

304 The word *maqʿad*, "seat," generally means a cushion.

305 This appointment is not noted in Sourdel, *Vizirat*.

306 For four months in the latter half of 321/933. See Sourdel, *Vizirat*, 476–78.

307 In the plural. Previously only one door was mentioned.

308 During the war for the caliphate between al-Amīn and al-Maʾmūn, when Ṭāhir ibn al-Ḥusayn fought for al-Maʾmūn against al-Amīn's general ʿAlī ibn ʿĪsā ibn Māhān, whom he defeated and killed in 195/811.

309 A play on the words dir*ham* (a silver coin) and *hamm* (care).

310 *Ghulām*, which in other contexts can mean "military slave," "pupil," or simply "boy."

311 Mūsā ibn ʿAbd al-Malik has already appeared in two stories, §§73.8–17 and 82.1.

312 The lady is in purdah, as her status requires.

313 See n. 132 on the connection between the Iraqi "peasantry" and Christian bureaucrats.

314 The *Book of Deliverance following Adversity and Straits.*

315 An echo of Q Tawbah 9:129.

316 Yazīd al-Raqqāshī is cited as a transmitter at §13.8.

317 See *EI2*, "Yazīd b. Abī Muslim," for a composite of these accounts.

318 In 102/720.

319 Like al-Tanūkhī, Abū Ṭālib ʿAbd al-ʿAzīz was part of the legal establishment. The vocalization of Danqash, his great-great-great-great-grandfather's name, is conjectural. It is sometimes spelled Danqīsh, and apparently is a nickname from *danqasha*, "to bow one's head in humility." See Cheikh-Moussa, "La négation d'Eros," 90–91.

320 See n. 131.

321 A paraphrase of Q Sharḥ 94:5–6; see §§1.1–4.

322 The term *qurrāʾ* was sometimes applied to Kharijites. It seems to be a false etymology, unconnected with the Qur'an.

323 Paraphrases of Q Raḥmān 55:29: «Every day He has some great task» (see §13.4) and of Q Sharḥ 94:5–6 (see §§1.1–4).

324 The *ṭaylasān* was worn over the headdress and shoulders by Abbasid functionaries.

325 *Rasm*, which I have translated as "embroidery," could also be a woven motif or a border, perhaps of *ṭirāz*, bearing the name of the giver, here perhaps Prince ʿAbbās. See Serjeant, *Islamic Textiles*, 139, 200.

326 People with no oven of their own would pay to use the baker's oven.

327 A paraphrase of Q Ṭalāq 65:3; see §1.4.

328 Meaning ʿĀʾishah; the honorific was applied to the wives of the Prophet.

329 Isḥāq ibn Ibrāhīm al-Mawṣilī, who was on familiar terms with al-Faḍl ibn al-Rabīʿ.

330 In the Berlin and Leiden MSS, the text is garbled. "These words" are spoken by "an unseen speaker" who declares: "I am your servant," like a jinni in the *Thousand and One Nights*. The prayer follows ungrammatically, omitting "in You."

Glossary

Words in boldface within the entries below denote other entries in the Glossary.

Abān ibn Taghlib (d. 141/758) Kufan Qur'an scholar and lexicographer.

al-ʿAbbās, son of Caliph al-Maʾmūn (d. 223/838) military commander, employer of **ʿAlī ibn Yazīd.** Murdered by his uncle **al-Muʿtaṣim** to prevent his being recognized as **al-Ma'mūn**'s successor.

Abbasids descendants of the Prophet's uncle al-ʿAbbās, their dynasty overthrew the **Umayyads** in 132/749 and reigned over the Islamic empire from **Iraq** until 656/1258. For a hundred years from 334/945 (thus, for the whole of al-Tanūkhī's adult lifetime), they fell under the tutelage of the **Buyids.**

ʿAbd al-Aʿlā ibn Ḥammād ibn Naṣr (d. ca. 237/852) Basran traditionist.

ʿAbd Allāh ibn ʿAbbās see **Ibn ʿAbbās.**

ʿAbd Allāh ibn Abī Awfā (d. 87/706) the last of the Prophet's **Companions** to die in **Kufa.**

ʿAbd Allāh ibn Abī l-Hudayl (d. between 105/723 and 120/738) Kufan traditionist.

ʿAbd Allāh ibn Abī Razīn (dates unknown) traditionist, possibly Kufan.

ʿAbd Allāh ibn Abī Saʿd ʿAbd Allāh ibn ʿAmr ibn ʿAbd al-Raḥmān (197–274/813–87), **stationer–copyist** and traditionist. His family were from **Balkh.** He was active in **Baghdad**, taught **Ibn Abī l-Dunyā**, and died in **Samarra** or **Wāsiṭ.**

ʿAbd Allāh ibn Aḥmad ibn ʿĀmir al-Ṭāʾī (d. 324/936) illiterate Baghdadi traditionist.

ʿAbd Allāh ibn Aḥmad ibn Dāsah a Basran acquaintance of **al-Tanūkhī**, who quotes twenty-eight anecdotes of his about animals, personalities, and curiosities in *Table Talk.*

ʿAbd Allāh ibn Ḍumayrah Medinan traditionist.

ʿAbd Allāh ibn al-Ḥārith ibn al-Sarrāj of Wāsiṭ unidentified; his grandfather was a saddler (*sarrāj*).

ʿAbd Allāh son of Ḥasan son of Ḥasan son of ʿAlī ibn Abī Ṭālib (70–145/690–763) great-grandson of **ʿAlī ibn Abī Ṭālib**, born **Medina**, imprisoned by **al-Manṣūr**, died **Kufa**.

ʿAbd Allāh ibn al-Ḥusayn ibn Saʿd unidentified.

ʿAbd Allāh ibn Jaʿfar unidentified.

ʿAbd Allāh ibn Jaʿfar ibn Abī Ṭālib (1–80/622–700) nephew of **ʿAlī ibn Abī Ṭālib.**

ʿAbd Allāh ibn Jaʿfar ibn Abī Ṭālib, daughter of unidentified **Alid.**

ʿAbd Allāh ibn Masʿūd (d. 32/653) servant and **Companion** of the Prophet; grandfather of **al-Qāsim ibn ʿAbd al-Raḥmān.**

ʿAbd Allāh ibn Mubashshir unidentified.

ʿAbd Allāh ibn Muḥammad probably ʿAbd Allāh ibn Muḥammad ibn Abī Shaybah (159–235/775–849), Iraqi traditionist and prolific historian.

ʿAbd Allāh ibn Muḥammad Ibn Abī l-Dunyā see **Ibn Abī l-Dunyā.**

ʿAbd Allāh ibn Muḥammad ibn Qarīʿah al-Azdī of Basra unidentified.

ʿAbd Allāh ibn Muḥammad al-Tamīmī or *ʿUbayd Allāh ibn Muḥammad al-Qurashī* unidentified; perhaps Ibn ʿĀʾishah the younger of **Baghdad** and **Basra** (d. 228/843), traditionist and historian.

ʿAbd Allāh ibn Muḥammad ibn Yaḥyā of Ahwaz (dates unknown) state **scribe**, maternal great-grandfather of **al-Tanūkhī.**

ʿAbd Allāh ibn al-Muʿtazz (247–96/861–908) **Abbasid** prince, son of al-Muʿtazz (r. 252–55/866–69), cousin of **al-Muʿtaḍid**, a pioneering **poet**, critic, and literary historian. He was famous for his aphorisms and was killed in an abortive coup against his nephew **al-Muqtadir.**

ʿAbd Allāh ibn Shaddād ibn al-Hādd (d. 81/700) Medinan traditionist.

ʿAbd Allāh ibn Ṭāhir (182–230/798–844) **al-Maʾmūn**'s governor of **Khurasan** from 214/829–30 in succession to his father, **Ṭāhir ibn al-Ḥusayn**, the founder of the **Ṭāhirid** dynasty. He was an active military commander under both **al-Maʾmūn** and **al-Muʿtaṣim**, and was the father of **ʿUbayd Allāh ibn ʿAbd Allāh ibn Ṭāhir.** He enjoyed a brilliant career and died immensely rich.

ʿAbd Allāh ibn ʿUmar see **Ibn ʿUmar.**

ʿAbd Allāh ibn Wahb (125–97/743–813) Egyptian legal scholar, admired for his accurate knowledge of a hundred thousand hadith.

ʿAbd Allāh ibn Yazīd unidentified.

ʿAbd Allāh ibn Zayd ibn Aslam (d. 164/781) Medinan traditionist, son of **Zayd ibn Aslam**, brother of **Usāmah ibn Zayd.**

ʿAbd al-ʿAzīz ibn ʿAbd Allāh a contemporary of the jurist **Mālik.**

ʿAbd al-ʿAzīz al-Qurashī also called ʿAbd al-ʿAzīz ibn Usayd al-Ṭalḥī, Basran traditionist.

ʿAbd al-ʿAzīz ibn ʿUmar ibn ʿAbd al-ʿAzīz (d. after 147/764) governor of **Mecca** and **Medina**, son of the caliph **ʿUmar ibn ʿAbd al-ʿAzīz.**

ʿAbd al-Jabbār unidentified.

ʿAbd al-Jalīl ibn ʿAṭiyyah Basran traditionist.

ʿAbd al-Malik ibn Marwān (r. 65–86/685–705) fifth **Umayyad** caliph, father of **al-Walīd ibn ʿAbd al-Malik** and **Yazīd ibn ʿAbd al-Malik.**

ʿAbd al-Malik ibn Mughīth unidentified.

ʿAbd al-Malik ibn ʿUmayr (d. ca. 136/753) Kufan traditionist who lived to the age of 130 (or 160).

ʿAbd al-Qays, a client of unidentified convert affiliate (***mawlā***) of an ancient Arab tribe.

ʿAbd al-Raḥmān ibn ʿAbd Allāh ibn Masʿūd (d. 77/696) son of **ʿAbd Allāh ibn Masʿūd.**

ʿAbd al-Raḥmān ibn Abī Bakrah (14–96/635–715) also called Ibn Nufayʿ; the first Muslim child to be born in **Basra**; appointed public treasurer by **ʿAlī ibn Abī Ṭālib.**

ʿAbd al-Raḥmān ibn ʿAlī unidentified.

ʿAbd al-Raḥmān ibn Ḥammād al-Shuʿaythī (d. 212/827) Basran traditionist.

ʿAbd al-Raḥmān al-Ḥimyarī unidentified.

ʿAbd al-Raḥmān ibn Isḥāq Basran traditionist.

ʿAbd al-Raḥmān ibn Ṣāliḥ al-Azdī (d. 235/850) Baghdadi traditionist.

ʿAbd al-Razzāq Abū Bakr ibn Hammām ibn Nāfiʿ of **Ṣanʿāʾ** (126–211/744–826).

ʿAbd al-Wāḥid ibn Ziyād (d. 176/792–93) Basran traditionist.

ʿAbdūs nephew of Abū ʿAlī al-Ḥasan ibn Ibrāhīm the **Christian**, **Muʿizz al-Dawlah**'s treasurer, otherwise unknown.

Abū l-ʿAbbās Muḥammad ibn Aḥmad ibn Ḥammād ibn Ibrāhīm ibn Thaʿlab the Gap-Toothed (240–336/854–947) born **Samarra**, died **Basra**; well-known Baghdadi Qurʾan scholar, a teacher of **al-Tanūkhī.**

Abū l-ʿAbbās Muḥammad ibn Ḥassān unidentified Basran traditionist.

Abū l-ʿAbbās Thaʿlab (200–91/815–904) Aḥmad ibn Yaḥyā; with **al-Mubarrad** one of the leading linguistic scholars of his day.

Abū l-ʿAbbās ibn Thawābah (d. 277/890–91) state **scribe**, **poet**, and expert on Arabic penmanship. At least four members of his family were prominent in the administration at the end of the third/ninth century. They were descended from a **Christian** who earned his living by the despised trade of **cupping**.

Abū ʿAbd Allāh ibn Abī ʿAwf the Grain Merchant (d. 297/910) merchant who won the esteem of the vizier **ʿUbayd Allāh ibn Sulaymān ibn Wahb**, who granted him lucrative state contracts. **Al-Tanūkhī** cites eight anecdotes about his commercial acumen, high standing with the political elite, and charitableness in *Table Talk*, adding that he cultivated a variety of melon that was named after him.

Abū ʿAbd Allāh Aḥmad ibn Abī Du'ād (d. 239/854) chief **judge** under successive caliphs and their trusted adviser, although his career and that of his son and deputy, **Abū l-Walīd**, ended in disgrace.

Abū ʿAbd Allāh of Bā Qaṭāyā al-Ḥasan ibn ʿAlī, state **scribe.**

Abū ʿAbd Allāh Ḥamd ibn Muḥammad of Dayr Qunnā son of **al-Ḥasan ibn Makhlad**'s paternal aunt or sister, he was a member of an originally **Christian** family of high officials and **viziers** from **Dayr Qunnā**, and a cousin of **ʿAlī ibn ʿĪsā**, the "good vizier" under whose vizierate of 301–4/913–17 he held a senior position in the bureaucracy. See Sourdel, *Vizirat*, 400, 739, 748.

Abū ʿAbd Allāh al-Ḥazunbal third/ninth-century Kufan linguistic scholar.

Abū ʿAbd Allāh Muḥammad Ibn ʿAbdūs al-Jahshiyārī see **Muḥammad ibn ʿAbdūs al-Jahshiyārī.**

Abū ʿAbd al-Raḥmān al-Farasī or al-Qurashī unidentified.

Abū ʿAbd al-Raḥmān of Kufa unidentified.

Abū ʿAbd al-Raḥmān al-Ṭā'ī unidentified.

Abū ʿAbd al-Ṣamad al-ʿAmmī (d. 187/803) Basran traditionist.

Abū Aḥmad unidentified Baghdadi Qur'an scholar and writer of **charms**, a "friend of a friend" of al-Tanūkhī's cousin **Abū l-Ḥasan Aḥmad ibn Yūsuf al-Azraq.** He typifies the "little man" who intervenes providentially in the lives of others.

Abū l-Aḥwas ʿAwf ibn Mālik ibn Nadalah al-Jushamī (d. early second/eighth century), Kufan traditionist.

Abū ʿAlī Aḥmad ibn Ismāʿīl (d. 290/903) originally from **al-Anbār**, nicknamed Naṭṭāḥah ("Always Locking Horns"), also known as Ibn al-Khaṣīb after an ancestor, al-Khaṣīb ibn ʿAbd al-Ḥamīd, who had been governor of **Egypt**, he was a state **scribe** in the service of **ʿUbayd Allāh ibn ʿAbd Allāh ibn Ṭāhir**, and an epistolographer and **poet** who corresponded with **ʿAbd Allāh ibn al-Muʿtazz.**

Abū ʿAlī of Dayr Qunnā son of the unidentified H.n.b.t.ā; state **scribe**, astrologer, cited in the *Book of Viziers* of Hilāl al-Ṣābi, who died 448/1056. One of a family of **Christian** or convert state **scribes** educated in **Dayr Qunnā**. Others are mentioned at §73.1.

Abū ʿAlī of Dayr Qunnā, grandfather of unidentified state **scribe.**

Abū ʿAlī al-Ḥasan ibn Ibrāhīm the Christian **Muʿizz al-Dawlah**'s trusted treasurer. The money he stole from the ruler's relatives and household was discovered buried in his house after his accidental death in 350/961. See Yāqūt, *Udabāʾ*, vol. 3, 982–83.

Abū ʿAlī al-Ḥasan ibn Muḥammad ibn ʿUthmān Basran, from **Fasā** in **Fars**, traditionist of the works of his fellow countryman and fellow Basran **Yaʿqūb ibn Sufyān** of Fasā.

Abū ʿAlī al-Muḥassin son of Judge Abū l-Qāsim ʿAlī ibn Muhammad ibn Abī l-Fahm al-Tanūkhī see **al-Tanūkhī, Judge Abū ʿAlī al-Muḥassin.**

Abū l-ʿĀliyah (d. ca. 90/709) Rufayʿ ibn Mihrān; a freed slave, Basran traditionist.

Abū ʿĀmir ʿAbd al-Malik ibn ʿAmr (d. ca. 204/819) Basran traditionist.

Abū ʿAqīl al-Khawlānī Anas ibn Sālim of **Antioch**, a teacher of **al-Tanūkhī's father.**

Abū l-Ashʿath (d. ca. 200/815) Basran traditionist.

Abū l-ʿAtāhiyah (131–211/748–826) Baghdadi **poet** famous for his melodious ascetic verse.

Abū l-ʿAwwām unidentified.

Abū Ayyūb Aḥmad ibn Muḥammad ibn Shujāʿ (d. 284/897), maternal nephew of **Abū l-Wazīr.** Served as a treasury official in **Egypt** at the end of the third/ninth century. **Abbasid** literature depicts him as foolish and deluded to the point of believing a female jinni was his lover, but he was prominent enough to have two poems addressed to him by the leading court **poet** al-Buḥturī. See al-Buḥturī, *Dīwān*, vol. 1, 491–92, 627–31.

Abū Ayyūb Khālid ibn Yazīd al-Khazrajī (d. 52/672), Medinan **Companion.**

Abū Ayyūb Sulaymān ibn Wahb (d. 272/885) from an originally **Christian** family of **Wāsiṭ** who had been state **scribes** since **Umayyad** times and claimed Arab ancestry from the leading pre-Islamic **Christian** tribe of **Najrān**, he served as secretary to **al-Ma'mūn**, was twice financial comptroller of **Egypt** and three times **vizier** (under **al-Muhtadī**, 256/860, and **al-Muʿtamid**, 263/877 and 264/878). He was on close terms with the Turkish military elite and a rival of **al-Ḥasan ibn Makhlad.** Imprisoned by **al-Muwaffaq**, he died in disgrace.

Abū Bakr ʿAbd Allāh ibn Muḥammad Ibn Abī l-Dunyā see **Ibn Abī l-Dunyā.**

Abū Bakr Aḥmad ibn Muḥammad of Sarakhs unidentified.

Abū Bakr al-Asadī Muḥammad ibn ʿAbd Allāh ibn Ibrāhīm, known as Son of the Shroud Maker (*akfānī*), traditionist, father of the Baghdadi **judge** ʿAbd Allāh ibn Muḥammad Ibn al-Akfānī.

Abū Bakr Ibn Abī Shaybah (159–235/775–849) ʿAbd Allāh ibn Muḥammad ibn Ibrāhīm, Iraqi traditionist and historian, some of whose works are extant.

Abū Bakr ibn Ḥafṣ ʿAbd Allāh ibn Ḥafṣ ibn ʿUmar, great-grandson of the conqueror of Iraq, **Saʿd ibn Abī Waqqāṣ.**

Abū Bakr Muḥammad son of ʿAbd Allāh the Fodder Merchant (d. 325/936–37) Baghdadi traditionist, known as al-Mustaʿīnī.

Abū Bakr Muḥammad ibn Isḥāq of Ahwaz (d. ca. 335/946) from Susa in **Khuzistan**, **legal witness** to **al-Tanūkhī's father**; he studied Hadith in **Baghdad** in 341/952–53.

Abū Bakr Muḥammad ibn Yaḥyā al-Ṣūlī **court companion**, chess master, author of a *Book of Viziers*, and leading literary scholar. Some of his editions of poetry are still extant, as is his *The Life and Times of Abū Tammām.*

Abū Bakr Mukarram ibn Aḥmad ibn ʿAbd al-Wahhāb ibn Mukarram (d. 345/956) Baghdadi **judge** and cloth merchant.

Abū Bakr al-Ṣayrafī ʿUthmān ibn Saʿīd, known as Ibn al-Ṣayrafī, the Son of the Money Changer, senior bureaucrat in charge of the army for periods between 303/915 and 321/933. See Sourdel, *Vizirat*, 742–43.

Abū Bakr ibn Shujāʿ Baghdadi Qur'an scholar, deputized for **al-Tanūkhī** as inspector of the **mint** at **Sūq al-Ahwāz** in 346/957–58, having served as a legal trustee for Judge **al-Aḥnaf** in East Baghdad 298–301/911–13.

Abū Bakr al-Thaqafī unidentified.

Abū Bakr the Undoubting so-called according to some traditions because he alone did not doubt the truth of the Prophet's Night Journey to heaven. A member of the Meccan ruling tribe of **Quraysh**, an early **convert** and close **Companion** of the Prophet, whose favourite wife was his daughter **ʿĀʾishah**. He was the first caliph (11–13/632–4).

Abū Bakrah (d. 52/672) Nufayʿ ibn al-Ḥārith, **Companion** of the Prophet.

Abū Balj al-Fazārī Yaḥyā ibn Sulaym, traditionist in **Wāsiṭ** and **Kufa**, contemporary with **Yazīd ibn Hārūn**; he kept pigeons.

Abū l-Dardāʾ (d. 32/652–53 in Damascus) ʿUwaymir ibn Zayd, **Companion** of the Prophet, **sage**, ascetic.

Abū Dāʾūd (202–75/817–89) Sulaymān ibn al-Ashʿath, leading Hadith scholar, author of *al-Sunan* (*Sound Traditions*); originally from **Sijistan** in Iran, he settled in **Basra**.

Abū Dhakwān al-Qāsim ibn Ismāʿīl (d. 238/852–53) grammarian, scholar of **poetry** and history; stepson of the linguistic scholar al-Tawwazī.

Abū Dharr (d. 32/652–53) Jundub ibn Janādah al-Ghifārī; ascetic and early **convert** to Islam.

Abū l-Faḍl Aḥmad ibn Sulaymān, Judge unidentified.

Abū l-Faḍl Muḥammad ibn ʿAbd Allāh ibn al-Marzubān of Shiraz state **scribe**; unidentified except through **al-Tanūkhī**'s citations. Al-Tanūkhī had known him at the court of his father's friend and his own patron, the Buyid vizier **al-Muhallabī**. He is his source for some dozen items in *Table Talk*. His father's uncle had been financial comptroller of **Shiraz**. See al-Tanūkhī, *Nishwār*, vol. 8, 240.

Abū l-Faraj ʿAbd al-Wāḥid ibn Naṣr al-Makhzūmī the Parrot (d. 398/1008) al-Babbaghāʾ, itinerant state **scribe, poet**, and epistolographer, esteemed for his talents and his character. See Hamori, "A Sampling of Pleasant Civilities."

Abū l-Faraj Muḥammad ibn al-ʿAbbās ibn Fasānjus a financial officer who came from a family of **Shirazi** state **scribes**. He must have known **al-Tanūkhī's father** when he served in **Basra** in **al-Muhallabī**'s adminstration, hence **al-Tanūkhī**'s shock at his malice toward him when he became **vizier**. After a year in office (359–60/970), he was deposed and subsequently jailed (366/977).

Abū l-Faraj Muḥammad ibn Jaʿfar ibn Ṣāliḥ al-Ṣāliḥī a descendant of **ʿAlī ibn Ṣāliḥ**, "owner of the Prophet's prayer mat."

Abū Ghassān Mālik ibn Ḍaygham unidentified.

Abū Ḥafṣ Aḥmad ibn Ḥamīd the Coppersmith unidentified.

Abū l-Ḥamd Dāwūd son of Aḥmad al-Nāṣir li-Dīn Allāh, son of al-Hādī li-l-Ḥaqq grandson of the founder of the **Zaydi** imamate of Yemen, whom **al-Tanūkhī** met.

Abū Ḥāmid Muḥammad ibn Hārūn al-Ḥaḍramī (225–321/840–933) Baghdadi traditionist.

Abū Hammām al-Ṣalt ibn Muḥammad of Kharg (d. ca. 210/825) Basran traditionist.

Abū l-Ḥasan ibn Abī l-Layth Baghdadi state **scribe** known only from **al-Tanūkhī**'s citations of his verse and anecdotes in *Deliverance* and *Table Talk*.

Abū l-Ḥasan ibn Abī l-Ṭāhir Muḥammad ibn al-Ḥasan known from **al-Tanūkhī**'s citation as a state **scribe** in charge of the army.

Abū l-Ḥasan Aḥmad ibn Muḥammad Ibn al-Mudabbir (d. ca. 264/877) state **scribe** and **poet**. Known for his financial exactions, first in **Syria**, then in **Egypt**, then again in Syria, he was twice arrested and his wealth confiscated. He eventually died in prison.

Abū l-Ḥasan Aḥmad ibn Yūsuf al-Azraq the Blue-Eyed (297–378/909–88) son of Yaʿqūb ibn Isḥāq ibn al-Buhlūl al-Tanūkhī, **al-Tanūkhī**'s first cousin once removed on his mother's side. State **scribe** and prominent **Muʿtazilī** intellectual, often cited by al-Tanūkhī in *Deliverance* and *Table Talk* for family and political history, and curiosities of human behavior and of the natural world.

Abū l-Ḥasan ʿAlī ibn al-Ḥasan (298–376/911–86) Baghdadi **legal witness**, known as al-Jarrāḥī.

Abū l-Ḥasan ʿAlī ibn Ibrāhīm ibn Ḥammād (d. 356/967) a judge in **Ahwaz** before moving to **Baghdad**.

Abū l-Ḥasan ʿAlī ibn Muḥammad al-Madāʾinī see **al-Madāʾinī**.

Abū l-Ḥasan Muḥammad ibn ʿAbd Allāh ibn al-Ḥusayn ibn Saʿd unidentified.

Abū l-Ḥasan Muḥammad ibn ʿAbd Allāh ibn Jayshān of Fam al-Ṣilḥ merchant, unidentified.

Abū Ḥātim of Rayy (195–277/810–890) Muḥammad ibn Idrīs, traditionist.

Abū Ḥāzim (d. 135/752) Salamah ibn Dīnār, Medinan traditionist and ascetic.

Abū Hishām al-Rifāʿī (d. 248/862) Muḥammad ibn Yazīd; Kufan, **Judge** of **Baghdad**, where he died in office.

Abū Hurayrah (d. ca. 58/678) **Companion** of the Prophet, a prolific, controversial, but popular traditionist. When he was a goatherd, his companion was a kitten (*hurayrah*), hence his nickname. At §13.8 he is cited as an authority in his own right.

Abū l-Ḥusayn ʿAbd al-Wāḥid ibn Muḥammad al-Khaṣībī member of a clan of state **scribes**, traditionist, and man of letters; grandson of **Abū l-Ḥasan Aḥmad ibn Muḥammad Ibn al-Mudabbir.**

Abū l-Ḥusayn son of the Doorman (d. 376/986) Qur'an scholar, traditionist.

Abū l-Ḥusayn ʿUmar al-Azdī, Judge ʿUmar ibn Muḥammad ibn Yūsuf ibn Yaʿqūb ibn Ismāʿīl ibn Ḥammād ibn Zayd ibn Dirham (291–328/904–40), cited by **al-Tanūkhī** as Judge Abū l-Ḥusayn. Member of a dynasty of Baghdadi **judges**, his father was Judge **Abū ʿUmar Muḥammad**, his grandfather Judge **Yūsuf.** A man of letters, he studied with **Abū Bakr Muḥammad ibn Yaḥyā al-Ṣūlī**, became judge aged twenty and died as chief judge of **Baghdad** aged thirty-seven. His *Book of Deliverance following Adversity* is now extant only in al-Tanūkhī's citations.

Abū Idrīs al-Khawlānī ʿĀʾidh Allāh ibn ʿAbd Allāh (8–80/630–700), preacher, judge of Damascus.

Abū ʿImrān al-Jawfī ʿAbd al-Malik ibn Ḥabīb (d. 123/740–41), Basran traditionist.

Abū ʿĪsā brother of Abū Ṣakhr senior state **scribe**, sometime deputy of the vizier **Ismāʿīl ibn Bulbul.**

Abū Isḥāq a prisoner of **al-Ḥajjāj ibn Yūsuf**, unidentified.

Abū Isḥāq ʿAmr ibn ʿAbd Allāh al-Hamdānī (d. 127/747), grandfather of **Isrāʿīl**, Kufan traditionist.

Abū Isḥāq Ibrāhīm ibn al-ʿAbbās ibn Muḥammad ibn Ṣūl (ca. 176–243/792–857) **poet** and state **scribe** of Turkic origin, great-uncle of **Abū Bakr Muḥammad ibn Yaḥyā al-Ṣūlī**, who edited his poetry, which is still extant.

Abū Ismāʿīl ibn Abī Fudayk (d. 200/815) traditionist.

Abū Jaʿfar Aḥmad ibn Isḥāq ibn al-Buhlūl al-Tanūkhī (231–318/845–930) judge, **al-Tanūkhī**'s great-grandfather on his mother's side, father of his grandfather **Abū Ṭālib Muḥammad.** One of the most prominent **judges** of his time, a model of rectitude.

Abū Jaʿfar Muḥammad ibn Muḥammad ibn Ḥibbān al-Anṣārī of Basra unidentified.

Abū Jahl (d. 2/624) Meccan, kinsman and enemy of the Prophet; died at the **Battle of Badr.**

Abū l-Jahm Aḥmad ibn al-Ḥusayn ibn Ṭallāb of Mashghrā unidentified.

Abū l-Jūd deputy of **ʿAjīb** over the Baghdad **police** and overseer of **prisons.**

Abū Khalīfah al-Faḍl ibn al-Ḥubāb al-Jumaḥī of Basra (d. 305/917–18) nephew of the famous historian of Arabic poetry Ibn Sallām al-Jumaḥī (d. 231/846), **judge**, blind man of letters.

Abū Khaythamah Zuhayr ibn Ḥarb (d. 234/848), Baghdadi traditionist.

Abū Khāzim, Judge Abū Ḥamīd ibn ʿAbd al-ʿAzīz (d. 292/905), held appointments in **Syria**, **Kufa**, and **Baghdad**; his rulings were studied and he was highly regarded for his probity.

Abū Marwān of Jāmidah or Ibn Marwān; unidentified.

Abū Muʿāwiyah unidentified.

Abū Muʿāwiyah Muḥammad ibn Ḥāzim (110–195/728–810), blind traditionist.

Abū Muḥammad ʿAbd Allāh ibn Aḥmad Ibn Ḥamdūn **court companion** of the caliphs **al-Mutawakkil**, in succession to his father, and **al-Muʿtaḍid.** See *EI2*, "Ibn Ḥamdūn."

Abū Muḥammad al-Ḥasan of Rāmhurmuz see **Ibn Khallād of Rāmhurmuz.**

Abū Muḥammad al-Ḥasan ibn Muḥammad al-Muhallabī (291–352/903–963) friend of **al-Tanūkhī's father** and **al-Tanūkhī.** He was the preeminent patron of letters of his day in **Iraq**, as well as a soldier, politician, and administrator who made the **Buyid** takeover of Iraq workable; his ascendancy lasted from 339/950 to 352/963. He was of an ancient noble Arab family with a long connection with **Basra**, but he also held court in **Baghdad.**

Abū Muḥammad al-Ḥasan ibn Muḥammad ibn ʿUthmān ibn Qanīf **al-Tanūkhī** records him as having been deputy **chamberlain** in the palace of the caliph **al-Muqtadir**; he was later in the service of the Lord of the Marshes **Muʿīn al-Dawlah**, but is otherwise unidentified.

Abū Muḥammad Sahl ibn ʿAbd Allāh of Tustar (ca. 203–83/818–96) the mystic Sahl al-Tustarī, born in **Khuzistan**, died in **Basra.**

Abū Muḥammad Wahb ibn Yaḥyā ibn ʿAbd al-Wahhāb al-Māzinī a Basran teacher of **al-Tanūkhī**, unidentified.

Abū Mujliz Lāḥiq ibn Ḥamīd ibn Saʿīd al-Sadūsī (d. ca. 106/724), Basran traditionist.

Abū Muṣʿab unidentified.

Abū Naṣr the Tutor unidentified.

Abū Naṣr Muḥammad ibn Muḥammad of Wāsiṭ friend of **al-Tanūkhī**, local government official, unidentified.

Abū Naṣr the Date Merchant ʿAbd al-Malik ibn ʿAbd al-ʿAzīz of **Nasā'** (d. 228/843).

Abū Nuʿaym ʿAmr ibn Ḥammād, known as al-Faḍl ibn Dukayn (d. ca. 219/834), Kufan shopkeeper and traditionist.

Abū Nuḥ ʿĪsā ibn Ibrāhīm secretary to **al-Fatḥ ibn Khāqān**, he held several high positions in the bureaucracy before being publicly tortured to death under **al-Muhtadī**.

Abū l-Qāsim secretary to **Nāzūk**, chief of the Baghdad **police**. Unidentified, his name is given differently in different manuscripts.

Abū l-Qāsim ʿAbd al-Raḥmān ibn al-ʿAbbās unidentified. Perhaps the Baghdadi traditionist known as Ibn al-Fāmī (d. 357/968).

Abū l-Qāsim ʿAbd al-Wahhāb ibn Abī Ḥayyah (d. 329/941) **stationer–copyist** to al-Jāḥiẓ (d. 255/869), the greatest prose writer of the third/ninth century.

Abū l-Qāsim Ibn Bint Manīʿ ʿAbd Allāh ibn Muḥammad (213–317/828–929), started life as a copyist and became a leading Baghdadi scholar of Hadith. His family was from **Baghshūr** near **Herat**.

Abū l-Qāsim ʿĪsā son of ʿAlī ibn ʿĪsā (d. 391/1001) one of two sons of the great vizier **ʿAlī ibn ʿĪsā**, he was a state **scribe**, a scholar of Greek philosophy, and a traditionist. He died in **Baghdad** aged ninety.

Abū l-Qāsim Ṭalḥah ibn Muḥammad ibn Jaʿfar (291–380/904–991) **legal witness** and Baghdadi Qur'an scholar, known as Ibn Mujāhid's Pupil (Ibn Mujāhid, d. 324/936, wrote the first book on the seven Qur'an readings).

Abū Rawḥ of Marw identity uncertain, perhaps ʿAbd al-Raḥmān ibn Qays of **Basra** or Khālid ibn Maḥdūj.

Abū Saʿd the Greengrocer Saʿīd ibn al-Marzubān, **freedman** of the **Companion** Ḥudhayfa ibn al-Yamān.

Abū Saʿīd, muezzin of Taif unidentified.

Abū Saʿīd Aḥmad ibn al-Ṣaqr ibn Thawbān **lecture-room assistant** to Bundār (**Ibn Bashshār**), studied tradition in **Baghdad** and settled in **Basra**.

Abū Saʿīd ibn Basīṭ unidentified.

Abū Saʿīd of Medina ʿAbd Allāh ibn Shabīb, traditionist, of **Baghdad** and **Basra**.

Abū Sāʿidah son of Abī l-Walīd son of Aḥmad ibn Abī Du'ād **Abū ʿAbd Allāh Aḥmad ibn Abī Du'ād al-Iyādī** and his son **Abū l-Walīd Muḥammad**, both **Muʿtazilīs**, had been chief **judges** and influential statesmen under **al-Muʿtaṣim**, but died in disgrace under **al-Mutawakkil**.

Abū Ṣakhr Ḥumayd ibn Ziyād the Tailor, born **Medina**, emigrated to **Egypt**.

Abū Salamah ʿAbd Allāh ibn Manṣūr unidentified.

Abū Salamah al-Juhanī unidentified.

Abū Ṣāliḥ Dhakwān of **Medina** (d. 101/719), muezzin, trader in oil and cooking fat in **Kufa.**

Abū Ṣāliḥ (owner of the Prophet's prayer mat) the ownership of this relic became hereditary in his family; see **Abū l-Faraj Muḥammad ibn Jaʿfar ibn Ṣāliḥ al-Ṣāliḥī** and **ʿAlī ibn Ṣāliḥ.**

Abū Ṣāliḥ ʿAbd Allāh ibn Muḥammad ibn Yazdād vizier to al-Mustaʿīn (r. 248–52/862–66) in **Samarra**; his four-month tenure ended in his fleeing to **Baghdad** in 249/863.

Abū l-Salīl Ḍurayb ibn Nuqayr, Basran traditionist.

Abū l-Sawdāʾ ʿAmr ibn ʿImrān, Kufan traditionist.

Abū Sawrah traditionist, nephew of an early Muslim warrior, Khālid ibn Zayd al-Anṣārī.

Abū Sufyān al-Ḥimyarī Saʿīd ibn Yaḥyā of **Wāsiṭ**, cobbler and traditionist.

Abū Sufyān Ṣakhr ibn Ḥarb (d. 31/652) leading Meccan commander, kinsman and enemy of the Prophet, then **Companion**; father of the first **Umayyad** caliph, **Muʿāwiyah ibn Abī Sufyān.**

Abū Sulaymān Dāwūd ibn al-Jarrāḥ see **Dāwūd ibn al-Jarrāḥ.**

Abū l-Ṭāhir Muḥammad ibn al-Ḥasan state **scribe** in charge of the army, unidentified.

Abū Ṭālib ʿAbd al-ʿAzīz ibn Aḥmad ibn Muḥammad ibn al-Faḍl ibn Aḥmad ibn Muḥammad ibn Ḥammād Danqash born **Baghdad** 302/914, he became judge of **Rāmhurmuz**; as well as citing **al-Tanūkhī's father**, he knew **al-Tanūkhī's son**, who quotes him in al-Khaṭīb al-Baghdādī's *Tārīkh Baghdād.*

Abū Ṭālib Muḥammad ibn Aḥmad ibn Isḥāq ibn al-Buhlūl (d. 348/959) **al-Tanūkhī**'s maternal grandfather. A **judge** like his father, **Abū Jaʿfar Aḥmad**, and his son **Jaʿfar ibn Abī Ṭālib**, he was also involved in politics.

Abū Tammām al-Ṭāʾī (ca. 189–232/805–45) famous court **poet** and anthologist, the subject of **Abū Bakr Muḥammad ibn Yaḥyā al-Ṣūlī**'s *The Life and Times of Abū Tammām.*

Abū ʿUbayd Allāh Muḥammad ibn ʿImrān al-Marzubānī (ca. 297–384/910–94) Baghdadi literary historian, critic, and anthologist. A few of al-Marzubānī's numerous works survive, notably his *Dictionary of Poets, Muʿjam al-shuʿarāʾ.*

Abū ʿUbaydah ibn al-Jarrāḥ (d. 18/40) the Prophet's general, he went on to play a leading role in the Muslim conquests under **ʿUmar ibn al-Khaṭṭāb.**

Abū ʿUbaydah Maʿmar ibn al-Muthannā (110–209/728–824) leading Basran philologist. Though of Persian parentage, he was an authority on the language and lore of the Bedouin **Arabs.** His numerous works, some of which survive, included treatises on the vocabulary of the Qur'an.

Abū ʿUmar Muḥammad ibn ʿAbd al-Wāḥid, "Thaʿlab's Pupil" (261–345/875–957) a teacher of **al-Tanūkhī**'s and student of the linguistic scholar **Abū l-ʿAbbās Thaʿlab,** who earned his living as an embroiderer. His speciality was Arabic vocabulary. See *EI2*, "Gh͟ulām Th͟aʿlab."

Abū ʿUmar Muḥammad al-Azdī Muḥammad ibn Yūsuf ibn Yaʿqūb (243–320/857–932); born in **Basra, judge** in **Baghdad** as well as holding many provincial appointments; great scholar of Hadith, father of Judge **Abū l-Ḥusayn ʿUmar al-Azdī.**

Abū Usāmah unidentified.

Abū l-ʿUyūf Ṣaʿb or Ṣuʿayb al-ʿAnazī unidentified.

Abū Wāʾil ʿAbd Allāh ibn Buḥayr of **Ṣanʿāʾ, popular preacher (*qāṣṣ*).**

Abū l-Walīd ibn Aḥmad ibn Abī Duʾād (d. 239/854) deputy and successor to his father, Chief Judge **Abū ʿAbd Allāh Aḥmad ibn Abī Duʾād**; both **Muʿtazilīs**, they fell from grace under **al-Mutawakkil.**

Abū l-Wazīr Aḥmad ibn Khālid al-Ṣarafīnī, state **scribe**, secretary to **al-Muʿtaṣim;** after periods of disgrace under succeeding caliphs he was put in charge of the **land tax** of **Egypt.**

Abū Yaḥyā Isḥāq al-ʿAdwānī unidentified.

Abū l-Yamān al-Ḥakam ibn Nāfiʿ (138–221/755–836) traditionist, of **Ḥimṣ.**

Abū Yazīd Unays ibn ʿImrān al-Nāfiʿī unidentified.

Abū Yūsuf Yaʿqūb ibn Bayān unidentified.

Abū Zunbūr Abū ʿAlī al-Ḥusayn ibn Rustum of **Mādharāʾ** (d. 314/926); member of the Mādharāʾī clan of state **scribes**, uncle of **Muḥammad ibn ʿAlī**, he served in **Egypt** overseeing the **land tax** under successive caliphs.

adages, aphorisms, proverbs an important branch of wisdom literature, through which known truths could be reflected upon and new ones discovered. From the second/eighth century, translators from Persian and Greek and scholars of Arabic competed in rediscovering the wisdom of the ancients and the **Arabs** through their sayings and systematizing it in book form. See Zakeri, *Persian Wisdom in Arabic Garb*.

ʿAḍud al-Dawlah Abū Shujāʿ Fanā Khusraw ibn Ḥasan, second **Buyid** ruler of **Fars** and **Khuzistan** (r. 338–72/949–83). **Al-Tanūkhī** was a member of his court and had mixed relations with him.

ʿAffān ibn Muslim (134–219/751–834) coppersmith, Basran traditionist.

al-Aghlab al-ʿIjlī (d. 21/641) early Muslim **poet**; died fighting in the conquest of **Iraq**.

Aḥmad ibn ʿAbd al-Aʿlā al-Shaybānī Baghdadi traditionist.

Aḥmad ibn ʿAbd Allāh ibn Aḥmad al-Warraq the Stationer-Copyist (299–379/911–90) Baghdadi **Shiʿi** traditionist.

Aḥmad ibn ʿAbd Allāh ibn al-Nuʿmān unidentified.

Aḥmad ibn Abī l-Aṣbagh state **scribe**, related to **Abū Ayyūb Sulaymān ibn Wahb** on the distaff side, secretary to the future **al-Muktafī**, governor of **Basra** in 311/923.

Aḥmad ibn Abī Khālid "the Cross-Eyed" (al-Aḥwal) (d. ca. 211/826), long-serving state **scribe**, influential with **al-Maʾmūn** whose secretary and close adviser he became for some ten years until his death. See Sourdel, *Vizirat*, 218–25.

Aḥmad ibn ʿAlī ibn Saʿīd of Kufa (d. 334/945) the Ḥamdānid **Nāṣir al-Dawlah**'s governor of **Wāsiṭ**, having previously served in the caliphal administration.

Aḥmad ibn ʿĀmir al-Ṭāʾī father of **ʿAbd Allāh ibn Aḥmad ibn ʿĀmir al-Ṭāʾī.**

Aḥmad ibn al-Ḥārith the Cobbler (d. 258/872) Baghdadi traditionist.

Aḥmad ibn Ibrāhīm al-ʿAbdī (d. 246/860) Baghdadi traditionist.

Aḥmad ibn Isrāʾīl (d. 255/869) high-ranking state **scribe** under several caliphs, he became **vizier** to al-Muʿtazz (r. 252–25/866–69) and was publicly tortured and executed by the **Turks** of **Samarra.**

Aḥmad ibn al-Khaṣīb state scribe whose career began under **al-Muʿtaṣim.** He was **vizier** for six months under al-Muntaṣir (247–48/861–62) before being banished to Crete by the **Turks** of **Samarra.**

Aḥmad ibn Muḥammad ibn Bakr Abū Rawq al-Hazzānī (d. ca. 324/936) Basran traditionist.

Aḥmad ibn Muḥammad ibn al-Faḍl, Abū ʿĪsā, son of Aḥmad ibn Muḥammad ibn Ḥammād Danqash **legal trustee** in **Baghdad.**

Aḥmad ibn Muḥammad ibn Ḥammād Danqash army chief and chief of **police** at **Samarra** under **al-Muhtadī.** .

Aḥmad ibn Muḥammad Ibn al-Jarrāḥ see **Ibn al-Jarrāḥ.**

Aḥmad ibn al-Rabīʿ al-Lakhmī the Silk Merchant of Kufa name and identification doubtful.

Aḥmad ibn Ṣāliḥ (170–248/786–863) son of an Iranian soldier, Qur'an scholar, transmitted in **Baghdad** and **Egypt**.

Aḥmad ibn Sulaymān of Ṭūs (240–322/854–934) Baghdadi traditionist.

Aḥmad ibn Yazīd ibn Muḥammad al-Muhallabī **court companion** of **al-Muʿtamid.**

al-Aḥnaf "the Lame" (d. 301/913) Judge Muḥammad ibn ʿAbd Allāh ibn ʿAlī ibn Muḥammad Ibn Abī l-Shawārib, member of a dynasty of **judges** of **Baghdad.**

Ahwaz or Sūq al-Ahwāz the main city of the province of **Khuzistan.**

ʿĀʾidh ibn Shurayḥ unidentified.

ʿĀʾishah (d. 58/678) daughter of **Abū Bakr the Undoubting**; favorite wife of **Muḥammad**; "Mother of the Faithful."

ʿAjīb, Nāzūk's henchman his deputy in charge of the **police**; executioner. Killed with **Nāzuk** in a coup (317/929).

al-Ajlaḥ al-Kindī Yaḥyā ibn ʿAbd Allāh (d. 145/762), Kufan traditionist.

ʿAjlān Medinan traditionist.

al-ʿAlāʾ ibn ʿAbd al-Jabbār the Druggist (d. 212/827) traditionist.

ʿAlī ibn ʿAbd Allāh the Stationer–Copyist, known as Ibn Abī Luʾluʾ unidentified.

ʿAlī ibn Abī ʿAlī al-Lahabī, Medinan traditionist.

ʿAlī ibn Abī Ṭālib (d. 40/660) cousin of the Prophet **Muḥammad**, husband of his daughter **Fāṭimah**; held by the **Shiʿis** to be his designated and only legitimate heir, the "Commander of the Faithful." He and his descendants were widely revered in **al-Tanūkhī**'s time by non-Shiʿi as well as Shiʿi and were believed by some to have powers of intercession. Known for his wisdom and eloquence, at §1.3 he is cited as a linguistic authority.

ʿAlī ibn Abī l-Ṭayyib al-Ḥasan ibn ʿAlī ibn Muṭrif of Rāmhurmuz see **ʿAlī ibn al-Ḥasan ibn ʿAlī ibn Muṭrif.**

ʿAlī ibn Bidhaymah (d. 133/750) transmitted in **Kufa** and northern **Syria.**

ʿAlī ibn Dubays state **scribe**, unidentified.

ʿAlī ibn Hammām unidentified.

ʿAlī ibn Ḥarb al-Ṭāʾī of Mosul (d. 265/877) traditionist.

ʿAlī ibn al-Ḥasan ibn ʿAlī ibn Muṭrif of Rāmhurmuz (298–376/911–86) **judge** who lived in **Baghdad**, cited as Alī ibn al-Ḥasan. It is through him, via Ibn al-Jarrāḥ, that **al-Tanūkhī** quotes **Ibn Abī l-Dunyā**'s *Book of Deliverance*, without naming it.

ʿAlī ibn Hishām known as Ibn Abī Qīrāṭ, he and his father Hishām ibn ʿAbd Allāh were state **scribes; al-Tanūkhī** cites him frequently in *Table Talk.*

ʿAlī ibn al-Ḥusayn Zayn al-ʿĀbidīn (d. 94/712–13), fourth imam of the **Twelver Shiʿi.**

ʿAlī ibn al-Ḥusayn ibn Muḥammad ibn Mūsā Ibn al-Furāt unidentified member of the Ibn al-Furāt family of state **scribes** and **viziers.**

ʿAlī ibn Ibrāhīm unidentified merchant from **Ahwaz.**

ʿAlī ibn ʿĪsā Alī ibn ʿĪsā ibn Dāwūd ibn al-Jarrāḥ, "the Good Vizier" (245–334/859–946), senior statesman, twice **vizier** under **al-Muqtadir**, he was regarded as the most capable and upright administrator of his day.

ʿAlī ibn ʿĪsā ibn Māhān (d. 195/811) leader of **al-Amīn**'s army, defeated and killed by **Ṭāhir ibn al-Ḥusayn.**

ʿAlī ibn al-Jaʿd (d. 230/845) Baghdadi traditionist.

ʿAlī son of Jaʿfar al-Ṣādiq son of Muḥammad al-Bāqir a son of the sixth **Twelver Shiʿi** imam.

ʿAlī al-Juʿfī Kufan traditionist.

ʿAlī ibn Muḥammad ibn Abī l-Fahm al-Tanūkhī see **al-Tanūkhī.**

ʿAlī ibn Muḥammad al-Madāʾinī see al-**Madāʾinī.**

ʿAlī ibn Naṣr ibn ʿAlī the Physician ʿAlī ibn Naṣr ibn ʿAlī ibn Bishr (d. 377/987), **Christian** physician, prolific author who died with many books unfinished; one on ethics, which contained adages, aphorisms, and proverbs, was reportedly 1,500 folios long.

ʿAlī al-Riḍā the son of Mūsā al-Kāẓim (d. 203/817) eighth imam of the **Twelver Shiʿi.**

ʿAlī ibn Ṣāliḥ one of a group of Iranian princes whom the caliph **al-Manṣūr** rewarded for their loyalty by offering them the pick of a treasure, ʿAlī ibn Ṣāliḥ took what was alleged to be the Prophet's prayer mat, on condition that he produced it on ceremonial occasions. It remained in the family until **al-Muʿtaṣim** reclaimed it. See al-Khaṭīb al-Baghdādī, *Tārīkh Baghdad*, vol. 11, 438–39.

ʿAlī ibn Yazīd **postmaster and intelligencer** of **Māsabadhān**, formerly secretary to **al-ʿAbbās, son of al-Maʾmūn.** Unidentified.

Alids **ʿAlī ibn Abī Ṭālib**, considered by the **Shiʿi** the true heir of the Prophet, and his descendants, the Alids, are all treated with reverence by **al-Tanūkhī** and his sources. They cite imams of the **Twelver Shiʿi** (who recognize eleven descendants of ʿAlī and the Prophet's daughter **Fāṭimah**): **ʿAlī ibn al-Ḥusayn** Zayn al-ʿĀbidīn, fourth imam; **ʿAlī al-Riḍā** son of Mūsā al-Kāẓim, eighth imam; **Ḥasan son of ʿAlī ibn Abī Ṭālib**, second imam; **al-Ḥusayn son of ʿAlī ibn Abī Ṭālib**, third imam; **Jaʿfar al-Ṣādiq**, sixth imam; **Muḥammad al-Bāqir**, fifth imam; and **Mūsā al-Kāẓim**, seventh imam (al-Tanūkhī, however, mocks the idea that the latter has miraculous powers of intercession on earth, §§80.3–4). Other Alids cited are: **ʿAbd Allāh son of Ḥasan son of Ḥasan son of ʿAlī ibn Abī Ṭālib**, ʿAbd Allāh ibn al-Ḥusayn ibn ʿAlī ibn Abī Ṭālib, **ʿAlī son of Jaʿfar al-Ṣādiq** son of Muḥammad al-Bāqir, Ḥasan ibn al-Ḥasan ibn ʿAlī ibn Abī Ṭālib, al-Ḥasan ibn Jaʿfar ibn ʿAbd Allāh ibn al-Ḥusayn ibn ʿAlī ibn Abī Ṭālib, Yaḥyā son of al-Ḥasan son of Jaʿfar son of ʿAbd Allāh son of al-Ḥusayn ibn ʿAlī ibn Abī Ṭālib, **Muḥammad ibn al-Ḥanafiyyah**; an unnamed Alid (§94.1–4); and **Abū l-Ḥamd Dāwūd**, son of the third **Zaydi** imam of Yemen. See Bernheimer, *The ʿAlids*.

al-Aʿmash Sulaymān ibn Mihrān al-Kāhilī (60–148/680–765), Kufan Qur'an scholar and traditionist.

al-Amīn sixth **Abbasid** caliph, he was defeated and killed in the war with his brother **al-Ma'mūn** for the succession to their father, **Hārūn al-Rashīd** (r. 193–98/809–13).

ʿAmr ibn al-ʿĀṣ (d. ca. 42/663) conqueror and governor of **Egypt**.

ʿAmr ibn Marzūq (d. 224/838–39) highly popular Basran traditionist.

ʿAmr ibn Maymūn (d. ca. 145/762) Kufan scholar and traditionist, the son and grandson of manumitted slaves.

ʿAmr ibn Muḥammad al-Qurashī (d. 199/814) traditionist.

ʿAmr ibn Murrah (d. ca. 118/736) blind Kufan traditionist.

ʿAmr of the Squadrons early Muslim warrior, unidentified.

ʿAmr ibn Uḥyaḥah al-Awsī **Companion.**

Anas ibn Mālik (d. 93/712) born **Medina**, servant and **Companion** of **Muḥammad**; father of **Mālik ibn Anas**; died in **Basra.**

al-Anbār an ancient settlement west of **Baghdad** on the left bank of the **Euphrates** in a fertile agricultural area; it had been the first **Abbasid** capital and was the ancestral home of the Buhlūlids, **al-Tanūkhī**'s maternal relatives, where they had farms and property.

Ancients a vague term for **sages** of past civilizations, often Greek philosophers.

angels (malā'ikah, sing. *malak)* the angels in chapters one and three of *Deliverance* petition God for human sufferers (§§13.8, 70.12), bring them aid and consolation (§§85.1–2., 86.1–2), and are invoked in prayer in His name (§§92.3, 93.2). Named angels are the Angel of Death, **Azrael**, **Gabriel**, **Israfel**, **Michael**, and the allegorical Benevolence (§70.12).

Anṣār the "Helpers," the people of **Medina** who invited **Muḥammad** to settle in their city, and aided him against the Meccans.

antechamber (dihlīz) a hall or complex of rooms forming the waiting area outside a grandee's audience chamber. Minor business is transacted there by members of the household, §§76.8–9.

Antioch in northern **Syria** on the Orontes near the Mediterranean coast, the home city of **al-Tanūkhī's father.**

Anūshirwān also Chosroes; Sasanian king, an emblematic rather than historical figure.

'Aqīl or 'Uqayl ibn Shihāb traditionist (the form of the name is speculative).

Arabs; Bedouin; Arabic while few members of the cultured **Abbasid** elite could trace their lineage back over several generations to Arab ancestors as could al-Tanūkhī, they wrote Arabic according to rules of grammar and lexicography derived by scholars such as **al-Aṣma'ī** and **Abū 'Ubaydah** (§47.8) from pre-Islamic Arabic poetry and from Bedouin informants. The Prophet and **'Alī ibn Abī Ṭālib** (§1.3) are exemplars of Arabic linguistic authority. The anonymous Bedouin of §§52.3, 53.1, and 82.3 are emblems of the moral authority embodied in Arab eloquence.

al-'Āṣ ibn Wā'il (d. ca. AD 620) kinsman and enemy of **Muḥammad.**

Aslam (d. 80/699) prisoner of war of unknown parentage, **freedman** of **'Umar ibn al-Khaṭṭāb.**

Asmā' bint 'Umays **Companion**, mother of **'Abd Allāh ibn Ja'far ibn Abī Ṭālib**, she had been married to **Ja'far ibn Abī Ṭālib**, **Abū Bakr the Undoubting**, and **'Alī ibn Abī Ṭālib.**

al-Aṣma'ī (122–213/740–828) Abū Sa'īd 'Abd al-Malik ibn Qurayb, scholar of **Arab** lore, **poetry**, and the Arabic language.

audience chamber (majlis) this is where members of the public or of the court came to present complaints or petitions to a **vizier** or other grandee, §80.2, and where **poets** performed, §102.3. Access to it was controlled by the **chamberlain.**

authorization to transmit (ijāzah) the authorization to transmit a teacher's material if he or she was satisfied that a pupil could quote it accurately.

Ayyūb, son of al-ʿAbbās ibn al-Ḥasan al-ʿAbbās ibn al-Ḥasan of Jarjarāyā, **vizier** to **al-Muktafī** (291–95/904–8), see Bowen, *The Life and Times of ʿAlí ibn ʿĪsà*, 65–67, and Sourdel, *Vizirat*, 359.

Āzarmihr Persian commander. Unidentified.

Azhar ibn Marwān al-Raqqāshī (d. 243/857) Basran traditionist.

Azrael the **Angel** of Death. See Burge, *Angels in Islam*, 132–45.

Bā Qaṭāyā village near **Baghdad.**

al-Babbaghā', "the Parrot" see **Abū l-Faraj al-Makhzūmī.**

Babylon in ancient **Iraq**, Nebuchadnezzar's capital.

Badr, Battle of southwest of **Medina**, in 2/624, following the **Hijrah**, the first victory of the Muslims over the Meccans.

Bāghand a village near **Wāṣit.**

Baghdad the richest and most populated city in **Iraq**, founded by the second **Abbasid** caliph **al-Manṣūr** in 145/762 as his capital. It remained the intellectual center even when the caliphs moved their court to **Raqqah** or **Samarra.**

Baghshūr or Bagh village near **Herat.**

al-Baḥrayn coastal strip and oasis in northeastern Arabia; **Kharijites** had a base there in **Umayyad** times.

Balkh the capital of **Khurasan** in late **Umayyad** and early **Abbasid** times.

Banū Sadūs sector of **Basra**, named after the tribe of that name.

Banū Yashkur sector of **Basra**, named after the tribe of that name.

Baqiyyah Abū Muḥammad Baqiyyah ibn al-Walīd ibn Ṣā'id al-Ḥimyarī of **Ḥimṣ** (d. 197/813), Syrian traditionist.

Barmakī family the descendants of the barmak (administrator) of the Buddhist monastery of Nawbahār near **Balkh**, who converted to Islam under the **Umayyads** and served as state **scribes** under the first five **Abbasid** caliphs, rising to great power under **Hārūn al-Rashīd** until 187/803, when, for reasons unexplained, he suddenly turned against them.

al-Barqī Abū ʿAbd Allāh Aḥmad ibn Jaʿfar, state **scribe** and Baghdadi traditionist, active 330/941 and after.

Bashīr ibn Nahīk unidentified.

basil or myrtle (rayḥānah) when Jacob calls Joseph a sweet-scented flower at §85.7, there is a play on the Qur'anic «breath» (*rīḥ*) or scent of Joseph

(Q Yūsuf 12:94), but also on the widespread idea of a child, living or dead, as a "fragrant plant." See Diem and Schöller, *The Living and the Dead*, vol. 3, 102.

Basra trading port and center of scholarship in lower **Iraq; al-Tanūkhī** was born and brought up there.

Basra, a holy woman of unidentified; **Basra** was an early center of asceticism and Sufism in which women were prominent.

bathhouse public and private bathhouses both had the same architecture and consisted of a suite of rooms. See *EI2*, "Ḥammām." The *ḥammāms* of §§73.14 and 78.7 are probably private baths in the Samarran mansion of **al-Mutawakkil**'s chief of **police** and in the palace of the governor of **Fars**. See Northedge, *The Historical Topography of Samarra*, 130, 269.

beardless boy (ghulām amrad) the beardlessness of the young soldier of §§76.1, 76.5–6 is the standard attribute of an object of homoerotic desire in both poetry and storytelling.

Bedouin see **Arab.**

Berbers the Arab conquest of **North Africa** had been difficult and left the indigenous Berbers unpacified. It was the governor **Yazīd ibn Abī Muslim**'s cruelty to his Berber bodyguard that led to his murder at their hands (§105.8). See Brett and Fentress, *The Berbers*, 86–88.

Bishr ibn Muʿādh blind Basran traditionist.

Bishr ibn Mūsā al-Asadī (190–288/806–901) Baghdadi traditionist.

Bishr ibn Rāfiʿ al-Ḥārithī Abū l-Asbāṭ of **Najrān**, traditionist.

Black Hole dungeon in **Iraq** used by **al-Ḥajjāj ibn Yūsuf.**

boat travel merchant seafaring played a major role in the **Abbasid** economy. The merchant of **Basra** who always took his daughter on his voyages (§16.1) may have sailed the Persian Gulf, the Arabian Sea, the Indian Ocean, and even as far as China. See Hourani, *Arab Seafaring*, 64. Within **Iraq**, whether by river or on the numerous canals, boats were the preferred means of travel (§80.1).

Bukhtakīn the Turk known as Āzād(h)rawayh, military governor of **Ahwaz** from ca. 356/967, he combined this position with **tax farming** the revenue of the region.

Bureaucratic Supervision, office of (al-zimām) sometimes referred to in the plural (*azimmah*) and sometimes in the singular, as at §73.8 (where *zimām* may be shorthand for *zimām al-azimmah*, the Supreme Office of

Supervision), this was a body or bodies that scrutinized the expenditure of one or more government bureaus or departments. Its functions and place within the administrative structure fluctuated in the course of the third/ninth century so that, Sourdel says, "one can never be sure what is meant by 'head of the *zimām*.'" See Sourdel, *Vizirat*, 599–605.

Burjulān village near **Wāsiṭ.**

Bursān village near **Samarqand.**

bushel the catchall term "bushel" has been used for the following dry measures, whose values fluctuated according to time and place: *ṣāʿ* and *mudd*, where a *ṣāʿ* is a measure of grain equal to eight handfuls or four *mudd*s (§13.3); *kurr* six donkey loads (§§77.1–2). See *EI2*, "Makāyīl."

Buyids or Buwayhids see **Daylamī.**

Buzurjmihr ibn al-Bakhtakān **vizier** to the Sasanian king Chosroes **Anūshirwān,** like him he is an emblematic rather than a historical figure.

chain of transmitters (isnād) the first three chapters of *Deliverance* include some complex chains of transmission and examples of *isnād* criticism by **al-Tanūkhī.** Most of his sources and transmitters are cited only once. Many are obscure. Some of the *isnād*s in which they figure may be feats of unassisted memory testifying to oral transmission (but see **notebook**). However, where al-Tanūkhī cites his predecessors in the *faraj* genre, with whose books he was familiar in written form since he says how many **folios** they contain, he may well be identifying as oral sources only the informant who read the book with him or in whose copy he read it (e.g., **ʿAlī ibn al-Ḥasan**), and consulting the book itself for the rest of the transmitters, and indeed for the text of the material cited. Although in modern scholarship *isnād*s have primarily been associated with hadith, for al-Tanūkhī and other scholars of his period they were proofs of textual accuracy and accuracy of attribution in all fields of knowledge. The references to *isnād*s that have been indexed here are to instances where al-Tanūkhī admits to not remembering an *isnād* or not wishing to pursue all the details of transmission.

chamberlain (ḥājib) chamberlains, who controlled access to caliphs, **viziers,** and commanders, occupied a position of trust. The family and professional connections of one early **Abbasid** chamberlain are enumerated at §106.1; the career of a later one is outlined at §59.3. The anonymous chamberlain whom **Hārūn al-Rashīd** tries to involve in the murder of an **Alid** at §§94.1–6 seems to be a figure of storytelling.

charms those described at §§76.1–3 are written (*kutub*), consist wholly of passages from the Qur'an, and are to be bound on to the right arm when the wearer is in a state of **ritual purity**. They have sympathetic qualities: their key words, "reconciliation" and "refuge," are supposed to ensure conciliation and protection.

Chosroes (kisrā) generic title given to Sasanian kings in Arabic writings.

Christians (Naṣārā) two sorts of **Christians** are mentioned in chapters one to three of *Deliverance*: on the one hand scriptural Christians (§§10, 11.1), uncontextualized Christians (§50.5), and **holy men** (§§50.2, 50.6); on the other, individuals known to **al-Tanūkhī** or his informants (§§14.4, 50.1). The proportion of Christians and other non-Muslims in the Iraqi population in the ninth and tenth centuries can only be guessed, but Muslims were probably not yet a majority. For a cultural analysis, see Morony, *Iraq*. A number of prominent state **scribes** were converts with Christian backgrounds (§§17.4, 103.1), and al-Tanūkhī's own family belonged to the originally Christian tribal confederation of Tanūkh and cherished the story of the conversion of its patriarch. See Bray, "Men, Women and Slaves," 127, and "Place and Self-Image," 41–44.

client see **freedman.**

Companions of the Prophet (Ṣaḥābah) anyone who had met the Prophet, even briefly, was a Companion and a source for eyewitness reports of his sayings and deeds. Companions cited as sources in this section of *Deliverance* are: **ʿAbd Allāh ibn Masʿūd, Abū Dharr, Abū Hurayrah, ʿAlī ibn Abī Ṭālib, Anas ibn Mālik, Asmā' bint ʿUmays, Ibn ʿAbbās, Ibn ʿUmar**, and **Maslamah ibn Mukhallad.**

converts see **Christians** and **freedman.**

cotton (quṭn) originally from India, cotton was cultivated, traded, and manufactured into ordinary and luxury textiles throughout the **Abbasid** empire. See Lombard, *Les textiles*, 61–79, and *EI2*, "Ḳuṭn."

court companion (nadīm) the job of court companions was to drink with the caliph, share in his leisure pursuits, and entertain him with verse recitation and storytelling. Their privileged access to the caliph made them sources of anecdote and keyhole history.

courtesy name (kunyah) for a man, a name consisting of Abū, "father of," followed by the name of a son or sometimes daughter. **Al-Tanūkhī**, whose *kunyah* was Abū ʿAlī, really did have a son called ʿAlī, but *kunyahs* were often given in childhood, without reference to offspring. A more polite form of address than the given name (as at §103.2, where the villain calls his prospective victim by his *kunyah*), the courtesy name, which accounts for a large number of the persons cited in *Deliverance*, was not necessarily the best way of identifying someone and could give rise to uncertainty, as at §104.1, where for the benefit of his readers al-Tanūkhī identifies "Abū Saʿīd" as **al-Aṣmaʿī.**

cupping (ḥijāmah) a cure (§§15.1–2) used in both traditional and Galenic humoral medicine, whereby a heated glass was applied to lightly scarified skin to remove blood; dry cupping was used to relieve pain without extracting blood. See Pormann and Savage-Smith, *Medieval Islamic Medicine*, 43–44, 72, 121.

cursing a form of prayer; §77.3 describes a ritual cursing (*duʿāʾ ʿalā*) that lasts for several sessions, in which a whole family takes part. See *EI3* "Cursing, Ritual."

curtain, purdah (sitr) at §103.1, a noblewoman speaks to the narrator from behind a curtain that has been rigged up in his audience chamber out of deference to her status. He suspects that the curtain also conceals a spy, which turns out to be the case. Here the curtain is both a social reality and a plot device. A curtain was usually put up between a **singing woman** and her audience; because it is a familiar procedure, this is implied but not spelled out at §78.3.

Dabīq in the suburbs of Damietta in the Nile Delta, a place famous for its high-quality woven fabrics.

Ḍabuʿ a settlement in the region of **Basra.**

al-Ḍaḥḥāk al-Ḍaḥḥāk ibn Muzāḥim of **Balkh** (d. 105/723), exegete and man of letters.

Damascus oasis (Ghūṭah) the gardens and orchards surrounding the city of Damascus, irrigated by the Baradā river.

Daniel Daniel is well known in tradition as a prophet but is not a Qurʾanic prophet. See Wheeler, *Prophets in the Quran*, 280–83.

Dāwūd ibn Abī Hind (d. 139/756) Egyptian traditionist.

Dāwūd ibn al-Jarrāḥ (dates unknown) state **scribe**, of **Dayr Qunnā**; grandfather of **ʿAlī ibn ʿĪsā** and uncle of **al-Ḥasan ibn Makhlad.** He was in charge of **bureaucratic supervision** under **al-Mutawakkil**, see §73.8.

Dāwūd ibn al-Muḥabbar Basran traditionist.

Dāwūd ibn Rushayd (d. 239/853) Khwarazmian traditionist.

Daylam the mountainous region southwest of the Caspian, home to the **Buyid** or Buwayhid dynasty.

Daylamī often use of the Buyid (or Buwayhid) **Shiʿi** soldier dynasty that seized power in Iraq in 334/945 and divided up the remaining eastern **Abbasid** provinces between three more branches of the family, which reigned concurrently. Their followers are recognizable by their Persian names at §§14.1, 80.2. Their regime brought about changes in government and society of which **al-Tanūkhī** was highly critical. See al-Tanūkhī, *Table Talk*, 7–8; Mottahedeh, *Loyalty and Leadership*; Donohue, *The Buwayhid Dynasty in Iraq*.

Dayr Qunnā monastery south of **Baghdad** where a number of **Abbasid** state **scribes** received their training. See *EI2*, "Dayr Ḳunnā."

dinar a gold coin, or money of account whose value in relation to the silver coinage (**dirham**) varies. The word *badrah*, meaning a skin or a purse, is also used of a sum of between a thousand and ten thousand dinars, and at §16.1 it is specified in the Arabic that "the two *badrah*s" the hero tosses into the sea "contained ten thousand dinars."

dirham a silver coin or money of account of which the gold coinage (**dinar**) is reckoned a multiple, though the ratio varies.

disembodied voice (hātif, pl. *hawātif)* the *hawātif* of §§16.1, 19.1, 95.1, and 112 are not the shrieks that frighten desert travelers in pre-Islamic Arabian folklore. See Fahd, "Hātif," *EI2*. They are Islamicized, in the tradition of **Ibn Abī l-Dunyā**'s book on the subject, which divides them into voices heard by the Prophet and **Companions**, voices in graveyards that address the living on behalf of the dead, and *hawātif* that teach prayers. Some are **angels**, but generally their status is ambiguous, and some are **jinn**. See Ibn Abī l-Dunyā, *Kitāb al-Hawātif*, 51, 58–111. **Al-Tanūkhī** and his sources do not speculate on the nature of the *hawātif* they encounter.

doctors of religion (ʿulamāʾ) at §67.2, **Ḥasan of Basra** means by *ʿulamāʾ* people like himself, who distanced themselves from the **Umayyad** regime and devoted themselves to asceticism and pondering the fundamentals of religion. He claims they have a divine mandate to denounce ungodliness. See Cook, *Commanding Right and Forbidding Wrong*, 52–53.

dreams modern studies of Islamic dreams and dream interpretation focus on Qur'anic and Prophetic paradigms of dream narrative and the symbols found in ancient dream books translated into Arabic. See Sirriyeh, *Dreams*. Chapters one and three of *Deliverance* do not conform to these patterns. We encounter dreams in which Qur'anic passages are recited by a being equivalent to or interchangeable with a **disembodied voice** (§§17.3, 18.1,19.1) and a dream consisting of a poem, equivalent to onomatomantic **fortune-telling** (§99).

Ḍumayrah ibn Saʿīd Medinan traditionist.

Egypt the Qur'anic land of Pharaoh, Joseph, and Moses; a province of the **Abbasid** empire, important as a source of revenue from the **land tax.**

elephants war elephants (§§96.1, 96.2) were familiar from the Qur'an, see Q 105, Sūrat al-Fīl, quoted by **al-Tanūkhī** at §18.1. Impressed by an elephant he had seen as a child, al-Tanūkhī included several elephant stories in *Deliverance* and *Table Talk*. See Bray, "Reading 'the Exotic.'"

embroidery, of Dabīq textiles were valuable, and those from **Dabīq** were much imitated. Dabīqī became a generic term for all sorts of luxury fabrics, brocaded or embroidered with patterns, images, or *ṭirāz* inscriptions. See Lombard, *Textiles*, 50, 160; Serjeant, *Islamic Textiles*, 136, 139, 141; and Mez, *Renaissance*, 460. As with many everyday objects, the Dabīqī kerchief or cloth (*mandīl*) of §109.2 is not described in enough detail to be easily visualized by a modern reader.

Estates, Bureau of the government department in charge of state and private properties subject to the property tax (*ṣadaqah*). Its functions, says Sourdel, were ill defined. See Sourdel, *Vizirat*, 591–92.

Euphrates the second great waterway of **Iraq**, connected to the **Tigris** by numerous canals.

execution mat (naṭʿ) a leather mat on which the victim knelt for his head to be struck off, §§67.5, 105.10.

eye salve (ithmid) an eye cosmetic or medicine that could be made of a variety of substances. See *EI2*, "al-Kuḥl."

al-Faḍl ibn Isḥāq al-Dūrī (d. 242/856) cloth merchant, Baghdadi traditionist.

al-Faḍl ibn Marwān (d. 250/864) appointed **vizier** by **al-Muʿtaṣim** in 218/833, he had wide powers, especially financial. Disgraced 211/838.

al-Faḍl ibn Muḥammad the Druggist of Antioch one of **al-Tanūkhī's father**'s teachers in **Antioch.**

al-Faḍl ibn Muḥammad al-Yazīdī (d. 278/891) uncle of **Muḥammad ibn al-ʿAbbās al-Yazīdī**; Baghdadi grammarian and traditionist.

al-Faḍl ibn al-Rabīʿ (d. ca. 207/823) Abū l-ʿAbbās. He succeeded **Yaḥyā ibn Khālid al-Barmakī** as **vizier** to **Hārūn al-Rashīd** after the disgrace of the Barmakids in 187/803, retained office under **al-Amīn**, and secured **al-Maʾmūn**'s favor after al-Amīn's defeat. In Sourdel's estimate, he was a scheming mediocrity. See *EI2*, "al-Faḍl b. al-Rabīʿ." At §11.4, he is all-powerful as **Hārūn al-Rashīd**'s vizier.

al-Faḍl ibn Sahl (d. 202/818) a Zoroastrian **convert**, trained by the **Barmakīs**, he became **al-Maʾmūn**'s mentor and first **vizier**, enjoying extensive military and administrative powers; he was murdered by the caliphal guard. See Sourdel, *Vizirat*, 196–213, and *EI2*, "al-Faḍl b. Sahl b. Za<u>dh</u>ānfarū<u>kh</u>."

al-Faḍl ibn Yaḥyā ibn Khālid al-Barmakī (147–93/764–808) he had extensive powers as a military commander and statesman, often deputizing as **vizier** for his father **Yaḥyā ibn Khālid**, and was **tutor** to **al-Amīn** when the latter was crown prince. As milk brother to **Hārūn al-Rashīd**, a bond considered almost as strong as blood brotherhood, he was especially well placed to grant favors. He shared in the downfall of the **Barmakīs**.

al-Faḍl ibn Yaʿqūb (d. 258/872) Baghdadi marble mason and traditionist.

Fam al-Ṣilḥ a village north of Wāsiṭ.

al-Farrāʾ (144–207/761–822) Yaḥyā ibn Ziyād, prominent grammarian, his works include a still extant grammatical commentary on the Qurʾan, *Maʿānī al-Qurʾān.*

Fars the **Abbasid** province covering the southwest of Iran; its capital was **Shiraz.**

al-Faryābī Abū ʿAbd Allāh Muḥammad ibn Yūsuf, traditionist from Faryāb near **Balkh.**

Fasā a city of **Fars.**

al-Fatḥ ibn Khāqān of Turkic origin, son of a military commander, he became **al-Mutawakkil**'s most intimate companion and adviser, and died with him when he was assassinated in 247/861.

Fāṭimah (AD 605–32) daughter of **Muḥammad** by his first wife, Khadījah; wife of **ʿAlī ibn Abī Ṭālib**; mother of al-Ḥasan and **al-Ḥusayn ibn ʿAlī ibn Abī Ṭālib.**

al-Fayḍ ibn Isḥāq traditionist, unidentified.

Firās ibn Yaḥyā (d. 129/747) Kufan jurist.

folio (waraqah) part of the structure of a book or booklet composed of sheets folded in two and gathered into quires (a codex). Each half sheet is a folio, the equivalent of two pages. Thus **al-Madāʾinī**'s five- or six-folio booklet (§0.5) was ten or twelve pages long, **Ibn Abī l-Dunyā**'s twenty-folio *Book of Deliverance* (§0.6) was forty pages long, and Judge **Abū l-Ḥusayn**'s fifty-folio work (§0.7) a hundred pages long. Arabic books were not transcribed identically in multiple copies, so in describing his predecessors' books **al-Tanūkhī** is either referring to specific copies or giving his readers a rough idea of length.

forfeiture payments (māl al-muṣādarah) it was normal to imprison, torture, and fine disgraced officials, on the assumption that they would have embezzled state monies while in office, or simply to make them forfeit their private fortunes.

fortune-telling the same word, *tafāʾul*, is used for inferring a good omen from the wording of a song (onomatomancy, §78.3) and for using chance-read passages of the Qurʾan as a guide to the future (§65.2) or to discovering the truth (§81.2). The case of the stork and the sparrow at §109.3 is an example of ornithomancy. See Fahd, *La divination*, 449–50. Other forms of prognostication in chapter three of *Deliverance* include **physiognomy** (§§68.4, 68.8) and omens taken from **graffiti** (§69.1) and from a message found underneath a seat (§98.1).

freedman (mawlā) *mawlā* has various meanings. Applied at §106.1 to someone with a non-Arab name, Danqash, it suggests a freed slave, whose position as captain of the guard also made him a trusted member of his master **al-Manṣūr**'s household. It can also mean a protégé, the likely sense of the word at §98.1. At §§38.1 and 105.1, *mawlā* means a client of an Arab or Arab tribe, a non-Arab who adopts an Arab identity on conversion.

al-Fuḍayl ibn ʿIyāḍ (105–87/723–803) ascetic and traditionist from **Samarqand**; died in **Mecca**.

Fuḍayl ibn Marzūq (d. ca. 160/776) Kufan traditionist.

Gabriel the **angel** who imparted the Qurʾan to **Muḥammad** (Q Baqarah 2:97). In tradition, he is the chief angel: see Burge, *Angels in Islam*, 120–27.

geometer on the flourishing of geometry in **Iraq** in the fourth/tenth century, see *EI2*, "ʿIlm al-Handasa." On the importance of mathematics to tax assessment, see **land tax.**

Ghālib the Cotton Merchant unidentified.

Gīlān part of **Daylam.**

God the descriptions of God in the Qur'an give rise to theological problems: should they be taken literally or figuratively? For example, does He really sit on a throne? Two such problem passages occur in this section of *Deliverance*: the prayer at §92.2 where God is said to have a "face," and §22, which implies that He has a physical existence in space ("Remember God, and He will be present to you," literally "you will find Him in front of you"). As a **Muʿtazilī, al-Tanūkhī** would have been hostile to anthropomorphism, but he refrains from comment, although a passage that might be understood as meaning that God predestines people to damnation rouses him to a piece of Muʿtazilī exegesis in defence of God's justice at §9.3. He also reflects on God's nature and the relationship between prophets and God at §8.5. God is made a protagonist in non-Qur'anic narratives at §§13.8, 70.4, 70.12, 85.1, 85.5, and 85.7.

Gospels (al-Injīl) at §§92.3 and 93.2, God is invoked as "He Who sent down the Gospels," that is, the scripture given to Jesus.

graffiti writings on walls form a distinct genre in medieval Arabic literature. See Abū l-Faraj al-Iṣfahānī (attrib.), *The Book of Strangers*.

grandfather of Abū ʿAlī of Dayr Qunnā, state scribe unidentified.

Graveyard of Quraysh a burial ground in **Baghdad.**

Ḥabash of Ṣanʿāʾ unidentified.

Ḥabīb ibn Maslamah (2–42/620–62) early Muslim commander, he took part in many campaigns against the Byzantines.

al-Hādī (r. 169–70/785–86) fourth **Abbasid** caliph, he wished his own son to succeed him in place of his brother **Hārūn al-Rashīd.** Notorious for his violent temper, he died suddenly in unexplained circumstances.

al-Ḥajjāj al-Ḥajjāj ibn Yūsuf al-Thaqafī (ca. 41–95/661–714), the ablest and most feared of **Umayyad** governors, he was appointed to **Iraq** in 75/694, aged thirty-three, where he quashed numerous rebellions, including that of the Kharijite **Qaṭarī ibn al-Fujāʾah.** He built the town of **Wāsiṭ** to house his **Syrian** troops.

al-Ḥakam ibn Hishām al-Thaqafī Kufan traditionist living in Damascus.

Haman in the Qur'an, the henchman of Pharaoh.

Ḥamdānids named after their ancestor Ḥamdān, a chieftain of the **Arab** tribe of Taghlib in **Mosul** in the second half of the third/ninth century, in the following century they served the **Abbasid** caliphs as miltary commanders, briefly ruling in **Iraq**, and established themselves as independent rulers in Mosul and Aleppo.

Ḥammād Danqash or Danqīsh (perhaps meaning "the Humble") captain of the guard under **al-Manṣūr**. Six generations of his descendants were in public service. See **Aḥmad ibn Muḥammad ibn al-Faḍl**, **Aḥmad ibn Muḥammad ibn Ḥammād Danqash**, and **Muḥammad ibn Ḥammād Danqash.**

Ḥammād Ḥammād ibn Zayd ibn Dirham (d. 197/813), Basran traditionist.

Ḥammād ibn Salamah (d. 167/783) Basran traditionist.

Ḥammād ibn Wāqid Basran coppersmith and traditionist.

Ḥanẓalah of Mecca Ḥanẓalah ibn Abī Sufyān, traditionist of mixed reputation.

(al-) Ḥaramī ibn Abī l-ʿAlāʾ Abū ʿAbd Allāh Aḥmad ibn Muḥammad, Baghdadi traditionist, secretary of Judge **Abū ʿUmar Muḥammad al-Azdī** (d. 317/929).

al-Ḥārith of Basra al-Ḥārith ibn ʿAṭiyyah, ascetic.

al-Ḥārith ibn Ḥabash of Ṣanʿāʾ unidentified.

Hārūn ibn ʿAbd Allāh (d. 243/857) Baghdadi porter, old-clothes dealer, and traditionist.

Hārūn al-Rashīd (r. 170–93/786–809) fifth **Abbasid** caliph, his father al-Mahdī (r. 158–69/775–85) designated him successor to his brother **al-Hādī**, who wished to be succeeded by his own son. His mentor before his accession was **Yaḥyā ibn Khālid al-Barmakī**, and for seventeen years Hārūn gave members of the **Barmakī** family a free hand in running the empire before suddenly turning on them in 187/803.

Hārūn al-Rashīd's chamberlain unidentified, probably fictional.

Hārūn ibn Sufyān (d. ca. 251/865) known as the Rooster, Baghdadi **lecture-room assistant** (*mustamlī*) and traditionist.

Ḥarūrī Ḥarūrīs were extreme **Kharijites** who took their name from the village of Ḥarūrāʾ near Kufa, where they rebelled against **ʿAlī ibn Abī Ṭālib** and declared their sole allegiance to God.

harvest assessment (taʿdīl) a complicated operation of evaluating the sources of all the kinds of tax levied on agricultural produce in a given tax district and calculating their monetary value (§§82.4, 82.6). See Cahen,

"Fiscalité." The case of **Abū l-Ḥasan Aḥmad ibn Muḥammad Ibn al-Mudabbir**, related at §§82.1–6, is studied in the original **papyrus** documents by Abbott, "Arabic Papyri of the Reign of Ǧaʿfar **al-Mutawakkil**." See Sourdel, *Vizirat*, 278–79.

al-Ḥasan ibn ʿAlī unidentified.

Ḥasan ibn ʿAlī ibn Abī Ṭālib (3–60/625–70) second imam of the **Twelver Shiʿi.** He renounced his claim to the caliphate to **Muʿāwiyah** and lived in **Medina** in seclusion.

al-Ḥasan ibn ʿAmr ibn Muḥammad al-Qurashī unidentified.

al-Ḥasan ibn Bakhtiyār or al-Ḥasan ibn Aḥmad ibn Bakhtiyār, **Daylamī** commander. Unidentified.

Ḥasan of Basra (d. 110/728) al-Ḥasan ibn Abī l-Ḥasan Yasār, early ascetic much cited as a model of piety and righteousness and for his compelling eloquence.

Ḥasan ibn Ḥasan ibn ʿAlī ibn Abī Ṭālib a son of the second imam of the **Twelver Shiʿi.**

al-Ḥasan ibn Jaʿfar ibn ʿAbd Allāh ibn al-Ḥusayn ibn ʿAlī ibn Abī Ṭālib **Alid.**

al-Ḥasan ibn Maḥbūb unidentified.

al-Ḥasan ibn Makhlad (209–69/824–82) al-Ḥasan ibn Makhlad ibn al-Jarrāḥ, nephew of **Dāwūd ibn al-Jarrāḥ** and cousin of **ʿAlī ibn ʿĪsā.** A recent convert from **Christian**ity, he was in charge of **Estates** under **al-Mutawakkil** and was twice **vizier** under **al-Muʿtamid** before being exiled to **Egypt.** He died in **Antioch**, possibly of poison.

al-Ḥasan ibn Mukarram (182–274/798–888) Baghdadi cloth merchant and traditionist.

al-Ḥasan ibn Sahl brother of **al-Maʾmūn**'s vizier **al-Faḍl ibn Sahl**, like him a state **scribe** trained by the **Barmakīs.** He occupied high positions in the administration but retired from public life after al-Faḍl's assassination. In 210/825, **al-Maʾmūn** married his daughter Būrān (d. 236/850–51).

al-Ḥasan ibn Wahb brother of **Abū Ayyūb Sulaymān ibn Wahb**, **poet** and secretary to the vizier **Ibn al-Zayyāt.**

Hāshim a forefather of the branch of **Quraysh** to which the Prophet belonged.

Herat city of **Khurasan**, now in Afghanistan.

al-Ḥijr city of north Arabia, now known as Madāʾin Ṣāliḥ.

Hijrah the Prophet's exodus when, in 1/622, persecuted by his own Meccan kinsmen (§12.3), he escaped with his followers to **Medina** (§12.2).

Hilāl **freedman** of **ʿUmar ibn ʿAbd al-ʿAzīz**; unidentified.

Ḥimṣ the modern Homs, Emesa in antiquity, a governorate of **Umayyad Syria.**

Hishām ibn Ismāʿīl (d. after 87/706) Hishām ibn Ismāʿīl al-Makhzūmī. The caliph **ʿAbd al-Malik ibn Marwān**, who was married to his daughter, appointed him governor of **Medina** in 82/701.

Hishām ibn Muḥammad Ibn al-Kalbī (ca. 120–204/737–819) member of a distinguished Kufan family. His father, Muḥammad, was a polymath; he himself was a prolific historian, some of whose works survive.

Hishām ibn ʿUrwah (d. ca. 145/762) son of **ʿUrwah** ibn al-Zubayr ibn al-ʿAwwām.

the Holy Land (al-arḍ al-muqaddasah) the dwelling place of Jeremiah.

holy man (ʿābid), holy woman (ʿābidah), literally "worshipers" Jaʿfar the holy man of **Rāmhurmuz** (§70.6), Jaʿfar ibn Mundhir the holy man of **Mahrūbān** (§70.9), Ḥumayd ibn ʿAbd Allāh (§§70.9–12), and the anonymous holy woman of §105.5 seem to be Muslims. We are not told about their way of life or how it fit into the spectrum of Muslim religious practices. Isaac (§§50.2, 50.6) appears to be a **Christian**; the faith of the holy man of §§70.1–5 is not identified, and the worshiper of §§70.7–8 is a Jew.

Ḥumayd ibn ʿAbd Allāh holy man, unidentified.

Ḥumayd ibn ʿAbd al-Raḥmān al-Ḥimyarī Basran jurist.

Ḥumayd ibn Ḥammād Ibn Khuwār or Ibn Abī l-Khuwār, Kufan or Basran traditionist.

Ḥunayn, Battle of in 8/630, following the Muslim conquest of **Mecca**, Mecca's rival **Taif** took to the field at Ḥunayn, a valley between Mecca and Taif, but were defeated in spite of vastly outnumbering the Muslims.

al-Ḥusayn ibn ʿAbd Allāh ibn Ḍumayrah Medinan traditionist.

al-Ḥusayn ibn ʿAbd al-Raḥmān of **Jarjarāyā** (d. 253/867), traditionist.

al-Ḥusayn ibn ʿAlī ibn Abī Ṭālib (4–61/626–80) third imam of the **Twelver Shiʿi**; died at **Karbalāʾ** defending his title to the caliphate against the **Umayyads**.

al-Ḥusayn ibn ʿAlī al-Juʿfī (d. 203/818) Kufan traditionist.

al-Ḥuṣayn ibn al-Ḥumām al-Murrī (d. ca. AD 612) pre-Islamic **poet.**

Ḥusayn ibn Ḥasan Ḥusayn ibn Ḥasan ibn Ḥarb al-Sulamī, traditionist of **Marw** and **Mecca.**

al-Ḥusayn ibn Numayr al-Khuzāʿī unidentified.

Ibn ʿAbbās, ʿAbd Allāh (d. 68/687) the Prophet's cousin, a highly respected authority. At §1.3 he is cited for his knowledge of the Qur'an and of the **Arabic** language. When he and **Muḥammad ibn al-Ḥanafiyyah** refused to recognize **Ibn al-Zubayr** as caliph, they were banished from **Mecca** in 64/684 and taken evenually to **Taif.**

Ibn Abī l-Dunyā (208–81/823–94) Abū Bakr ʿAbd Allāh ibn Muḥammad, polymath, traditionist, preacher, **tutor** to the sons of caliphs, and prolific compiler. Like many of his edifying works, his *Book of Deliverance* is extant.

Ibn Abī Fudayk Muḥammad ibn Ismāʿīl ibn Muslim ibn Abī Fudayk Dīnār (d. ca. 200/815), Medinan traditionist.

Ibn Abī Maryam unidentified.

Ibn Abī ʿUdayy (d. 194/ 809–10) Muḥammad ibn Ibrāhīm al-Sulamī of **Basra.**

Ibn al-Azhar Muḥammad ibn Jaʿfar (d. 300/913) traditionist nicknamed "the Kufan liar."

Ibn Baqiyyah (314–67/926–977) Muḥammad ibn Muḥammad ibn Baqiyyah, Iraqi peasant turned soldier, became vizier to the **Buyid** ʿIzz al-Dawlah Bakhtiyār (r. Iraq 356–67/967–78) in 362/972. By trying to win over **Muʿīn al-Dawlah** with gifts, he aroused the suspicions of Bakhtiyār, who had him arrested and blinded. He was finally trampled to death by **elephants.**

Ibn Bashshār Abū Bakr Muḥammad, known as Bundār (d. 252/866), Basran traditionist.

Ibn Durayd Abū Bakr Muḥammad ibn al-Ḥasan (223–321/838–933), leading Basran and Baghdadi linguistic scholar. Many of his works are extant.

Ibn al-Jarrāḥ Aḥmad ibn Muḥammad (d. 381/991), silk merchant, traditionist, transmitter of **Ibn Abī l-Dunyā**, and a wealthy and flamboyant figure in **Buyid Baghdad.**

Ibn Jubayr Saʿīd ibn Jubayr, Kufan of Abyssinian extraction, scholar and chess player, executed for rebellion by **al-Ḥajjāj** (d. 95/714).

Ibn Jurayj ʿAbd al-Malik ibn ʿAbd al-ʿAzīz (80–150/699–767), Meccan jurist of Byzantine extraction.

Ibn Khallād of Rāmhurmuz, Abū Muḥammad al-Ḥasan ibn ʿAbd al-Raḥman judge, deputy to **al-Tanūkhī's father**, **poet**, traditionist, and author of two extant works, the seminal *al-Muḥaddith al-fāṣil bayn al-rāwī wa l-wāʿī,* on distinguishing between accurate and inaccurate chains of transmission, and *Amthāl al-Nabī,* on proverbs and wise sayings attributed to the Prophet.

Ibn al-Munkadir Abū ʿAbd Allāh Muḥammad (d. 130/747), Medinan traditionist.

Ibn Muqlah Muḥammad ibn ʿAlī (272–328/885–940) began his career as a collector of **land taxes** in **Fars**, and was **vizier** in 304–6/917–19, again briefly in 320–21/932–33 and for a third and last time in 322–24/934–36. His career ended in disgrace and prison; a famous calligrapher, he was tortured by having his right hand cut off.

Ibn al-Sarrāj unidentified.

Ibn Shubrumah ʿAbd Allāh (d. 144/761), son or grandson of the **Companion** Shubrumah ibn al-Ṭufayl, Kufan **judge**, jurist, and **poet.**

Ibn ʿUmar ʿAbd Allāh ibn ʿUmar ibn al-Khaṭṭāb (d. 73/693), son of the second caliph, renowned for his sanctity.

Ibn Wahb ʿAbd Allāh, Egyptian traditionist.

Ibn al-Zayyāt (d. 233/847) Muḥammad ibn ʿAbd al-Malik. From a merchant family (his surname means Son of the Oil Merchant), he became a state **scribe**, was made **vizier** under **al-Muʿtaṣim**, and remained in office under **al-Wāthiq**, demanding forfeiture payments from officials such as **Abū Ayyūb Sulaymān ibn Wahb. Al-Mutawakkil** tortured him to death in a device he himself had invented.

Ibn al-Zubayr (2–73/624–692) ʿAbd Allāh ibn al-Zubayr ibn al-ʿAwwām, a member of **Quraysh.** He made his base in **Mecca** and declared himself caliph in 64/684, imprisoned **Ibn ʿAbbās** and **Muḥammad ibn al-Ḥanafiyyah** for refusing to recognize him, and was defeated by **al-Ḥajjāj.**

Ibrāhīm ibn al-Haytham al-Baladī unidentified.

Ibrāhīm ibn Khallād al-Azdī unidentified.

Ibrāhīm ibn Masʿūd unidentified.

Ibrāhīm ibn Muḥammad al-Anṣārī known as the **Eye-Salve** Merchant. Unidentified.

Ibrāhīm ibn Muḥammad Ibn Saʿd grandson of **Saʿd ibn Abī Waqqās**, Kufan traditionist.

Ibrāhīm ibn Rabāḥ state **scribe**, briefly in charge of the Bureau of **Estates** under **al-Wāthiq.**

Ibrāhīm ibn Rāshid (d. 264/878) Baghdadi traditionist.

Ibrāhīm ibn Saʿīd unidentified.

Ibrāhīm ibn Saʿīd (d. 249/863) Baghdadi jeweler and traditionist.

Ibrāhīm al-Taymī Ibrāhīm ibn Yazīd (d. 94/713), Kufan ascetic, executed by **al-Ḥajjāj.**

Ibrāhīm ibn Yūḥannā **steward** of **al-ʿAbbās son of al-Maʾmūn**; otherwise unidentified.

ʿImrān ibn al-Nuʿmān early Muslim commander, unidentified.

incense (bakhūr) used to **perfume** clothes, as at §73.14. The word can be applied to several substances and compounds. See al-Washshāʾ, *Le Livre de brocart*, 169–70.

inkwell (dawāt) surviving early-**Abbasid** inkwells (§73.13) are made of glass. See *EI2*, "Dawāt."

intention (niyyah) actions are invalid unless preceded by a declaration of good intent and corresponding focusing of the mind (§9.10). See *EI2*, "Niyya" and "Ikhlāṣ."

Iraq at §11.3, ancient "Iraq in the land of Babylon"; elsewhere, the land between and around the lower course of the **Euphrates** and **Tigris**, from north of **Samarra** to the Gulf.

Iraqis Iraqi support for **Alid** claimants to the caliphate made them a constant source of suspicion to the **Umayyads.**

ʿĪsā ibn ʿAbd al-ʿAzīz al-Ẓāhirī unidentified.

Isaac **holy man**, unidentified.

Isḥāq (150–235/767–850) Iṣhāq ibn Ibrāhīm al-Mawṣilī, the leading musician of his day, scholar, courtier, and witness to much keyhole history.

Isḥāq ibn Abī Isrāʾīl Isḥāq ibn Ibrāhīm ibn Kāmjar of **Marw** (151–246/768–860), Baghdadi traditionist.

Isḥāq ibn al-Buhlūl al-Tanūkhī Ishāq ibn al-Buhlūl ibn Hassān ibn Sinān (164–252/780–867), **al-Tanūkhī**'s maternal great-great-grandfather, traditionist, and state **scribe**, of **al-Anbār** and **Baghdad.**

Isḥāq ibn al-Ḍayf Basran traditionist.

Isḥāq ibn Ibrāhīm of Kūfa (d. after 130/748).

Isḥāq ibn Ibrāhīm ibn Muṣʿab (207–35/822–50) a nephew of **Ṭāhir ibn al-Ḥusayn.** Soldier, chief of **police** of **Baghdad**, and governor of **Iraq** under successive caliphs.

Isḥāq ibn ʿĪsā son of the daughter of Dāwūd ibn Abī Hind Basran traditionist.

Isḥāq ibn Ismāʿīl of **Ṭāliqān** (d. 230/845), known as the Incomparable, Baghdadi traditionist.

Isḥāq ibn Sulaymān of **Kufa** (d. 200/815), Baghdadi traditionist.

Ismāʿīl ibn Bulbul (230–78/844–92) appointed **vizier** by **al-Muwaffaq** in 265/878, from 272/885 he extended his authority and tried to prevent al-Muwaffaq's son **al-Muʿtaḍid** from taking part in public affairs.

Ismāʿīl ibn Umayyah (d. 139/756) Meccan jurist.

Israfel not mentioned in the Qur'an, in tradition Israfel is the **Angel** of the Trumpet, who will announce the Last Day, and a bearer of the Throne of God. See Burge, *Angels in Islam*, 128–32.

Isrāʾīl unidentified.

Isrāʾīl (d. 162/779) Isrāʾīl ibn Yūnus al-Sabīʿī.

Ītākh Abū Manṣūr (d. 235/849), **Turk** soldier, had been raised by **al-Muʿtaṣim** from kitchen boy to general. His power base was in **Samarra.** He held high office in the caliphal household under **al-Wāthiq**, whose son he supported as his successor. When **al-Mutawakkil** became caliph, he threw him into prison, where he died of thirst. See Kennedy, *The Court of the Caliphs*, 237–38.

al-Jabal probably synonymous with **al-Jibāl**, the province to the north and west of **Khuzistan** and **Fars.**

Jaʿfar ibn ʿAbd Allāh ibn al-Ḥusayn ibn ʿAlī ibn Abī Ṭālib **Alid.**

Jaʿfar ibn Abī Ṭālib ibn Abī Jaʿfar Ibn al-Buhlūl al-Tanūkhī, Judge Jaʿfar ibn Muḥammad ibn Aḥmad ibn Isḥāq ibn al-Buhlūl ibn Ḥassān (303–77/916–87), **al-Tanūkhī**'s uncle on his mother's side, Baghdadi traditionist.

Jaʿfar the holy man unidentified.

Jaʿfar ibn Maymūn seller of felts and traditionist.

Jaʿfar ibn Muḥammad ibn ʿUyaynah unidentified.

Jaʿfar ibn Mundhir al-Ṭāʾī the holy man unidentified.

Jaʿfar al-Ṣādiq (83–148/702–65) Jaʿfar ibn Muḥammad, sixth imam of the **Twelver Shiʿi**, Medinan jurist.

Jaʿfar ibn Sulaymān (d. 178/794) Basran **Shiʿi** ascetic and traditionist.

Jaʿfar ibn Sulaymān al-Hāshimī (d. 177/793) cousin of **al-Manṣūr**, governor of **Medina**, **Mecca**, and other cities.

Jāmidah large village between **Wāsiṭ** and **Basra.**

Jarīr ibn Ḥafṣ (d. 170/786) Basran traditionist.

Jarjarāyā town on the **Tigris** between **Baghdad** and **Wāsiṭ**.

Jazīrat Ibn ʿUmar port city on the **Tigris** north of **Mosul.**

Jerusalem (Bayt al-Maqdis) city in **Syria.**

al-Jibāl a province corresponding to today's northwestern Iran.

jinn part of the gamut of intelligent creation, jinn are made of fire or vapor (humans are made of clay, **angels** of light), and are often mentioned in the Qur'an, where surah 72 is named after them. They can be good or bad, like humans.

Joseph's shirt Joseph's shirt (§§85.1, 85.2) and the bond it forms between him and his father Jacob is an important theme in the Qur'anic story of Joseph (Q Yūsuf 12:18, 12:93, 12:96) and was much developed in early Muslim storytelling. See Thaʿlabī, *Lives of the Prophets*, 192–93, 223–29.

judge (qāḍī) and deputy judge (khalīfah) judges were appointed to towns, quarters of large cities, provinces, and districts, to administer Shariah law (personal, family, and contract law). They could accumulate appointments and appoint deputies and other officers of the court such as **legal witnesses** and **legal trustees**, and thereby built up professional and social networks. The law often ran in families, which might intermarry, as did the two branches of **al-Tanūkhī**'s. Al-Tanūkhī and his father (who were Ḥanafīs, the legal school originally favored by the **Abbasid** elite) held their appointments during one of the growth periods of both jurisprudence and the theory of the administration of law, on which there is a large body of modern scholarship. Actual legal practice has been less studied, and we know little about where judges sat, how much of their time their duties took, and so on. See Tyan, *Histoire*, for legal procedure; Tillier, *Les cadis d'Iraq*, for the sociopolitical importance of Abbasid judges; and Tillier, "L'exemplarité," for judges in al-Tanūkhī's *Table Talk*, a unique insider source.

Juwaybir Juwaybir ibn Saʿīd of **Balkh** (d. after 140/757), exegete.

Kaaba in **Mecca**, the Sacred House where Hagar and Ishmael settled (Q Ibrāhīm 14:37) and to which Muslims make pilgrimage.

Kahmas ibn al-Ḥasan (d. 149/766) Basran traditionist.

al-Kalwadhānī Abū l-Qāsim ʿUbayd Allāh. As well as deputizing for **Ibn Muqlah** in 320/932, he briefly deputized for **ʿAlī ibn ʿĪsā** in 314/927 and was **vizier** in his own right for two months in 319/931. His home town of Kalwadhā lay to the east of **Baghdad**.

al-Karaj (perhaps al-Kīrāj) a city of **Sind**.

Karbalāʾ northwest of Kufa, the battlefield where **al-Ḥusayn ibn ʿAlī ibn Abī Ṭālib** was killed in 61/680.

al-Karkh a commercial district of **Baghdad**.

Kathīr ibn Hishām (d. 207/822) Baghdadi traditionist.

Khālid ibn Khidāsh (d. 223/838) Baghdadi traditionist.

al-Khalīl ibn Murrah of **Raqqah** (d. 160/777), Basran traditionist.

Kharg island in the Gulf, a port of call between **Basra** and Oman.

Kharijite after rebelling against **ʿAlī ibn Abī Ṭālib** for agreeing to accept arbitration over his claim to the caliphate, the Kharijites became perpetual rebels against all authority. They were feared for their bloodthirstiness, but their **poets** were admired. **Qaṭarī ibn al-Fujāʾah** (§53.2) was one of the most famous.

al-Khaṭṭāb ibn ʿUthmān holy man, of **Ḥimṣ**.

Khulayd ibn Diʿlaj of **Mosul** and **Jerusalem** (d. 166/783), Basran traditionist.

Khurasan the easternmost province of the **Abbasid** empire until the overthrow of its **Ṭāhirid** governors in 259/873.

Khuzistan rich agricultural and manufacturing province, situated between the Zagros mountains and the Gulf in southwestern Iran.

Khwarazm eastern province, to the north of **Khurasan.**

Kufa important city on the **Tigris**, midway between **Basra** and **Baghdad.**

Kurdūs ibn ʿAmr also ibn al-ʿAbbās or ibn Hāniʾ. Unidentified.

land tax (kharāj) the main source of government income. As at §§14.4 and 80.2, its collection was often delegated to private individuals (see **tax farming**). Its assessment was complicated (see **harvest assessment**) and called for a high degree of knowledge of geometry and arithmetic, in order to measure land surfaces and estimate crop yields, as well as to convert yields into their cash value, since in the highly monetarized **Abbasid** economy taxes were remitted in cash, not in kind. See Cahen, "Quelques problèmes économiques et fiscaux."

Lashkarwarz ibn Sahlān the Daylamī (d. 348/959) commander in the army of **Muʿizz al-Dawlah**, who married his daughter.

lecture-room assistant (mustamlī) in large gatherings of hadith transmission, the *mustamlī* repeated the teacher's words for those out of earshot.

legal trustee (amīn, pl. *umanāʾ)* an officer of the court appointed by the **judge** as guardian of the goods of minor orphans. See Tyan, *Histoire*, 259–60.

legal witness (shāhid, pl. *shuhūd)* appointed by the **judge** as fixed witnesses, they sit with him and testify to the validity of court procedures and of the judge's verdicts. They also deputize for him in visiting incapacitated witnesses to take depositions, etc. See Tyan, *Histoire*, 236–50, and Cahen, "A propos des *shuhūd*."

al-Madāʾinī Abū l-Ḥasan ʿAlī ibn Muḥammad (135–228/752–843), historian, author of some two hundred works including *The Book of Deliverance following Adversity and Straits*, of which only two survive in part.

Mādharāʾ village near **Wāsiṭ**.

Maḥmūd ibn ʿUmar of **ʿUkbarā**. Unidentified.

Mahrūbān prosperous port in southern **Fars**, the first harbor reached by ships heading from **Basra** to India.

majlis a general term for any assembly, large or small, formal or informal, whether its purpose is business or entertainment. At §31.4 it refers to a Hadith session. At §78.3 it refers to a private music party. See Ali, *Arabic Literary Salons*.

Mālik ibn Anas (d. 179/796) son of **Anas ibn Mālik**, Medinan traditionist and jurist, author of *al-Muwaṭṭā*, a survey of the legal and ritual practice of **Medina**, and eponym of the Mālikī school of law.

Mālik ibn Dīnār (d. 131/749) Basran traditionist and Qurʾan copyist.

Mālik ibn Suʿayr (d. 198/813) traditionist.

al-Maʾmūn (r. 198–218/813–33) seventh **Abbasid** caliph, he defeated his brother **al-Amīn** in their war for the throne after the death of their father **Hārūn al-Rashīd**.

al-Maʾmūniyyah village near **Sūq al-Ahwāz**.

al-Manṣūr (r. 136–58/754–75) second **Abbasid** caliph, founder of **Baghdad** in 145/762.

manure (tabūdhak) a fertilizer made from chicken droppings and offal. See Ziriklī, *Aʿlām*, vol. 7, 320, "Al-Minqarī, Mūsā ibn Ismāʿīl."

Marshes, of southern Iraq (al-Baṭīḥah) the swampland between the **Euphrates** and **Tigris**, reaching south of **Kufa** and **Wāsiṭ** to **Basra**.

Marw the main city of **Khurasan**.

Māsabadhān a district in Jibāl province (see **al-Jabal**).

Mashghrā village in the **Damascus oasis**.

Maslamah ibn ʿAlqamah Basran traditionist.

Maslamah ibn Mukhallad (1–62/622–682) early Muslim commander. **Muʿāwiyah** appointed him governor of **Egypt** and **North Africa**.

Masrūr ibn ʿAbd Allāh al-Ustādī identity uncertain. Possibly Masarrah ibn ʿAbd Allāh (d. 322/934), a eunuch in the household of **al-Mutawakkil**.

mawlā see **freedman.**

maydān the "Great Square" in **Baghdad.**

Maymūn ibn Hārūn unidentified.

Mecca pre-Islamic trading city and religious center in western Arabia, under the dominance of **Quraysh**; in Islam, the city of the Pilgrimage. In early Islamic times troublesome as the residence of politically important relatives and descendants of the Prophet opposed to the ruling regimes.

Medina oasis city north of **Mecca** to which the Prophet and the first Muslims emigrated in 1/622; the first Muslim capital, superseded by Damascus under the **Umayyads** and **Baghdad** under the **Abbasids.**

Michael in tradition, the **angel** Michael is second to **Gabriel** in rank. See Burge, *Angels in Islam*, 127–28. Next in rank are **Israfel** and **Azrael.**

Midian the Land of Midian of the Old Testament and the Qur'an.

mint (dār al-ḍarb), inspector of the in the highly monetarized **Abbasid** economy, there were numerous local mints. Young **al-Tanūkhī** was appointed to the inspection (*ʿiyār*, §19.1) of the mint of **Sūq al-Ahwāz** and his deputy inspector was also a legal dignitary.

Miʿsar (d. ca. 153/770) Miʿsar ibn Kidām, Kufan traditionist.

mosque of al-Manṣūr the first mosque in **Baghdad**, built by the city's founder **al-Manṣūr**, used for Friday prayer.

Mosul city of northern Mesopotamia on the west bank of the **Tigris.**

al-Muʿallā ibn ʿAbd Allāh ibn al-Muʿallā ibn Ayyūb grandson of **al-Muʿallā ibn Ayyūb.**

al-Muʿallā ibn Ayyūb (d. 255/869) state **scribe**, maternal cousin of **al-Faḍl ibn Sahl.** He served **al-Ma'mūn** and went on to serve **al-Muʿtaṣim** and several of his successors, dying some thirty years after the episode at §§17.1–4. At §82.7 he comes to the aid of a fellow scribe in the reign of **al-Mutawakkil.**

Mu'ammal ibn Ihāb of **Ramlah** (d. 254/868), Kufan traditionist.

al-Muʿammar ibn Sulaymān of **Raqqah** (d. 191/807).

Muʿāwiyah Muʿāwiyah ibn Abī Sufyān (r. 41–60/661–80), first **Umayyad** caliph.

Muʿāwiyah ibn Qurrah (d. 113/731) Basran traditionist.

Muʿāwiyah ibn Yaḥyā Damascene traditionist.

al-Mubarrad Abū l-ʿAbbās Muḥammad ibn Yazīd (ca. 210–86/826–900), born in **Basra**, was called to the court of **al-Mutawakkil** in **Samarra** in 246/860, then taught in **Baghdad.** His *al-Kāmil* (*Comprehensive Corpus*) remains a classic, as do other works.

Mudlij ibn ʿAbd al-ʿAzīz unidentified.

Mughīth unidentified.

al-Muhallabī see **Abū Muḥammad al-Ḥasan ibn Muḥammad al-Muhallabī.**

Muḥammad (d. 11/632) Prophet and teacher, the founder of Islam through revelation and example. The Qur'an often refers to situations and events in Muḥammad's mission. His own example and precepts are recorded independently as hadith (traditions) and passed down by the **Companions** who witnessed them, the **Successors** who heard the Companions' accounts, and then by traditionists (any Muslim interested in Hadith) to each other, hence the chains of transmitters that introduce any report about the Prophet.

Muḥammad ibn ʿAbbād ibn Mūsā (d. 234/848) Baghdadi traditionist.

Muḥammad ibn al-ʿAbbās al-Yazīdī (ca. 228–310/843–922) Baghdadi traditionist, scholar of early **Arabic** poetry, **tutor** to the sons of **al-Muqtadir.**

Muḥammad ibn ʿAbd Allāh al-Anṣārī (118–215/736–830) **judge** in **Basra** and **Baghdad.**

Muḥammad ibn ʿAbd Allāh al-Azdī of **Baghdad** and **Mosul** (d. 252/866).

Muḥammad ibn ʿAbd al-Karīm traditionist of **Marw.**

Muḥammad ibn ʿAbd al-Malik ibn Mughīth unidentified.

Muḥammad ibn ʿAbd al-Raḥmān al-Juʿfī (d. 160/777) Kufan traditionist.

Muḥammad ibn ʿAbdūs al-Jahshiyārī (d. 331/942) his *Book of Viziers*, which continued until 296/908, survives only until the start of the reign of **al-Ma'mūn.** He also wrote a lost chronicle of the reign of **al-Muqtadir.** He was **chamberlain** to the vizier **ʿAlī ibn ʿĪsā** and a friend of **Ibn Muqlah.**

Muḥammad ibn Abī Rajā' unidentified.

Muḥammad ibn ʿAjlān (d. 148/765) Medinan traditionist.

Muḥammad ibn ʿAlī Muḥammad ibn ʿAlī ibn Aḥmad ibn Rustum of **Mādharā'** (258–354/872–956), state **scribe,** nephew of **Abū Zunbūr.**

Muḥammad ibn ʿAmr ibn al-Bakhtarī the Rice Merchant (251–339/865–950) Baghdadi traditionist.

Muḥammad ibn Bakr of Bursān Basran traditionist.

Muḥammad ibn Bakr ibn Dāsah unidentified contemporary of **al-Tanūkhī.**

Muḥammad al-Bāqir ibn ʿAlī (57–114/677–732) fifth imam of the **Twelver Shiʿi,** Medinan jurist.

Muḥammad ibn al-Ḥajjāj al-Ḍabbī unidentified.

Muḥammad ibn Ḥammād Danqash or Danqīsh (d. 240/855) **chamberlain** to **al-Muʿtaṣim** and **Hārūn al-Rashīd**; well known in **Abbasid** literary circles, having been secretary to the state **scribe** and **poet** Abū Ḥukaymah Rāshid ibn Isḥāq.

Muḥammad ibn al-Ḥanafiyyah (d. 81/700–1) a son of **ʿAlī ibn Abī Ṭālib** by a woman of the tribe of Ḥanīfah, he attracted the hostility of **Ibn al-Zubayr.**

Muḥammad ibn al-Ḥasan unidentified.

Muḥammad ibn al-Ḥasan ibn al-Muẓaffar (d. 388/998) known as al-Ḥātimī, Baghdadi man of letters and critic, some of whose works have been published.

Muḥammad ibn al-Ḥusayn (d. 261/875) possibly Abū Jaʿfar, Baghdadi traditionist.

Muḥammad ibn al-Ḥusayn of Burjulān (d. 238/852–53) author of works on asceticism and devotion; a teacher of **Ibn Abī l-Dunyā.**

Muḥammad ibn al-Ḥusayn al-Anṣārī unidentified.

Muḥammad ibn Ibrāhīm ibn al-Muṭṭalib ibn Abī Wadāʿah al-Sahmī Medinan traditionist.

Muḥammad ibn Ibrāhīm of Fam al-Ṣilḥ (d. 310/922–23) Baghdadi traditionist.

Muḥammad ibn Ismāʿīl al-Sulamī (d. 270/883).

Muḥammad ibn Jarīr al-Ṭabarī see **al-Ṭabarī.**

Muḥammad ibn Kaʿb al-Quraẓī (d. ca. 117/735) Medinan traditionist.

Muḥammad Ibn al-Kalbī Muḥammad ibn al-Sāʾib al-Kalbī (d. 146/763), Kufan historian often cited by his son **Hishām ibn Muḥammad Ibn al-Kalbī.**

Muḥammad ibn Muʿammar (d. after 250/864) traditionist of **al-Baḥrayn.**

Muḥammad ibn Muhājir (d. 170/786) traditionist.

Muḥammad ibn Muḥammad (d. 312/924) known as the Son of the Man from **Bāghand, Baghdadi** traditionist.

Muḥammad ibn Muḥammad, known as the Son of the Geometer Abū l-Ḥasan Muḥammad ibn Muḥammad ibn ʿUthman of **Ahwaz**, state **scribe**. Unidentified.

Muḥammad ibn al-Munkadir (54–130/674–747) Medinan ascetic.

Muḥammad ibn Numayr Muḥammad ibn ʿAbd Allāh ibn Numayr known as al-Numayrī, minor love **poet** in the courtly Hijazi tradition (second half of first/seventh century).

Muḥammad ibn al-Qāsim al-Thaqafī (62–98/681–716) early Muslim commander, conquered **Sind** for his kinsman **al-Ḥajjāj**, who later had him executed.

Muḥammad ibn al-Qāsim ibn ʿUbayd Allāh ibn Sulaymān ibn Wahb great-grandson of **Abū Ayyūb Sulaymān ibn Wahb**, the last of four generations to hold vizieral office, was briefly **vizier** to **al-Qāhir** in 321/933.

Muḥammad ibn Saʿd son of **Saʿd ibn Abī Waqqāṣ**; executed by **al-Ḥajjāj**.

Muḥammad ibn Saʿīd unidentified.

Muḥammad ibn Ṣāliḥ al-Naṭṭāḥ Basran traditionist.

Muḥammad ibn ʿUmārah al-Asadī cited by **al-Ṭabarī** in his *History*.

Muḥammad ibn Wāsiʿ (d. 127/745) Basran ascetic.

Muḥammad ibn Yaʿqūb ibn Isḥāq the Lame unidentified.

Muḥammad ibn Yazīd (d. after 101/720) **client** of the **Anṣār**, secretary to **ʿAbd al-Malik ibn Marwān**, was made governor of **North Africa.** He incurred the enmity of **Yazīd ibn ʿAbd al-Malik**, who replaced him with **Yazīd ibn Abī Muslim**; his later career is unknown.

Muḥammad ibn Yūnus al-Kudaymī (183–286/799–899) Baghdadi traditionist.

Muḥammad ibn al-Zubayr al-Tamīmī unidentified.

al-Muḥammadiyyah formerly al-Ītākhiyyah, a pleasure resort near **Samarra**, which the caliph **al-Mutawakkil** seized from the Turkish commander **Ītākh** and renamed after his own son.

al-Muḥassin ibn ʿAlī ibn Muḥammad ibn Abī l-Fahm al-Tanūkhī see **al-Tanūkhī, al-Muḥassin ibn ʿAlī.**

al-Muhtadī (r. 255–56/869–70) fourteenth **Abbasid** caliph.

Muʿīn al-Dawlah Abū l-Ḥusayn ʿImrān ibn Shāhīn (d. 369/979) Lord of the **Marshes of southern Iraq**, a bandit who claimed kinship with the venerable **Arab** tribe of Sulaym. Unable to put him down, the **Buyids** recognized him as governor.

Muʿizz al-Dawlah Abū l-Ḥusayn Aḥmad ibn Būyah, first **Buyid** ruler of **Iraq** (r. 334–56/945–67).

Mujāhid Mujāhid ibn Jabr (ca. 21–100/642–718), famous Meccan Qurʾan scholar.

Mujālid and Mujāshiʿ al-Sulamī (d. 36/656) sons of Masʿūd ibn Thaʿlabah al-Sulamī; **Companions** who died in the same battle.

Mujammiʿ ibn Yaḥyā unidentified.

al-Muktafī seventeenth **Abbasid** caliph (r. 289–95/902–8).

al-Mundhir ibn Ziyād al-Ṭāʾī Basran traditionist.

al-Muqtadir eighteenth **Abbasid** caliph (r. 295–320/908–32). Temporarily ousted by **ʿAbd Allāh ibn al-Muʿtazz** in 296/908, and then by his brother **al-Qāhir** in 317/929, he died opposing an armed uprising.

Mūsā ibn ʿAbd al-Malik Abū ʿImrān of Isfahan, state **scribe**, head of the office of **land tax** and holder of other offices under **al-Mutawakkil**; said to have died 245/859.

Mūsā ibn Ismāʿīl the Manure Seller (d. 223/838) Basran scholar.

Mūsā al-Kāẓim (128–83/744–99) seventh imam of the **Twelver Shiʿi**; buried in **Baghdad**.

al-Muʿtaḍid sixteenth **Abbasid** caliph (r. 279–89/892–902).

al-Muʿtamid fifteenth **Abbasid** caliph (r. 256–79/870–92) with his brother the regent **al-Muwaffaq**.

al-Muʿtaṣim eighth **Abbasid** caliph (r. 218–27/833–42).

al-Mutawakkil tenth **Abbasid** caliph (r. 232–47/847–61). Not the expected successor to his brother **al-Wāthiq**, he took revenge on those who had mistreated him during the latter's reign and that of **al-Muʿtaṣim**.

Muʿtazilism a rationalist school of theology, which emphasized God's absolute oneness (hence the Qur'an, although the Word of God, must be created, not coeternal with Him) and His justice, which means that humans are freely responsible for their own choices and fates. Nevertheless, He may assist them with grace, an idea that seems to underpin **al-Tanūkhī**'s conception of the deliverance that follows adversity. See *EQ*, "Muʿtazila" and *EI2*, "Luṭf."

al-Muthannā ibn ʿAbd al-Karīm unidentified.

al-Muwaffaq also called **al-Nāṣir** (d. 278/891), soldier; father of the future **al-Muʿtaḍid**, brother and regent of the fifteenth **Abbasid** caliph **al-Muʿtamid**, who was confined in **Samarra** while al-Muwaffaq ruled from **Baghdad**. He had his own **viziers**, of whom **Ismāʿīl ibn Bulbul** was the last.

al-Naḍr ibn Anas (d. after 101/714) son of **Anas ibn Mālik**, Basran.

al-Naḍr ibn Ismāʿīl al-Bajlī (d. 182/798) Kufan popular preacher (*qāṣṣ*), Baghdadi traditionist.

Nāfiʿ (d. 119/737) client of **Ibn ʿUmar**.

Nahr Tīrā a place near **Ahwaz** in **Khuzistan**.

Najāḥ ibn Salamah state **scribe** who accused **Mūsā ibn ʿAbd al-Malik** and **al-Ḥasan ibn Makhlad** of financial malfeasance; in revenge, the vizier

ʿUbayd Allāh ibn Yaḥyā ibn Khāqān had him tortured to death and his and his sons' estates confiscated. (There is a ten-year discrepancy between the dating of this event to 245/859 and the chronology of the narrative at §§73.1–6.)

Najrān in the century before Islam, agricultural and trading city of northern Yemen, a center of **Christian**ity.

Nasāʾ a city of **Khurasan.**

Naṣībīn modern Nusaybin, Nisibis in Antiquity, city of upper Mesopotamia.

al-Nāṣir see **al-Muwaffaq.**

Nāṣir al-Dawlah al-Ḥasan ibn Abī l-Hayjāʾ ibn Ḥamdān, **Ḥamdānid** ruler of **Mosul** (r. 317–56/929–67). After the caliph al-Muttaqī (r. 329–33/940–44) appointed him supreme commander (*amīr al-umarāʾ*) in 330/942, he briefly ruled in **Baghdad** and **Iraq.**

Naṣr ibn ʿAlī al-Jahḍamī of **Basra** (d. 250/864), Baghdadi traditionist.

Naṣr ibn al-Qāsim unidentified.

Nasr ibn Ziyād identity uncertain.

Nawf of Syria or Nawf al-Bikālī (d. ca. 90/714) stepson of the Jewish **convert** Kaʿb al-Aḥbār (d. ca. 32/652), the source of much Jewish lore in Qurʾanic exegesis. Damascene traditionist.

Nāzūk Abū Manṣūr (d. 317/929), appointed chief of **police** in **Baghdad** ca. 311/923. Brutal, a brave soldier, he played a leading role in politics until his death in a military coup.

North Africa **Umayyad** province corresponding to today's geographical North Africa.

notebook (kitāb/aṣl kitābih) one of various terms in use for the written notes that assisted the oral transmission of hadith. In some circumstances, written sources are routinely designated (see **reading, reading back for verification, authorization to transmit**); in others, the written nature of a source is concealed under an ostensibly oral **chain of transmitters.**

Nuʿaym ibn Muwarriʿ unidentified.

al-Nuʿmān ibn Bashīr al-Anṣārī (2–65/623–84) **Companion, poet** and orator, **judge** in Damascus, holder of governorships under **Muʿāwiyah.**

oath of allegiance (mubāyaʿah; bayʿah) an oral contract and vow formula, confirmed by a handclasp, whereby the new caliph was acknowledged and proclaimed by his supporters in the military or bureaucratic elite. See Marsham, *Rituals of Islamic Monarchy*, 297–98, 315.

outlaw someone declared a criminal who can be killed by any member of the public without the killer or their community incurring the normal legal penalty of blood money (literally by "making the criminal's blood non-avengeable," *ahdara damahu*, §71.1). It can also be declared lawful, or imperative, to kill a person who is considered a heretic or infidel (*tabarra'a*, §88.1).

paper; papyrus paper had become common in **Iraq** by the periods in which the stories in *Deliverance* are set. See Bloom, *Paper before Print*. Papyrus remained in use, however, as attested by surviving administrative documents (§82.6). The terminology of writing materials is not clear-cut. The word *ruqʿah* (pl. *riqāʿ*) is used of a slip of any writing material. See Gaček, *The Arabic Manuscript Tradition: A Glossary*, 57. At §76.3 it is applied to a **charm**, at §§79.1–2 and 80.5 to a deposition in a lawsuit (*qiṣṣah*), at §98.1 to a message found underneath a seat, and at §111.4 to **petitions**. The word *qirṭās* at §§73.13, 76.8, and 76.9 may refer to a sheet of papyrus, paper, or even parchment. See Gaček, *Arabic Manuscripts*, 186; *The Arabic Manuscript Tradition: A Glossary*, 114; Supplement, 61.

peasant (nabaṭī) an insulting name for descendants of the pre-conquest inhabitants of **Iraq**.

perfumed unguent (ghāliyah) and scent (ṭīb) both men and women used perfumes and scents, solid or liquid. They were expensive, hence **al-Ḥajjāj**'s gift of *ghāliyah* (§67.3) to **Ḥasan of Basra** is a mark of esteem.

perfumes (mashāmm) room perfumes that, together with **wine** and music, were held to have a physically and psychologically therapeutic effect. See Bray, "Bleeding Poetry."

petition (ruqʿah, pl. *riqāʿ)* petitions would be presented by an intermediary, generally in a bundle, to a bureaucrat above him in the hierarchy for signature (*tawqīʿ*). If the grandee signed them without reading them, it was a mark of his regard for the intermediary.

physician like the father or forebear of **ʿAlī ibn Naṣr ibn ʿAlī the Physician** (§§50.1, 51.1), many of the leading **Abbasid** physicians were **Christians**. They practiced Galenic, humoral medicine.

physiognomy (firāsah; qiyāfah) the art of reading hidden truths from physical signs or appearances (§§68.4, 68.8) was reputed to be one of the skills native to **Arabs**. See Fahd, *La divination*, 370–87 and Müller, *Der Beduine und die Regenwolke*.

poets; poetry most professional poets were freelancers, but even when attached to a court or a household, they composed opportunistically and extemporized in order to attract attention and win rewards (§§101.2, 102.3). As amateur poets, **al-Tanūkhī** (§59.3) and various state **scribes** demonstrate by extemporizing that they are men of culture and sensibility (§§61, 66.1, 106.1, 111.3–4); and poetry, of one's own or in quotation, is a natural vent for strong feelings (§§19.1, 107.1–2, 108.1, 110.1, 110.4, 40, 57). As poetry was held to be of supernatural inspiration, it is not surprising that **dream** apparitions, **disembodied voices**, and other unseen messengers may express themselves in verse (§§99, 19.1–3, 97.1, 98.1).

police (shurṭah); police chief (ṣāḥib al-shurṭah) the police consisted of separate forces that operated in individual cities. Police chiefs were appointed by the governor of a city or province and could carry out not only Shariah physical punishments after due legal process (see **judge**) but summary chastisement and execution. See Tyan, *Histoire*, 585–88, 598–99.

popular preacher (qāṣṣ) see **tales of the prophets.**

postmaster and intelligencer (ṣāḥib al-barīd) the **Abbasid** government's messenger service and spy network shared the same mounted couriers. See *EI3*, "Barīd." Overseeing a postal hub was a lucrative position: the **poet Abū Tammām** was granted the postmastership of **Mosul** (see al-Ṣūlī, *The Life and Times of Abū Tammām*, xiv), so **ʿAlī ibn Yazīd**'s postmastership of **Māsabadhān** (§109.1) shows that his story ended happily.

prayer the five daily prayers (*ṣalāt*) and other prayers, such as personal prayers of supplication (*duʿāʾ*), must be performed in a state of **ritual purity** and after forming the **intention** (*niyyah*) of prayer. They consist of several sequences of bowing, utterances, and prostration (*rakʿah*s).

prayers, answered some individuals were believed to be *mustajāb al-daʿwah*, to have the gift of having their prayers answered, and were asked to pray for others (§74.1). Others were believed to be granted the gift on particular occasions (§§76.8, 95.2).

prison little is known about medieval Islamic prisons. See *EI2*, "Sidjn." Most of our knowledge comes from narratives like those in *Deliverance*. **Al-Ḥajjāj**'s dungeon, the **Black Hole**, was a public prison; people were also imprisoned in their custodians' houses, including their privies (§73.5). Sometimes they were given luxurious accommodation and allowed visitors (§§73.15, 78.1–4).

psalms (al-zabūr) at §§92.3 and 93.2, God is invoked as "He Who sent down the Psalms," that is, the scripture given to David (Q Nisāʾ 4:163, Isrāʾ 17:54). See *EI2*, "Zabūr."

pulpit (minbar) the Prophet's pulpit (§13.3) is said to have consisted of two wooden steps and a seat. As well as a platform for preaching, the *minbar* was a symbol of authority and a place from which caliphal rulings were read out to the public (§68.4).

al-Qāhir (d. 339/950) nineteenth **Abbasid** caliph. Figurehead in an abortive palace coup against his brother **al-Muqtadir** in 317/929, given the **oath of allegiance** after his death in 320/932. He was overthrown, imprisoned, and blinded in 322/934.

al-Qāsim ibn ʿAbd al-Raḥmān (d. 110/728) a grandson of **ʿAbd Allāh ibn Masʿūd; judge** of **Mecca.**

al-Qāsim ibn Hāshim (d. 259/873) Baghdadi broker and traditionist.

al-Qāsim ibn Ismāʿīl Abū l-Mundhir al-Sawramī unidentified.

Qatādah (ca. 60–117/680–735) Qatādah ibn Diʿāmah, blind Basran traditionist and exegete, a pupil of **Ḥasan of Basra.**

Qaṭarī ibn al-Fujāʾah (d. ca. 78/698) tribal chief; **Kharijite poet** and caliph.

Qazʿah ibn Suwayd Basran traditionist.

Qudāmah unidentified.

Qur'an, unambiguous (muḥkam) passages the Qur'an states that it consists of unambiguous and ambiguous (*mutashābih*) passages (Q Āl ʿImrān 3:7). Identifying them was controversial; theological opinions could differ diametrically as to which is which. See *EQ*, "Ambiguous."

Qur'an, used in prognostication see **fortune-telling.**

"Qur'an reader" (qāriʾ) probably a misnomer. The word is applied to **Kharijites** and may derive from early Muslim settlers in the villages (*qurā*) of Iraq. See *EI2*, "Ḳurrāʾ."

Ramadan the ninth month, when Muslims fast between sunrise and sunset.

Rāmhurmuz city and district of **Khuzistan**, southeast of **Ahwaz.**

Ramlah town of Palestine, north of **Jerusalem** on the coastal plain.

Raqqah an important city on the northern **Euphrates**, once adopted by **Hārūn al-Rashīd** as his capital.

Rawḥ ibn al-Ḥārith ibn Ḥabash of Ṣanʿāʾ unidentified.

Rawḥ ibn ʿUbādah (d. ca. 205/820) Basran traditionist.

Rayy city near the site of modern Tehran.

reading (wajada) to "find" something that has been written down, through independent reading, as opposed to being taught it by word of mouth. This method of learning precludes the possibility of **reading back for verification.**

reading back for verification (qirāʾah ʿalā) when a teacher has dictated a text, the student reads back to him or her what he or she has written down for correction or confirmation.

rice (aruzz) already cultivated in parts of the Middle East in late antiquity, by **Abbasid** times it was an established cash crop in lower **Iraq** and **Khuzistan** and was a staple of the diet of the poor in the form of rice bread, as well as an ingredient in elite cuisine. **Al-Tanūkhī**'s *Deliverance* and *Table Talk* are among the sources for its economic role. See Canard, "Le riz," 115, 120–25, and *EI2*, "al-Ruzz."

ritual ablution (wuḍūʾ, taṭahhur) the ritual cleansing required before prayer.

ritual purity (ṭahārah) the avoidance of unclean matter and activities and the use of ablution if necessary.

robe of honor (khilʿah) a valuable garment bestowed as a mark of favor, usually in public in the **audience chamber.** Rulers and grandees had a stock of them ready for bestowal, often embroidered in ***ṭirāz*** with their name and titles. See Serjeant, *Islamic Textiles*, 16–27.

Sābūr eunuch of the caliph **al-Qāhir**, employed by him to arrest officers of state.

Saʿd ibn Abī Waqqāṣ (d. ca. 50/670) **Companion**, commander in the conquest of Iraq.

Saʿd ibn Saʿīd (d. 41/661) Medinan traditionist.

Ṣaʿdah city of northern Yemen, capital of the **Zaydī imams** of Yemen.

Saʿdawayh (d. 225/840) Saʿīd ibn Sulaymān al-Ḍabbī of **Wāsiṭ**, Baghdadi cloth merchant and traditionist.

Ṣafwān ibn ʿAmr of **Ḥimṣ** (d. ca. 155/772), traditionist.

sage (ḥakīm, pl. *ḥukamāʾ)* since wisdom (*ḥikmah*) was held to be universal, many wise sayings are conventionally attributed to "a sage" rather than a named source, without distinction between people of antiquity and more recent periods. See **Ancients.**

Sahl ibn Muḥammad Abū Ḥātim al-Sijistānī (d. 255/869), from the village of **Sijistān** near **Basra**, Basran philologist.

Sahl al-Tustarī see **Abū Muḥammad Sahl ibn ʿAbd Allāh of Tustar.**

Sahl ibn Saʿd al-Sāʿidī (d. 91/710) the last **Companion** to die in **Medina.**

Saʿīd ibn ʿAbd al-ʿAzīz al-Tanūkhī of Damascus (d. 228/843), jurist.

Saʿīd ibn Abī Ayyūb perhaps Saʿīd ibn Miqlāṣ (100–61/718–77), Egyptian traditionist.

Saʿīd ibn Abī ʿUrūbah Saʿīd ibn Mihrān (d. 156/773), Basran traditionist.

Saʿīd ibn ʿĀmir of Ḍabuʿ (d. 188/804) Basran traditionist.

Saʿīd ibn ʿAnbasah unidentified.

Saʿīd ibn Ḥumayd (d. after 257/871 or 260/874) state **scribe**, famous as a love **poet** and above all as a prose stylist. Fragments of his writings have been edited.

Saʿīd ibn Manṣūr of Balkh (d. 227/842) traditionist.

al-Sakan ibn Saʿīd unidentified.

Ṣāliḥ ibn ʿAbd Allāh al-Muzanī governor of **Medina** under the caliph **al-Walīd ibn ʿAbd al-Malik**, unidentified.

Ṣāliḥ ibn Ḥassān of **Medina** and **Basra** or **Baghdad.** Said to have lived into the reign of al-Mahdī (r. 158–69/775–85) and to have damaged his reputation as a traditionist by consorting with **singing women.**

Ṣāliḥ ibn Mismār of **Marw** (d. 246/860), traditionist.

Ṣāliḥ ibn Waṣīf (d. 256/870) **Turk** commander, played a prominent part in the bloody politics of **Samarra** and was murdered by a rival.

Sālim ibn ʿAbd Allāh ibn ʿUmar (d. 106/725) son of **Ibn ʿUmar**; Medinan scholar.

Samarqand a city of Soghdia in central Asia.

Samarra city on the east bank of the **Tigris**, founded by **al-Muʿtaṣim** in 221/836 to house his troops. It remained the caliphal capital until 279/892, when **al-Muʿtaḍid** reestablished **Baghdad** as the capital.

Ṣanʿāʾ the chief city of Yemen from ancient times.

Sarakhs city of northern **Khurasan.**

al-Sayārī **poet**, unidentified.

seal see **signet ring.**

sergeant (ʿarīf) a petty officer in the army or **police.** At §88.1 one of his functions is the denunciation of heresy. See *EI3*, "ʿArīf."

Seth in the Qurʾan, Seth is a prophet. See Wheeler, *Prophets in the Quran*, 43–44.

seven earths see **seven heavens.**

seven heavens God is invoked as the Lord of the Qur'anic seven heavens and «Lord of the mighty throne» (Q Tawbah 9:129) at §§68.3, 68.10, 83.3, and as Lord of the seven heavens, seven earths, and the «mighty throne» at §30. The Qur'an describes the creation of the seven heavens (Q Baqarah 2:29, Fuṣṣilat 41:11–12) and refers to «as many» earths (Q Ṭalāq 65:12). See *EQ*, "Heaven and Sky." There were various ways of plotting the cosmological relationship of the seven heavens and earths and the celestial ocean beneath the Throne of God, as well as Hellenized versions of Qur'anic cosmology and alternative cosmologies. See *EI2*, "Samāʾ."

al-Shaʿbī (ca. 40–103/660–721) ʿĀmir ibn Sharaḥīl al-Ḥimyarī, Kufan jurist and historian involved in anti-**Umayyad** movements.

Shaqshā a town in the **Marshes of southern Iraq**, large enough to have a Friday Mosque (§59.2) but not noted by the geographers.

Sharīk Sharīk ibn ʿAbd Allāh ibn Abī Sharīk (95–177/713–94), Kufan judge born in **Bukhara.**

Shaybah ibn Rabīʿah (d. 2/624) kinsman and enemy of the Prophet, killed at the **Battle of Badr.**

Shiʿi a label applied to those who recognize only **ʿAlī ibn Abī Ṭālib** as the true heir of the Prophet. They are the "party" (*shīʿah*) of ʿAlī. See **Alids; Twelver Shiʿism; Zaydī imams of Yemen.**

Shiraz capital of the province of **Fars.**

shrine of Mūsā al-Kāẓim place of pilgrimage in the **Graveyard of Quraysh** in **Baghdad.**

Shuʿayb ibn Abī Ḥamzah of **Ḥimṣ** (d. 163/780), traditionist.

Shuʿayb ibn Ṣafwān Kufan state **scribe** and traditionist.

Shuʿbah Shuʿbah ibn al-Ḥajjāj (d. ca. 160/776), Basran ascetic and traditionist.

Shurayḥ Shurayḥ ibn al-Ḥārith (d. 78/697), celebrated Kufan **judge.**

signet ring (khātam) signet rings were often engraved with a phrase of special significance to the wearer, as at §72. Some were made in one piece; others consisted of a bezel set with a gem, as at §§102.2–3. See al-Washshāʾ, *Le Livre de brocart*, 168, 210–18. At §81.3, the wife's signet ring is used as a seal and mark of ownership.

Sijistan modern Sistan, region of eastern Iran.

Sijistān a village near **Basra.**

Simeon unidentified.

Sind the lower part of the Indus valley, now in Pakistan, invaded by the Muslims in 93/711.

singing woman (mughanniyah) heard but not seen at §§78.3–4, the female slave musician was a major cultural figure in elite **Abbasid** circles as entertainer, woman of fashion, and object of desire. See al-Jāḥiẓ, *The Epistle on Singing Girls*; al-Washshā', *Le Livre de brocart*, 135–48; and Ibn al-Sāʿī, *Consorts of the Caliphs.*

slave woman (jāriyah) as well as meaning a girl or young woman, *jāriyah* can mean a female domestic, but applied to a concubine (*ḥaẓiyyah*, §81.1) in a rich household, it implies a woman trained in the arts of pleasing and entertaining. See Ibn al-Sāʿī, *Consorts of the Caliphs.*

sleeve (kumm) sleeves were put to the same use as modern pockets.

state scribe (kātib, pl. *kuttāb)* an administrator of any rank. **Abbasid** bureaucrats were salaried professionals. Their training began young, as junior clerks under an experienced senior (§17.2), and took place in-house, with no examination system. The highest position in the bureaucracy was that of **vizier**. The profession of *kātib* often ran in families, and patronage was essential to advancement. See van Berkel, *Crisis and Continuity*, 93–109. As well as many of his informants, a number of **al-Tanūkhī**'s relatives were state scribes. See Bray, "Place and Self-Image."

stationer–copyist (warrāq) the same term is used of an individual working for a patron or author, an employee in a bookshop, or the owner of a book and stationery shop. With the advent of cheap **paper**, the book trade in Baghdad expanded, and stationer–copyists were the equivalent of publishers, copying books to order or on spec. See Toorawa, *Ibn Abī Ṭāhir Ṭayfūr*, 56–59.

steward (wakīl) person who manages an estate (§80.2) or household (§109.4) for another.

stole of office the *ṭaylasān*, worn over the shoulders or pulled over the head, was part of the costume of **judges** and jurists and is so described in Dozy, *Noms*, 279, and Mez, *Renaissance*, 83, 171, 226, but at §109.1 it is all that remains of the wardrobe of a disgraced secretary.

Successors (Tābiʿūn) in the terminology of hadith transmission, the next generation or generations after the **Companions**.

Sufyān see **Sufyān ibn ʿUyaynah.**

Sufyān ibn Ibrāhīm Kufan traditionist.

Sufyān ibn Saʿīd al-Thawrī (97–161/716–78) Kufan jurist; anti-**Abbasid**, he fled to Arabia to avoid being made a **judge** by **al-Manṣūr**.

Sufyān ibn ʿUyaynah of **Kufa** (d. 196/811), Meccan traditionist.

Sulaymān ibn ʿAbd al-Malik (r. 96–99/715–17) seventh **Umayyad** caliph.

Sulaymān ibn Salamah of **Ḥimṣ**, traditionist.

Sulaymān ibn Yaḥyā ibn Muʿādh secretary to **ʿAbd Allāh ibn Ṭāhir**, under whom he rose to high office.

al-Ṣūlī see **Abū Bakr Muḥammad ibn Yaḥyā al-Ṣūlī.**

al-Ṣūlī see **Abū Isḥāq Ibrāhīm ibn al-ʿAbbās ibn Muḥammad ibn Ṣūl.**

Sūq al-Ahwāz see **Ahwaz.**

Syria the biblical land of Syria; the **Umayyad** and **Abbasid** province. Syria was the stronghold of **Umayyad** loyalism and Syrian troops were greatly feared elsewhere in the **Umayyad** empire.

al-Ṭabarī Muḥammad ibn Jarīr (ca. 224–314/839–923), best known for his monumental *History* and Qur'an commentary.

Ṭāhir ibn al-Ḥusayn (159–207/776–822) founder of the **Ṭāhirid** dynasty of governors of **Baghdad** and **Khurasan.** He was **al-Ma'mūn**'s general in his war with **al-Amīn**, whom he defeated and had killed (198/813), becoming chief of **police** of Baghdad and then governor of Khurasan.

Ṭāhir son of Yaḥyā son of al-Ḥasan son of Jaʿfar son of ʿAbd Allāh son of al-Ḥusayn son of ʿAlī ibn Abī Ṭālib **Alid.**

Ṭāhirids a dynasty of **police** chiefs and governors of **Baghdad** and **Khurasan** who owed the power they held in the **Abbasid** state for most of the third/ninth century to the part played by **Ṭāhir ibn al-Ḥusayn** (§§101.1–2) in defeating **al-Ma'mūn**'s brother **al-Amīn**, and to the military and administrative skills of his son **ʿAbd Allāh ibn Ṭāhir** (§45.2). Immensely wealthy, some Ṭāhirids were also prominent patrons of literature.

Taif town southeast of **Mecca.**

tales of the prophets (qiṣaṣ al-anbiyā') elaborations on Qur'anic accounts of the prophets, they develop themes such as that of **Joseph's shirt**, and introduce new details, such as the maggots that afflicted Job (§7.1) and the locusts of gold that God showered on him (§7.2). They were taken up by **popular preachers** (*quṣṣāṣ*, sing. *qāṣṣ*), but were also extensively quoted by learned exegetes. For example, the *Lives of the Prophets* of al-Thaʿlabī (d. 427/1035) (see 244n287 and 245n289) is the work of a scholar.

Ṭāliqān a city of **Khurasan.**

al-Tanūkhī, Judge Abū l-Qāsim ʿAlī ibn Muḥammad ibn Abī l-Fahm (also "my father"; in full, his genealogy goes back a further twenty-five generations to the mythical **Arab** tribal ancestor Quḍāʿah) (278–342/892–953); born in **Antioch**, died in **Basra**, traditionist, man of letters, **poet**, courtier, **judge**, and local politican. Al-Tanūkhī appears to have been his only child.

al-Tanūkhī, Judge Abū ʿAlī al-Muḥassin, son of the judge Abū l-Qāsim ʿAlī ibn Muḥammad ibn Abī l-Fahm (also "the author," "the author of this book") (327–84/939–94) born **Basra**, died **Baghdad**; his only child appears to have been ʿAlī ibn Abī ʿAlī. See **al-Tanūkhī, ʿAlī.**

al-Tanūkhī, Judge ʿAlī son of Abū ʿAlī al-Muḥassin Abū l-Qāsim, generally known as ʿAlī ibn Abī ʿAlī (365–447/976–1055), born **Basra**, died **Baghdad**, **judge**, man of letters and historian, major contributor to all literary and biographical records of the period. He had one son, who was the last of the family.

Ṭāwūs (33–106/653–724) Ṭāwūs ibn Kaysān al-Khawlānī; Yemeni traditionist renowned for shunning those in power.

tax (or revenue) farming in order to have cash in hand, the **Abbasid** government sold individuals a contract (*ḍamān*) whereby they guaranteed to pay a fixed sum against the estimated value of a district's taxable yield. See Bowen, *The Life and Times of ʿAlí ibn ʿĪsà*, 16, 123. Some contracts were for enormous sums. The relatively trivial deficit for which **Abū l-Ḥasan ibn Abī l-Layth** is imprisoned at §14.4 suggests that they could also be small scale. Under the **Buyids**, **Bukhtakīn the Turk** combined a governorship with tax farming (§80.6).

Thābit or Thābit al-Banānī Thābit ibn Aslam (d. 127/745), Basran traditionist.

Themistius Greek philosopher, fourth century AD. Well known in **Baghdad** as a commentator on Aristotle, he was translated by Ḥunayn ibn Isḥāq (194–260/809–73) and Mattā ibn Yūnus (d. 328/940).

throne (dast) this Persian loan word clearly refers to a seat of honor at §76.5. It was probably some sort of cushion, like most seating at this period (§98.1). See Sadan, *Mobilier*, 107.

Throne of God (ʿarsh) God is invoked as «the Lord of the mighty throne» (Q Tawbah 9:129) at §§30, 31.4, 31.9, 32, 34.2, 63.2, 68.3, 68.7, 68.10, and 83.3 (and as "Lord of the throne" at §104.2). The throne of God is also mentioned as the place to which Jonah's supplication rose and was intercepted by the **angels** (§13.8), "underneath" which the human world exists (§92.2), and in a version of the Lord's Prayer beginning "Our Lord, Whose throne is in heaven" (§29.1). In the Qur'an, the angels are described as circling the throne of God (Q Zumar 39:75), Who is «throned above the waters» (Q Hūd 11:6). The Qur'anic word for the throne of God is *'arsh* except in the Throne Verse (Q Baqarah 2:255, see §76.2), where it is called *kursī* and is described as extending across the heavens and the earth. There were both literalist and figurative interpretations of where the throne has its being and what the Qur'an means by throne. See *EQ*, "Throne of God" and *EI2*, "Samā'."

Tigris river of **Iraq**, the main waterway of **Baghdad**, **Samarra**, and **Basra**.

ṭirāz the word *rasm*, used of the tattered embroidered or figured remains of the narrator's **Dabīqī** kerchief at §109.2, sometimes refers to *ṭirāz*, an inscription bearing the name of the ruler. See **robe of honor**.

Torah (al-Tawrāh) at §§92.3 and 93.2, God is invoked as "He Who sent down the Torah," that is, the scripture of the Jews.

Turks (Atrāk) for nearly thirty years from 833 to 861, **Samarra**, north of **Baghdad**, was the **Abbasid** caliphs' capital, a mixture of pleasure palaces and military cantonments in which the Turkic slave soldiers (*ghilmān*), also known simply as "the **Turks**," became kingmakers. At §73.3, they oppose **al-Mutawakkil**. At §65.6, they throw their weight behind **al-Mu'taḍid**.

Ṭūs a district of **Khurasan**.

Tustar the second main city of **Khuzistan**.

tutor (mu'addib) usually a private instructor in a wealthy family.

Twelver Shi'ism (ithnā' 'ashariyyah; madhhab al-imāmiyyah) the Twelvers or imamis believe in a line of descendants of the Prophet's daughter **Fāṭimah** and her husband and cousin **'Alī ibn Abī Ṭālib**, the Prophet's heir and the true Commander of the Faithful (*amīr al-mu'minīn*), that ends with the disappearance (occultation) of the twelfth imam, Muḥammad al-Mahdī, in around 260/873–74.

'Ubayd ibn Muḥammad al-Muḥāribī, Kufan traditionist.

'Ubayd Allāh ibn 'Abd Allāh ibn Ṭāhir (223–300/838–913) hereditary chief of **police** and governor of **Baghdad** in succession to **'Abd Allāh ibn Ṭāhir**, he was also a **poet**, musician, and patron.

'Ubayd Allāh ibn Mūsā (d. 213/828) Kufan traditionist.

'Ubayd Allāh ibn Sulaymān ibn Wahb (d. 288/901) son of **Abū Ayyūb Sulaymān ibn Wahb**, he was disgraced with him in 272/885 but became **vizier** in 278/891, dying in office.

'Ubayd Allāh ibn 'Umar (d. 37/657) a son of **'Umar ibn al-Khaṭṭāb**, brother of **Ibn 'Umar.**

'Ubayd Allāh ibn Yaḥyā ibn Khāqān (209–63/824–77) **vizier** for some ten years ca. 237–47/851–61 under **al-Mutawakkil**, and again for seven years under **al-Mu'tamid**, he died of an accidental blow received while riding in the ***maydān*** of **Baghdad.**

'Ubayd Allāh ibn Ziyād unidentified.

'Ukbarā town on the **Tigris** between **Baghdad** and **Samarra.**

'Umar ibn 'Abd al-'Azīz 'Umar II, eighth **Umayyad** caliph (r. 99–101/717–20), renowned for his piety and righteousness.

'Umar ibn Ḥamzah al-'Umarī a grandson of **Ibn 'Umar.**

'Umar ibn al-Khaṭṭāb second caliph (r. 13–23/634–44), known for his piety and austerity; organizer of the Muslim wars of conquest.

'Umar ibn Shabbah (173–262/789–878) influential historian, his works survive in quotation.

Umayyads descended from a collateral branch of the Prophet's tribe of **Quraysh**, they ruled the Islamic empire from their bases in **Syria** from 41/661 to 132/749.

Umayyah ibn Abī l-Ṣalt (d. ca. 9/631) pre-Islamic **poet** believed to have had foreknowledge of Islam.

Umayyah ibn Khālid probably two individuals (§§21.1, 105.9), both unidentified.

Umm Salamah (d. ca. 59/679) Hind bint Abī Umayyah, she married the Prophet **Muḥammad** in 4/626.

'Uqbah ibn Abī Mu'ayṭ (d. 2/624) Meccan, enemy of the Prophet; executed after the **Battle of Badr.**

al-Urdunn Transjordan, a province of **Umayyad** and **Abbasid Syria.**

'Urwah (22–93/643–712) 'Urwah ibn al-Zubayr ibn al-'Awwām, brother of **Ibn al-Zubayr**; Medinan jurist.

Usāmah ibn Zayd (d. in the reign of **al-Manṣūr**) son of **Zayd ibn Aslam**, brother of **'Abd Allāh ibn Zayd ibn Aslam**; Medinan traditionist.

'Utbah ibn Rabī'ah (d. 2/624) kinsman and enemy of the Prophet, killed fighting the Muslims at the **Battle of Badr.**

ʿUthmān ibn Ḥayyān al-Murrī name uncertain; an **Umayyad** governor of **Medina.**

ʿUthmān ibn Sulaymān Ibn Abī Khaythamah al-ʿAdawī, unidentified.

visiting of shrines (ziyārah) visiting the tombs of one's own dead, or those of holy people, was a widespread custom to which people attached different beliefs, as illustrated in the story **al-Tanūkhī** tells against himself at §§80.3–5.

vizier the chief minister of state under the **Abbasids**. See Sourdel, *Vizirat*, and van Berkel, *Crisis and Continuity*, 65–86. The function is attributed by **Abbasid** writers to other civilizations (see §§97.1–2), especially the Sasanians, **Buzurjmihr ibn al-Bakhtakān** being the perfect Sasanian vizier (§§49.1, 49.2, 50.7). "Books of Viziers" were an **Abbasid** genre that interpreted history from the viewpoint of viziers and state **scribes. Al-Tanūkhī**'s quotations from the Books of Viziers of **Abū Bakr Muḥammad ibn Yaḥyā al-Ṣūlī** and **Muḥammad ibn ʿAbdūs al-Jahshiyārī**, and the stories he quotes from personal informants, make him a major source for modern historians of the Abbasid state.

Wadāʿah al-Sahmī unidentified.

Waḍḍāḥ ibn Khaythamah **chamberlain** of **ʿUmar ibn ʿAbd al-ʿAzīz**, whose dying wish to him was that he empty the prisons.

wajada see **reading.**

Wakīʿ, Judge Muḥammad ibn Khalaf (d. 306/918), **judge** of **Ahwaz** and historian.

al-Wakīʿī Aḥmad ibn Jaʿfar (d. 215/830), called al-Wakīʿī from his association with the Kufan traditionist Wakīʿ ibn al-Jarrāḥ (d. 197/812); blind Baghdadi traditionist.

al-Walīd ibn ʿAbd al-Malik ibn Marwān sixth **Umayyad** caliph (r. 86–96/705–15).

al-Walīd ibn Muslim (d. 195/811) Basran traditionist.

Wāsiṭ city of lower **Iraq**, halfway between **Basra** and **Baghdad**, founded by **al-Ḥajjāj** as the seat of **Umayyad** government in Iraq.

al-Wāthiq ninth **Abbasid** caliph, son of **al-Muʿtaṣim** (r. 227–32/842–47).

wine and drinking at §78.3, date wine (*nabīdh*) is debatably licit, whereas grape wine is not, but the word can also be used euphemistically of grape wine. "Drinking" (*shurb*) always implies alcohol. Wine drinking, accompanied by food, was an important feature of social life that often went with listening to music, as at §§78.2–3. The morning drink (*ṣubūḥ*) with which Prince ʿ**Abbās** begins his day at §109.4 is nothing unusual in elite circles.

woolen garments (ṣūf) hot, scratchy, and smelly, garments of coarse wool were used as a form of punishment or torture (§§49.1, 49.3, 73.5).

Yaḥyā ibn ʿAbd al-Malik Kufan traditionist.

Yaḥyā ibn Ayyūb (157–234/774–848) known as al-Maqābirī from his habit of lingering in graveyards (*maqābir*) as a spiritual exercise, Baghdadi traditionist.

Yaḥyā son of al-Ḥasan son of Jaʿfar son of ʿAbd Allāh son of al-Ḥusayn son of ʿAlī ibn Abī Ṭālib **Alid.**

Yaḥyā ibn Khālid the Blue-Eyed of **Ahwaz** (dates unknown), grandfather of **ʿAbd Allāh ibn Muḥammad ibn Yaḥyā of Ahwaz**, state **scribe**, maternal forebear of **al-Tanūkhī.**

Yaḥyā ibn Khālid al-Barmakī (115 or 119–190/733 or 737–805) foster father and **tutor** of **Hārūn al-Rashīd**, who addressed him as "father," later his **vizier**; his sons occupied all the main offices of state until the family's downfall in 187/803. He died in prison in **Raqqah.**

Yaḥyā ibn Sulaym of **Wāsiṭ**, traditionist.

Yaʿqūb ibn ʿAbd al-Raḥmān (d. 331/943) Baghdadi plasterer and traditionist.

Yaʿqūb ibn Isḥāq ibn al-Buhlūl al-Tanūkhī Yaʿqūb ibn Isḥāq ibn al-Buhlūl ibn Ḥassān ibn Sinān, of **al-Anbār** (187–251/803–65), a maternal great-uncle of **al-Tanūkhī**, traditionist and devout recluse.

Yaʿqūb ibn Isḥāq ibn Ziyād (d. 271/884) Basran traditionist, **judge** of **Naṣībīn.**

Yaʿqūb ibn Sufyān of Fasā (d. 277/890) an ascetic and leading religious scholar who lived in **Basra.**

Yāqūt (d. 324/936) Abū l-Muẓaffar, high-ranking Turkic soldier in **al-Muqtadir**'s army. He held a number of court, fiscal, and military positions.

Yazīd ibn ʿAbd al-Malik Yazīd II, ninth **Umayyad** caliph (r. 101–5/720–24).

Yazīd ibn Abī Muslim Yazīd ibn Dīnār al-Thaqafī (d. 102/720), **al-Ḥajjāj**'s **scribe** and foster brother, later governor of **North Africa**, notorious for his cruelty, murdered by his **Berber** bodyguard.

Yazīd al-Ḍabbī unidentified.

Yazīd ibn Hārūn of **Wāsiṭ** (118–206/736–821). Blind in old age, when his memory for traditions weakened, he would make his maid check them in his **notebook.**

Yazīd ibn Muḥammad al-Muhallabī **poet, court companion** of **al-Mutawakkil**, al-Muntaṣir (r. 247–48/861–62), and al-Muʿtazz (r. 252–55/866–69).

Yazīd al-Raqqāshī (d. before 120/738) Basran **popular preacher** (*qāṣṣ*).

Yūnus ibn ʿAbd al-Aʿlā (170–264/787–877) Egyptian traditionist.

Yūnus ibn Maysarah (d. 132/749) Damascene ascetic.

Yūsuf, Judge Yūsuf ibn Yaʿqūb ibn Ismāʿīl (208–297/823–910), **judge** in **Basra**, then in **Baghdad**; succeeded by his son Abū ʿUmar Muḥammad, father of Judge **Abū l-Ḥusayn ʿUmar**, author of the *Book of Deliverance following Adversity*.

Yūsuf ibn Mūsā (d. 253/867) Kufan **cotton** merchant with a business in **Rayy** and Baghdadi traditionist.

Zāfir ibn Sulaymān importer of textiles from his native **Rayy** to **Baghdad**; traditionist.

Zamzam the sacred spring of **Mecca**, dug by an **angel** for Hagar and Ishmael.

Zayd ibn Akhzam al-Ṭāʾī (d. 257/871) Basran traditionist.

Zayd ibn Aslam (d. 136/753) Medinan jurist and exegete, companion of **ʿUmar ibn ʿAbd al-ʿAzīz.**

Zaydi imams of Yemen the Zaydīs split from **Twelver Shiʿism** by recognizing **Muḥammad al-Bāqir**'s half-brother Zayd (d. 122/740) as fifth imam in his place. Al-Hādī ilā l-Ḥaqq Yaḥyā founded a Zaydī dynasty in Yemen in 284/897. **Al-Tanūkhī** does not say where he met his grandson **Abū l-Ḥamd Dāwūd**, who taught him two "family" prayers. (§§32, 33). See *EI2*, "Zaydiyya" and *EI3*, "ʿAlids."

Ziyād ibn Abīhi (ca. 1–53/622–73) governor of **Iraq** and the eastern provinces under **Muʿāwiyah**, feared for his severe treatment of disobedience.

al-Zubayr ibn Bakkār (172–256/788–870) Medinan **judge** and man of letters, he also visted **Baghdad** and **Samarra** and composed for the regent **al-Muwaffaq** a collection of reports about historical celebrities, *al-Akhbār al-Muwaffaqiyyāt*, which is partly extant.

Zuhrah Ibn ʿAmr al-Taymī identity uncertain.

al-Zuhrī (d. 124/722) Abū Bakr Muḥammad ibn Muslim, a founder of the science of tradition.

Zurārah ibn Awfā (d. 93/712) Basran **judge**.

Bibliography

Abbott, Nabia. "Arabic Papyri of the Reign of Ǧaʿfar al-Mutwakkil ʿAlā-llāh (A.H. 232–47/ A.D. 847–61." *Zeitschrift der Deutschen Morgenländsichen Gesellschaft* 92 (1938): 88–135.

Abū l-Faraj al-Iṣfahānī (attrib.). *The Book of Strangers: Medieval Arabic Graffiti on the Theme of Nostalgia.* Translated by Patricia Crone and Shmuel Moreh. Princeton: Markus Wiener, 2000.

Ali, Samer. *Arabic Literary Salons in the Islamic Middle Ages: Poetry, Performance and the Presentation of the Past.* Notre Dame, IN: University of Notre Dame Press, 2010.

Ashtor, E. "Ḳutn (1)." In *EI2*.

Ashtor, E. and Burton-Page, J. "Makāyil." In *EI2*.

Baer, E. "Dawāt." In *EI2*.

Beaumont, Daniel. "In the Second Degree: Fictional Technique in at-Tanūkhī's *Al-Faraj baʿd ash-shidda*." *Arabic and Middle Eastern Literatures* 1 (1998): 125–39.

Behzadi, Lale. "Standardizing Emotions: Aspects of Classification and Arrangement in Tales with a Good Ending." *Asiatische Studien–Etudes Asiatiques* 71 (2017): 811–31.

Bernheimer, Teresa. *The ʿAlids: The First Family of Islam 750–1200*. Edinburgh: Edinburgh University Press, 2013.

Bloom, Jonathan. *Paper before Print: The History and Impact of Paper in the Islamic World.* New Haven: Yale University Press, 2001.

Bosworth, C. E. "Wahb, Banū." In *EI2*.

Bowen, Harold. *The Life and Times of ʿAlí ibn ʿÍsà , "the Good Vizier."* Cambridge: Cambridge University Press, 1928.

Böwering, G. "Sahl al-Tustarī." In *EI2*.

Bray, Julia. "Third and Fourth Century Bleeding Poetry." *Arabic and Middle Eastern Literatures* 2 (1999): 75–92.

———. "Ibn al-Muʿtazz and Politics: The Question of the *Fuṣūl Qiṣār*." *Oriens* 38 (2010): 107–43.

[Ashtiany] Bray, Julia. "*Isnād*s and Models of Heroes: Abū Zubayd al-Ṭāʾī, Tanūkhī's Sundered Lovers and Abū l-ʿAnbas al-Ṣaymarī," *Arabic and Middle Eastern Literatures* 1 (1998): 7–30.

Bray, Julia. "Men, Women and Slaves in Abbasid Society." In *Gender in the Early Medieval World: East and West, 300–900*, edited by Leslie Brubaker and Julia M. H. Smith, 121–46. Cambridge: Cambridge University Press, 2004.

———. "Place and Self-Image: The Buhlūlids and Tanūhids and Their Family Traditions." *Quaderni di Studi Arabi* n.s. 3 (2008): 39–66.

———. "Practical Mu'tazilism: The Case of al-Tanūkhī." In *'Abbasid Studies*. Occasional Papers of the School of 'Abbasid Studies, Cambridge 6–10 July 2002, edited by James E. Montgomery, 111–26. Leuven and Dudley, MA: Peeters, 2004.

———. "Reading 'the Exotic' and Organising the Production of Knowledge: Al-Tanūkhī on Indians and Their Elephants." Putting the House of Wisdom in Order: *Asiatische Studien —Etudes Asiatiques* 71 (2017): 833–56.

Brett, Michael, and Elizabeth Fentress. *The Berbers*. Oxford: Blackwell Publishing, 1997.

Al-Buḥturī. *Dīwān*. Edited by Ḥasan Kāmil al-Ṣayrafī. 5 vols. Cairo: Dār al-Ma'ārif, 1972–78.

Burge, S. R. *Angels in Islam. Jalāl al-Dīn al-Suyūṭī's al-Ḥabā'ik fī akhbār al-malā'ik*. London and New York: Routledge, 2012.

Burnett, Charles. "Astrology." In *EI3*.

Cahen, Claude. "A propos des *shuhūd*." *Studia Islamica* 31 (1970): 71–79. Reprinted in idem, *Les peuples musulmans dans l'histoire médiévale*. Damascus: Presses de l'IFPO, 2014. Online resource.

———. "Fiscalité, propriété, antagonismes sociaux en Haute-Mésopotamie au temps des premiers 'Abbāsides d'après Denys de Tell-Mahré." *Arabica* 1 (1953): 136–52. Reprinted in idem, *Les peuples musulmans dans l'histoire médiévale*. Damascus: Presses de l'IFPO, 2014. Online resource.

———. "Quelques problèmes économiques et fiscaux de l'Iraq būyide d'après un traité de mathématiques." Annales de L'iInstitut d'Études Orientales, Université d'Alger 10 (1952), 326–63. Reprinted in idem, *Les peuples musulmans dans l'histoire médiévale*. Damascus: Presses de l'IFPO, 2014. Online resource.

Canard, M. "Le riz dans le Proche Orient aux premiers siècles de l'Islam." *Arabica* 6 (1959): 113–31.

Cheikh-Moussa, A. "La négation d'Éros ou Le *'išq* d'après deux épîtres d'al-Ǧāḥiẓ." *Studia Islamica* 72 (1990): 71–119.

Cook, Michael. *Commanding Right and Forbidding Wrong in Islamic Thought*. Cambridge: Cambridge University Press, 2000.

Crone, P. "'Arīf." In *EI3*.

Daftary, Farhad. "'Alids." In *EI3*.

Diem, Werner, and Marco Schöller. *The Living and the Dead: Studies in Arabic Epitaphs*. 3 vols. Wiesbaden: Harrassowitz Verlag, 2004.

Dietrich, A. "Al-Ḥadjdjādj b. Yūsuf." In *EI2*.

Donohue, John J. *The Buwayhid Dynasty in Iraq 334 H./945 to 403 H./1012: Shaping Institutions for the Future*. Leiden and Boston: Brill, 2003.

Dozy, R. *Dictionnaire détaillé des noms des vêtements chez les Arabes*. Amsterdam: Jean Müller, 1845.

EI2. See The Encyclopaedia of Islam, Second Edition.

EI3. See Encyclopaedia of Islam, Three.

Elias, Jamal. "Throne of God." In *EQ*.

The Encyclopaedia of Islam, Second Edition. Eleven vols. with supplement vol. and index vol. Edited by P. Bearman, Th. Bianquis, C. E. Bosworth, E. van Donzel, and W. P. Heinrichs. Leiden: Brill, 1960–2009. All references are to the unpaginated electronic resource.

Encyclopaedia of Islam, Three. Edited by Kate Fleet, Gudrun Krämer, Denis Matringe, John Nawas, and Everett Rowson. Leiden: Brill, 2007. All references are to the unpaginated electronic resource.

Encyclopedia of the Qurʾān. 6 vols. Edited by Jane Dammen McAuliffe. Leiden: Brill, 2001–6. All references are to the unpaginated electronic resource.

Enzyklopädie des Märchens. Edited by Kurt Ranke and Hermann Bausinger. Berlin: W. de Gruyter, 1975–2015.

EQ. See Encyclopedia of the Qurʾān.

Fahd, Toufic. *La divination arabe: Etudes religieuses, sociologiques et folkloriques sur le milieu natif de l'Islam*. Paris: Sindbad, 1987.

Fakkar, Rouchdi. *At-Tanûẖî et son livre: La délivrance après l'angoisse*. Cairo: Institut Français d'Archéologie Orientale, 1955.

Franssen, Elise. "A *Maġribī* Copy of the *Kitāb al-Faraj baʿd aš-Šidda*, by the ʿIrāqī *Qāḍī* at-Tanūẖī: Study of a Manuscript of Liège University (Belgium)." *Journal of Islamic Manuscripts* 1 (2010): 61–78.

———. "Une copie en *maġribī* du *Kitāb al-Faraj baʿd aš-Šidda*, d'at-Tanūẖī: Analyse d'un manuscrit de l'Université de Liège." Master's diss., Liège University, 2009.

Gaček, Adam. *Arabic Manuscripts: A Vademecum for Readers*. Leiden: Brill, 2009. Reprinted 2012.

———. *The Arabic Manuscript Tradition: A Glossary of Technical Terms and Bibliography*. Leiden: Brill, 2001. Reprinted 2012.

———. *The Arabic Manuscript Tradition: A Glossary of Technical Terms and Bibliography*. Supplement. Leiden: Brill, 2008. Reprinted 2012.

Gardet, L. "Ikhlāṣ." In *EI2*.

Garulo, Teresa. "Erudición y nostalgia: Al-Ḥanīn ilà l-awṭān en el editor de al-Faray ba'd al-šidda de al-Tanūjī." *Al-Qanṭara* 33 (2012): 107–46.

Ghersetti, Antonella. "Il *qāḍī* al-Tanūḫī e il *Kitāb al-farağ ba'd al-šidda.*" *Annali.* Istituto Universitario Orientale Napoli 51 (1991): 33–51.

———. *Sollievo.* See: Translations of *al-Faraj ba'd al-shiddah.*

———. "La 'storia del uomo e del serpente' nell'opera di Al-Tanūḫī: L'elaborazione letteraria del motivo e la sua diffusione nella letteratura araba. "*Annali della Facoltà di Lingue e Letterature Straniere di Cà Foscari* 21 (1990); 37–53.

Hamori, Andras. "A Sampling of Pleasant Civilities: A 4th/10th Century *Qiṣṣa* by al-Babbaghā'." *Studia Islamica* 95 (2002): 57–69.

Heinen, A. "Samā'." In *EI2*.

Heinrichs, W. P. "Sa'īd b. Ḥumayd." In *EI2*.

Horovitz, J., and R. Firestone "Zabūr." In *EI2*.

Hourani, George Fadlo. *Arab Seafaring in the Indian Ocean in Ancient and Early Medieval Times.* Princeton, NJ: Princeton University Press, 1951. Reprinted New York: Octagon Books, 1975.

Ibn Abī l-Dunyā. *Al-Faraj ba'd al-shiddah.* In *Mawsū'at Rasā'il Ibn Abī l-Dunyā,* vol. 3. Edited by Muṣṭafā 'Abd al-Qādir 'Aṭā. Beirut: Mu'assasat al-Kutub al-Thaqāfiyyah, 1993.

———. *Kitāb al-Hawātif.* In *Mawsū'at Rasā'il Ibn Abī l-Dunyā,* vol. 4. Edited by Muṣṭafā 'Abd al-Qādir 'Aṭā. Beirut: Mu'assasat al-Kutub al-Thaqāfiyyah, 1993.

Ibn al-Sā'ī. *Consorts of the Caliphs: Women and the Court of Baghdad.* Edited by Shawkat M. Toorawa. Translated by the editors of the Library of Arabic Literature. New York and London: New York University Press, 2015.

Al-Jāḥiẓ. *The Epistle on Singing-Girls.* Edited and translated by A. F. L. Beeston. Warminster: Aris & Phillips, 1980.

Jarrar, Maher. "Heaven and Sky." In *EQ*.

Kennedy, Hugh. *The Court of the Caliphs: The Rise and Fall of Islam's Greatest Dynasty.* London: Weidenfeld & Nicolson, 2004. Published in the USA as *When Baghdad Ruled the Muslim World: The Rise and Fall of Islam's Greatest Dynasty.* Cambridge, MA: Da Capo Press, 2005.

———. *The Prophet and the Age of the Caliphates: The Islamic Near East from the Sixth to the Eleventh Century.* London and New York: Longman, 1986.

Key, Alexander. Review of *Khalifa, Hardship and Deliverance. Journal of Islamic Studies* 24 (2013): 212–16.

Khalifa, Nouha. *Hardship and Deliverance in the Islamic Tradition: Theology and Spirituality in the Works of al-Tanūkhī.* London: I. B. Tauris, 2010.

Al-Khaṭīb al-Baghdādī. *Tārīkh Baghdād aw Madīnat al-salām.* 14 vols. Cairo, Maktabat al-Khānjī, 1931.

Kilpatrick, Hilary. *Making the Great Book of Songs: Compilation and the Author's Craft in Abū l-Faraj al-Iṣbahānī's Kitāb al-aghānī.* London and New York: RoutledgeCurzon, 2003.

Kinberg, Leah. "Ambiguous." In *EQ.*

Leaman, O. N. H. "Luṭf." In *EI2.*

Lombard, Maurice. *Les Textiles dans le monde musulman du VIIe au XIIe siècle.* Mouton: The Hague, 1978.

Madelung, W. "Zaydiyya." In *EI2.*

Marlow, Louise. *Counsel for Kings: Wisdom and Politics in Tenth-Century Iran.* 2 vols. Edinburgh: Edinburgh University Press, 2016.

Marsham, Andrew. *Rituals of Islamic Monarchy: Accession and Succession in the First Muslim Monarchy.* Edinburgh: Edinburgh University Press, 2009.

Mez, Adam. *The Renaissance of Islam.* Translated by S. Khuda Bukhsh and D. S. Margoliouth. London: Luzac, 1937.

Miskawayh. *The Eclipse of the Abbasid Caliphate.* 3 vols. Translated by D. S. Margoliouth. Oxford: Basil Blackwell, 1920. Reprinted London: I. B. Tauris, 2015.

Moebius, Marc Helmuth. "Narrative Judgments: The *Qāḍī* al-Tanūkhī and the *Faraj* Genre in Medieval Arabic Literature." PhD diss. Princeton University, 2008.

Morony, Michael G. *Iraq after the Muslim Conquest.* Princeton, NJ: Princeton University Press, 1984.

Mottahedeh, Roy. *Loyalty and Leadership in an Early Islamic Society.* Princeton, NJ: Princeton University Press, 1980. Reprinted London: I. B. Tauris, 2001.

Mourad, Suleiman. *Early Islam between Myth and History: Al-Ḥasan al-Baṣrī (d.110H/728 CE) and the Formation of His Legacy in Classical Islamic Scholarship.* Leiden and Boston: Brill, 2006.

Al-Mubarrad. *Al-Kāmil.* Edited by Muḥammad Aḥmad al-Dālī. 4 vols. Beirut: Mu'assasat al-Risālah, 1986.

Müller, Kathrin. *Der Beduine und die Regenwolke. Ein Beitrag zur Erforschung der altarabischen Anekdote.* Munich: Bayerische Akademie der Wissenschaften. In Kommission bei C. H. Beck, 1995.

Nagel, T. "Ḳurrā'." In *EI2.*

Northedge, Alastair. *The Historical Topography of Samarra*. Samarra Studies I. Second, revised, ed. London: British School of Archaeology in Iraq. Fondation Max van Berchem, 2007.

Özkan, Hakan. *Narrativität im Kitāb al-Farağ ba'da aš-Šidda des Abū 'Alī al-Muḥassin al-Tanūhī*. Berlin: Klaus Schwarz, 2008.

Pellat, Charles. "Ghulām Tha'lab." In *EI2*.

Périer, Jean Baptiste. *Vie d'al-Hadjdjâdj ibn Yousof (41–95 de l'hégire = 661–714 de J.-C.) d'après les sources arabes*. Paris: É. Bouillon, 1904.

Pormann, Peter, and Emilie Savage-Smith. *Medieval Islamic Medicine*. Edinburgh: Edinburgh University Press, 2007.

Sadan, J. *Le Mobilier au Proche Orient médiéval*. Leiden: E. J. Brill, 1976.

Schippers, Arie. "Changing Narrativity in a Changing Society: The Dichotomy between the 'Early' and the 'Later' Stories in Tanūkhī's 'Relief after Adversity.'" *Quaderni di Studi Arabi* 20–1 (2002–3): 39–51.

Schmidtke, Sabine. "Mu'tazila." In *EQ*.

Schneider, I. "Sidjn." In *EI2*.

Schoeler, Gregor. *Écrire et transmettre dans les débuts de l'islam*. Paris: Presses Universitaires de France, 2002.

Serjeant, R. B. *Islamic Textiles: Material for a History Up to the Mongol Conquest*. Beirut: Librairie du Liban, 1972. Reprinted from *Ars Islamica* 9–16 (1942–51).

Sezgin, U. "Al-Madā'inī." In *EI2*.

Silverstein, Adam. "Barīd." In *EI3*.

Sirriyeh, Elizabeth. *Dreams and Visions in the World of Islam: A History of Muslim Dreaming and Foreknowing*. London and New York: I. B. Tauris, 2015.

Souag, Lameen. "Archaic and Innovative Islamic Prayer Names around the Sahara." *Bulletin of the School of Oriental and African Studies* 78 (2015): 357–74.

Souissi, M. "'Ilm al-Handasa". In *EI2*.

Sourdel, Dominique. "Dayr Ḳunnā." In *EI2*.

———. "Al-Faḍl b. Marwān."

———. "Al-Faḍl b. al-Rabī'." In *EI2*.

———. "Al-Faḍl b. Sahl b. Zadhānfarūkh." In *EI2*.

———. "Fragments d'al-Ṣūlī sur l'histoire des vizirs 'Abbāsides." *Bulletin d'Études Orientales* 15 (1955–57): 98–108.

———. "Al-Muwaffaḳ." In *EI2*.

———. "Nouvelles recherches sur la deuxième partie du 'Livre des Vizirs' d'al-Ğahšiyārī." *Mélanges Louis Massignon* 3 (1957): 271–99.

———. Review of Fakkar, Rouchdi. *At-Tanûhî et son livre: La délivrance après l'angoisse. Arabica* 4 (1957): 88–90.

———. "Une lettre inédite de ʿAlī b. ʿĪsā (317/929)." *Arabica* 3 (1956): 80–90.

———. *Le Vizirat abbāside de 749 à 936 (132 à 324 de l'Hégire)*. 2 vols. Institut Français de Damas, 1959–60.

Sourdel-Thomine, J., and A. Louis. "Ḥammām." In *EI2*.

Al-Ṣūlī, Abū Bakr. *The Life and Times of Abū Tammām*, edited and translated by Beatrice Gruendler. New York and London: New York University Press, 2015.

Szombathy, Zoltan. "Cursing, Ritual." In *EI3*.

Al-Ṭabarī. *The History of al-Ṭabarī*. 40 vols. General editor Ehsan Yarshater. Albany: State University of New York Press, 1985–99. Reprinted 2007.

Al-Tanūkhi, al-Muḥassin ibn ʿAlī. *Al-Faraj baʿd al-shiddah*. 5 vols. Edited by ʿAbbūd al-Shāljī. Beirut: Dār Ṣādir, 1978.

———. *Nishwār al-muḥāḍarah*. 8 vols. Edited by ʿAbbūd al-Shāljī. Beirut: Dār Ṣādir, 1971–73.

———. *The Table-Talk of a Mesopotamian Judge: Part 1*. Translated by D. S. Margoliouth. London: The Royal Asiatic Society, 1922. Parts 8 and 2. Translated by D. S. Margoliouth. *Islamic Culture* 3–6 (1929–32).

Al-Thaʿlabī. *ʿArāʾis al-majālis fī qiṣaṣ al-anbiyāʾ* or *Lives of the Prophets*. Translated by William M. Brinner. Leiden and Boston: Brill, 2002.

Tillier, Mathieu. *Les cadis d'Iraq et l'état abbasside (132/750–334/945)*. Damascus: Institut français du Proche-Orient, 2009.

———. "L'exemplarité chez al-Tanūḫī: Les cadis dans le *Nišwār al-Muḥāḍara*." *Arabica* 54 (2007): 1–24.

Toorawa, Shawkat M. *Ibn Abī Ṭāhir Ṭayfūr and Arabic Writerly Culture: A Ninth-Century Bookman in Baghdad*. London: RoutledgeCurzon, 2004.

Tyan, Émile. *Histoire de l'organisation judiciaire en pays d'Islam*. Second, revised, ed. Leiden: Brill, 1960.

Vadet, J.-C. "Ibn Ḥamdūn." In *EI2*.

Van Berkel, Maaike, Nadia Maria El Cheikh, Hugh Kennedy, and Letizia Osti. *Crisis and Continuity at the Abbasid Court: Formal and Informal Politics in the Caliphate of al-Muqtadir (295–320/908–32)*. Leiden and Boston: Brill, 2013.

Waines, D. "Al-Ruzz." In *EI2*.

Al-Washshāʾ. *Le Livre de brocart ou La Société raffinée de Bagdad au Xe siècle*. Translated by Siham Bouhlal. Paris: Gallimard, 2004.

Weaver, James, Letizia Osti, and Ulrich Rudolph (eds). *Putting the House of Wisdom in Order: The Fourth Islamic Century and the Impulse to Classify, Arrange and Inventory.* Special issue of *Asiatische Studien–Etudes Asiatiques* 71 (2017).

Wensinck, A. J. "Niyya." In *EI2*.

Wheeler, Brannon. *Prophets in the Quran: An Introduction to the Quran and Muslim Exegesis.* London and New York: Continuum, 2002.

Wiedemann, E., and J. Allan. "Al-Kuḥl." In *EI2*.

Wiener, Alfred. "Die *Farağ ba'd aš-Šidda*-Literatur: Von Madā'inī († 225 H) bis Tanūhī († 384 H): Ein Beitrag zur arabischen Literaturgeschichte." *Der Islam* 4 (1913), 270–98, 387–420.

Yāqūt. *Mu'jam al-udabā': Irshād al-arīb ilā ma'rifat al-adīb.* Edited by Iḥsān 'Abbās. 7 vols. Beirut: Dār al-Gharb al-Islāmī, 1993.

Zakeri, Mohsen. *Persian Wisdom in Arabic Garb: 'Alī b. 'Ubayda al-Rayḥānī (d. 219/834) and His Jawāhir al-kilam wa-farā'id al-ḥikam.* 2 vols. Leiden: Brill: 2007.

Zetterstéen, K. V. and C. E. Bosworth. "Al-Muhallabī." In *EI2*.

Al-Ziriklī, Khayr al-Dīn. *Al-A'lām.* 8 vols. 10th ed. Beirut: Dār al-'Ilm li-l-Malāyīn, 1992.

Translations of *al-Faraj ba'd al-shiddah*

Al-Tanūhī. *Il Sollievo dopo la distretta.* Translated by Antonella Ghersetti. Milan: Edizioni Ariele, 1995. Annotated selections, from 'Abbūd al-Shāljī's edition.

At-Tanūkhī. *Ende Gut, Alles Gut: Das Buch der Erleichterung nach der Bedrängnis.* Zürich: Manesse-Verlag, 1979. Translated by Arnold Hottinger. Unannotated selections, from the Cairo 1955 edition.

Tanûkhî. *La Délivrance après l'épreuve.* Translated by Jean-Jacques Schmidt. Arles: Actes Sud Sindbad, 2007. Annotated selections, from an unspecified edition.

Further Reading

Beaumont, Daniel. "Hard-Boiled: Narrative Discourse in Early Muslim Traditions." *Studia Islamica* 83 (1996), 5–31.

Bosworth, C. E. "The Ṭāhirids and Arabic Culture." *Journal of Semitic Studies* 14 (1969): 45–79.

Elias, Jamal J., ed. *Key Themes for the Study of Islam*. Oxford: Oneworld, 2010.

Gutas, Dimitri. *Greek Thought, Arabic Culture: The Graeco-Arabic Translation Movement in Baghdad and Early ʿAbbāsid Society (2nd–4th/8th–10th centuries)*. London: Routledge, 1998.

———. *Greek Wisdom Literature in Arabic Translation: A Study of the Graeco-Arabic Gnomologia*. New Haven, CT: American Oriental Society, 1975.

Hamori, Andras. "Folklore in al-Tanūkhī: The Collector of Ramlah." *Studia Islamica* 71 (1990): 65–75.

———. "The House of Brotherly Love: A Story in al-Tanūḫī and in the Thousand and One Nights." In *Problems in Arabic Literature*, edited by Miklós Maroth, 15–26. Piliscsaba: Avicenna Institute for Middle Eastern Studies, 2004.

Kraemer, Joel L. *Humanism in the Renaissance of Islam: The Cultural Revival during the Buyid Age*. Leiden: Brill, 1986.

Marzolph, U. "Motiv-Index der arabischen literarischen Anekdote." *Fabula* 24 (1983), 275–76.

Nielson, Lisa. "Gender and the Politics of Music in Early Islamic Courts." *Early Music History* 31 (2012), 235–61.

Padwick, Constance E. *Muslim Devotions: A Study of Prayer-Manuals in Common Use*. London: Society for the Promotion of Christian Knowledge, 1961. Reprinted Oxford: Oneworld, 1997.

Silverstein, Adam. *Postal Systems in the Pre-Modern Islamic World*. Cambridge: Cambridge University Press, 2007.

Schoeler, Gregor. *The Genesis of Literature in Arabic: From the Aural to the Read*. Revised edition. Translated by and in collaboration with Shawkat M. Toorawa. Edinburgh: Edinburgh University Press, 2009.

Index of Qur'anic Quotations

Index of Prophetic Hadith

من ستر أخاه المسلم . . .

من ستر مسلمًا . . .

من كان في حاجة أخيه . . .

ياحيّ يا قيوم برحمتك أستغيث .

ياكائنًا قبل كل شيء . . .

Index of Poems

	Poet	No. of lines	Meter	Rhyme
§57	a poet, anon.	2	*basīṭ*	يُؤَنِّبُهُ
§59.3	al-Tanūkhī	2	*munsariḥ*	أَدَبِهِ
§9.3	Abū l-ʿAtāhiyah	1	*wāfir*	ذَهَابِ
§78.4	al-Numayrī	2	*ṭawīl*	ٱلسَّبْتُ
§19.1	a God-fearing man	1	*wāfir*	أَصْلَحْ
§19.1	a disembodied voice	2	*wāfir*	بَرِّحْ
§19.3	a disembodied voice	1	*wāfir*	تَبْرَحْ
§61	al-Muhallabī	2	*ṭawīl*	مُنَاصِحُ
§13.10	Umayyah ibn Abī l-Ṣalt	1	*ṭawīl*	ضَاحِيا
§97.1	a man, anon.	2	*ramal*	أَوَدَكْ
§60.5	ʿAlī ibn Abī Ṭālib	2	*ṭawīl*	ٱجْتِهَادُهُ
§108.1	a "Qurʾan reader"	2	*ṭawīl*	أَمْرُ
§111.3	al-Faḍl ibn al-Rabīʿ	2	*ṭawīl*	يَدُورُ
§111.4	al-Faḍl ibn al-Rabīʿ	1	*ṭawīl*	عُثُورُ
§111.6	al-Faḍl ibn al-Rabīʿ	1	*ṭawīl*	عُثُورُ
§111.4	al-Faḍl ibn al-Rabīʿ	1	*ṭawīl*	أُمُورُ
§106.1	Ibn Thawābah	2	*ṭawīl*	قِصَارُ
§66.1	al-Ḥasan ibn Wahb	4	*kāmil*	لَهَا
§66.1	Sulaymān ibn Wahb	2	*kāmil*	لَعَلَّهَا
§107.1	Jaʿfar al-Ṣādiq	1	*wāfir*	ٱلطَّوِيلِ
§107.2	Jaʿfar al-Ṣādiq	3	*wāfir*	ٱلطَّوِيلِ
§107.3	al-Ḥusayn ibn ʿAlī	1	*wāfir*	قِيلِ
§107.3	al-Ḥusayn ibn ʿAlī	1	*wāfir*	ٱلْعُقُولِ
§53.3	al-Ḥuṣayn ibn al-Ḥumām	1	*ṭawīl*	أَتَقَدَّمَا
§102.3	al-Sayārī	2	*kāmil*	ٱلْخَاتِمِ
§101.2	a poet in the army of Ṭāhir ibn al-Ḥusayn	2	*kāmil*	ٱلْهَمِّ
§53.2	Qaṭarī ibn al-Fujāʾah	4	*kāmil*	لِحِمَامِ
§0.3	al-Aghlab al-ʿIjlī	1	*rajaz*	يَجِينَا

	Poet	No. of lines	Meter	Rhyme
§0.3	al-Aghlab al-ʿIjlī	1	*rajaz*	يَجِينَهْ
§40	al-Aghlab al-ʿIjlī	0.5	*rajaz*	يَنْجَلِينَ
§110.1	an Arab woman	1	*ṭawīl*	نَجَّانِي
§110.4	an Arab woman	1	*ṭawīl*	نَجَّانِي
§98.1	written on a piece of paper	1	*basīṭ*	آللّٰهُ
§99	someone in a dream	2	*kāmil*	تَكْرَهُ
§82.3	a Bedouin	1	*rajaz*	كَارِهُ

General Index

About the NYU Abu Dhabi Institute

NYU
ABU DHABI
INSTITUTE

The Library of Arabic Literature is supported by a grant from the NYU Abu Dhabi Institute, a major hub of intellectual and creative activity and advanced research. The Institute hosts academic conferences, workshops, lectures, film series, performances, and other public programs directed both to audiences within the UAE and to the worldwide academic and research community. It is a center of the scholarly community for Abu Dhabi, bringing together faculty and researchers from institutions of higher learning throughout the region.

NYU Abu Dhabi, through the NYU Abu Dhabi Institute, is a world-class center of cutting-edge research, scholarship, and cultural activity. The Institute creates singular opportunities for leading researchers from across the arts, humanities, social sciences, sciences, engineering, and the professions to carry out creative scholarship and conduct research on issues of major disciplinary, multidisciplinary, and global significance.

About the Typefaces

The Arabic body text is set in DecoType Naskh, designed by Thomas Milo and Mirjam Somers, based on an analysis of five centuries of Ottoman manuscript practice. The exceptionally legible result is the first and only typeface in a style that fully implements the principles of script grammar (*qawāʿid al-khaṭṭ*).

The Arabic footnote text is set in DecoType Emiri, drawn by Mirjam Somers, based on the metal typeface in the naskh style that was cut for the 1924 Cairo edition of the Qur'an.

Both Arabic typefaces in this series are controlled by a dedicated font layout engine. ACE, the Arabic Calligraphic Engine, invented by Peter Somers, Thomas Milo, and Mirjam Somers of DecoType, first operational in 1985, pioneered the principle followed by later smart font layout technologies such as OpenType, which is used for all other typefaces in this series.

The Arabic text was set with WinSoft Tasmeem, a sophisticated user interface for DecoType ACE inside Adobe InDesign. Tasmeem was conceived and created by Thomas Milo (DecoType) and Pascal Rubini (WinSoft) in 2005.

The English text is set in Adobe Text, a new and versatile text typeface family designed by Robert Slimbach for Western (Latin, Greek, Cyrillic) typesetting. Its workhorse qualities make it perfect for a wide variety of applications, especially for longer passages of text where legibility and economy are important. Adobe Text bridges the gap between calligraphic Renaissance types of the 15th and 16th centuries and high-contrast Modern styles of the 18th century, taking many of its design cues from early post-Renaissance Baroque transitional types cut by designers such as Christoffel van Dijck, Nicolaus Kis, and William Caslon. While grounded in classical form, Adobe Text is also a statement of contemporary utilitarian design, well suited to a wide variety of print and on-screen applications.

Titles Published by the Library of Arabic Literature

For more details on individual titles, visit www.libraryofarabicliterature.org

Classical Arabic Literature: A Library of Arabic Literature Anthology
Selected and translated by Geert Jan van Gelder (2012)

A Treasury of Virtues: Sayings, Sermons, and Teachings of ʿAlī, by al-Qāḍī al-Quḍāʿī, with the **One Hundred Proverbs** attributed to al-Jāḥiẓ
Edited and translated by Tahera Qutbuddin (2013)

The Epistle on Legal Theory, by al-Shāfiʿī
Edited and translated by Joseph E. Lowry (2013)

Leg over Leg, by Aḥmad Fāris al-Shidyāq
Edited and translated by Humphrey Davies (4 volumes; 2013–14)

Virtues of the Imām Aḥmad ibn Ḥanbal, by Ibn al-Jawzī
Edited and translated by Michael Cooperson (2 volumes; 2013–15)

The Epistle of Forgiveness, by Abū l-ʿAlāʾ al-Maʿarrī
Edited and translated by Geert Jan van Gelder and Gregor Schoeler (2 volumes; 2013–14)

The Principles of Sufism, by ʿĀʾishah al-Bāʿūniyyah
Edited and translated by Th. Emil Homerin (2014)

The Expeditions: An Early Biography of Muḥammad, by Maʿmar ibn Rāshid
Edited and translated by Sean W. Anthony (2014)

Two Arabic Travel Books
Accounts of China and India, by Abū Zayd al-Sīrāfī
Edited and translated by Tim Mackintosh-Smith (2014)
Mission to the Volga, by Aḥmad ibn Faḍlān
Edited and translated by James Montgomery (2014)

Disagreements of the Jurists: A Manual of Islamic Legal Theory, by al-Qāḍī al-Nuʿmān
Edited and translated by Devin J. Stewart (2015)

Consorts of the Caliphs: Women and the Court of Baghdad, by Ibn al-Sāʿī
Edited by Shawkat M. Toorawa and translated by the Editors of the Library of Arabic Literature (2015)

What ʿĪsā ibn Hishām Told Us, by Muḥammad al-Muwayliḥī
Edited and translated by Roger Allen (2 volumes; 2015)

The Life and Times of Abū Tammām, by Abū Bakr Muḥammad ibn Yaḥyā al-Ṣūlī
Edited and translated by Beatrice Gruendler (2015)

The Sword of Ambition: Bureaucratic Rivalry in Medieval Egypt, by ʿUthmān ibn Ibrāhīm al-Nābulusī
Edited and translated by Luke Yarbrough (2016)

Brains Confounded by the Ode of Abū Shādūf Expounded, by Yūsuf al-Shirbīnī
Edited and translated by Humphrey Davies (2 volumes; 2016)

Light in the Heavens: Sayings of the Prophet Muḥammad, by al-Qāḍī al-Quḍāʿī
Edited and translated by Tahera Qutbuddin (2016)

Risible Rhymes, by Muḥammad ibn Maḥfūẓ al-Sanhūrī
Edited and translated by Humphrey Davies (2016)

A Hundred and One Nights
Edited and translated by Bruce Fudge (2016)

The Excellence of the Arabs, by Ibn Qutaybah
Edited by James E. Montgomery and Peter Webb
Translated by Sarah Bowen Savant and Peter Webb (2017)

Scents and Flavors: A Syrian Cookbook
Edited and translated by Charles Perry (2017)

Arabian Satire: Poetry from 18th-Century Najd, by Ḥmēdān al-Shwēʿir
Edited and translated by Marcel Kurpershoek (2017)

In Darfur: An Account of the Sultanate and Its People, by Muḥammad ibn ʿUmar al-Tūnisī
Edited and translated by Humphrey Davies **(2 volumes; 2018)**

War Songs, by ʿAntarah ibn Shaddād
Edited by James E. Montgomery
Translated by James E. Montgomery with Richard Sieburth **(2018)**

Arabian Romantic: Poems on Bedouin Life and Love, by ʿAbdallah ibn Sbayyil
Edited and translated by Marcel Kurpershoek **(2018)**

Dīwān ʿAntarah ibn Shaddād: A Literary-Historical Study
By James E. Montgomery **(2018)**

Stories of Piety and Prayer: Deliverance Follows Adversity, by al-Muḥassin ibn ʿAlī al-Tanūkhī
Edited and translated by Julia Bray **(2019)**

English-only Paperbacks

Leg over Leg, by Aḥmad Fāris al-Shidyāq **(2 volumes; 2015)**
The Expeditions: An Early Biography of Muḥammad, by Maʿmar ibn Rāshid **(2015)**
The Epistle on Legal Theory: A Translation of al-Shāfiʿī's *Risālah*, by al-Shāfiʿī **(2015)**
The Epistle of Forgiveness, by Abū l-ʿAlāʾ al-Maʿarrī **(2016)**
The Principles of Sufism, by ʿĀʾishah al-Bāʿūniyyah **(2016)**
A Treasury of Virtues: Sayings, Sermons, and Teachings of ʿAlī, by al-Qāḍī al-Quḍāʿī, with the **One Hundred Proverbs** attributed to al-Jāḥiẓ **(2016)**
The Life of Ibn Ḥanbal, by Ibn al-Jawzī **(2016)**
Mission to the Volga, by Aḥmad ibn Faḍlān **(2017)**
Accounts of China and India, by Abū Zayd al-Sīrāfī **(2017)**
A Hundred and One Nights (2017)
Disagreements of the Jurists: A Manual of Islamic Legal Theory, by al-Qāḍī al-Nuʿmān **(2017)**
What ʿĪsā ibn Hishām Told Us, by Muḥammad al-Muwayliḥī **(2018)**
War Songs, by ʿAntarah ibn Shaddād **(2018)**

The Life and Times of Abū Tammām, by Abū Bakr Muḥammad ibn Yaḥyā al-Ṣūlī (2018)

The Sword of Ambition, by ʿUthmān ibn Ibrāhīm al-Nābulusī (2019)

Brains Confounded by the Ode of Abū Shādūf Expounded: Volume One, by Yūsuf al-Shirbīnī (2019)

Brains Confounded by the Ode of Abū Shādūf Expounded: Volume Two, by Yūsuf al-Shirbīnī and **Risible Rhymes**, by Muḥammad ibn Maḥfūẓ al-Sanhūrī (2019)

About the Editor–Translator

Julia Bray became the Laudian Professor (now the AS AlBabtain-Laudian Professor) of Arabic at the University of Oxford and a fellow of St. John's College in 2012, having previously taught at the universities of Manchester, Edinburgh, St. Andrews and Paris 8-Vincennes—Saint-Denis. She writes on medieval to early modern Arabic literature, life-writing, and social history; has contributed to the *New Cambridge History of Islam* (2010), to *Essays in Arabic Literary Biography 1350–1850* (2009), and to cross-cultural studies such as *Approaches to the Byzantine Family* (2013); and edited *Writing and Representation in Medieval Islam* (2006). With Wen-chin Ouyang, she edits the monograph series Edinburgh Studies in Classical Arabic Literature. With Helen Blatherwick, she is editing a special issue of the journal *Cultural History* on the history of emotions in Arabic.